Critical Essays of the
Seventeenth Century

1650-1685

Critical Essays of the Seventeenth Century

Edited by

J. E. SPINGARN

VOLUME II

1650 – 1685

INDIANA UNIVERSITY PRESS
Bloomington

820.9

5757c

82128

FIRST PUBLISHED BY THE CLARENDON PRESS, OXFORD
REISSUED 1957 BY INDIANA UNIVERSITY PRESS
MANUFACTURED IN THE UNITED STATES OF AMERICA

CONTENTS

Contents

SIR WILLIAM DAVENANT

PREFACE TO *GONDIBERT, AN HEROICK POEM*

1650

The AUTHOR'S
PREFACE
To his much Honour'd FRIEND
Mr HOBS.

SIR,

Since you have done me the honour to allow this Poem a daily examination as it was writing, I will presume, now it hath attain'd more length, to give you a
5 longer trouble, that you may yeild me as great advantages by censuring the Method as by judging the Numbers and the matter. And because you shall pass through this new Building with more ease to your disquisition, I will acquaint you what care I took of my materials ere I began to work.
10 But first give me leave (remembring with what difficulty the world can shew any Heroick Poem that in a perfect glass of Nature gives us a familiar and easie view of our selves) to take notice of those quarrels which the Living have with the Dead; and I will (according as all times
15 have apply'd their reverence) begin with *Homer*, who though he seems to me standing upon the Poets famous hill, like the eminent Sea-mark by which they have in former ages steer'd, and though he ought not to be removed from that eminence, least Posterity should
20 presumptously mistake their course, yet some (sharply observing how his successors have proceeded no farther

then a perfection of imitating him) say that, as Sea-marks are chiefly useful to Coasters, and serve not those who have the ambition of Discoverers, that love to sail in untry'd Seas, so he hath rather prov'd a Guide for those whose satisfy'd Wit will not venture beyond the track of others, then to them who affect a new and remote way of thinking, who esteem it a deficiency and meaness of minde to stay and depend upon the authority of example.

Some there are that object that, even in the likelyhoods of Story (and Story, where ever it seems most likely, growes most pleasant), he doth too frequently intermixe such Fables as are objects lifted above the Eyes of Nature; and as he often interrogates his Muse, not as his rational Spirit, but as a *Familiar*, separated from his body, so her replys bring him where he spends time in immortal conversation, whilest supernaturally he doth often advance his men to the quality of Gods, and depose his Gods to the condition of men.

His Successor to fame, and consequently to censure, is *Virgil*, whose toyles nor vertue cannot free him from the peevishness, or rather curiosity, of divers Readers.   He is upbrayded by some (who perhaps are affected Antiquaries, and make priority of time the measure of excellence) for gaining his renown by immitation of *Homer* : Whilst others, no less bold with that ancient Guide, say He hath so often led him into Heaven and Hell, till by conversation with Gods and Ghosts he sometimes deprives us of those natural probabilities in Story which are instructive to humane life : And others affirm (if it be not irreverence to record their opinion) That even in wit he seems deficient by many omissions, as if he had design'd a pennance of gravity to himself and to posterity : And by their observing that continued gravity, me thinks they look upon him as on a Musitian composing of Anthemes, whose excellence consists more in the solemnness then in the fancy, and upon the body of his Work as on the body of a Giant, whose force hath more of strength then quickness, and of patience then activity.

But these bold Censure⟨r⟩s are in danger of so many
5 Enemies, as I shall wisely shrink from them, and only observe, That if any Disciples of unimitable *Virgil* can prove so formal as to esteem wit (as if it were levity) an imputation to the Heroick Muse (by which malevolent word, Wit, they would disgrace her extraordinary heights),
10 yet if those grave Judges will be held wise, they must endure the fate of Wise men, who always have but few of their society ; for many more then consist of their number (perhaps not having the sullenness to be of it) are taken with those bold flights, and think 'tis with the Muse, whose
15 noble Quarry is men, as with the Eagle, who when he soares high stoops more prosperously and is most certain of his prey. And surely Poets, whose business should represent the Worlds true image often to our view, are not less prudent then Painters, who when they draw Land-
20 schaps entertain not the Eye wholy with even Prospect and a continued Flat, but for variety terminate the sight with lofty Hills, whose obscure heads are sometimes in the clouds.

Lucan, who chose to write the greatest actions that ever
25 were allowed to be true, which for fear of contemporary witnesses oblig'd him to a very close attendance upon Fame, did not observe that such an enterprize rather beseem'd an Historian then a Poet : For wise Poets think it more worthy to seek out truth in the Passions then to
30 record the truth of Actions, and practise to describe Man-kinde just as we are perswaded or guided by instinct, not particular persons as they are lifted or levell'd by the force of Fate, it being nobler to contemplate the general History of Nature then a selected Diary of Fortune : And Painters
35 are no more then Historians, when they draw eminent

persons, though they terme that drawing to the life ; but when, by assembling divers figures in a larger volumn, they draw Passions, though they terme it but Story, then they increase in dignity and become Poets.

I have been thus hardy to call him to account for the 5 choice of his Argument, not meerly as it was Story, but because the actions he recorded were so eminent, and so neer his time, that he could not assist Truth with such ornaments as Poets, for useful pleasure, have allowed her, least the fained complexion might render the true suspected. 10 And now I will leave to others the presumption of measuring his Hyperboles, by whose space and height they malitiously take the dimension of wit, and so mistake him in his boyling Youth, which had marvellous forces, as we disrellish excellent Wine when fuming in the Lee. 15

Statius, with whom we may conclude the old Heroicks, is as accomptable to some for his obligations to *Virgill*, as *Virgill* is to others for what he owes to *Homer*; and more closely then *Virgill* waits on *Homer* doth *Statius* attend *Virgill*, and follows him there also where Nature never comes, even into 20 Heaven and Hell : and therefore he cannot escape such as approve the wisdom of the best Dramaticks, who, in representation of examples, beleeve they prevail most on our manners, when they lay the Scene at home in their own Country ; so much they avoid those remote Regions of Heaven and 25 Hell, as if the People, whom they make civill by an easie communication with reason (and familiar reason is that which is call'd the civility of the Stage), were become more discreet than to have their eyes perswaded by the descending of Gods in gay Clouds, and more manly than to be frighted with the 30 rising of Ghosts in Smoke.

Tasso, who reviv'd the Heroick flame after it was many ages quench'd, is held, both in time and merit, the first of the Moderns,—an honour by which he gains not much, because the number he excels must needs be few, which 35

affords but one fit to succeed him ; for I will yeeld to their
opinion who permit not *Ariosto*, no, nor *Du Bartas*, in this
eminent rank of the Heroicks, rather than to make way by
their admission for *Dante, Marino,* and others.   *Tasso's*
5 honour, too, is chiefly allow'd him, where he most
endevours to make *Virgill* his Pattern ; and again, when
we consider from whom *Virgill*'s spirit is deriv'd, we may
observe how rarely humane excellence is found ; for
Heroick Poesie (which, if exact in it self, yeelds not to any
10 other humane work) flow'd but in few, and even those
streams descended but from one Grecian Spring ; and 'tis
with Originall Poems as with the Originall Pieces of Painters, whose Copies abate the excessive price of the first Hand.

   But *Tasso*, though he came late into the world, must
15 have his share in that Criticall warr which never ceases
amongst the Learned ; and he seems most vnfortunate,
because his errors, which are deriv'd from the Ancients,
when examin'd, grow in a great degree excusable in them,
and by being his, admit no pardon.   Such as are his Coun-
20 cell assembled in Heaven, his Witches Expeditions through
the Air, and enchanted Woods inhabited with Ghosts.   For
though the elder Poets, which were then the sacred Priests,
fed the world with supernaturall Tales, and so compounded
the Religion of Pleasure and Mysterie, two Ingredients
25 which never fail'd to work upon the People, whilst for the
eternity of their Chiefs, more refin'd by education, they
surely intended no such vain provision : Yet a Christian
Poet, whose Religion little needs the aids of Invention,
hath less occasion to imitate such Fables as meanly
30 illustrate a probable Heaven by the fashion and dignity of
Courts, and make a resemblance of Hell out of the Dreams
of frighted Women, by which they continue and increase
the melancnoly mistakes of the People.

   Spencer may stand here as the last of this short File of
35 Heroick Poets,—Men whose intellectuals were of so great

a making (though some have thought them lyable to those few Censures we have mentioned) as perhaps they will in worthy memory outlast even Makers of Laws and Founders of Empires, and all but such as must therefore live equally with them because they have recorded their names; and consequently with their own hands led them to the Temple of Fame. And since we have dar'd to remember those exceptions which the Curious have against them, it will not be expected I should forget what is objected against *Spencer*, whose obsolete Language we are constrain'd to mention, though it be grown the most vulgar accusation that is laid to his charge.

Language, which is the onely Creature of Man's creation, hath like a Plant seasons of flourishing and decay, like Plants is remov'd from one soile to another, and by being so transplanted doth often gather vigour and increase. But as it is false husbandry to graft old branches upon young stocks, so we may wonder that our Language (not long before his time created out of a confusion of others, and then beginning to flourish like a new Plant) should as helps to its increase receive from his hand new grafts of old wither'd words. But this vulgar exception shall only have the vulgar excuse, which is, That the unlucky choice of his *Stanza* hath by repetition of Rime brought him to the necessity of many exploded words.

If we proceed from his Language to his Argument, we must observe with others, that his noble and most artfull hands deserv'd to be employ'd upon matter of a more naturall and therefore of a more usefull kinde: His allegoricall Story, by many held defective in the connexion, resembling, methinks, a continuance of extraordinary Dreams, such as excellent Poets and Painters, by being over-studious, may have in the beginning of Feavers: And those moral Visions are just of so much use to humane application as painted History, when with the cousenage of lights it is represented in Scenes, by which we are much lesse inform'd then by actions on the Stage.

Thus, Sir, I have perhaps taken paines to make you think me malicious, in observing how far the Curious have look'd
5 into the errors of others,—Errors which the natural humor of imitation hath made so like in all, even from *Homer* to *Spencer*, as the accusations against the first appear but little more then repetition in every process against the rest; & comparing the resemblance of error in persons of one
10 generation to that which is in those of another age, we may find it exceeds not any where notoriously the ordinary proportion. Such limits to the progress of every thing, even of worthiness as well as defect, doth Imitation give; for whilst we imitate others, we can no more excel them, then
15 he that sailes by others Mapps can make a new discovery; and to Imitation, Nature (which is the onely visible power and operation of God) perhaps doth needfully encline us to keep us from excesses. For though every man be capable of worthiness and unworthiness, as they are defined by
20 Opinion, yet no man is built strong enough to bear the extremities of either without unloading himself upon others shoulders, even to the weariness of many. If courage be worthiness, yet where it is overgrown into extremes it becomes as wilde and hurtful as ambition, and so what was
25 reverenced for protection grows to be abhorr'd for oppression. If *Learning* (which is not Knowledge, but a continu'd Sayling by fantastick and uncertain winds towards it) be worthiness, yet it hath bounds in all Philosophers; and Nature, that measur'd those bounds, seems not so partial
30 as to allow it in any one a much larger extent then in another, as if in our fleshy building she consider'd the furniture and the room alike and together; for as the compass of Diadems commonly fits the whole succession of those Kings that wear them, so throughout the whole World
35 a very few inches may distinguish the circumference of

the heads of their Subjects. Nor need we repine that
Nature hath not some Favorites to whom she doth dispence
this Treasure, *Knowledge*, with a prodigious Liberality : For
as there is no one that can be said vastly to exceed all mankinde, so divers that have in learning transcended all in some 5
one Province have corrupted many with that great quantity
of false gold, and the authority of their stronger Science
hath often serv'd to distract or pervert their weaker disciples.

And as the qualities which are term'd good are bounded,
so are the bad, and likewise limited as well as gotten by 10
imitation ; for amongst those that are extraordinary either
by birth or brain (for with the usual pride of Poets I pass
by common crowds as negligently as Princes move from
throngs that are not their own Subjects), we cannot finde any
one so egregious (admitting cruelty and avarice for the 15
chiefest evils, and errors in government or doctrin to be
the greatest errors) but that divers of former or succeeding
times may enter the scales with them and make the
Ballance even ; though the passion of Historians would
impose the contrary on our beleef, who in dispraise of evil 20
Princes are often as unjust and excessive as the common
People : for there was never any Monarch so cruel but he
had living Subjects, nor so avaritious but that his Subjects
were richer then himself, nor ever any disease in Government so extremely infectious as to make universal Anarchy, 25
or any error in Doctrin so strong by the Maintainer but
that Truth (though it wrastled with her often & in many
places) hath at some season and on some ground made her
advantages and success apparent. Therefore we may
conclude that Nature, for the safety of mankinde, hath as 30
well, by dulling and stopping our progress with the constant humor of imitation, given limits to courage and to
learning, to wickedness and to error, as it hath ordain'd
the shelves before the shore to restrain the rage and
excesses of the Sea. 35

But I feel, Sir, that I am falling into the dangerous Fit of a hot Writer; for in stead of performing the promise which begins this Preface, and doth oblige me, after I had given you the judgement of some upon others, to present 5 my self to your censure, I am wandring after new thoughts; but I shall ask your pardon, and return to my undertaking.

My Argument I resolv'd should consist of Christian persons; for since Religion doth generally beget and govern manners, I thought the example of their actions 10 would prevail most upon our own by being deriv'd from the same doctrin and authority, as the particular Sects educated by Philosophers were diligent and pliant to the dictates and fashions of such as deriv'd themselves from the same Master, but lazy and froward to those who 15 convers'd in other Schools: Yet all these Sects pretended to the same beauty, *Vertue*, though each did court her more fondly when she was dress'd at their own homes by the hands of their acquaintance: And so Subjects bred under the Laws of a Prince,—though Laws differ not 20 much in Morality or priviledge throughout the civil World, being every where made for direction of Life more then for sentences of Death,—will rather dye neer that Prince, defending those they have been taught, then live by taking new from another.

25 These were partly the reasons why I chose a Story of such persons as profess'd Christian Religion; but I ought to have been most enclin'd to it, because the Principles of our Religion conduce more to explicable vertue, to plain demonstrative justice, and even to Honor (if Vertue, the 30 Mother of Honour, be voluntary and active in the dark, so as she need not Laws to compel her, nor look for witnesses to proclaim her), then any other Religion that e're assembled men to Divine Worship. For that of the *Jews* doth still consist in a sullen separation of themselves from the 35 rest of humane flesh, which is a fantastical pride of their

own cleaness, and an uncivil disdain of the imagined contagiousness of others ; and at this day, their cantonizing in Tribes, and shyness of allyance with neighbours, deserves not the terme of mutual love, but rather seems a bestial melancholy of herding in their own Walks. That 5 of the Ethnicks, like this of *Mahomet*, consisted in the vain pride of Empire, and never enjoyn'd a Jewish separation, but drew all Nations together, yet not as their companions of the same species, but as slaves to a Yoke : Their sanctity was Honor, and their Honor onely an impudent 10 courage or dexterity in destroying. But Christian Religion hath the innocence of Village neighbourhood, and did anciently in its politicks rather promote the interest of Mankinde then of States, and rather of all States then of one ; for particular endeavours onely in behalf of our own 15 homes are signes of a narrow moral education, not of the vast kindness of Christian Religion, which likewise ordain'd as well an universal communion of bosomes as a community of Wealth. Such is Christian Religion in the precepts, and was once so in the practise. But I resolv'd 20 my Poem should represent those of a former age, perceiving 'tis with the servants of Christ as with other servants under temporal power, who with all cleanness, and even with officious diligence, perform their duty in their Masters sight, but still as he grows longer absent become more 25 slothful, unclean, and false. And this who ever compares the present with the Primitive times may too palpably discern.

When I consider'd the actions which I meant to describe (those inferring the persons), I was again perswaded rather 30 to chuse those of a former age then the present, and in a Century so far remov'd, as might preserve me from their improper examinations, who know not the requisites of a Poem, nor how much pleasure they lose (and even the pleasures of Heroick Poesy are not unprofitable) who take 35

away the liberty of a Poet, and fetter his feet in the shackles
of an Historian : For why should a Poet doubt in Story to
mend the intrigues of Fortune by more delightful convei-
ances of probable fictions, because austere Historians have
5 enter'd into bond to truth,—an obligation which were in
Poets as foolish and unnecessary as is the bondage of false
Martyrs, who lye in chains for a mistaken opinion ; but by
this I would imply that Truth narrative and past is the Idol
of Historians, who worship a dead thing, and truth
10 operative, and by effects continually alive, is the Mistris of
Poets, who hath not her existence in matter but in reason.

I was likewise more willing to derive my Theme from
elder times, as thinking it no little mark of skilfulness to
comply with the common Infirmity ; for men, even of the
15 best education, discover their eyes to be weak when they
look upon the glory of Vertue, which is great actions, and
rather endure it at distance then neer, being more apt to
beleeve and love the renown of Predecessors then of Contemporaries, whose deeds, excelling theirs in their own
20 sight, seem to upbraid them, and are not reverenc'd as
examples of Vertue, but envy'd as the favours of Fortune.
But to make great Actions credible is the principall Art of
Poets, who, though they avouch the utility of Fictions,
should not, by altering and subliming Story, make use of
25 their priviledg to the detriment of the Reader, whose
incredulity, when things are not represented in proportion,
doth much allay the rellish of his pity, hope, joy, and other
Passions ; For we may descend to compare the deceptions
in Poesie to those of them that professe dexterity of Hand
30 which resembles Conjuring, and to such we come not with
the intention of *Lawyers* to examine the evidence of Facts,
but are content, if we like the carriage of their feign'd
motion, to pay for being well deceiv'd.

As in the choice of time, so of place I have comply'd
35 with the weakness of the generality of men, who think the

best objects of their own country so little to the size of
those abroad, as if they were shew'd them by the wrong
end of a Prospective ; for Man, continuing the appetites of
his first Childhood till he arive at his second, which is
more froward, must be quieted with somthing that he 5
thinks excellent wch he may call his own, but when he
sees the like in other places, not staying to compare them,
wrangles at all he has. This leads us to observe the
craftiness of the *Comicks*, who are only willing when they
describe humor (& humor is the drunkeness of a Nation 10
which no sleep can cure) to lay the Scæne in their own
Country, as knowing we are, like the Son of *Noah*, so little
distasted to behold each others shame, that we delight to
see even that of a Father ; yet when they would set forth
greatness and excellent vertue, which is the Theme of 15
Tragedy, publiquely to the people, they wisely, to avoid the
quarrels of neighbourly envy, remove the Scene from
home. And by their example I travail'd too ; and *Italie*,
which was once the Stage of the World, I have made the
Theater where I shew, in either Sex, some patterns of 20
humane life that are perhaps fit to be follow'd.

Having told you why I took the actions that should be
my Argument from men of our own Religion, and given
you reasons for the choyce of the time and place design'd
for those actions, I must next acquaint you with the 25
Schooles where they were bred ; not meaning the Schooles
where they took their Religion, but Morality ; for I know
Religion is universally rather inherited then taught, and
the most effectual Schools of Morality are Courts and
Camps : yet towards the first the people are unquiet 30
through envie, and towards the other through fear, and
always jealous of both for Injustice, which is the naturall
scandal cast upon authority and great force. They look
upon the outward glory or blaze of Courts, as wilde Beasts
in dark nights stare on their Hunters Torches ; but though 35

the expences of Courts, whereby they shine, is that consuming glory in which the people think their liberty is wasted,—for wealth is their liberty, and lov'd by them even to jealousie, being themselves a courser sort of Princes,
5 apter to take then to pay,—yet Courts (I mean all abstracts of the multitude, either by King or Assemblies) are not the Schools where men are bred to oppression, but the Temples where sometimes Oppressors take sanctuary, a safety which our reason must allow them. For the ancient laws of
10 Sanctuary, deriv'd from God, provided chiefly for actions that proceeded from necessity ; and who can imagine less then a necessity of oppressing the people, since they are never willing either to buy their Peace or to pay for Warr ?

Nor are Camps the Schools of wicked Destroyers, more
15 then the *Inns of Court*, being the Nursery of Judges, are the Schools of Murderers ; for as Judges are avengers of private men against private Robbers, so are Armies the avengers of the publique against publique Invaders, either civill or forraign, and Invaders are Robbers, though more
20 in countenance then those of the high-way because of their number. Nor is there other difference between Armies when they move towards Sieges or Battail, and Judges moving in their Circuit, during the danger of extraordinary malefactors, with the guards of the County, but that the
25 latter is a lesse Army, and of lesse Discipline. If any man can yet doubt of the necessary use of Armies, let him study that which was anciently call'd a Monster, the Multitude,— for Wolves are commonly harmlesse when they are met alone, but very uncivill in Herds,—and he will not finde
30 that all his kindred by *Adam* are so tame and gentle as those Lovers that were bred in *Arcadia* ; or to reform his opinion, let him ask why, during the utmost age of History, Cities have been at the charge of defensive Walls, and why Fortification hath been practic'd so long till it is grown
35 an Art ?

I may now beleeve I have usefully taken from Courts
and Camps the patterns of such as will be fit to be imitated
by the most necessary men ; and the most necessary men
are those who become principall by prerogative of blood,
which is seldom unassisted with education, or by greatnesse 5
of minde, which in exact definition is Vertue.   The common
Crowd, of whom we are hopelesse, we desert, being rather
to be corrected by laws, where precept is accompanied
with punishment, then to be taught by Poesy ; for few
have arriv'd at the skill of *Orpheus* or at his good fortune, 10
whom we may suppose to have met with extraordinary
Grecian Beasts, when so successfully he reclaim'd them with
his Harp.   Nor is it needfull that Heroick Poesy should
be levell'd to the reach of Common men : for if the examples
it presents prevail upon their Chiefs, the delight of Imita- 15
tion (which we hope we have prov'd to be as effectuall to
good as to evill) will rectify, by the rules which those
Chiefs establish of their own lives, the lives of all that
behold them ; for the example of life doth as much surpasse
the force of Precept as Life doth exceed Death.   20

In the choice of these Objects which are as Seamarks to
direct the dangerous voyage of life, I thought fit to follow
the rule of Coasting Mapps, where the Shelves and Rocks
are describ'd as well as the safe Channell, the care being
equall how to avoid as to proceed ; and the Characters of 25
men whose passions are to be eschew'd I have deriv'd from
the distempers of Love or Ambition, for Love and Ambition
are too often the raging Feavers of great minds.   Yet
Ambition, if the vulgar acception of the word were corrected,
would signifie no more then an extraordinary lifting of the 30
feet in the rough ways of Honor over the impediments of
Fortune, and hath a warmth, till it be chaf'd into a Feaver,
which is necessary for every vertuous breast : for good
men are guilty of too little appetite to greatness, and it
either proceeds from that they call contentednesse (but 35

contentednesse when examin'd doth mean something of
Lasynesse as well as moderation) or from some melancholy
precept of the Cloyster, where they would make life, for
which the world was only made, more unpleasant then
5 Death; as if Nature, the Vicegerent of God,—who, in
providing delightfull varieties which vertuous greatnesse
can best possesse or assure peaceably to others, implicitly
commanded the use of them,—should in the necessaries of
life (life being her chief business), though in her whole
10 reign she never committed one error, need the counsell of
Fryars, whose solitude makes them no more fit for such
direction then Prisoners long fetter'd are for a race.

In saying this I onely awaken such retir'd men as
evaporate their strength of minde by close and long think-
15 ing, and would every where separate the soul from the
body ere we are dead, by perswading us (though they
were both created and have been long companions
together) that the preferment of the one must meerly consist in deserting the other,—teaching us to court the Grave,
20 as if during the whole lease of life we were like Moles to
live under ground, or as if long and well dying were the
certain means to live in Heaven. Yet Reason (which,
though the most profitable Talent God hath given us, some
Divines would have Philosophers to bury in the Napkin,
25 and not put it to use) perswades us that the painful active-
ness of Vertue (for Faith, on which some wholly depend,
seems but a contemplative boast till the effects of it grow
exemplary by action) will more probably acquire everlasting dignities. And surely if these severe Masters, who,
30 though obscure in Cells, take it ill if their very opinions
rule not all abroad, did give good men leave to be
industrious in getting a Share of governing the world, the
Multitudes, which are but Tenants to a few Monarchs,
would endure that subjection which God hath decreed
35 them, with better order and more ease; for the world is

onely ill govern'd because the wicked take more paines to
get authority then the vertuous, for the vertuous are often
preach'd into retirement, which is to the publick as ⟨un-⟩
profitable as their sleep; and the erroneousnesse of such
lazy rest let Philosophers judge, since Nature, of whose 5
body man thinks himself the chiefest member, hath not any
where, at any time, been respited from action (in her call'd
motion) by which she universally preserves and makes Life.
Thus much of Ambition, which should have succeeded
something I was saying of Love.   10

Love, in the Interpretation of the Envious, is Softnesse;
in the Wicked, good men suspect it for Lust; and in the
Good, some spiritual men have given it the name of Charity.
And these are but terms to this which seems a more considered definition, that indefinite Love is Lust, and Lust 15
when it is determin'd to one is Love. This definition, too,
but intrudes it self on what I was about to say, which is
(and spoken with sobernesse though like a *Lay-man*) that
Love is the most acceptable imposition of Nature, the cause
and preservation of Life, and the very healthfulnesse of the 20
mind as well as of the Body, but Lust, our raging Feaver,
is more dangerous in Cities then the Calenture in Ships.

Now, Sir, I again ask you pardon, for I have again
digressed, my immediate business being to tell you, That the
distempers of Love and Ambition are the only Characters 25
I design'd to expose as objects of terrour, and my purpose
was also to assure you that I never meant to prostitute
Wickednesse in the Images of low and contemptible
people, as if I expected the meanest of the multitude for
my Readers, since only the Rabble is seen at common 30
executions, nor intended to raise iniquity to that height of
horrour, till it might seem the fury of something worse then
a beast. In order to the first, I beleeve the *Spartans*, who,
to deter their children from Drunkennesse, accustom'd
their Slaves to vomit before them, did by such fulsome 35

examples rather teach them to disdain the Slaves then to loath Wine, for Men seldom take notice of the vice in abject persons, especially where necessity constrains it. And in observation of the second, I have thought that
5 those horrid spectacles, when the latter race of *Gladiators* made up the excesses of Roman feasts, did more induce the Guests to detest the cruelty of mankinde then increase their courage by beholding such an impudent scorne of Life.

I have now given you the accompt of such provisions as
10 I made for this new Building ; and you may next please, having examin'd the substance, to take a view of the forme, and observe if I have methodically and with discretion dispos'd of the materialls which with some curiosity I had collected. I cannot discerne by any help from reading or
15 learned men, who have been to me the best and briefest Indexes of Books, that any Nation hath in representment of great actions, either by *Heroicks* or *Dramaticks*, digested Story into so pleasant and instructive a method as the English by their *Drama* ; and by that regular species,
20 though narratively and not in Dialogue, I have drawn the body of an Heroick Poem ; In which I did not only observe the Symmetry,—proportioning five Books to five *Acts*, & *Canto's* to *Scenes*, the *Scenes* having their number ever govern'd by occasion,—but all the *shadowings, happy*
25 *strokes, secret graces*, and even the *drapery*, which together make the second beauty, I have, I hope, exactly follow'd ; and those compositions of second beauty I observe in the *Drama* to be the under-walks, interweaving, or correspondence of lesser design in *Scenes*, not the great motion of the
30 main plot and coherence of the *Acts*.

The first *Act* is the general preparative, by rendring the chiefest characters of persons, and ending with something that looks like an obscure promise of design. The second begins with an introducement of new persons, so finishes
35 all the characters, and ends with some little performance

of that design which was promis'd at the parting of the
first *Act*.   The third makes a visible correspondence in the
under-walks, or lesser intrigues, of persons, and ends with
an ample turn of the main design and expectation of a new.
The fourth, ever having occasion to be the longest, gives a 5
notorious turn to all the under-walks, and a counterturn to
that main design which chang'd in the third.   The fifth
begins with an intire diversion of the main and dependant
Plotts, then makes the general correspondence of the persons
more discernable, and ends with an easy untying of those 10
particular knots which made a contexture of the whole,
leaving such satisfaction of probabilities with the Spectator
as may perswade him that neither Fortune in the fate of
the Persons, nor the Writer in the Representment, have
been unnatural or exorbitant.   To these Meanders of the 15
English Stage I have cut out the Walks of my Poem, which
in this description may seem intricate and tedious, but will,
I hope, when men take pains to visit what they have heard
describ'd, appear to them as pleasant as a summer passage
on a crooked River, where going about and turning back 20
is as delightful as the delayes of parting Lovers.

In placing the Argument, as a *P⟨r⟩oem*, before every
Canto, I have not wholly follow'd the example of the
Moderns, but averted it from that purpose to which I
found it frequently us'd ; for it hath been intended by 25
others as the contents of the Chapter, or as a Bill of Fare
at a Venetian Feast, which is not brought before the meat
to raise an expectation, but to satisfie the longing curiosity
of the Guests.   And that which I have call'd my Argument
is onely meant as an assistance to the readers memory, by 30
containing brief hints, such as, if all the Arguments were
successively read, would make him easily remember the
mutual dependancies of the general design ; yet each
rather mentions every person acting then their actions :
But he is very unskilful that by Narratives before an 35

Historical Poem prevents expectation ; for so he comes to
have as little success over the Reader (whom the Writer
should surprize, and, as it were, keep prisoner for a time)
as he hath on his Enemies, who commanding a party out
5 to take them (and commonly Readers are justly Enemies to
Writers) imparts openly the design ere he begins the action :
Or he may be said to be as unluckily officious as he that
leads a wooing to a Mistriss one that already hath newly
enjoy'd her.

10   I shall say a little why I have chosen my interwoven
Stanza of four, though I am not oblig'd to excuse the
choice ; for numbers in Verse must, like distinct kinds of
Musick, be expos'd to the uncertain and different taste of
several Eares.   Yet I may declare that I beleev'd it would
15 be more pleasant to the Reader, in a Work of length, to
give this respite or pause between every *Stanza*, having
endeavour'd that each should contain a period, then to run
him out of breath with continu'd *Couplets*. Nor doth
alternate Rime by any lowliness of Cadence make the
20 sound less Heroick, but rather adapt it to a plain and
stately composing of Musick ; and the brevity of the
Stanza renders it less subtle to the Composer and more
easie to the Singer, which, in *stilo recitativo*, when the
Story is long, is chiefly requisite. And this was, indeed, if
25 I shall not betray vanity in my Confession, the reason that
prevail'd most towards my choice of this *Stanza* and my
division of the main work into *Canto's*, every *Canto*
including a sufficient accomplishment of some worthy
design or action ; for I had so much heat (which you, Sir,
30 may call pride, since pride may be allow'd in *Pegasus*, if it
be a praise to other Horses) as to presume they might, like
the Works of *Homer* ere they were joyn'd together and made
a Volumn by the Athenian King, be sung at Village-feasts,
though not to Monarchs after Victory, nor to Armies before
35 battel.   For so, as an inspiration of glory into the one, and

of valour into the other, did *Homer's* Spirit, long after his
bodies rest, wander in musick about *Greece*.

Thus you have the *Model* of what I have already built,
or shal hereafter join to the same frame.   If I be accus'd
of Innovation, or to have transgressed against the method 5
of the Ancients, I shall think my self secure in beleeving
that a Poet, who hath wrought with his own instruments at
a new design, is no more answerable for disobedience to
Predecessors, then *Law-makers* are liable to those old Laws
which themselves have repealed.   10

Having describ'd the outward frame, the large rooms
within, the lesser conveyances, and now the furniture, it
were orderly to let you examine the matter of which that
furniture is made.   But though every Owner who hath the
Vanity to shew his ornaments or Hangings must endure 15
the curiosity and censure of him that beholds them, yet I
shall not give you the trouble of inquiring what is, but tell
you of what I design'd, their substance, which is, *Wit*:
And *Wit* is the laborious and the lucky resultances of
thought, having towards its excellence, as we say of the 20
strokes of Painting, as well a happinesse as care.   It is a
Webb consisting of the subt'lest threds ; and like that of
the *Spider* is considerately woven out of our selves ; for
a *Spider* may be said to consider, not only respecting his
solemnesse and tacit posture (like a grave Scout in ambush 25
for his Enemy), but because all things done are either from
consideration or chance, and the works of Chance are
accomplishments of an instant, having commonly a dis-
similitude, but hers are the works of time, and have their
contextures alike.   30

Wit is not only the luck and labour, but also the dexterity of thought, rounding the world, like the Sun, with
unimaginable motion, and bringing swiftly home to the
memory universall surveys.   It is the Souls *Powder*, which
when supprest, as forbidden from flying upward, blows up 35

the restraint, and loseth all force in a farther ascension
towards Heaven (the region of God), and yet by nature is
much less able to make any inquisition downward towards
Hell, the Cell of the Devill ; But breaks through all about
5 it as farr as the utmost it can reach, removes, uncovers,
makes way for Light where darkness was inclos'd, till great
bodies are more examinable by being scatter'd into parcels,
and till all that find its strength (but most of mankind are
strangers to *Wit*, as *Indians* are to *Powder*) worship it for
10 the effects as deriv'd from the Deity.   It is in Divines,
Humility, Exemplarinesse, and Moderation ; in Statesmen,
Gravity, Vigilance, Benigne Complacency, Secrecy, Patience, and Dispatch ; in Leaders of Armies, Valor, Painfulness, Temperance, Bounty, Dexterity in punishing and
15 rewarding, and a sacred Certitude of promise.   It is in
Poets a full comprehension of all recited in all these, and
an ability to bring those comprehensions into action, when
they shall so far forget the true measure of what is of greatest consequence to humanity (which are things righteous,
20 pleasant, and usefull) as to think the delights of greatness
equall to that of Poesy, or the Chiefs of any Profession
more necessary to the world then excellent Poets.   Lastly,
though *Wit* be not the envy of ignorant Men, 'tis often of
evill Statesmen, and of all such imperfect great spirits as
25 have in it a lesse degree then Poets ; for though no man
envies the excellence of that which in no proportion he
ever tasted, as men cannot be said to envy the condition of
Angels, yet we may say the Devill envies the Supremacy of
God, because he was in some degree partaker of his Glory.
30   That which is not, yet is accompted, *Wit*, I will but
sleightly remember, which seems very incident to imperfect
youth and sickly age.   Yong men, as if they were not
quite deliver'd from Childhood, whose first exercise is
Language, imagine it consists in the Musick of words, and
35 beleeve they are made wise by refining their Speech above

the vulgar Dialect, which is a mistake almost as great as that of the people who think Orators (which is a title that crowns at riper years those that have practis'd the dexterity of tongue) the ablest men, who are indeed so much more unapt for governing as they are more fit for Sedition ; and it 5 may be said of them as of the Witches of *Norway*, who can sell a Storm for a *Doller*, which for Ten Thousand they cannot allay. From the esteem of speaking they proceed to the admiration of what are commonly call'd *Conceits*, things that sound like the knacks or toyes of ordinary *Epigram-* 10 *matists*, and from thence, after more conversation and variety of objects, grow up to some force of *Fancy* ; Yet even then, like young Hawks, they stray and fly farr off, using their liberty as if they would ne're return to the Lure, and often goe at check ere they can make a stedy view and know 15 their game.

Old men, that have forgot their first Childhood and are returning to their second, think it lyes in *agnominations*, and in a kinde of an alike tinkling of words, or else in a grave telling of wonderfull things, or in comparing of 20 times without a discover'd partiality : which they perform so ill by favoring the past, that, as 'tis observ'd, if the bodies of men should grow less, though but an unmeasurable proportion in Seaven years, Yet, reckoning from the *Flood*, they would not remain in the Stature of Froggs, so if States 25 and particular persons had impair'd in government and increas'd in wickedness proportionably to what Old men affirm they have done from their own infancy to their age, all publique Policy had been long since Confusion, and the Congregated World would not suffise now to people a Village. 30

The last thing they suppose to be *Wit* is their bitter Morals, when they almost declare themselves Enemies to Youth and Beauty, by which severity they seem cruel as *Herod* when he surpris'd the sleeping Children of *Bethlem* : for Youth is so far from wanting Enemies that it is mortally 35

its own, so unpractised that it is every where cosen'd more
then a Stranger among *Jews*, and hath an Infirmity of sight
more hurtful then Blindness to Blinde men, for though it
cannot chuse the way it scorns to be led. And Beauty,
5 though many call themselves her Friends, hath few but
such as are fals to her : though the World sets her in a
Throne, yet all about her, even her gravest Councellors,
are Traytors, though not in conspiracy, yet in their distinct
designs ; and to make her certain not onely of distress but
10 ruine, she is ever pursu'd by her most cruel enemy, the
great Destroyer, *Time*. But I will proceed no farther
upon old men, nor in recording mistakes, least finding so
many more then there be Verities, we might beleeve we
walk in as great obscurity as the Egyptians when Darkness
15 was their Plague. Nor will I presume to call the matter of
which the Ornaments or Substantial parts of this Poem are
compos'd, *Wit*; but onely tell you my endeavour was, in
bringing Truth, too often absent, home to mens bosoms, to
lead her through unfrequented and new ways, and from
20 the most remote Shades, by representing Nature, though
not in an affected, yet in an unusual dress.

'Tis now fit, after I have given you so long a survay of
the Building, to render you some accompt of the Builder,
that you may know by what time, pains, and assistance I
25 have already proceeded, or may hereafter finish my work ;
and in this I shal take occasion to accuse and condemn, as
papers unworthy of light, all those hasty digestions of
thought which were published in my Youth,—a sentence
not pronounc'd out of melancholy rigour, but from a cheerful
30 obedience to the just authority of experience : For that
grave Mistris of the World, *Experience*, (in whose profitable
School those before the Flood stay'd long, but we like
wanton children come thither late, yet too soon are call'd
out of it and fetch'd home by Death) hath taught me that the
35 engendrings of unripe age become abortive and deform'd,

and that after obtaining more years, those must needs prophecy with ill success who make use of their Visions in Wine ; That, when the ancient Poets were vallew'd as Prophets, they were long and painfull in watching the correspondence of Causes ere they presum'd to foretell effects, and that 'tis a high presumption to entertain a Nation (who are a Poets standing Guest, and require Monarchicall respect) with hasty provisions ; as if a Poet might imitate the familiar dispatch of Faulkoners, mount his *Pegasus*, unhood his *Muse*, and with a few flights boast he hath provided a feast for a Prince. Such posting upon *Pegasus* I have long since forborne, and during my Journey in this worke have mov'd with a slow pace, that I might make my survays as one that travaild not to bring home the names, but the proportion and nature, of things ; and in this I am made wise by two great examples, for the friends of *Virgill* acknowledge he was many years in doing honor to *Æneas*, still contracting at night into a closer force the abundance of his morning strengths, and *Statius* rather seems to boast then blush, when he confesses he was twice Seaven in renowning the war between *Argos* and *Thebes*.

Next to the usefulness of Time, which here implys ripe age, I beleev'd pains most requisite to this undertaking : for though painfulness in Poets (according to the usual negligence of our Nation in Examining, and their diligence to censure) seems always to discover a want of natural force, and is traduc'd, as if Poesy concern'd the world no more then Dancing, whose onely grace is the quickness and facility of motion, and whose perfection is not of such publique consequence that any man can merit much by attaining it with long labour ; yet let them consider, and they will finde (nor can I stay long ere I convince them in the important use of Poesy) the natural force of a Poet more apparent by but confessing that great forces aske great labor in managing, then by an arrogant braving the World when

he enters the field with his undisciplin'd first thoughts : For
a wise Poet, like a wise General, will not shew his strengths
till they are in exact government and order, which are not
the postures of chance, but proceed from Vigilance and
5 labour.

Yet to such painfull Poets some upbraid the want of
extemporary fury, or rather *inspiration*, a dangerous word
which many have of late successfully us'd ; and *inspiration*
is a spiritual Fitt, deriv'd from the ancient Ethnick Poets,
10 who then, as they were Priests, were Statesmen too, and
probably lov'd dominion ; and as their well dissembling of
inspiration begot them reverence then equall to that which
was paid to Laws, so these who now profess the same
fury may perhaps by such authentick example pretend
15 authority over the people, It being not unreasonable to
imagine they rather imitate the *Greek* Poets then the
Hebrew Prophets, since the later were inspir'd for the use
of others, and these, like the former, prophecy for themselves. But though the ancient Poets are excus'd, as
20 knowing the weak constitution of those Deities from whom
they took their Priesthood, and the frequent necessity of
dissembling for the ease of government, yet these, who also
from the chief to the meanest are Statesmen and Priests,
but have not the luck to be Poets, should not assume such
25 saucy familiarity with a true God.

From the time and labour requir'd to my Poem, let me
proceed to my Assistants, by which I shall not so much
attest my own weakness as discover the difficulties and
greatness of such a work ; For when *Solomon* made use of
30 his Neighbours towards his Building he lost no reputation,
nor by demanding those aids was thought a lesser Prince,
but rather publish'd his Wisdom in rightly understanding
the vast extent of his enterprise, who likewise with as much
glory made use of Fellers of Wood and Hewers of Stone
35 as of learned Architects ; Nor have I refrain'd to be oblig'd

to men of any Science, as well mechanicall as liberall ; Nor
when Memory (from that various and plentifull stock with
which all observers are furnish'd that have had diversity of
life) presented me by chance with any figure, did I lay it
aside as useless, because at that instant I was not skilfull to 5
manage it artfully, but I have staid and recorded such
objects, till by consulting with right Masters I have dispos'd
of them without mistake ; It being no more shame to get
Learning at that very time and from the same Text when
and by which we instruct others, then for a forward Scout, 10
discovering the Enemy, to save his own life at a Pass,
where he then teaches his Party to escape.

In remembring mine own helps, I have consider'd
those which others in the same necessity have taken, and
finde that Writers, contrary to my inclination, are apter to 15
be beholding to Bookes then to Men, not only as the first
are more in their possession, being more constant Companions then dearest friends, but because they commonly
make such use of treasure found in Books· as of other
treasure belonging to the Dead and hidden under ground ; 20
for they dispose of both with great secrecy, defacing the
shape or images of the one as much as of the other, through
fear of having the originall of their stealth or abundance
discover'd. And the next cause why Writers are more in
Libraries then in company is that Books are easily open'd, 25
and learned men are usually shut up by a froward or envious
humor of retention, or else unfold themselves so as we
may read more of their weakness and vanity then Wisdom,
imitating the Holyday-custom in great Cities, where the
shops of Chaundry and slight wares are familiarly open, but 30
those of solid and staple Merchandise are proudly lock'd up.

Nor indeed can it be expected that all great Doctors are
of so benigne a nature as to take pains in gaining treasure
(of which Knowledge is the greatest) with intent to inrich
others so easily as if they stood every where with their 35

Pockets spred and ready to be pickt : nor can we read of any
Father who so far and secretly adopted his Sonn to a Book
of his own writing, as that his Sonn might be thought Author
of that written Wit as much as his Father was Author of
5 him : Nor of any Husband that to his darling Wife would
so far surrender his Wisdom, as that in publique he could
endure to let her use his Dictates, as if she would have
others think her wiser then himself. By this remembrance
of that usual parsimony in owners of Wit towards such as
10 would make use of their plenty, I lament the fortune of
others, and may wish the Reader to congratulate mine ; for
I have found Friends as ready as Books to regulate my
conceptions, or make them more correct, easie, and apparent. But though I am become so wise, by knowing my
15 self, as to beleeve the thoughts of divers transcend the best
which I have written, yet I have admitted from no man any
change of my Design, nor very seldom of my sense : For I
resolv'd to have this Poem subsist and continue throughout
with the same complexion and spirit, though it appear but
20 like a plain Family, of a neighbourly alliance, who marry
into the same moderate quality and garbe, and are fearfull
of introducing strangers of greater ranke, least the shining
presence of such might seem to upbraid and put all about
them out of countenance.
25 And now, Sir, that the Reader may (whom Writers are
fain to court, draw in, and keep with artifice, so shy men
grow of Books) beleeve me worthy of him, I cannot forbear
to thank you in publique for examining, correcting, and
allowing this Poem in parcels ere it arriv'd at the contex-
30 ture : by which you have perform'd the just degrees of
proceeding with Poets, who during the gayety and wantonness of the Muse are but as children to Philosophers
(though of some Giant race), whose first thoughts, wilde,
and roaming farr off, must be brought home, watch'd, and
35 interrogated, and after they are made more regular, be

encourag'd and prais'd for doing well, that they may
delight in aiming at perfection. By such a Method the
Muse is taught to become Master of her own and others
strength ; and who is he so learn'd (how proud so ever with
being cherish'd in the bosome of Fame) that can hope, when 5
through the severall ways of Science he seeks Nature in
her hidden walks, to make his Journy short, unless he call
you to be his Guide ? and who so guided can suspect his
safety, even when he travails through the Enemy's Country ?
for such is the vast field of Learning, where the Learned, 10
though not numerous enough to be an Army, lye as small
Parties malitiously in Ambush to destroy all new Men that
look into their Quarters. And from such, you, and those
you lead, are secure, because you move not by common
Mapps, but have painfully made your own Prospect, and 15
travail now like the Sun, not to inform your self, but
enlighten the world.

And likewise, when by the strict survey and Government
that hath been had over this Poem I shall think to govern
the Reader,—who, though he be noble, may perhaps judg 20
of supreme Power like a very Commoner, and rather
approve authority when it is in many then in one,—I must
acquaint him that you had not alone the trouble of establishing and destroying, but enjoy'd your intervals and ease
by Two Colleagues : Two that are worthy to follow you 25
into the Closets of Princes, if the knowledg of Men past,
of whom Books are the remaining minds, or of the present,
of whom Conversation is the usefull and lawfull Spy, may
make up such greatnesse as is fit for great Courts, or if the
rayes that proceed from the Poetick Planet be not a little 30
too strong for the sight of modern Monarchs, who now are
too seldom taught in their youth like Eaglets to fortifie their
eyes by often soaring near the Sun. And though this be
here but my testimony, it is too late for any of you to dis-
claim it ; for since you have made it valid by giving yours 35

of GONDIBERT under your hands, you must be content to be us'd by me as Princes are by their preferr'd Subjects, who in the very act of taking honor return it to the Giver, as benefits receiv'd by the Creature manifest the power
5 and redound to the glory of the Creator.

I am now, Sir, to your great comfort, that have bin thus ill and long diverted, arriv'd at my last consideration, which is to satisfie those who may inquire why I have taken so much paines to become an Author. Or why any
10 man stays so long sweating at the fire of Invention, to dress the food of the Minde, when Readers have so imperfect Stomacks, as they either devour Books with over hasty Digestion or grow to loath them from a surfet? And why I more especially made my task an Heroick Poem? I
15 shall involve the two first Questions in one, as submitting to be concern'd amongst the generality of Writers, whose Enemies being many, and now mine, we must joyn forces to oppose them.

Men are chiefly provok'd to the toyl of compiling Books
20 by love of Fame, and often by officiousness of Conscience, but seldom with expectation of Riches; for those that spend time in writing to instruct others may finde leasure to inform themselves how mean the provisions are which busy and studious minds can make for their own sedentary
25 bodies: And Learned men, to whom the rest of the world are but Infants, have the same foolish affection in nourishing others minds as Pellicans in feeding their young, which is at the expence of the very subsistance of Life. 'Tis then apparent they proceed by the instigation of Fame or
30 Conscience; and I believe many are perswaded by the first (of which I am One) and some are commanded by the second. Nor is the desire of Fame so vain as divers have rigidly imagin'd, Fame being, when belonging to the Living, that which is more gravely call'd a steddy and
35 necessary reputation, and without it hereditary Power or

acquir'd greatness can never quietly govern the World.
'Tis of the dead a musical glory, in which God, the author
of excellent goodness, vouchsafes to take a continual
share : For the remember'd vertues of great men are
chiefly such of his works, mention'd by King *David*, as 5
perpetually praise him ; and the good fame of the Dead
prevails by example much more then the reputation of the
Living, because the later is alwayes suspected by our Envy,
but the other is cheerfully allow'd and religiously admir'd ;
for Admiration, whose Eyes are ever weak, stands still 10
and at gaze upon great things acted far off, but when they
are neer, walks slightly away as from familiar objects.
Fame is to our Sons a solid Inheritance, and not unuseful
to remote Posterity ; and to our Reason, tis the first
though but a little taste of Eternity.   15

Those that write by the command of Conscience, thinking
themselves able to instruct others, and consequently
oblig'd to it, grow commonly the most voluminous, because
the pressures of Conscience are so incessant that she is
never satisfy'd with doing enough ; for such as be newly 20
made the Captives of God (many appearing so to themselves
when they first begin to weare the Fetters of Conscience)
are like common slaves when newly taken, who, terrify'd
with a fancy of the severity of absolute Masters, abuse
their diligence out of fear, and do ill rather then appear 25
idle. And this may be the cause why Libraries are more
then double lin'd with Spiritual Books or Tracts of
Morality, the latter being the Spiritual Counsels of *Lay-
men* ; and the newest of such great volumns, being usually
but transcriptions or translations, differ so much from the 30
Ancients as later daies from those of old, which difference
is no more then an alteration of names by removing the
Ethnicks to make way for the *Saints*. These are the
effects of their labours who are provok'd to become
Authors meerly out of Conscience ; and Conscience we 35

may again averre to be often so unskilful and timerous
that it seldom gives a wise and steddy account of God,
but grows jealous of him as of an Adversary, and is after
melancholy visions like a fearfull Scout, after he hath ill
5 survey'd the Enemy, who then makes incongruous, long,
and terrible Tales.

Having confess'd that the desire of Fame made me
a Writer, I must declare why in my riper age I chose to
gain it more especially by an Heroicall Poem ; and the
10 Heroick being by most allow'd to be the most beautifull of
Poems, I shall not need to decide the quarrels of Poets
about the Degrees of Excellence in Poesy. But 'tis not
amiss, ere I avow the usefulnesse of the Science in generall,
which was the cause of my undertaking, to remember the
15 value it had from the greatest and most worthy spirits in
all Ages ; for I will not abstain, though it may give me the
reputation but of common reading, to mention that *Pisi-
stratus*, though a Tyrant, liv'd with the praise and dy'd with
the blessing of all *Greece* for gathering the scatter'd limbs of
20 *Homer's* Works into a Body, and that great *Alexander*, by
publiquely conversing with it, attain'd the universall opinion
of Wit, the fame of such inward forces conducing as much
to his Conquests as his Armies abroad : That the *Athenian*
Prisoners were thought worthy of life and liberty for
25 singing the Tragedies of *Euripides* : That *Thebes* was sav'd
from destruction by the Victors reverence to the memory
of *Pindar* : That the elder *Scipio*, who govern'd all the
civill world, lay continually in the bosome of *Ennius* :
That the great *Numantin* and *Lælius*, no less renownd,
30 were openly proud when the Romans beleev'd they assisted
Terence in his Comedies : That *Augustus*, to whom the
mysteries of universall Empire were more familiar then
domestick Dominion to Modern Kings, made *Virgill* the
partner of his joyes, and would have divided his business
35 with *Horace* : And that *Lucan* was the fear and envy of

Nero.   If we approach nearer our own times, we may add
the triumphall Entry which the Papacy gave to *Petrarch*,
and how much *Tasso* is stil the glory and delight of *Italy*.

But as in this hasty Muster of Poets and listing their
confederates, I shall by omitting many deprive them of that 5
pay which is due from Fame, so I may now by the opinion
of some Divines, whom notwithstanding I will reverence
in all their distinct habits and fashions of the mind, be
held partiall and too bold, by adding to the first number
(though I range them upon holy ground, and aside) *Moses,* 10
David, and *Solomon,* for their Songs, Psalmes, and
Anthemes,—the Second being the acknowledg'd Favorite of
God, whom he had gain'd by excellent Praises in sacred
Poesy.   And I fear, since Poesy is the clearest light by
which they finde the soul who seek it, that Poets have in 15
their fluent kindnesse diverted from the right use, and spent
too much of that spirituall talent in the honor of mortall
Princes ; for divine Praise (when in the high perfection,
as in Poets, and only in them) is so much the uttermost
and whole of Religious worship that all other parts of 20
Devotion serve but to make it up.

89.

Gondibert,   Praise *is Devotion fit for mighty Mindes,*
lib. 2,   *The diff'ring World's agreeing Sacrifice,*
canto 6. *Where Heaven divided, Faiths united findes ;*
    But Pray'r *in various discord upward flyes.*   25

90.

For Pray'r *the Ocean is, where diversly*
    Men steer their course, each to a sev'ral Coast,
Where all our Int'rests so discordant be,
    That half beg windes by which the rest are lost.

91.

By Penitence *when We our selves forsake,*   30
  'Tis but in wise design on piteous Heaven ;
In Praise *We nobly give what God may take,*
    And are without a Beggars blush forgiven.

92.

Its utmost force, like Powder's, *is unknown ;*
  And though weak Kings excess of Praise *may fear,*
  Yet when 'tis here, like Powder *dang'rous grown,*
5   *Heaven's Vault receives what would the Palace tear.*

After this contemplation how acceptable the voice of
Poesy hath been to God, we may, by descending from
Heaven to Earth, consider how usefull it is to Men ; and
among Men Divines are the chief, because ordain'd to
10 temper the rage of humane power by spirituall menaces,
as by suddain and strange threatnings madnesse is frighted
into Reason ; and they are sent hither as Liegers from
God, to conserve in stedfast motion the slippery joints of
Government, and to perswade an amity in divided Nations :
15 therefore to Divines I first addresse my self, and presume
to ask them why, ever since their dominion was first
allow'd at the great change of Religions, though ours
more then any inculcates obedience as an easie Medicine
to cool the impatient and raging world into a quiet rest,
20 mankinde hath been more unruly then before,—it being
visible that Empire decreas'd with the increase of
Christianity, and that one weak Prince did anciently
suffice to govern many strong Nations ; but now one little
Province is too hard for their own wise King, and a small
25 Republique hath Seventy years maintain'd their revolt to
the disquiet of many Monarchs. Or if Divines reply we
cannot expect the good effects of their office because their
spirituall Dominion is not allow'd as absolute, then it may
be ask'd them more severely, why 'tis not allow'd ? for
30 where ever there hath been great degrees of power, which
hath been often and long in the Church, it discovers,
though worldly vicissitude be objected as an excuse, that
the managers of such power, since they endeavor'd not
to enlarge it, beleev'd the increase unrighteous, or were in
35 acting or contriving that endeavor either negligent or

weak : For Power, like the hasty Vine, climbes up apace
to the Supporter, but if not skilfully attended and dress'd,
instead of spreading and bearing fruit, grows high and
naked, and then, like empty title, being soon useless to
others, becomes neglected and unable to support it self.   5

But if Divines have faild in governing Princes, that is,
of being intirely beleev'd by them, yet they might obliquely
have rul'd them in ruling the People, by whom of late
Princes have been govern'd ; and they might probably
rule the People, because the heads of the Church, where   10
ever Christianity is preach'd, are Tetrarchs of Time, of
which they command the fourth Division, for to no less
the Sabbaths and Daies of Saints amount; and during
those daies of spiritual triumph Pulpits are Thrones, and
the people oblig'd to open their Eares, and let in the   15
ordinances and commands of Preachers, who likewise are
not without some little Regency throughout the rest of the
Year ; for then they may converse with the Laity, from
whom they have commonly such respect (and respect soon
opens the door to perswasion) as shews their Congregations   20
not deaf in those holy seasons when speaking predominates.

But notwithstanding these advantages, the Pulpit hath
little prevail'd ; for the world is in all Regions revers'd or
shaken by disobedience, an Engine with which the great
Angels (for such were the Devils, and had faculties much   25
more sublim'd then Men) beleev'd they could disorder
Heaven. And it is not want of capacity in the lower
Auditory that makes Doctrin so unsuccesful ; for the
people are not simple, since the Gentry, even of strongest
education, lack sufficient defence against them, and are   30
hourly surpris'd in their common Ambushes, their Shops :
For on sacred Daies they walk gravely and sadly from
Temples, as if they had newly bury'd their sinful Fathers,
at night sleep as if they never needed forgiveness, and rise
with the next Sun to lie in wait for the Noble & the   35

Studious. And though these quiet Cousners are amongst
the People esteem'd their steddy Men, yet they honor
the courage and more active parts of such disobedient
Spirits as, disdaining thus tamely to deceive, attempt
5 bravely to robb the State; and the State, they beleeve,
though the Helme were held by Apostles, would always
consist of such Arch-robbers, as who ever stripps them but
waves the tedious satisfaction which the Lasy expect from
Laws, and comes a shorter way to his own.

10 Thus unapt for obedience,—in the condition of Beasts
whose appetite is Liberty, and their Liberty a license of
Lust,—the People have often been since a long and
notorious power hath continu'd with Divines, whom though
with reverence we accuse for mistaken lenity, yet are we
15 not so cruel to expect they should behave themselves to
Sinners like fierce *Phineas*, or preach with their Swords
drawn, to kill all they cannot perswade: But our meaning
is to shew how much their Christian meekness hath
deceiv'd them in taming this wilde monster, the People,
20 and a little to rebuke them for neglecting the assistance of
Poets, and for upbraiding the Ethnicks because the Poets
mannag'd their Religion, as if Religion could walk more
prosperously abroad then when Morality, respectfully and
bare-headed as her Usher, prepares the way: it being no
25 lesse true that during the dominion of Poesy a willing and
peacefull obedience to Superiors becalm'd the world, then
that obedience, like the marriage yoke, is a restraint more
needful and advantagious then liberty, and hath the same
reward of pleasant quietnesse which it anciently had, when
30 *Adam*, till his disobedience, enjoy'd Paradise. Such are
the effects of sacred Poesy, which charms the People
with harmonious precepts, and whose aid Divines should
not disdain, since their Lord, the Saviour of the World,
vouchsaf'd to deliver his Doctrine in Parabolicall Fictions.
35 Those that be of next importance are Leaders of Armies,

and such I measure not by the suffrages of the People, who give them respect as Indians worship the evill Spirit, rather for fear of harm then for affection, but esteem them as the painfull Protectors and enlargers of Empire, by whom it actively moves ; and such active motion of Empire 5 is as necessary as the motion of the Sea, where all things would putrifie and infect one another if the Element were quiet : so is it with mens minds on shore, when that Element of greatness and honor, *Empire*, stands still, of which the largeness is likewise as needfull as the vastness 10 of the Sea ; For God ordain'd not huge Empire as proportionable to the Bodies but to the Mindes of Men, and the Mindes of Men are more monstrous and require more space for agitation and the hunting of others then the Bodies of Whales. But he that beleeves men such 15 moderate Sheep, as that many are peacefully contain'd in a narrow Folde, may be better inform'd in *America*, where little Kings never enjoy a harmlesse neighbourhood, unless protected defensively amongst themselves by an Emperor that hath wide possessions and priority over 20 them, as in some few places ; but when restrain'd in narrow dominion, where no body commands and hinders their nature, they quarrell like Cocks in a Pitt ; and the Sun in a dayes travail there sees more battails (but not of consequence, because their Kings, though many, are little) 25 then in *Europe* in a Year.

To *Leaders of Armies*, as to very necessary Men, whose Office requires the uttermost aids of art and Nature, and rescues the sword of Justice when 'tis wrested from supreme Power by Commotion, I am now address'd, 30 and must put them in minde, though not upbraidingly, how much their Mighty Predecessors were anciently oblig'd to Poets, whose Songs, recording the praises of Conduct and Valour, were esteem'd the chiefest rewards of Victory ; And since Nature hath made us prone to 35

Imitation, by which we equall the best or the worst, how
much those Images of Action prevail upon our mindes
which are delightfully drawn by Poets. For the greatest
of the Grecian Captains have confess'd that their Counsels
5 have bin made wise and their Courages warm by *Homer* ;
and since Praise is a pleasure which God hath invited, and
with which he often vouchsaf'd to be pleas'd when it was
sent him by his own Poet, why is it not lawfull for
vertuous men to be cherish'd and magnify'd with hearing
10 their vigilance, Valour, and good Fortune (the latter being
more the immediate gift of Heaven, because the effect of
an unknown Cause) commended and made eternall in
Poesy ? But perhaps the art of praising Armies into great
and instant action by singing their former deeds (an Art
15 with which the Ancients made *Empire* so large) is too
subtle for modern *Leaders*, who, as they cannot reach the
heights of Poesy, must be content with a narrow space of
Dominion ; and narrow Dominion breeds evil, peevish, and
vexatious mindes and a Nationall self-opinion, like simple
20 Jewish arrogance ; and the Jews were extraordinary
proud in a very little Country: For men in contracted
governments are but a kinde of Prisoners, and Prisoners
by long restraint grow wicked, malitious to all abroad, and
foolish esteemers of themselves, as if they had wrong in
25 not enjoying every thing which they can only see out of
Windows.

Our last application is to *Statesmen* and Makers of
Laws, who may be reasonably reduc'd to one, since the
second differ no more from the first then Judges, the
30 Copies of *Law-makers*, differ from their Originals: For
Judges, like all bold interpreters, by often altering the
Text make it quite new, and *Statesmen*, who differ not
from Law-makers in the act but in the manner of doing,
make new Lawes presumptuously without the consent of
35 the people : but *Legislators* more civilly seem to whistle

to the Beast, and stroak him into the Yoke; and in the Yoke of State, the People, with too much pampering, grow soon unruly and draw awry: Yet *Statesmen* and *Judges*, whose businesse is governing, and the thing to be govern'd is the people, have amongst us—we being more 5 proud and mistaken then any other famous Nation—look'd gravely upon Poetry, and with a negligence that betray'd a Northerly ignorance, as if they beleev'd they could perform their work without it. But Poets, who with wise diligence study the People, and have in all ages by an 10 insensible influence governd their manners, may justly smile when they perceive that *Divines, Leaders of Armies, Statesmen,* and *Judges* think *Religion,* the *Sword,* or (which is unwritten *Law* and a secret Confederacy of Chiefs) *Policy,* or *Law* (which is written, but seldom rightly read) 15 can give without the help of the *Muses* a long and quiet satisfaction in government. For *Religion* is to the wicked and faithless, who are many, a jurisdiction against which they readily rebell, because it rules severely, yet promiseth no worldly recompence for obedience,—obedience being 20 by every humane Power invited with assurances of visible advantage. The good, who are but few, need not the Power of *Religion* to make them better, the power of *Religion* proceeding from her threatnings, which, though mean weapons, are fitly us'd, since she hath none but base 25 Enemies. We may observe, too, that all Vertuous men are so taken up with the rewards of Heaven that they live as if out of the World; and no government receives assistance from any man meerly as he is good, but as that goodness is active in temporal things.   30

The *Sword* is in the hand of *Justice* no guard to Govern-ment, but then when *Justice* hath an Army for her own defence; and Armies, if they were not pervertible by Faction, yet are to Common-wealths like Kings Physitians to poor Patients, who buy the cure of their disorder'd 35

bodies at so high a rate that they may be said to change their Sickness for Famine. *Policy* (I mean of the Living, not of the Dead : the one being the last rules or designs governing the Instant, the other those Laws that began
5 Empire) is as mortal as *States-men* themselves, whose incessant labors make that Hectick feaver of the minde which insensibly dispatches the Body ; and when We trace *States-men* through all the Histories of Courts, we finde their Inventions so unnecessary to those that succeed
10 at the Helme, or so much envy'd, as they scarce last in authority till the Inventors are buried ; and change of designs in *States-men* (their designs being the weapons by which States are defended) grows as destructive to Govern-ment as a continual change of various weapons is to
15 Armies, which must receive with ruine any suddain assault, when want of practise makes unactiveness. We cannot urge that the Ambition of *States-men*, who are obnoxious to the people, doth much disorder government, because the Peoples anger, by a perpetual coming in of new
20 Oppressors, is so deverted in considering those whom their Eyes but lately left, as they have not time enough to rise for the Publick ; and evil successors to power are in the troubled stream of State like succeeding Tides in Rivers, where the Mudd of the former is hidden by the filth of
25 the last.

Laws, if very ancient, grow as doubtful and difficult as Letters on buryd Marble, which only Antiquaries read ; but if not Old, they want that reverence which is therefore paid to the vertues of Ancestors, because their crimes
30 come not to our remembrance ; and yet great Men must be long dead whose ills are forgotten. If *Laws* be New, they must be made either by very Angels or by Men that have some vices, and those being seen make their Vertues suspected ; for the People no more esteem able men whose
35 defects they know, though but errors incident to Humanity,

then an Enemy values a strong Army having experience
of their Errors.   And new Laws are held but the projects
of necessitous Power, new Nets spred to intangle Us, the
Old being accounted too many, since most are beleev'd to
be made for Forfeitures ; and such letting of blood, though 5
intended by Lawmakers for our health, is to the People
always out of Season, for those that love life with too
much Passion (and Mony is the life blood of the People)
ever fear a Consumption.   But be Law-makers as able as
Nature or Experience, which is the best Art, can make 10
them, yet, though I will not yeeld the Wicked to be wiser
then the Vertuous, I may say offences are too hard for the
Laws, as some Beasts are too wylie for their Hunters, and
that Vice overgrows Vertue as much as Weeds grow faster
then Medicinable Herbs ; or rather that Sin, like the 15
fruitfull slime of *Nilus*, doth increase into so many various
shapes of Serpents, whose walks and retreats are winding
and unknown, that even *Justice*, the painfull pursuer of
Mischief, is become weary and amaz'd.

After these Meditations, me thinks Government resembles 20
a Ship, where though *Divines*, *Leaders* of *Armies*, *States-*
men, and *Judges* are the trusted Pilots, yet it moves by the
means of winds as uncertain as the breath of Opinion, and
is laden with the People, a Fraight much loosser and more
dangerous then any other living stowage, being as trouble- 25
some in fair weather as Horses in a Storm.   And how can
these Pilots stedily maintain their course to the Land of
Peace and Plenty, since they are often divided at the
Helm ?   For *Divines*, when they consider great *Chiefs*,
suppose Armies to be sent from God for a temporary 30
Plague, not for continuall Jurisdiction, and that Gods
extreme punishments, of which Armies be the most
violent, are ordain'd to have no more lastingness, then the
extremes in Nature.   They think, when they consider
Statesmen, Policy hath nothing of the Dove, and, being all 35

Serpent, is more dangerous then the dangers it pretends to
prevent, and that out-witting by falshood and corruption
adverse States or the People (though the people be often
the greater enemy, and more perilsome, being nearest) is
5 but giving reputation to Sinn, and that to maintain the
Publique by politique evils, is a base prostitution of
Religion, and the prostitution of Religion is that unpardonable whoredom which so much anger'd the Prophets.
They think *Law* nothing but the Bible forcibly usurp'd by
10 covetous Lawyers and disguis'd in a Paraphrase more
obscure then the Text, and that 'tis only want of just
reverence to Religion which doth expose us to the charges
and vexations of *Law*.

The *Leaders of Armies* accuse *Divines* for unwisely
15 raising the War of the World by opposite Doctrine, and
for being more indiscreet in thinking to appease it by
perswasion, forgetting that the dispatchful ending of War
is blows, and that the naturall region for Disputes when
Nations are engag'd, though by Religion, is the Field of
20 Battail, not Schools and Academies, which they beleeve, by
their restless controversies, less civill then Camps, as
intestine Quarrell is held more barbarous then foraign
War. They think *Statesmen* to them, unlesse dignify'd
with military Office, but mean Spys, that like *African
25 Foxes*, who attend on *Lyons*, ranging before and about for
their valiant prey, shrink back till the danger be subdu'd,
and then with insatiate hunger come in for a share : Yet
sometimes with the Eye of Envie, which enlarges objects
like a multiplying glass, they behold these *Statesmen*, and
30 think them immense as *Whales*, the motion of whose vast
bodies can in a peacefull calm trouble the Ocean till it boyl;
After a little hasty wonder, they consider them again with
disdain of their low constraints at Court, where they must
patiently endure the little follies of such small Favorites as
35 wait even near the wisest Thrones ; so fantastically weak

seem Monarchs in the sicknesse of Care, a feaver in the head, when for the humorous pleasure of Diversity they descend from purple Beds, and seek their ease upon the ground.   These great *Leaders* say also that *Law* moves slowly as with fetter'd feet, and is too tedious in redresse of 5 wrongs, whilst in Armies *Justice* seems to ride poste, and overtakes Offenders er'e the contagion of crimes can infect others ; and though in Courts and Cities great men fence often with her, and with a forcive sleight put by her sword, yet when she retires to *Camps* she is in a posture not only 10 to punish the offences of particular Greatnesse but of injurious Nations.

States-men look on *Divines* as men whose long solitude and Meditations on Heaven hath made them Strangers upon Earth, and tis acquaintance with the World and 15 knowledge of Man that makes abilities of Ruling; for though it may be said that a sufficient belief of Doctrin would beget obedience, which is the uttermost design of governing, yet since diversity of Doctrin doth distract all Auditors, and makes them doubtfully dispose their obedience 20 even towards spiritual powers, on which many would have the temporal depend, therefore *States-men* think themselves more fit to manage *Empire* then *Divines*, whose usefulness consists in perswasion; and perswasion is the last medicine, being the most desperate, which *States-men* apply to the 25 distemper of the People, for their distemper is madness, and madness is best cur'd with terror and force.   They think that *Leaders* of *Armies* are to great Empire as great Rivers to the continent, which make an easie access of such benefits as the Metropolis, the seat of power, would 30 else at vast distances with difficulty reach ; yet often like proud Rivers when they swell, they destroy more by once overflowing their borders at home then they have in long time acquir'd from abroad :   They are to little Empire like the Sea to low Islands, by nature a defence from Forreign- 35

ers, but by accident when they rage a deluge to their own
shore. And at all seasons *States-men* beleeve them more
dangerous to government then themselves; for the popularity of *States-men* is not so frequent as that of *Generals*,
5 or if by rare sufficiency of Art it be gain'd, yet the force of
crowds in Cities, compar'd to the validity of men of Armes
and discipline, would appear like the great number of
Sheep to a few Wolves, rather a cause of Comfort then of
Terror. They think that chief *Ministers of Law*, by un-
10 skilful integrity or love of popularity (which shews the
Minde as meanly born as bred), so earnestly pursue the
protection of the Peoples right, that they neglect the publick
Interest; and though the Peoples right and publick Interest
be the same, yet usually by the People the Ministers of
15 Law mean private men, and by the other the State; and
so the State and the People are divided, as we may say a man
is divided within himself, when reason and Passion (and
Passion is folly) dispute about consequent actions; and if
we were call'd to assist at such intestine war, we must side
20 with Reason, according to our duty, by the Law of Nature;
and Natures Law, though not written in Stone, as was the
Law of Religion, hath taken deep impression in the Heart
of Man, which is harder then marble of *Mount-Sinai.*

Cheef *Ministers* of *Law* think *Divines* in government
25 should, like the *Penal Statutes*, be choicely and but seldom
us'd; for as those Statutes are rigorously inquisitive after
venial faults, punishing our very manners and weak constitution as well as insolent appetite, so Divines, that are made
vehement with contemplating the dignity of the Offended
30 (which is God) more then the frailty of the Offender, govern
as if men could be made Angels ere they come to Heaven.

Great *Ministers* of *Law* think likewise that Leaders of
Armies are, like ill Physitians, onely fit for desperate cures,
whose boldness calls in the assistance of Fortune during
35 the fears and troubles of Art; Yet the health they give to

a distemper'd State is not more accidental then the preservation of it is uncertain, because they often grow vain with
success, and encourage a restor'd State to such hazards as
shew like irregularity of life in other recover'd bodies, such
as the cautious and ancient gravity of *Law* disswaded: For ₅
Law, whose temperate design is safety, rather prevents by
constancy of Medicine (like a continu'd Diet) diseases in
the body-politick then depends after a permitted Sickness
upon the chance of recovery. They think *States-men* strive
to be as much Judges of Law as themselves, being chief ₁₀
Ministers of Law, are Judges of the People, and that even
good *States-men* pervert the Law more then evil Judges:
For Law was anciently meant a defensive Armor, and the
people took it as from the Magazin of Justice to keep them
safe from each others violence; but *States-men* use it as ₁₅
offensive Armes, with which, in forraging to get relief for
Supreme Power, they often wound the Publick.

　　Thus we have first observ'd the Four chief aids of
Government, *Religion*, *Armes*, *Policy*, and *Law*, defectively
apply'd, and then we have found them weak by an emulous ₂₀
war amongst themselves: it follows next we should introduce to strengthen those principal aids (still making the
people our direct object) some collateral help, which I will
safely presume to consist in Poesy.

　　We have observ'd that the People, since the latter time ₂₅
of Christian Religion, are more unquiet then in former
Ages,—so disobedient and fierce, as if they would shake
off the ancient imputation of being Beasts by shewing their
Masters they know their own strength; and we shall not
erre by supposing that this conjunction of fourfold Power ₃₀
hath fail'd in the effects of authority by a mis-application;
for it hath rather endeavour'd to prevail upon their bodies
then their mindes, forgetting that the martiall art of
constraining is the best, which assaults the weaker part;
and the weakest part of the people is their mindes, for ₃₅

want of that which is the mindes only strength, *Education*,
but their Bodies are strong by continuall labour, for Labour
is the Education of the Body. Yet when I mention the
misapplication of force, I should have said they have not
5 only fail'd by that, but by a main error; Because the
subject on which they should work is the Minde, and the
Minde can never be constrain'd, though it may be gain'd
by perswasion: And since Perswasion is the principal
instrument which can bring to fashion the brittle and
10 mishapen mettal of the Minde, none are so fit aids to this
important work as Poets, whose art is more then any
enabled with a voluntary and chearfull assistance of Nature,
and whose operations are as resistlesse, secret, easy, and
subtle as is the influence of Planets.

15 I must not forget, least I be prevented by the vigilance
of the Reader, that I have profess'd not to represent the
beauty of Vertue in my Poem with hope to perswade
common men; and I have said that *Divines* have fail'd in
discharging their share of Government by depending upon
20 the effects of perswasion, and that Statesmen in managing
the people rely not upon the perswasion of Divines, but
upon force. In my despair of reducing the mindes of
Common men, I have not confest any weaknesse of Poesy
in the generall Science, but rather inferr'd the particular
25 strength of the Heroick, which hath a force that over-
matches the infancy of such mindes as are not enabled by
degrees of Education; but there are lesser forces in other
kinds of Poesy, by which they may train and prepare
their understandings; and Princes and Nobles, being
30 reform'd and made Angelicall by the Heroick, will be
predominant lights, which the people cannot chuse but
use for direction, as Gloworms take in and keep the Suns
beams till they shine and make day to themselves.

In saying that *Divines* have vainly hop'd to continue
35 the peace of Government by perswasion, I have imply'd

such perswasions as are accompany'd with threatnings
and seconded by force, which are the perswasions of
Pulpits, where is presented to the obstinate Hell after
Death ; and the civill Magistrate during life constrains
such obedience as the Church doth ordain.   But the Per- 5
swasions of Poesy, in stead of menaces, are Harmonious
and delightful insinuations, and never any constraint,
unless the ravishment of Reason may be call'd Force. And
such Force, contrary to that which *Divines*, *Commanders*,
States-men, and *Lawyers* use, begets such obedience as 10
is never weary or griev'd.

In declaring that *Statesmen* think not the State wholly
secure by such manners as are bred from the perswasions
of *Divines*, but more willingly make Government rely upon
military force, I have neither concluded that Poets are 15
unprofitable nor that *Statesmen* think so ; for the wisdom
of Poets would first make the Images of Vertue so amiable
that her beholders should not be able to look off, rather
gently and delightfully infusing then inculcating Precepts ;
and then when the minde is conquer'd like a willing Bride, 20
Force should so behave it self as noble Husbands use their
power, that is, by letting their Wives see the Dignity and
prerogative of our Sex (which is the Husbands harmless
conquest of Peace) continually maintain'd to hinder Disobedience rather then rigorously impose Duty : But to 25
such an easy government, neither the People, which are
subjects to Kings and States, nor Wives, which are subject
to Husbands, can peacefully yeild, unless they are first
conquer'd by Vertue ; and the Conquests of Vertue be
never easy but where her forces are commanded by 30
Poets.

It may be objected that the education of the Peoples
mindes (from whence Vertuous manners are deriv'd) by
the several kindes of Poesy, of which the *Dramatick* hath
been in all Ages very successful, is opposite to the receav'd 35

opinion that the People ought to be continu'd in ignorance,—a Maxime sounding like the little subtilty of one
that is a Statesman only by Birth or Beard, and merits
not his place by much thinking : For ignorance is rude,
5 sensorious, jealous, obstinate, and proud, these being
exactly the ingredients of which Disobedience is made,
and Obedience proceeds from ample consideration, of
which knowledge consists ; and knowledge will soon put
into one Scale the weight of oppression, and in the other
10 the heavy burden which Disobedience lays on us in the
effects of civil War ; and then even Tyranny will seem
much lighter, when the hand of supreme Power binds up
our Load and lays it artfully on us, then Disobedience,
the Parent of Confusion, when we all load one another, in
15 which every one irregularly increases his fellows burden
to lessen his own.

Others may object that Poesy on our Stage or the
Heroick in Musick (for so the latter was anciently us'd)
is prejudicial to a State, as begetting Levity, and giving
20 the People too great a diversion by pleasure and mirth.
To these, if they be worthy of satisfaction, I reply, That
whoever in Government endeavours to make the People
serious and grave, which are attributes that may become
the Peoples *Representatives* but not the People, doth
25 practise a new way to enlarge the State, by making every
Subject a *Statesman* ; and he that means to govern so
mournfully (as it were, without any Musick in his Dominion)
must lay but light burdens on his Subjects, or else he
wants the ordinary wisdom of those who to their Beasts
30 that are much loaden whistle all the day to encourage their
Travail.   For that supreme power which expects a firm
obedience in those who are not us'd to rejoycing, but live
sadly, as if they were preparing for the funeral of Peace,
hath little skil in contriving the lastingness of Govern-
35 ment, which is the principal work of Art : And less hath

that Power consider'd Nature, as if such new austerity did seem to tax even her for want of gravity in bringing in the Spring so merrily with a Musical variety of Birds: And such sullen power doth forget that Battails, the most solemne and serious business of Death, are begun with 5 Trumpets and Fifes, and anciently were continu'd with more diversity of Musick: And that the Grecian Laws,— Laws being the gravest endevor of humane Councels for the ease of Life,—were long before the dayes of *Lycurgus*, to make them more pleasant to memory, published in 10 Verse: And that the wise *Athenians*, dividing into Three parts the publique Revenue, expended one in Plays and Showes, to divert the People from meeting to consult of their Rulers merit and the defects of Government: And that the *Romans* had not so long continu'd their Empire 15 but for the same diversions at a vaster charge.

Againe, it may be objected, that the Precepts of Christian Religion are sufficient towards our regulation by appointment of manners, and towards the ease of Life by imposing obedience, so that the moral assistance of Poesy is but 20 vainly intruded. To this I may answer that as no man should suspect the sufficiency of Religion by its insuccessfulness, so if the insuccessfulness be confess'd, we shall as little disparage Religion by bringing in more aids when 'tis in action as a General dishonours himself by en- 25 deavouring with more of his own Forces to make sure an attempt that hath a while miscarry'd: For Poesy, which like contracted *Essences* seems the utmost strength & activity of Nature, is as all good Arts subservient to Religion, all marching under the same Banner though 30 of less discipline and esteem. And as Poesy is the best Expositor of Nature, Nature being misterious to such as use not to consider, so Nature is the best Interpreter of God, and more cannot be said of Religion. And when the Judges of Religion, which are the Chiefs of the 35

Church, neglect the help of Moralists in reforming the People (and Poets are of all Moralists the most useful), they give a sentence against the Law of Nature : For Nature performs all things by correspondent aids and 5 harmony. And 'tis injurious not to think Poets the most useful Moralists, for as Poesy is adorn'd and sublim'd by Musick, which makes it more pleasant and acceptable, so Morality is sweetned and made more amiable by Poesy. And the Austerity of some Divines may be the cause why 10 Religion hath not more prevaild upon the manners of Men ; for great Doctors should rather comply with things that please, as the wise Apostle did with Ceremonies, then lose a Proselyte. And even *Honor*, taught by moral Philosophers, but more delightfully infusd by Poets, will 15 appear (notwithstanding the sad severity of some latter Divines) no unsafe Guide towards Piety ; for it is as wary and nice as *Conscience*, though more cheerful and coura-gious. And however *Honor* be more pleasing to flesh and blood because in this World it find's applause, yet 'tis 20 not so mercenarie as Piety ; for Piety, being of all her expectations inwardly assur'd, expects a reward in Heaven to which all earthly payments compar'd are but Shaddows and Sand.

And it appears that Poesy hath for its natural prevailings 25 over the Understandings of Men (sometimes making her conquests with easy plainnesse, like native country Beauty) been very succesful in the most grave and important occasions that the necessities of States or Mankinde have produc'd. For it may be said that *Demosthenes* sav'd the 30 *Athenians* by the Fable or Parable of the Doggs and Wolves, in answer to King *Philip's* Proposition ; And that *Menenius Agrippa* sav'd the Senate, if not *Rome*, by that of the Belly and the Hands ; and that even our Saviour was pleas'd, as the most prevalent way of Doctrine, wholly 35 to use such kinde of Parables in his converting or saving of Souls,—it being written, *Without a Parable spake he not to them*. And had not the learned Apostle thought the wisdom of Poets worthie his remembrance, and instructive not only to Heathens but to Christians, he had not cited *Epimenides* to the *Cretans* as well as *Aratus* to the 5 *Athenians*.

I cannot also be ignorant that divers, whose conscientious Melancholy amazes and discourages others Devotion, will accuse Poets as the admirers of Beauty, and Inventors or Provokers of that which by way of 10 aspersion they call *Love*. But such, in their first accusation, seem to look carelesly and unthankfully upon the wonderful works of God, or else through low education or age become incompetent Judges of what is the chief of his works upon Earth. And Poets, when they 15 praise Beauty, are at least as lawfully thankfull to God as when they praise Seas, Woods, Rivers, or any other parts that make up a prospect of the World. Nor can it be imagin'd but that Poets in praising them praise wholly the Maker, and so in praising beauty: For that Woman who 20 beleeves she is prais'd when her beauty is commended may as well suppose that Poets think she created her self: And he that praises the inward beauty of Women, which is their Vertue, doth more perform his duty then before ; for our envious silence in not approving & so encouraging 25 what is good is the cause that vice is more in fashion and countenance then Vertue. But when Poets praise that which is not beauty or the minde which is not vertuous, they erre through their mistake or by flattery ; and flattery is a crime so much more prosperous in others who are 30 Companions to greatnesse, that it may be held in Poets rather Kindnesse then designe.

They who accuse Poets as provokers of Love are Enemies to Nature ; and all affronts to Nature are offences to God, as insolencies to all subordinate officers of the 35

Crown are rudenesses to the King. *Love*, in the most
obnoxious interpretation, is Natur's Preparative to her
greatest work, which is the making of *Life*. And since
the severest Divines of these latter times have not been
5 asham'd publiquely to command and define the most
secret dutys and entertainments of Love in the Married,
why should not Poets civilly endeavour to make a Friendship between the Guests before they meet, by teaching
them to dignifie each other with the utmost of estimation ?
10 And Mariage in Mankinde were as rude and unprepar'd
as the hasty elections of other Creatures, but for acquaintance and conversation before it ; and that must
be an acquaintance of Mindes, not of bodys ; and of the
Minde Poesy is the most natural and delightfull Interpreter.
15 When neither Religion (which is our art towards God)
nor Nature (which is Gods first Law to Man, though by
Man least study'd), nor when Reason (which is Nature,
and made art by Experience) can by the enemies of Poesy
be sufficiently urg'd against it, then some, whose froward-
20 nesse will not let them quitt an evil cause, plead written
Authority. And though such authority be a Weapon
which even in the War of Religion distres'd disputers
take up as their last shift, yet here we would protest
against it, but that we finde it makes a false defence and
25 leaves the Enemy more open. This authority, which is
but single too, is from *Plato*, and him some have malitiously
quoted as if in his feign'd Common-wealth he had banish'd
all Poets ; But *Plato* says nothing against Poets in general,
and in his particular quarrel, which is to *Homer* and *Hesiod*,
30 only condemns such errors as we mention'd in the beginning
of this *Preface* when we look'd upon the Ancients. And
those errors consist in their abasing Religion by representing the Gods in evil proportion and their *Heroes* with
as unequal Characters, and so brought Vices into fashion
35 by intermixing them with the vertues of great Persons.

Yet even during this divine anger of *Plato*, he concludes, not against Poesy, but the Poems then most in request ; for these be the words of his Law : *If any Man, having ability to imitate what he pleases, imitate in his Poems both good and evil, let him be reverenc'd as a sacred, admirable, and pleasant* 5 *Person ; but be it likewise known, he must have no place in our Common-wealth.* And yet before his banishment he allows him *the honor of a Diadem, and sweet Odours to anoint his Head* ; And afterwards says : *Let us make use of more profitable, though more severe and less pleasant Poets,* 10 *who can imitate that which is for the honor and benefit of the Common-wealth.* But those who make use of this just indignation of *Plato* to the unjust scandal of Poesy have the common craft of False Witnesses, inlarging every circumstance when it may hurt, and concealing all things 15 that may defend him they oppose. For they will not remember how much the Scholler of *Plato*, who like an absolute Monarch over Arts hath almost silenc'd his Master throughout the Schools of *Europe*, labours to make Poesy universally current by giving Laws to the Science : 20 Nor will they take notice in what dignitie it continu'd whilst the *Greeks* kept their dominion or Language ; and how much the *Romans* cherish'd even the publique repetition of *Verses* : Nor will they vouchsafe to observe, though *Juvenall* take care to record it, how gladly all *Rome* during 25 that exercise ran to the voice of *Statius*.

Thus having taken measure, though hastily, of the extent of those great Professions that in Government contribute to the necessities, ease, and lawfull pleasures of Men, and finding Poesy as usefull now as the Ancients 30 found it towards perfection and happinesse, I will, Sir, unless with these Two Books you returne me a discouragement, cheerfully proceed ; and though a little time would make way for the Third, and make it fit for the Presse, I am resolv'd rather to hazard the inconvenience 35

which expectation breeds (for divers with no ill satisfaction
have had a taste of *Gondibert*) then endure that violent
envie which assaults all Writers whilst they live, though
their Papers be but fill'd with very negligent and ordinary
5 thoughts; and therefore I delay the publication of any
part of the Poem till I can send it you from *America*,
whither I now speedily prepare, having the folly to hope
that when I am in another World (though not in the
common sense of dying) I shall finde my Readers, even the
10 Poets of the present Age, as temperate and benigne as we
are all to the Dead, whose remote excellence cannot hinder
our reputation. And now, Sir, to end with the Allegory
which I have so long continu'd, I shall, after all my busy
vanitie in chewing and describing my new Building, with
15 great quietness (being almost as weary as your self) bring
you to the Backdore, that you may make no review but in
my absence; and steale hastely from you, as one who is
asham'd of all the trouble you have receiv'd from,

SIR,

20 Your most humble and most affectionate Servant,
WILL. D'AVENANT.

From the Louure *in Paris*,
January 2, 1650.

THOMAS HOBBES

I. ANSWER TO DAVENANT'S PREFACE
TO *GONDIBERT*

1650

THE ANSWER

OF

MR HOBBES

TO

S^R WILL. D'AVENANT'S
PREFACE

Before *GONDIBERT*

SIR,

I F to commend your Poem I should onely say, in general
Termes, that in the choice of your Argument, the disposition of the parts, the maintenance of the Characters of
your Persons, the dignity and vigor of your expression,
you have performed all the parts of various experience, 5
ready memory, clear judgement, swift and well govern'd
fancy, though it were enough for the truth, it were too
little for the weight and credit of my testimony. For I lie
open to two Exceptions, one of an incompetent, the other
of a corrupted Witness. Incompetent, because I am not 10
a Poet; and corrupted with the Honor done me by your
Preface. The former obliges me to say something, by the
way, of the Nature and differences of Poesy.

As Philosophers have divided the Universe, their subject,
into three Regions, *Celestiall*, *Aëriall*, and *Terrestriall*, so 15
the Poets (whose worke it is, by imitating humane life
in delightful and measur'd lines, to avert men from vice

and incline them to vertuous and honorable actions)
have lodg'd themselves in the three Regions of mankinde,
Court, City, and *Country,* correspondent in some proportion
to those three Regions of the World. For there is in
5 Princes and men of conspicuous power, anciently called
Heroes, a lustre and influence upon the rest of men
resembling that of the Heavens; and an insincereness,
inconstancy, and troublesome humor of those that dwell in
populous Cities, like the mobility, blustring, and impurity
10 of the Aire; and a plainness, and though dull, yet a nutri-
tive faculty in rurall people, that endures a comparison with
the Earth they labour.

From hence have proceeded three sorts of Poesy,
Heroique, Scommatique, and *Pastorall.* Every one of these
15 is distinguished again in the manner of *Representation,*
which sometimes is *Narrative,* wherein the Poet himself
relateth, and sometimes *Dramatique,* as when the persons
are every one adorned and brought upon the Theater
to speak and act their own parts. There is therefore
20 neither more nor less then six sorts of Poesy. For
the Heroique Poem narrative, such as is yours, is called
an *Epique Poem.* The Heroique Poem Dramatique is
Tragedy. The Scommatique Narrative is *Satyre,* Dramatique is *Comedy.* The Pastorall narrative is called simply
25 *Pastorall,* anciently *Bucolique;* the same Dramatique,
Pastorall Comedy. The Figure therefore of an Epique
Poem and of a Tragedy ought to be the same, for they
differ no more but in that they are pronounced by one or
many Persons. Which I insert to justifie the figure of
30 yours, consisting of five books divided into Songs, or
Cantoes, as five Acts divided into Scenes has ever been
the approved figure of a Tragedy.

They that take for Poesy whatsoever is writ in Verse
will think this Division imperfect, and call in Sonets,
35 Epigrams, Eclogues, and the like peeces, which are but

Essayes and parts of an entire Poem, and reckon *Empedocles* and *Lucretius* (natural Philosophers) for Poets, and the moral precepts of *Phocylides, Theognis,* and the Quatraines of *Pybrach* and the History of *Lucan,* and others of that kind amongst Poems, bestowing on such Writers for honor 5 the name of Poets rather then of Historians or Philosophers. But the subject of a Poem is the manners of men, not natural causes ; manners presented, not dictated ; and manners feigned, as the name of Poesy imports, not found in men. They that give entrance to Fictions writ in 10 Prose err not so much, but they err : For Prose requireth delightfulness, not onely of fiction, but of stile, in which, if Prose contend with Verse, it is with disadvantage and, as it were, on foot against the strength and wings of *Pegasus.*

For Verse amongst the *Greeks* was appropriated anciently 15 to the service of their Gods, and was the Holy stile, the stile of the Oracles, the stile of the Laws, and the stile of men that publiquely recommended to their Gods the vowes and thanks of the people, which was done in their holy songs called Hymnes, and the Composers of them were called 20 Prophets and Priests before the name of Poet was known. When afterwards the majestie of that stile was observed, the Poets chose it as best becoming their high invention. And for the Antiquity of Verse, it is greater then the antiquity of Letters. For it is certain *Cadmus* was the 25 first that from *Phœnicia,* a country that neighboureth *Judea,* brought the use of Letters into *Greece.* But the service of the Gods and the Laws, which by measured Sounds were easily committed to the memory, had been long time in use before the arrivall of *Cadmus* there. 30

There is, besides the grace of stile, another cause why the ancient Poets chose to write in measured language, which is this. Their Poems were made at first with intention to have them sung, as well Epique as Dramatique,—which custom hath been long time laid aside, but 35

began to be revived, in part, of late years in *Italy*,—and
could not be made commensurable to the Voyce or Instruments in Prose, the ways and motions whereof are so
uncertain and undistinguished, like the way and motion of
5 a Ship in the Sea, as not onely to discompose the best
Composers, but also to disappoint some times the most
attentive Reader and put him to hunt counter for the sense.
It was therefore necessary for Poets in those times to write
in Verse.

10 The verse which the *Greeks* and *Latines*, considering
the nature of their own Languages, found by experience
most grave, and for an Epique Poem most decent, was
their *Hexameter*, a Verse limited not onely in the length
of the line, but also in the quantity of the syllables.
15 In stead of which we use the line of ten Syllables, recom-
pencing the neglect of their quantity with the diligence of
Rime. And this measure is so proper for an Heroique
Poem as without some losse of gravity and dignity it was
never changed. A longer is not far from ill Prose, and
20 a shorter is a kinde of whisking, you know, like the unlacing
rather then the singing of a Muse. In an Epigram or
a Sonnet a man may vary his measures, and seek glory
from a needlesse difficulty, as he that contrived Verses into
the formes of an Organ, a Hatchet, an Egg, an Altar, and
25 a paire of Wings; but in so great and noble a worke as is
an Epique Poem, for a man to obstruct his own way with
unprofitable difficulties is great imprudence. So likewise
to chuse a needlesse and difficult correspondence of Rime
is but a difficult toy, and forces a man sometimes for the
30 stoping of a chink to say somewhat he did never think;
I cannot therefore but very much approve your *Stanza*,
wherein the syllables in every Verse are ten, and the Rime
Alternate.

For the choyce of your subject, you have sufficiently
35 justified your self in your Preface. But because I have

observed in *Virgil*, that the Honor done to *Æneas* and his companions has so bright a reflection upon *Augustus Cæsar* and other great *Romans* of that time as a man may suspect him not constantly possessed with the noble spirit of those his *Heroes*, and beleeve you are not acquainted with any great man of the Race of *Gondibert*, I add to your justification the purity of your purpose, in having no other motive of your labour but to adorn vertue and procure her Lovers, then which there cannot be a worthier designe, and more becoming noble Poesy.

In that you make so small account of the example of almost all the approved Poets, ancient and modern, who thought fit in the beginning, and sometimes also in the progress of their Poems, to invoke a Muse or some other Deity that should dictate to them or assist them in their writings, they that take not the laws of Art from any reason of their own but from the fashion of precedent times will perhaps accuse your singularity. For my part, I neither subscribe to their accusation, nor yet condemn that Heathen custom otherwise then as accessary to their false Religion. For their Poets were their Divines, had the name of Prophets; Exercised amongst the People a kinde of spiritual Authority, would be thought to speak by a divine spirit, have their works which they writ in Verse (the divine stile) pass for the word of God and not of man, and to be hearkened to with reverence. Do not our Divines (excepting the stile) do the same, and by us that are of the same Religion cannot justly be reprehended for it? Besides, in the use of the spiritual calling of Divines, there is danger sometimes to be feared from want of skill, such as is reported of unskilful Conjurers, that mistaking the rites and cerimonious points of their art, call up such spirits as they cannot at their pleasure allay again, by whom storms are raised that overthrow buildings and are the cause of miserable wracks at sea. Unskilful Divines do often times

the like: For when they call unseasonably for *Zeal* there
appears a Spirit of *Cruelty*; and by the like error, instead
of *Truth* they raise *Discord*; instead of *Wisdom, Fraud*;
instead of *Reformation, Tumult*; and *Controversie* instead of
5 *Religion*.   Whereas in the Heathen Poets, at least in those
whose works have lasted to the time we are in, there are
none of those indiscretions to be found that tended to
subversion or disturbance of the Common-wealths wherein
they lived.   But why a Christian should think it an ornament
10 to his Poem, either to profane the true God or invoke
a false one, I can imagin no cause but a reasonless
imitation of Custom, of a foolish custome, by which a man,
enabled to speak wisely from the principles of nature and
his own meditation, loves rather to be thought to speak by
15 inspiration, like a Bagpipe.

   Time and Education begets experience ; Experience
begets memory; Memory begets Judgement and Fancy:
Judgment begets the strength and structure, and Fancy
begets the ornaments of a Poem.   The Ancients therefore
20 fabled not absurdly in making memory the Mother of the
Muses.   For memory is the World (though not really, yet
so as in a looking glass) in which the Judgment, the
severer Sister, busieth her self in a grave and rigid
examination of all the parts of Nature, and in registring
25 by Letters their order, causes, uses, differences, and
resemblances ; Whereby the Fancy, when any work of
Art is to be performed, findes her materials at hand and
prepared for use, and needs no more then a swift motion
over them, that what she wants, and is there to be had,
30 may not lie too long unespied.   So that when she seemeth
to fly from one *Indies* to the other, and from Heaven to
Earth, and to penetrate into the hardest matter and
obscurest places, into the future and into her self, and all
this in a point of time, the voyage is not very great, her
35 self being all she seeks ; and her wonderful celerity con-

sisteth not so much in motion as in copious Imagery discreetly ordered & perfectly registred in the memory, which most men under the name of Philosophy have a glimpse of, and is pretended to by many that, grosly mistaking her, embrace contention in her place. But so far forth as the Fancy of man has traced the ways of true Philosophy, so far it hath produced very marvellous effects to the benefit of mankinde. All that is beautiful or defensible in building, or marvellous in Engines and Instruments of motion, whatsoever commodity men receive from the observations of the Heavens, from the description of the Earth, from the account of Time, from walking on the Seas, and whatsoever distinguisheth the civility of *Europe* from the Barbarity of the *American* savages, is the workmanship of Fancy but guided by the Precepts of true Philosophy. But where these precepts fail, as they have hitherto failed in the doctrine of Moral vertue, there the Architect, *Fancy*, must take the Philosophers part upon her self. He therefore that undertakes an Heroick Poem, which is to exhibite a venerable & amiable Image of Heroick vertue, must not only be the Poet, to place & connect, but also the Philosopher, to furnish and square his matter, that is, to make both Body and Soul, colour and shadow of his Poem out of his own Store: Which how well you have performed I am now considering.

Observing how few the Persons be you introduce in the beginning, and how in the course of the actions of these (the number increasing) after several confluences they run all at last into the two principal streams of your Poem, *Gondibert* and *Oswald*, methinks the Fable is not much unlike the Theater. For so, from several and far distant Sources, do the lesser Brooks of *Lombardy*, flowing into one another, fall all at last into the two main Rivers, the *Po* and the *Adice*. It hath the same resemblance also with a mans veins, which, proceeding from different parts, after the like concourse insert themselves at last into the two principal veins of the Body. But when I considered that also the actions of men, which singly are inconsiderable, after many conjunctures grow at last either into one great protecting power or into two destroying factions, I could not but approve the structure of your Poem, which ought to be no other then such as an imitation of humane life requireth.

In the Streams themselves I finde nothing but setled Valor, cleane Honor, calm Counsel, learned diversion, and pure Love, save onely a torrent or two of Ambition, which, though a fault, has somewhat Heroick in it, and therefore must have place in an Heroick Poem. To shew the reader in what place he shall finde every excellent picture of vertue you have drawn is too long. And to shew him one is to prejudice the rest; yet I cannot forbear to point him to the Description of Love in the person of *Birtha*, in the seventh *Canto* of the second Book. There has nothing been said of that Subject neither by the Ancient nor Modern Poets comparable to it. Poets are Painters: I would fain see another Painter draw so true, perfect, and natural a Love to the Life, and make use of nothing but pure Lines, without the help of any the least uncomely shadow, as you have done. But let it be read as a piece by it self, for in the almost equal height of the whole the eminence of parts is Lost.

There are some that are not pleased with fiction, unless it be bold, not onely to exceed the *work*, but also the *possibility* of nature: they would have impenetrable Armors, Inchanted Castles, invulnerable bodies, Iron Men, flying Horses, and a thousand other such things, which are easily feigned by them that dare. Against such I defend you (without assenting to those that condemn either *Homer* or *Virgil*) by dissenting onely from those that think the Beauty of a Poem consisteth in the exorbitancy of the fiction. For as truth is the bound of Historical, so the Resemblance of truth is the utmost limit of Poeticall Liberty. In old time amongst the Heathen such strange fictions and Metamorphoses were not so remote from the Articles of their Faith as they are now from ours, and therefore were not so unpleasant. Beyond the actual works of nature a Poet may now go ; but beyond the conceived possibility of nature, never. I can allow a Geographer to make in the Sea a Fish or a Ship which by the scale of his Mapp would be two or three hundred mile long, and think it done for ornament, because it is done without the precincts of his undertaking ; but when he paints an *Elephant* so, I presently apprehend it as ignorance, and a plain confession of *Terra incognita*.

As the description of Great Men and Great Actions is the constant designe of a Poet, so the descriptions of worthy circumstances are necessary accessions to a Poem, and being well performed are the Jewels and most precious ornaments of Poesy. Such in *Virgil* are the Funeral games of *Anchises*, The duel of *Æneas* and *Turnus, &c.* ; and such in yours are *The Hunting, The Bataile, The City Mourning, The Funeral, The House of Astragon, The Library, and the Temple*, equal to his, or those of *Homer* whom he imitated.

There remains now no more to be considered but the Expression, in which consisteth the countenance and colour of a beautiful Muse, and is given her by the Poet out of his own provision, or is borrowed from others. That which he hath of his own is nothing but experience and knowledge of Nature, and specially humane nature, and is the true and natural Colour. But that which is taken out of Books (the ordinary boxes of Counterfeit Complexion) shews well or ill, as it hath more or less resemblance with the natural, and are not to be used without examination unadvisedly. For in him that professes the imitation of

Nature, as all Poets do, what greater fault can there be then to bewray an ignorance of nature in his Poem,—especially having a liberty allowed him, if he meet with any thing he cannot master, to leave it out?

5 That which giveth a Poem the true and natural Colour consisteth in two things, which are, *To know well*, that is, to have images of nature in the memory distinct and clear, and *To know much*. A signe of the first is perspicuity, property, and decency, which delight all sorts of men,
10 either by instructing the ignorant or soothing the learned in their knowledge. A signe of the latter is novelty of expression, and pleaseth by excitation of the minde; for novelty causeth admiration, and admiration curiosity, which is a delightful appetite of knowledge

15 There be so many words in use at this day in the English Tongue, that though of magnifique sound, yet (like the windy blisters of a troubled water) have no sense at all, and so many others that lose their meaning by being ill coupled, that it is a hard matter to avoid them; for having
20 been obtruded upon youth in the Schools by such as make it, I think, their business there (as 'tis exprest by the best Poet)

With terms to charm the weak and pose the wise,   Gondibert, Lib. I.
they grow up with them, and, gaining reputation with the Cant. 5.
25 ignorant, are not easily shaken off.

To this palpable darkness I may also add the ambitious obscurity of expressing more then is perfectly conceived, or perfect conception in fewer words then it requires. Which Expressions, though they have had the honor to
30 be called strong lines, are indeed no better then Riddles, and, not onely to the Reader but also after a little time to the Writer himself, dark and troublesome.

To the property of Expression I referr that clearness of memory by which a Poet, when he hath once introduced any person whatsoever speaking in his Poem, maintaineth in him to the end the same character he gave him in the beginning. The variation whereof is a change of pace that argues the Poet tired.

Of the Indecencies of an Heroick Poem the most re- markable are those that shew disproportion either between the persons and their actions, or between the manners of the Poet and the Poem. Of the first kinde is the un-comliness of representing in great persons the inhumane vice of Cruelty or the sordid vice of Lust and Drunkenness. To such parts as those the Ancient approved Poets thought it fit to suborn, not the persons of men, but of monsters and beastly Giants, such as *Polyphemus, Cacus,* and the *Centaures.* For it is supposed a Muse, when she is invoked to sing a song of that nature, should maidenly advise the Poet to set such persons to sing their own vices upon the Stage, for it is not so unseemly in a *Tragedy.* Of the same kinde it is to represent scurrility or any action or language that moveth much laughter. The delight of an *Epique* Poem consisteth not in mirth, but admiration. Mirth and Laughter is proper to *Comedy* and *Satyre.* Great persons that have their mindes employed on great designes have not leasure enough to laugh, and are pleased with the contemplation of their own power and vertues, so as they need not the infirmities and vices of other men to recommend themselves to their own favour by comparison, as all men do when they laugh. Of the second kinde, where the disproportion is between the Poet and the Persons of his Poem, one is in the Dialect of the Inferior sort of People, which is alwayes different from the language of the Court. Another is to derive the Illustration of any thing from such Metaphors or Comparisons as cannot come into mens thoughts but by mean conversation and experience of humble or evil Arts, which the Person of an *Epique* Poem cannot be thought acquainted with.

From *Knowing much*, proceedeth the admirable variety and novelty of Metaphors and Similitudes, which are not possible to be lighted on in the compass of a narrow knowledge. And the want whereof compelleth a Writer to
5 expressions that are either defac'd by time or sullied with vulgar or long use. For the Phrases of Poesy, as the airs of musick, with often hearing become insipide, the Reader having no more sense of their force then our Flesh is sensible of the bones that sustain it. As the sense we
10 have of bodies consisteth in change and variety of impression, so also does the sense of language in the variety and changeable use of words. I mean not in the affectation of words newly brought home from travail, but in new and with all significant translation to our purposes of those
15 that be already received, and in far fetch't but withal apt, instructive, and comly similitudes.

Having thus, I hope, avoided the first Exception against the incompetency of my Judgement, I am but little moved with the second, which is of being bribed by the honor
20 you have done me by attributing in your Preface somewhat to my Judgment. For I have used your Judgment no less in many things of mine, which coming to light will thereby appear the better. And so you have your bribe again.

Having thus made way for the admission of my Testi-
25 mony, I give it briefly thus : I never yet saw Poem that had so much shape of Art, health of Morality, and vigour and beauty of Expression as this of yours. And but for the clamour of the multitude, that hide their Envy of the present under a Reverence of Antiquity, I should say
30 further that it would last as long as either the *Æneid* or *Iliad*, but for one. Disadvantage ; and the Disadvantage is this : The languages of the *Greeks* and *Romans*, by their Colonies and Conquests, have put off flesh and blood, and are becom immutable, which none of the modern tongues
35 are like to be. I honor Antiquity, but that which is

commonly called *old time* is *young time*.　The glory of
Antiquity is due, not to the Dead, but to the Aged.

And now, whilst I think on't, give me leave with a short
discord to sweeten the Harmony of the approaching close.
I have nothing to object against your Poem, but dissent 5
onely from something in your Preface sounding to the
prejudice of Age.　'Tis commonly said that old Age is
a return to childhood : Which methinks you insist on so
long, as if you desired it should be believed.　That's the
note I mean to shake a little.　That saying, meant onely 10
of the weakness of body, was wrested to the weakness of
minde by froward children, weary of the controulment of
their parents, masters, and other admonitors.　Secondly,
the dotage and childishness they ascribe to Age is never
the effect of Time, but sometimes of the excesses of youth, 15
and not a returning to, but a continual stay with, childhood.
For they that, wanting the curiosity of furnishing their
memories with the rarities of nature in their youth, and
pass their time in making provision onely for their ease
and sensual delight, are children still at what years soever, 20
as they that coming into a populous City, never going out
of their Inn, are strangers still, how longsoever they have
bin there.　Thirdly, there is no reason for any man to
think himself wiser to day then yesterday, which does not
equally convince he shall be wiser to morrow then to day. 25

Fourthly, you will be forced to change your opinion
hereafter when you are old ; and in the mean time you
discredit all I have said before in your commendation,
because I am old already.　But no more of this.

I beleeve, Sir, you have seen a curious kinde of perspec- 30
tive, where he that looks through a short hollow pipe upon a
picture containing divers figures sees none of those that
are there painted, but some one person made up of their
parts, conveyed to the eie by the artificial cutting of a glass.
I finde in my imagination an effect not unlike it from your 35

Poem. The vertues you distribute there amongst so many
noble Persons represent in the reading the image but of
one mans vertue to my fancy, which is your own, and that
so deeply imprinted as to stay for ever there, and govern
5 all the rest of my thoughts and affections in the way of
honouring and serving you to the utmost of my power,
that am,

Sir,

Your most humble and obedient Servant,
10   THOMAS HOBBES.
Paris, Ian. 10, 1650.

II. PREFACE TO *HOMER'S ODYSSES, TRANSLATED BY THO. HODDES OF MALMSBURY*

1675

TO THE

READER,

concerning

The VERTUES of an

HEROIQUE POEM

THe Vertues required in an Heroick Poem, and indeed
in all Writings published, are comprehended all in this
one word, *Discretion*.
15   And Discretion consisteth in this, That every part of the
Poem be conducing, and in good order placed, to the End
and Designe of the Poet. And the Designe is not only
to profit, but also to delight the Reader.

By Profit, I intend not here any accession of Wealth,
20 either to the Poet, or to the Reader; but accession of
Prudence, Justice, Fortitude, by the example of such
Great and Noble Persons as he introduceth speaking, or

describeth acting.   For all men love to behold, though not
to practise, Vertue.   So that at last the work of an Heroique
Poet is no more but to furnish an ingenuous Reader (when
his leisure abounds) with the diversion of an honest
and delightful Story, whether true or feigned.   5

But because there be many men called Critiques, and
Wits, and Vertuosi, that are accustomed to censure the
Poets, and most of them of divers Judgments : How is it
possible (you'l say) to please them all ? Yes, very well ; if
the Poem be as it should be.   For men can judge what's 10
good, that know not what is best.   For he that can judge
what is best, must have considered all those things (though
they be almost innumerable) that concur to make the
reading of an Heroique Poem pleasant.   Whereof I'll
name as many as shall come into my mind.   15

And they are contained, first, in the choice of words.
Secondly, in the construction.   Thirdly, in the contrivance
of the Story or Fiction.   Fourthly, in the Elevation of the
Fancie.   Fifthly, in the Justice and Impartiality of the
Poet. Sixthly, in the clearness of Descriptions.   Seventhly, 20
in the Amplitude of the Subject.

And (to begin with words) the first Indiscretion is,
The use of such words as to the Readers of Poesie (which
are commonly Persons of the best Quality) are not
sufficiently known.   For the work of an Heroique Poem is 25
to raise admiration, principally, for three Vertues, Valour,
Beauty, and Love ; to the reading whereof Women no less
than Men have a just pretence, though their skill in
Language be not so universal.   And therefore forein
words, till by long use they become vulgar, are unintelligi- 30
ble to them.   Also the names of Instruments and Tools
of Artificers, and words of Art, though of use in the Schools,
are far from being fit to be spoken by a Heroe.   He
may delight in the Arts themselves, and have skill in some
of them ; but his Glory lies not in that, but in Courage, 35

Nobility, and other Vertues of Nature, or in the Command
he has over other men. Nor does *Homer* in any part
of his Poem attribute any praise to *Achilles,* or any blame
to *Alexander,* for that they had both learnt to play upon the
5 Ghittarre. The character of words that become a Heroe
are Property and Significancy, but without both the malice
and lasciviousness of a Satyr.

Another Vertue of an Heroique Poem is the Perspicuity
and the Facility of Construction, and consisteth in a
10 natural contexture of the words, so as not to discover
the labour but the natural ability of the Poet; and this
is usually called a good Style. For the order of words,
when placed as they ought to be, carries a light before
it, whereby a man may foresee the length of his period, as
15 a torch in the night shews a man the stops and unevenness
in his way. But when plac'd unnaturally, the Reader will
often find unexpected checks, and be forced to go back and
hunt for the sense, and suffer such unease, as in a Coach a
man unexpectedly finds in passing over a furrow. And
20 though the Laws of Verse (which have bound the Greeks
and Latines to number of Feet and quantity of Syllables,
and the English and other Nations to number of Syllables
and Rime) put great constraint upon the natural course of
Language, yet the Poet, having the liberty to depart from
25 what is obstinate, and to chuse somewhat else that is more
obedient to such Laws, and no less fit for his purpose,
shall not be, neither by the measure nor by the necessity of
Rime, excused ; though a Translation often may.

A third Vertue lies in the Contrivance. For there
30 is difference between a Poem and a History in Prose. For
a History is wholly related by the Writer ; but in a
Heroique Poem the Narration is, a great part of it, put upon
some of the persons introduced by the Poet. So *Homer*
begins not his *Iliad* with the injury done by *Paris,* but
35 makes it related by *Menelaus,* and very briefly, as a thing

notorious ; nor begins he his *Odysses* with the departure of
Ulysses from *Troy*, but makes *Ulysses* himself relate the
same to *Alcinous*, in the midst of his Poem ; which I think
much more pleasant and ingenious than a too precise
and close following of the time.   5

A fourth is in the Elevation of Fancie, which is generally
taken for the greatest praise of Heroique Poetry ; and is so,
when governed by discretion. For men more generally
affect and admire Fancie than they do either Judgment, or
Reason, or Memory, or any other intellectual Vertue ; and 10
for the pleasantness of it, give to it alone the name of Wit,
accounting Reason and Judgment but for a dull entertainment. For in Fancie consisteth the Sublimity of a Poet,
which is that Poetical Fury which the Readers for the most
part call for. It flies abroad swiftly to fetch in both 15
Matter and Words ; but if there be not Discretion at home
to distinguish which are fit to be used and which not, which
decent and which undecent for Persons, Times, and Places,
their delight and grace is lost. But if they be discreetly
used, they are greater ornaments of a Poem by much than 20
any other. A Metaphor also (which is a Comparison
contracted into a word) is not unpleasant ; but when they
are sharp and extraordinary, they are not fit for an Heroique
Poet, nor for a publique consultation, but only for an
Accusation or Defence at the Bar.   25

A fifth lies in the Justice and Impartiality of the Poet,
and belongeth as well to History as to Poetry. For both
the Poet and the Historian writeth only (or should do)
matter of Fact. And as far as the truth of Fact can defame
a man, so far they are allowed to blemish the reputation 30
of Persons. But to do the same upon Report, or by inference, is below the dignity not only of a Heroe but of a
Man. For neither a Poet nor an Historian ought to
make himself an absolute Master of any mans good name.
None of the Emperors of *Rome* whom *Tacitus* or any other 35

Writer hath condemned, was ever subject to the Judgment of any of them, nor were they ever heard to plead for themselves, which are things that ought to be antecedent to condemnation. Nor was, I think, *Epicurus* the Philosopher (who is transmitted to us by the Stoicks for a man of evil and voluptuous life) ever called, convented, and lawfully convicted, as all men ought to be before they be defamed. Therefore 'tis a very great fault in a Poet to speak evil of any man in their Writings Historical.

A sixth Vertue consists in the perfection and curiosity of Descriptions, which the ancient writers of Eloquence called *Icones*, that is, *Images*. And an Image is always a part, or rather the ground, of a Poetical comparison. As, for example, when *Virgil* would set before our eyes the fall of *Troy*, he describes perhaps the whole Labour of many men together in the felling of some great Tree, and with how much ado it fell. This is the Image. To which if you but add these words, So fell *Troy*, you have the Comparison entire ; the grace whereof lieth in the lightsomness, and is but the description of all, even of the minutest, parts of the thing described ; that not onely they that stand far off, but also they that stand near, and look upon it with the oldest spectacles of a Critique, may approve it. For a Poet is a Painter, and should paint Actions to the understanding with the most decent words, as Painters do Persons and Bodies with the choicest colours to the eye ; which, if not done nicely, will not be worthy to be plac'd in a Cabinet.

The seventh Vertue which lying in the Amplitude of the Subject, is nothing but variety, and a thing without which a whole Poem would be no pleasanter than an Epigram, or one good Verse ; nor a Picture of a hundred figures better than any one of them asunder, if drawn with equal art. And these are the Vertues which ought especially to be looked upon by the Critiques, in the comparing of the Poets,

Homer with *Virgil*, or *Virgil* with *Lucan*. For these only, for their excellencie, I have read or heard compared.

If the comparison be grounded upon the first and second Vertues, which consist in known words and Style unforc'd, they are all excellent in their own Language, though 5 perhaps the Latin than the Greek is apter to dispose it self into an Hexameter Verse, as having both fewer Monosyllables and fewer Polysyllables. And this may make the Latin Verse appear more grave and equal, which is taken for a kind of Majesty; though in truth there be 10 no Majesty in words, but then when they seem to proceed from an high and weighty imployment of the minde. But neither *Homer*, nor *Virgil*, nor *Lucan*, nor any Poet writing commendably, though not excellently, was ever charged much with unknown words, or great constraint 15 of Style, as being a fault proper to Translators, when they hold themselves too superstitiously to their Authors words.

In the third Vertue, which is Contrivance, there is no doubt but *Homer* excels them all. For their Poems, 20 except the Introduction of their Gods, are but so many Histories in Verse; whereas *Homer* has woven so many Histories together as contain the whole Learning of his time (which the Greeks called *Cyclopœdia*), and furnished both the Greek and Latin Stages with all the 25 Plots and Arguments of their Tragedies.

The fourth Vertue, which is the height of Fancie, is almost proper to *Lucan*, and so admirable in him, that no Heroique Poem raises such admiration of the Poet as his hath done, though not so great admiration of the persons he 30 introduceth. And though it be the mark of a great Wit, yet it is fitter for a Rhetorician than a Poet, and rebelleth often against Discretion, as when he says,

Victrix causa Diis placuit, sed victa Catoni ;

that is,

> *The Side that Won the Gods approved most,*
> *But* Cato *better lik'd the Side that lost.*

Than which nothing could be spoken more gloriously
to the Exaltation of a man, nor more disgracefully to
the Depression of the Gods.   *Homer* indeed maketh some
Gods for the *Greeks*, and some for the *Trojans*, but always
makes *Jupiter* impartial : And never prefers the judgment
of a man before that of *Jupiter*, much less before the judgment of all the Gods together.

The fifth Vertue, which is the Justice and Impartiality of
a Poet, is very eminent in *Homer* and *Virgil*, but the
contrary in *Lucan*. *Lucan* shews himself openly in the
Pompeyan Faction, inveighing against *Cæsar* throughout
his Poem, like *Cicero* against *Cataline* or *Marc Antony*, and
is therefore justly reckon'd by *Quintilian* as a Rhetorician
rather than a Poet. And a great part of the delight
of his Readers proceedeth from the pleasure which too
many men take to hear Great persons censured. But
Homer and *Virgil* (especially *Homer*) do every where what
they can to preserve the Reputation of their Heroes.

If we compare *Homer* and *Virgil* by the sixth Vertue,
which is the clearness of Images, or Descriptions, it is
manifest that *Homer* ought to be preferr'd, though *Virgil*
himself were to be the Judge. For there are very few
Images in *Virgil* besides those which he hath translated
out of *Homer ;* so that *Virgils* Images are *Homers* Praises.
But what if he have added something to it of his own ?
Though he have, yet it is no addition of praise, because 'tis
easie. But he hath some Images which are not in *Homer*,
and better than his. It may be so ; and so may other
Poets have which never durst compare themselves with
Homer. Two or three fine sayings are not enough to
make a Wit. But where is that Image of his better

done by him than *Homer*, of those that have been done by
them both? Yes, *Eustathius*, as Mr. *Ogilby* hath observ'd,
where they both describe the falling of a Tree, prefers
Virgil's description. But *Eustathius* is in that, I think,
mistaken. The place of *Homer* is in the fourth of the ₅
Iliads, the sense whereof is this:

> *As when a man hath fell'd a Poplar Tree*
> *Tall, streight, and smooth, with all the fair boughs on ;*
> *Of which he means a Coach-wheel made shall be,*
> *And leaves it on the Bank to dry i' th' Sun :* ₁₀
> *So lay the comely* Simoisius,
> *Slain by great* Ajax, *Son of* Telamon.

It is manifest that in this place *Homer* intended no more
than to shew how comely the body of *Simoisius* appeared
as he lay dead upon the Bank of *Scamander*, streight ₁₅
and tall, with a fair head of hair, and like a streight
and high Poplar with the boughs still on; and not at all
to describe the manner of his falling, which, when a man
is wounded through the breast, as he was with a Spear, is
always sudden. ₂₀

The description of how a great Tree falleth, when many
men together hew it down, is in the second of *Virgil's*
Æneads. The sense of it, with the comparison, is in
English this ;

> *And* Troy, *methought, then sunk in fire and smoke,* ₂₅
> *And overturned was in every part :*
> *As when upon the mountain an old Oak*
> *Is hewn about with keen steel to the heart,*
> *And pli'd by Swains with many heavy blows,*
> *It nods and every way it threatens round,* ₃₀
> *Till overcome with many wounds, it bows,*
> *And leisurely at last comes to the ground.*

And here again it is evident that *Virgil* meant to compare
the manner how *Troy* after many Battles, and after the
losses of many Cities, conquer'd by the many nations under ₃₅

Agamemnon in a long War, and thereby weaken'd, and at last overthrown, with a great Tree hewn round about, and then falling by little and little leisurely.

So that neither these two Descriptions nor the two Comparisons can be compared together. The Image of a man lying on the ground is one thing; the Image of falling, especially of a Kingdom, is another. This therefore gives no advantage to *Virgil* over *Homer*. 'Tis true that this Description of the Felling and Falling of a Tree is exceeding graceful. But is it therefore more than *Homer* could have done if need had been? Or is there no Description in *Homer* of somewhat else as good as this? Yes, and in many of our English Poets now alive. If it then be lawful for *Julius Scaliger* to say, that if *Jupiter* would have described the fall of a Tree, he could not have mended this of *Virgil*, it will be lawful for me to repeat an old Epigram of *Antipater*, to the like purpose, in favour of *Homer:*

> *The Writer of the famous* Trojan *War,*
> *And of* Ulysses *Life, O* Jove, *make known,*
> *Who, whence he was; for thine the Verses are,*
> *And he would have us think they are his own.*

The seventh and last commendation of an Heroique Poem consisteth in Amplitude and Variety; and in this *Homer* exceedeth *Virgil* very much, and that not by superfluity of words, but by plenty of Heroique matter, and multitude of Descriptions and Comparisons (whereof *Virgil* hath translated but a small part into his *Æneads*), such as are the Images of Shipwracks, Battles, Single Combats, Beauty, Passions of the mind, Sacrifices, Entertainments, and other things, whereof *Virgil* (abating what he borrows of *Homer*) has scarce the twentieth part. It is no wonder therefore if all the ancient Learned men both of *Greece* and *Rome* have given the first place in Poetry to *Homer*. It is rather strange that two or three, and of late time and but Learners of the Greek tongue, should dare to contradict so many competent Judges both of Language and Discretion. But howsoever I defend *Homer*, I aim not thereby at any reflection upon the following Translation. Why then did I write it? Because I had nothing else to do. Why publish it? Because I thought it might take off my Adversaries from shewing their folly upon my more serious Writings, and set them upon my Verses to shew their wisdom. But why without Annotations? Because I had no hope to do it better than is already done by Mr. *Ogilby*.

T. Hobbes.

ABRAHAM COWLEY

PREFACE TO *POEMS*

1656

AT my return lately into *England*, I met by great accident
(for such I account it to be, that any Copy of it should
be extant any where so long, unless at his house who
printed it) a *Book* entituled, *The Iron Age*, and published
under *my name* during the time of my absence. I wondred
very much how one who could be so *foolish* to write so ill
Verses, should yet be so *Wise* to set them forth as another
Mans rather than his *own*; though perhaps he might have
made a better choice, and not fathered the *Bastard* upon
such a person, whose stock of Reputation is, I fear, little
enough for maintenance of his own numerous *Legitimate
Off-spring* of that kinde. It would have been much less
injurious, if it had pleased the *Author* to put forth some of
my Writings under his *own name*, rather then his own
under *mine*. He had been in that a more pardonable
Plagiary, and had done less wrong by *Robbery* then he
does by such a *Bounty*; for no body can be *justified* by the
Imputation even of anothers *Merit*, and our own course
Cloathes are like to become us better then those of another
mans, though never so *rich*: but these, to say the truth,
were so *beggarly*, that I my self was ashamed to *wear* them.
It was in vain for me that I avoided censure by the con-
cealment of my own writings, if my reputation could be
thus *Executed in Effigie*; and impossible it is for any good
Name to be in safety, if the malice of *Witches* have the
power to consume and destroy it in an *Image* of their own
making. This indeed was so ill made, and so *unlike*, that

I hope the *Charm* took no effect.　So that I esteem my
self less prejudiced by it then by that which has been done
to me since, almost in the same kinde, which is the publication of some things of mine without my consent or
knowledge, and those so mangled and imperfect that I
could neither with honor acknowledge nor with honesty
quite disavow them.　Of which sort was a *Comedy* called
The Guardian, printed in the year 1650, but made and
acted before the *Prince*, in his passage through *Cambridge*
towards *York*, at the beginning of the late unhappy War;
or rather neither *made* nor *acted*, but *rough-drawn* onely,
and *repeated*; for the haste was so great that it could
neither be *revised* or *perfected* by the *Author*, nor *learnt
without-Book* by the *Actors*, nor set forth in any measure
tolerably by the *Officers* of the *College*.　After the *Representation* (which, I confess, was somewhat of the *latest*)
I began to look it over, and changed it very much, striking
out some whole parts, as that of the *Poet* and the *Souldier*;
but I have lost the *Copy*, and dare not think it deserves the
pains to write it again, which makes me omit it in this
publication, though there be some things in it which I am
not ashamed of, taking in the excuse of my age and small
experience in humane conversation when I made it.　But
as it is, it is onely the hasty *first-sitting* of a *Picture*, and
therefore like to resemble me accordingly.　From this
which had hapned to my self, I began to reflect upon the
fortune of almost all *Writers*, and especially *Poets*, whose
Works (commonly printed after their deaths) we finde
stuffed out, either with *counterfeit pieces*, like *false Money*
put in to fill up the *Bag*, though it adde nothing to the
sum, or with such, which though of their own *Coyn*, they
would have called in themselves for the baseness of the
Alloy: whether this proceed from the indiscretion of their
Friends, who think a vast *heap* of Stones or Rubbish a
better *Monument* then a little *Tomb* of *Marble*, or by the

unworthy avarice of some *Stationers*, who are content to
diminish the value of the *Author*, so they may encrease
the price of the *Book*, and like *Vintners* with sophisticate
mixtures, spoil the whole vessel of wine, to make it yield
5 more *profit*. This has been the case with *Shakespear*,
Fletcher, *Johnson*, and many others, part of whose *Poems*
I should take the boldness to prune and lop away, if the
care of replanting them in print did belong to me; neither
would I make any scruple to cut off from some the un-
10 necessary yong *Suckars*, and from others the old withered
Branches; for *a great Wit* is no more tyed to live in a
Vast Volume then in a *Gigantic Body*; on the contrary,
it is commonly more vigorous, the less space it animates.
And as *Statius* says of little *Tydeus*,

15   —— *Totos infusa per artus*   *Stat.* i. *l.*
      Major in exiguo regnabat corpore virtus.   *Theb.*

I am not ignorant that, by saying this of others, I expose
my self to some Raillery, for not using the same severe
discretion in my own case, where it concerns me nearer.
20 But though I publish here more then in strict wisdom I
ought to have done, yet I have supprest and cast away
more then I *publish*; and for the ease of my self and others,
have *lost*, I believe, too, more then *both*. And upon these
considerations I have been perswaded to overcome all the
25 just repugnances of my own *modesty*, and to produce these
Poems to the light and view of the World; not as a thing
that I approved of in it self, but as a lesser evil, which I
chose rather then to stay till it were done for me by some
body else, either surreptitiously before, or avowedly after,
30 my death; and this will be the more excusable, when the
Reader shall know in what respects he may look upon me
as a *Dead*, or at least a *Dying Person*, and upon my *Muse*
in this action, as appearing, like the *Emperor Charles the
Fifth*, and *assisting* at her own *Funeral*.

35   For to make my self absolutely dead in a *Poetical* capacity,

my resolution at present is never to exercise any more that faculty. It is, I confess, but seldom seen that the *Poet* dyes before the *Man*; for when we once fall in love with that bewitching *Art*, we do not use to court it as a *Mistress*, but marry it as a *Wife*, and take it for better or worse, as 5 an *Inseparable Companion* of our whole life. But as the *Mariages* of *Infants* do but rarely prosper, so no man ought to wonder at the diminution or decay of my affection to *Poesie*, to which I had contracted my self so much under *Age*, and so much to my own prejudice in regard of those 10 more profitable matches which I might have made among the *richer Sciences*. As for the *Portion* which this brings of *Fame*, it is an *Estate* (if it be any, for men are not oftner deceived in their hopes of *Widows* then in their opinion of *Exegi monumentum ære perennius*) that hardly ever comes 15 in whilst we are *Living* to enjoy it, but is a *fantastical kind of Reversion to our own selves*; neither ought any man to envy *Poets* this posthumous and imaginary happiness, since they finde commonly so little in present, that it may be truly applyed to them, which S. *Paul* speaks of the first *Christians*, 20 *If their reward be in this life, they are of all men the most miserable*.

And if in quiet and flourishing times they meet with so small encouragement, what are they to expect in rough and troubled ones? if *wit* be such a *Plant* that it scarce receives 25 heat enough to preserve it alive even in the *Summer* of our cold *Clymate*, how can it choose but wither in a long and a sharp *winter*?—a warlike, various, and a tragical age is best to *write of*, but worst to *write in*. And I may, though in a very unequal proportion, assume that to my self which 30 was spoken by *Tully* to a much better person, upon occasion of the *Civil Wars* and Revolutions in his time, *Sed in te intuens, Brute, doleo, cujus in adolescentiam per medias laudes quasi quadrigis vehentem transversa incurrit misera fortuna Reipublicæ.* 35

Cic. de Clar. Orator.

Neither is the present constitution of my *Mind* more proper then that of the *Times* for this exercise, or rather divertisement. There is nothing that requires so much serenity and chearfulness of *Spirit*; it must not be either
5 overwhelmed with the cares of *Life*, or overcast with the *Clouds* of *Melancholy* and *Sorrow*, or shaken and disturbed with the storms of injurious *Fortune*; it must, like the *Halcyon*, have *fair weather* to breed in. The *Soul* must be filled with bright and delightful *Idœa's*, when it undertakes
10 to communicate delight to others, which is the main end of *Poesie*. One may see, through the stile of *Ovid de Trist.*, the humbled and dejected condition of *Spirit* with which he wrote it; there scarce remains any footsteps of that *Genius*,

Quem nec Iovis ira, nec ignes, &c.

15 The *cold* of the Countrey had strucken through all his faculties, and benummed the very *feet* of his *Verses*. He is himself, methinks, like one of the *Stories* of his *own Metamorphosis*; and though there remain some weak *resemblances* of *Ovid* at *Rome*, It is but as he says of *Niobe*,

20   *In vultu color est sine sanguine, lumina mœstis*   Ovid.
    Stant immota genis; nihil est in Imagine vivum;—   Metam.
    Flet tamen.—   l. 6.

The truth is, for a man to write well it is necessary to be in good humor; neither is *Wit* less eclypsed with the unquiet-
25 ness of *Mind* then *Beauty* with the *Indisposition* of *Body*. So that 'tis almost as hard a thing to be a *Poet* in despight of *Fortune*, as it is in despight of *Nature*. For my own part, neither my obligations to the *Muses*, nor expectations from them are so great, as that I should suffer my self upon
30 no considerations to be *divorced*, or that I should say, like *Horace*,

    Quisquis erit vitœ, Scribam, color.   Hor. Sat.
    1. l. 2. Ser.

I shall rather use his words in another place,

*Vixi Camœnis nuper idoneus,
Et militavi non sine gloriâ,
Nunc arma defunctùmque bello
Barbiton hic paries habebit.*

And this resolution of mine does the more befit me, because 5
my desire has been for some years past (though the execution has been accidentally diverted) and does stil vehemently
continue, to retire my self to some of our *American Plantations*, not to seek for *Gold* or inrich my self with the traffique
of those parts (which is the end of most men that travel 10
thither, so that of *these Indies* it is truer then it was of the
former,

> *Improbus extremos currit Mercator ad Indos
> Pauperiem fugiens—*)

But to forsake this world for ever, with all the *vanities* and 15
Vexations of it, and to bury my self in some obscure retreat
there (but not without the consolation of *Letters* and *Philosophy*),

> *Oblitúsque meorum, obliviscendus & illis,*

As my former *Author* speaks too, who has inticed me here, 20
I know not how, into the *Pedantry* of this heap of *Latine
Sentences*.   And I think *Doctor Donnes Sun Dyal in a grave*
is not more useless and ridiculous then *Poetry* would be in
that *retirement.*   As this therefore is in a true sense a kind
of *Death* to the *Muses*, and a real *literal quitting* of this 25
World : So, methinks, I may make a just claim to the
undoubted priviledge of *Deceased Poets*, which is to be
read with more *favor* then the *Living* :

> *Tanti est ut placeam tibi, Perire.*

Having been forced for my own necessary justification 30
to trouble the *Reader* with this long Discourse of the
Reasons why I trouble him also with all the rest of the *Book*,
I shall only add some what concerning the several parts
of it and some other pieces which I have thought fit to

reject in this publication : As first, all those which I wrote
at *School* from the age of ten years till after fifteen, for
even so far backward there remain yet some *traces* of me
in the little *footsteps* of a *childe* ; which though they were
5 then looked upon as *commendable extravagances* in a *Boy*
(men setting a value upon *any kind* of *fruit* before the usual
season of it), yet I would be loth to be bound now to read
them all over *my self*, and therefore should do ill to expect
that patience from *others*. Besides, they have already past
10 through several *Editions*, which is a longer *Life* then uses
to be enjoyed by *Infants* that are born before the ordinary
terms. They had the good fortune then to find the world
so *indulgent* (for considering the time of their production,
who could be so hard-hearted to be *severe* ?) that I scarce
15 yet apprehend so much to be censured for *them* as for not
having made *advances* afterwards proportionable to the
speed of my *setting out*, and am obliged too in a maner by
Discretion to conceal and suppress them, as *Promises* and
Instruments under my own hand, whereby I stood *engaged*
20 for more then I have been able to *perform* ; in which truly,
if I have failed, I have the real excuse of the *honestest* sort
of *Bankrupts*, which is to have been made *Unsolvable*, not
so much by their own *negligence* and ill-husbandry, as by
some notorious accidents and publike disasters. In the
25 next place, I have cast away all such pieces as I wrote
during the time of the late troubles, with any relation to
the differences that caused them, as among others, *three
Books of the Civil War it self*, reaching as far as the first
Battel of *Newbury*, where the succeeding *misfortunes* of the
30 *party* stopt the *work*; for it is so uncustomary as to become
almost *ridiculous*, to make *Lawrels* for the *Conquered*.
Now, though in all *Civil Dissentions*, when they break into
open hostilities, the *War* of the *Pen* is allowed to accompany
that of the *Sword*, and every one is in a maner obliged with
35 his *Tongue* as well as *Hand* to serve and assist the side

which he engages in ; yet when the event of battel and the unaccountable *Will* of *God* has determined the controversie, and that we have submitted to the conditions of the *Conqueror*, we must lay down our *Pens* as well as *Arms*, we must *march* out of our *Cause* it self, and *dismantle* that, 5 as well as our *Towns* and *Castles*, of all the *Works* and *Fortifications* of *Wit* and *Reason* by which we defended it. *We* ought not, sure, to begin our selves to revive the remembrance of those times and actions for which we have received a *General Amnestie* as a *favor* from the *Victor*. 10 The truth is, neither *We* nor *They* ought by the *Representation* of *Places* and *Images* to make a kind of *Artificial Memory* of those things wherein we are all bound to desire, like *Themistocles*, the *Art* of *Oblivion*. The *enmities* of *Fellow-Citizens* should be, like that of *Lovers*, the *Redinte-* 15 *gration* of their *Amity*. The Names of *Party* and *Titles* of *Division*, which are sometimes in effect the whole quarrel, should be extinguished and forbidden in peace under the notion of *Acts* of *Hostility*. And I would have it accounted no less unlawful to *rip up old wounds* then to *give new ones*; 20 which has made me not onely abstain from printing any things of this kinde, but to burn the very copies, and inflict a severer punishment on them my self then perhaps the most rigid Officer of *State* would have thought that they deserved. 25

As for the ensuing Book, it consists of four parts : The first is a *Miscellanie* of several Subjects, and some of them made when I was very young, which it is perhaps *superfluous* to tell the *Reader* ; I know not by what chance I have kept *Copies* of them, for they are but a very few in comparison 30 of those which I have lost, and I think they have no extra-ordinary virtue in them, to deserve more care in preservation then was bestowed upon their *Brethren*, for which I am so little concerned that I am ashamed of the *arrogancy* of the *word*, when I said *I had lost them*. 35

The *Second* is called, *The Mistress*, or *Love-Verses*; for
so it is that *Poets* are scarce thought *Free-men* of their
Company, without paying some duties and obliging themselves to be true to *Love*. Sooner or later they must all
5 pass through that *Tryal*, like some *Mahumetan Monks*, that
are bound by their Order, once at least in their life, to
make a *Pilgrimage* to *Meca*,—

In furias ignémque ruunt; Amor omnibus idem.

But we must not always make a judgement of their *manners*
10 from their *writings* of this kind, as the *Romanists* uncharit-
ably do of *Beza* for a few lascivious *Sonnets* composed by
him in his youth. It is not in this sense that *Poesie* is
said to be a kind of *Painting*; it is not the *Picture* of the
Poet, but of *things* and *persons* imagined by him. He may
15 be in his own practice and disposition a *Philosopher*, nay
a *Stoick*, and yet speak sometimes with the softness of an
amorous *Sappho*.

Feret & rubus asper Amomum.

He professes too much the use of *Fables* (though without
20 the malice of deceiving) to have his testimony taken even
against himself. Neither would I here be misunderstood,
as if I affected so much gravity as to be ashamed to be
thought really in *Love*. On the contrary, I cannot have
a good opinion of any man who is not at least capable of
25 being so. But I speak it to excuse some expressions (if
such there be) which may happen to offend the severity of
supercilious *Readers*; for much *Excess* is to be allowed in
Love, and even more in *Poetry*, so we avoid the two unpardonable vices in both, which are *Obscenity* and *Pro-*
30 *phaneness*, of which I am sure, if my *words* be ever guilty,
they have ill-represented my *thoughts* and *intentions*. And
if, notwithstanding all this, the lightness of the matter here
displease any body, he may finde wherewithal to content

his more serious inclinations in the weight and height of the ensuing Arguments.

For as for the *Pindarick Odes* (which is the third part) I am in great doubt whether they will be understood by most *Readers*; nay, even by very many who are well enough acquainted with the common Roads and ordinary Tracks of *Poesie*. They either are, or at least were meant to be, of that kinde of *Stile* which *Dion. Halicarnasseus* calls, Μεγαλοφνὲς καὶ ἡδὺ μετὰ δεινότητος, and which he attributes to *Alcæus*. The digressions are many and sudden, and sometimes long, according to the fashion of all *Lyriques*, and of *Pindar* above all men living. The *Figures* are un-usual and *bold*, even to *Temeritie*, and such as I durst not have to do withal in any other kinde of *Poetry*. The *Numbers* are various and irregular, and sometimes (especially some of the long ones) seem harsh and uncouth, if the just measures and cadencies be not observed in the *Pronunciation*. So that almost all their *Sweetness* and *Numerosity* (which is to be found, if I mistake not, in the roughest, if rightly repeated) lies in a maner wholly at the *Mercy* of the *Reader*. I have briefly described the nature of these Verses in the *Ode* entituled, *The Resur-rection*: And though the *Liberty* of them may incline a man to believe them easie to be composed, yet the undertaker will finde it otherwise.

> *—Vt sibi quivis*
> *Speret idem, multum sudet frustràque laboret*
> *Ausus idem.—*

I come now to the last Part, which is, *Davideis*, or an *Heroical Poem* of the *Troubles of David*, which I designed into *Twelve Books*, not for the *Tribes* sake but after the *Patern* of our Master *Virgil*, and intended to close all with that most Poetical and excellent *Elegie* of *Davids* upon the death of *Saul* and *Jonathan*. For I had no mind to carry him quite on to his *Anointing* at *Hebron*, because it is the

custom of *Heroick Poets* (as we see by the examples of
Homer and *Virgil,* whom we should do ill to forsake to
imitate others) never to come to the full end of their *Story,*
but onely so near that every one may see it; as men
commonly play not out the game, when it is evident that
they can win it, but lay down their *Cards* and take up
what they have won. This, I say, was the *whole Designe,*
in which there are many noble and fertile Arguments behinde; as, The barbarous cruelty of *Saul* to the *Priests* at
Nob, the several flights and escapes of *David,* with the
maner of his living in the *Wilderness,* the *Funeral* of
Samuel, the love of *Abigal,* the sacking of *Ziglag,* the loss
and recovery of *Davids* wives from the *Amalekites,* the
Witch of *Endor,* the war with the *Philistines,* and the
Battel of *Gilboa;* all which I meant to interweave upon
several occasions with most of the illustrious *Stories* of
the *Old Testament,* and to embellish with the most remarkable *Antiquities* of the *Jews* and of other Nations before or
at that *Age.* But I have had neither *Leisure* hitherto nor
have *Appetite* at present to finish the work, or so much as
to revise that part which is done with that care which
I resolved to bestow upon it, and which the *Dignity* of the
Matter well deserves. For what worthier *subject* could
have been chosen among all the *Treasuries* of past times
then the Life of this young *Prince,* who from so small
beginnings, through such infinite troubles and oppositions,
by such miraculous virtues and excellencies, and with such
incomparable variety of wonderful actions and accidents,
became the greatest *Monarch* that ever sat upon the most
famous Throne of the whole Earth? whom should a *Poet*
more justly seek to *honor* then the highest person who ever
honored his Profession? whom a *Christian Poet,* rather then
the man after Gods own heart, and the man who had that
sacred pre-eminence above all other *Princes,* to be the best
and mightiest of that Royal Race from whence *Christ*

himself according to the flesh disdained not to descend ?
When I consider this, and how many other bright and
magnificent subjects of the like nature the *Holy Scripture*
affords and *proffers*, as it were, to *Poesie*, in the wise
managing and illustrating whereof the *Glory* of *God*
Almighty might be joyned with the singular utility and
noblest delight of *Mankinde*: It is not without grief and
indignation that I behold that *Divine Science* employing all
her inexhaustable riches of *Wit* and *Eloquence*, either in
the wicked and beggarly *Flattery* of great persons, or the
unmanly *Idolizing* of *Foolish Women*, or the wretched
affectation of scurril *Laughter*, or at best on the confused
antiquated *Dreams* of senseless *Fables* and *Metamorphoses*.
Amongst all holy and consecrated things which the *Devil*
ever stole and alienated from the service of the *Deity*, as
Altars, Temples, Sacrifices, Prayers, and the like, there is
none that he so universally and so long usurpt as *Poetry*.
It is time to recover it out of the *Tyrants* hands, and to
restore it to the *Kingdom* of *God*, who is the *Father* of it.
It is time to *Baptize* it in *Jordan*, for it will never become
clean by bathing in the *Waters* of *Damascus*. There wants,
methinks, but the *Conversion* of *That* and the *Jews*, for the
accomplishing of the *Kingdom of Christ*. And as men
before their receiving of the *Faith* do not without some
carnal reluctancies apprehend the *bonds* and *fetters* of it,
but finde it afterwards to be the truest and greatest *Liberty* :
It will fare no otherwise with this *Art*, after the *Regenera-*
tion of it ; it will meet with wonderful variety of new, more
beautiful, and more delightful *Objects*; neither will it want
Room, by being *confined to Heaven*. There is not so great
a *Lye* to be found in any *Poet* as the vulgar conceit of men
that *Lying* is *Essential* to good *Poetry*. Were there never
so wholesome *Nourishment* to be had (but, alas, it breeds
nothing but *Diseases*) out of these boasted *Feasts* of *Love*
and *Fables*, yet, methinks, the unalterable continuance of

the *Diet* should make us *Nauseate* it : For it is almost impossible to serve up any *new Dish* of that kinde. They
are all but the *Cold-meats* of the *Antients*, new-heated, and
new set forth. I do not at all wonder that the old Poets
made some rich crops out of these grounds ; the heart of
the *Soil* was not then wrought out with continual *Tillage*.
But what can we expect now, who come a *Gleaning*, not
after the first *Reapers*, but after the very *Beggars* ? Besides,
though those mad stories of the *Gods* and *Heroes* seem in
themselves so ridiculous, yet they were then the *whole
Body* (or rather *Chaos*) of the *Theologie* of those times.
They were believed by all but a few *Philosophers* and
perhaps some *Atheists*, and served to good purpose among
the *vulgar* (as pitiful things as they are) in strengthening
the authority of *Law* with the terrors of *Conscience*, and
expectation of certain rewards and unavoidable punishments. There was no other *Religion*, and therefore *that*
was better then *none at all*. But to us who have no need
of them, to us who deride their *folly* and are wearied with
their *impertinencies*, they ought to appear no better arguments for *Verse* then those of their worthy *Successors*, the
Knights Errant. What can we imagine more proper for
the ornaments of *Wit* or *Learning* in the story of *Deucalion*
then in that of *Noah* ? why will not the actions of *Sampson*
afford as plentiful matter as the *Labors* of *Hercules* ?
why is not *Jeptha's Daughter* as *good a woman* as *Iphigenia*,
and the friendship of *David* and *Jonathan* more worthy
celebration then that of *Theseus* and *Perithous* ? Does not
the passage of *Moses* and the *Israelites* into the *Holy Land*
yield incomparably more Poetical variety then the voyages
of *Ulysses* or *Æneas* ? Are the obsolete threadbare tales
of *Thebes* and *Troy* half so stored with great, heroical, and
supernatural actions (since *Verse* will needs *finde* or *make*
such) as the wars of *Joshua*, of the *Judges*, of *David*, and
divers others ? Can all the *Transformations* of the *Gods*

give such copious hints to flourish and expatiate on as the true *Miracles* of *Christ,* or of his *Prophets* and *Apostles*? What do I instance in these few particulars? All the *Books* of the *Bible* are either already most admirable and exalted pieces of Poesie, or are the best *Materials* in the world for it. Yet, though they be in themselves so proper to be made use of for this purpose, None but a good *Artist* will know how to do it; neither must we think to cut and polish *Diamonds* with so little pains and skill as we do *Marble.* For if any man design to compose a *Sacred Poem* by onely turning a story of the *Scripture,* like Mr. *Quarles's,* or some other godly matter, like Mr. *Heywood of Angels,* into *Rhyme,* He is so far from elevating of *Poesie* that he onely *abases Divinity.* In brief, he who can write a *prophane Poem well* may write a *Divine one better*; but he who can do that but ill will do this much worse. The same fertility of *Invention,* the same wisdom of *Disposition,* the same *Judgement* in observance of *Decencies,* the same lustre and vigor of *Elocution,* the same modesty and majestie of *Number,* briefly, the same kinde of *Habit,* is required to both; only this latter allows better *stuff,* and therefore would look more deformedly, if *ill drest* in it. I am farre from assuming to my self to have fulfilled the duty of this weighty undertaking: But sure I am that there is nothing yet in our *Language* (nor perhaps in *any*) that is in any degree answerable to the *Idea* that I conceive of it. And I shall be ambitious of no other fruit from this weak and imperfect attempt of mine but the opening of a way to the courage and industry of some other persons, who may be better able to perform it throughly and succesfully.

RICHARD FLECKNOE

A SHORT DISCOURSE OF THE ENGLISH STAGE

1664

To his Excellency, the Lord Marquess of NEWCASTLE.

My Noble Lord,

I SEND your Excellency here a short Discourse of the *English Stage*, which if you pleas'd you could far better treat of then my self; but before I begin it, I will speak a word or two of those of other Countreys.

5 About the midst of the last Century, Playes, after a long discontinuance and civil death in a manner, began to be reviv'd again, first in *Italy* by *Guarino, Tasso, de Porta*, and others, and afterwards in *Spain* by *Lopes de Vega*; the French beginning later by reason of their Civil Wars,
10 Cardinal *Richlieu* being the first that brought them into Vouge and Esteem as now they are, well knowing how much the Acting noble and heroick Playes conferr'd to the instilling a noble and heroick Spirit into the Nation. For us, we began before them, and if since they seem to have
15 out-strip us, 'tis because our Stage ha's stood at a stand this many years; nor may we doubt, but now we shall soon out-strip them again, if we hold on but as we begin. Of the Dutch I speak nothing, because they are but slow, and follow other Nations onely afar off. But to return
20 unto our present subject.

Playes (which so flourisht amongst the Greeks, and afterwards amongst the Romans) were almost wholly abolished when their Empire was first converted to

Christianity, and their Theaters, together with their Temples, for the most part demolished as Reliques of Paganisme, some few onely reserved and dedicate to the service of the True God, as they had been to their false gods before; from which time to the last Age, they Acted 5 nothing here but Playes of the holy Scripture or Saints Lives, and that without any certain Theaters or set Companies, till about the beginning of Queen *Elizabeths* Reign they began here to assemble into Companies, and set up *Theaters*, first in the City (as in the Inn-yards of 10 the *Cross-Keyes* and *Bull* in *Grace* and *Bishops-Gate Street* at this day is to be seen), till that Fanatick Spirit which then began with the Stage, and after ended with the Throne, banisht them thence into the Suburbs, as after they did the Kingdom, in the beginning of our Civil Wars. 15 In which time Playes were so little incompatible with Religion, and the Theatre with the Church, as on Week-dayes after Vespers both the Children of the Chappel and St. *Pauls* Acted Playes, the one in *White-Friers*, the other behinde the Convocation-house in *Pauls*, till people growing 20 more precise, and Playes more licentious, the Theatre of *Pauls* was quite supprest, and that of the Children of the Chappel converted to the use of the Children of the Revels.

In this time were Poets and Actors in their greatest flourish, *Johnson, Shakespear*, with *Beaumont* and *Fletcher* 25 their Poets, and *Field* and *Burbidge* their Actors.

For Playes, *Shakespear* was one of the first who inverted the Dramatick Stile from dull History to quick Comedy, upon whom *Johnson* refin'd; as *Beaumont* and *Fletcher* first writ in the Heroick way, upon whom *Suckling* and 30 others endeavoured to refine agen; one saying wittily of his *Aglaura* that 'twas full of fine flowers, but they seem'd rather stuck then growing there; as another, of *Shakespear's* writings, that 'twas a fine Garden, but it wanted weeding.

There are few of our English Playes (excepting onely 35

some few of *Johnsons*) without some faults or other; and
if the French have fewer then our English, 'tis because
they confine themselves to narrower limits, and consequently have less liberty to erre.

5 The chief faults of ours are our huddling too much
matter together, and making them too long and intricate;
we imagining we never have intrigue enough till we lose
our selves and Auditors, who shu'd be led in a Maze, but
not a Mist; and through turning and winding wayes, but
10 so still as they may finde their way at last.

A good Play shu'd be like a good stuff, closely and
evenly wrought, without any breakes, thrums, or loose
ends in 'um, or like a good Picture well painted and
designed; the Plot or Contrivement, the Design, the
15 Writing, the Coloris, and Counterplot, the Shaddowings,
with other Embellishments: or finally, it shu'd be like
a well contriv'd Garden, cast into its Walks and Counter-
walks, betwixt an Alley and a Wilderness, neither too
plain nor too confus'd. Of all Arts, that of the Dramatick
20 Poet is the most difficult and most subject to censure; for
in all others, they write onely of some particular subject,
as the Mathematician of Mathematicks, or Philosopher of
Philosophy; but in that, the Poet must write of every
thing, and every one undertakes to judge of it.

25 A Dramatick Poet is to the Stage as a Pilot to the Ship,
and to the Actors as an Architect to the Builders, or
Master to his Schollars: he is to be a good moral Philosopher, but yet more learned in Men then Books. He is
to be a wise as well as a witty Man, and a good man as
30 well as a good Poet; and I'de allow him to be so far
a good fellow too, to take a chearful cup to whet his wits,
so he take not so much to dull 'um, and whet 'um quite
away.

To compare our English Dramatick Poets together,
35 without taxing them, *Shakespear* excelled in a natural

Vein, *Fletcher* in Wit, and *Johnson* in Gravity and ponder-
ousness of Style, whose onely fault was he was too
elaborate, and had he mixt less erudition with his Playes,
they had been more pleasant and delightful then they are.
Comparing him with *Shakespear*, you shall see the 5
difference betwixt Nature and Art ; and with *Fletcher*, the
difference betwixt Wit and Judgement : Wit being an
exuberant thing, like *Nilus*, never more commendable then
when it overflowes ; but Judgement, a stayed and reposed
thing, alwayes containing it self within its bounds and 10
limits.

Beaumont and *Fletcher* were excellent in their kinde,
but they often err'd against *Decorum*, seldom representing
a valiant man without somewhat of the *Braggadoccio*, nor
an honourable woman without somewhat of *Dol Common* 15
in her ; to say nothing of their irreverent representing
Kings persons on the Stage, who shu'd never be represented but with Reverence.   Besides, *Fletcher* was the
first who introduc't that witty obscenity in his Playes,
which like poison infused in pleasant liquor is alwayes the 20
more dangerous the more delightful.   And here to speak
a word or two of Wit, it is the spirit and quintessence of
speech, extracted out of the substance of the thing we
speak of, having nothing of the superfice, or dross of
words, as clenches, quibbles, gingles, and such like trifles 25
have : it is that, in pleasant and facetious discourse, as
Eloquence is in grave and serious, not learnt by Art and
Precept, but Nature and Company.   'Tis in vain to say
any more of it ; for if I could tell you what it were, it
would not be what it is ; being somewhat above expression, 30
and such a volatil thing, as 'tis altogether as volatil to
describe.

It was the happiness of the Actors of those Times to
have such Poets as these to instruct them and write for
them ; and no less of those Poets, to have such docile and 35

excellent Actors to Act their Playes, as a *Field* and
Burbidge, of whom we may say that he was a delightful
Proteus, so wholly transforming himself into his Part, and
putting off himself with his Cloathes, as he never (not so
5 much as in the Tyring-house) assum'd himself again until
the Play was done; there being as much difference betwixt
him and one of our common Actors, as between a Ballad-
singer who onely mouths it, and an excellent singer, who
knows all his Graces, and can artfully vary and modulate
10 his Voice, even to know how much breath he is to give to
every syllable. He had all the parts of an excellent
Orator, animating his words with speaking, and Speech
with Action; his Auditors being never more delighted
then when he spake, nor more sorry then when he held
15 his peace; yet even then he was an excellent Actor still,
never falling in his Part when he had done speaking, but
with his looks and gesture maintaining it still unto the
heighth, he imagining *Age quod agis* onely spoke to him:
so as those who call him a Player do him wrong, no man
20 being less idle then he whose whole life is nothing else but
action; with only this difference from other mens, that as
what is but a Play to them is his Business, so their
business is but a play to him.

Now, for the difference betwixt our Theaters and those
25 of former times, they were but plain and simple, with no
other Scenes nor Decorations of the Stage, but onely old
Tapestry, and the Stage strew'd with Rushes, with their
Habits accordingly, whereas ours now for cost and
ornament are arriv'd to the heighth of Magnificence; but
30 that which makes our Stage the better makes our Playes
the worse perhaps, they striving now to make them more
for sight then hearing, whence that solid joy of the interior
is lost, and that benefit which men formerly receiv'd from
Playes, from which they seldom or never went away but
35 far better and wiser then they came.

The Stage being a harmless and innocent Recreation, where the minde is recreated and delighted, and that *Ludus Literarum*, or School of good Language and Behaviour, that makes Youth soonest Man, and man soonest good and vertuous, by joyning example to precept, 5 and the pleasure of seeing to that of hearing: Its chiefest end is to render Folly ridiculous, Vice odious, and Vertue and Noblenesse so amiable and lovely, as every one shu'd be delighted and enamoured with it ; from which when it deflects, as *corruptio optimi pessima*, of the best it becomes 10 the worst of Recreations.   And this his Majesty well understood, when after his happy Restauration he took such care to purge it from all vice and obscenity ; and would to God he had found all bodies and humours as apt and easie to be purg'd and reform'd as that.   15

For Scenes and Machines they are no new invention, our Masks and some of our Playes in former times (though not so ordinary) having had as good or rather better then any we have now.

They are excellent helps of imagination, most grateful 20 deceptions of the sight, and graceful and becoming Ornaments of the Stage, transporting you easily without lassitude from one place to another, or rather by a kinde of delightful Magick, whilst you sit still, does bring the place to you.   Of this curious Art the *Italians*, this latter 25 age, are the greatest masters, the *French* good proficients, and we in *England* onely Schollars and Learners yet, having proceeded no further then to bare painting, and not arriv'd to the stupendious wonders of your great Ingeniers, especially not knowing yet how to place our 30 Lights, for the more advantage and illuminating of the Scenes.

And thus much suffices it briefly to have said of all that concerns our Modern Stage, onely to give others occasion to say more.   35

SIR ROBERT HOWARD

I. PREFACE TO *FOUR NEW PLAYS*

1665

To The
READER.

THERE is none more sensible than I am, how great a
Charity the most Ingenious may need, that expose
their private Wit to a publique Judgment ; since the same
Phansie from whence the Thoughts proceed must probably
5 be kind to its own Issue.   This renders Men no perfecter
Judges of their own Writings than Fathers are of their
own Children, who find out that Wit in them which another
discerns not, and see not those Errors which are evident to
the unconcern'd.   Nor is this self-kindness more fatal to
10 Men in their Writings than in their Actions, every Man
being a greater Flatterer to himself than he knows how to
be to another ; otherwise it were impossible that things of
such distant Natures shou'd find their own Authors so
equally kind in their affections to them, and Men so
15 different in Parts and Virtues should rest equally contented in their own Opinions.

This Apprehension, added to that greater which I have
of my own Weakness, may, I hope, incline the Reader to
believe me when I assure him that these Follies were
20 made publique as much against my Inclination as Judgment.   But being pursu'd with so many Sollicitations of
Mr Herringman's, and having received Civilities from him

(if it were possible) exceeding his Importunities, I at last
yielded to prefer that which he believed his Interest before
that which I apprehended my own Disadvantage : Considering withal, That he might pretend it would be a real
Loss to him, and could be but an imaginary Prejudice to 5
me ; since things of this nature, though never so excellent
or never so mean, have seldom prov'd the Foundation of
Mens new-built Fortunes or the Ruine of their old ; it
being the Fate of Poetry, though of no other good Parts,
to be wholly separated from Interest ; and there are few 10
that know me but will easily believe I am not much
concern'd in an unprofitable Reputation. This clear
account I have given the Reader of this seeming Contradiction, to offer that to the World which I dislike my
self ; and in all things I have no greater an ambition than 15
to be believ'd a Person that would rather be unkind to my
self than ungrateful to others.

I have made this excuse for my self ; I offer none for
my Writings, but freely leave the Reader to condemn that
which has receiv'd my Sentence already. Yet I shall 20
presume to say somthing in the justification of our Nations
Plays, though not of my own ; since in my Judgment,
without being partial to my Country, I do really prefer our
Plays as much before any other Nations as I do the best of
ours before my own.   25

The manner of the Stage-Entertainments have differ'd
in all Ages ; and as it has encreas'd in use, it has enlarg'd
it self in business. The general manner of Plays among
the Ancients we find in *Seneca*'s Tragedies for serious
Subjects, and in *Terence* and *Plautus* for the Comical, in 30
which latter we see some pretences to Plots, though certainly short of what we have seen in some of Mr *Johnson*'s
Plays ; and for their Wit, especially *Plautus*, I suppose it
suited much better in those days than it would do in ours,
for were their Plays strictly Translated and Presented on 35

our Stage, they would hardly bring as many Audiences as
they have now Admirers.

The serious Plays were anciently compos'd of *Speeches*
and *Choruses*, where all things are related, but no matter
5 of Fact presented on the Stage.   This Pattern the *French*
do at this time neerly follow, only leaving out the *Chorus*,
making up their Plays with almost entire and discoursive
Scenes, presenting the business in Relations.   This way
has very much affected some of our Nation, who possibly
10 believe well of it more upon the account that what the
French do ought to be a Fashion than upon the Reason of
the thing.   *82128*

It is first necessary to consider why probably the Compositions of the Ancients, especially in their serious Plays,
15 were after this manner ; and it will be found that the
Subjects they commonly chose drove them upon the
necessity, which were usually the most known Stories and
Fables : Accordingly, *Seneca* making choice of *Medea*,
Hyppolitus, and *Hercules Oetus*, it was impossible to shew
20 *Medea* throwing old mangled *Æson* into her Age-renewing
Caldron, or to present the scattered Limbs of *Hyppolitus*
upon the Stage, or shew *Hercules* burning upon his own
Funeral Pyle : And this the judicious *Horace* clearly
speaks of in his *Arte Poetica*, where he says,

25   *non tamen intus*
    Digna geri promes in Scenam ; multaque tolles
    Ex oculis, quæ mox narret facundia præsens.
    Nec pueros coram populo Medea *trucidet,*
    Aut humana palàm coquat exta nefarius Atreus,
30   *Aut in avem* Procne *vertatur,* Cadmus *in anguem.*
    Quodcunque ostendis mihi sic, incredulus odi.

So that it appears a fault to chuse such Subjects for the
Stage, but much greater to affect that Method which those
Subjects enforce ; and therefore the *French* seem much
35 mistaken, who without the necessity sometimes commit the

Error ; and this is as plainly decided by the same Author
in his preceding words :

> *Aut agitur res in Scenis aut acta refertur :*
> *Segnius irritant animos demissa per aurem,*
> *Quam quæ sunt oculis subjecta fidelibus, & quæ*   5
> *Ipse sibi tradit spectator,—*

By which he directly declares his Judgment, That every
thing makes more impression Presented than Related :
Nor indeed can any one rationally assert the contrary, for
if they affirm otherwise, they do by consequence maintain,   10
That a whole Play might be as well Related as Acted.
Therefore, whoever chuses a Subject that inforces him to
Relations is to blame, and he that does it without the
necessity of the Subject is much more.

If these Premises be granted, 'tis no partiality to con-   15
clude, That our *English* Plays justly challenge the
Preheminence ; yet I shall as candidly acknowledg, That
our best Poets have differed from other Nations (though
not so happily) in usually mingling and interweaving Mirth
and Sadness through the whole Course of their Plays,   20
Ben. Johnson only excepted, who keeps himself entire to
one Argument ; and I confess I am now convinc'd in my
own Judgment, That it is most proper to keep the Audience
in one entire disposition both of Concern and Attention ;
for when Scenes of so different Natures immediately   25
succeed one another, 'tis probable the Audience may not so
suddenly recollect themselves as to start into an enjoyment
of the Mirth or into a concern for the Sadness. Yet I
dispute not but the variety of this World may afford
pursuing Accidents of such different Natures ; but yet   30
though possible in themselves to be, they may not be so
proper to be Presented,—an entire Connexion being the
natural Beauty of all Plays, and Language the Ornament
to dress them in, which in serious Subjects ought to be
great and easie, like a high-born Person that expresses   35

Greatness without pride or affectation ; the easier dictates of Nature ought to flow in Comedy, yet separated from obsceneness, there being nothing more impudent than the immodesty of Words : Wit should be chaste, and those 5 that have it can only write well.

> *Si modo—*
> *Scimus in Urbanum Lepido seponere dicto.*

Another way of the Ancients which the *French* follow, and our Stage has now lately practis'd, is to write in 10 Rhime ; and this is the dispute betwixt many ingenious Persons, Whether Verse in Rhime, or Verse without the sound, which may be call'd Blank Verse (though a hard Expression), is to be preferr'd ? But take the Question largely, and it is never to be decided, but by right applica- 15 tion I suppose it may ; for in the general they are both proper, that is, one for a Play, the other for a Poem or Copy of Verses,—a Blank Verse being as much too low for one as Rhime is unnatural for the other. A Poem, being a premeditated form of Thoughts upon design'd 20 Occasions, ought not to be unfurnish'd of any harmony in Words or Sound : The other is presented as the present Effect of Accidents not thought of ; so that 'tis impossible it should be equally proper to both these, unless it were possible that all Persons were born so much more than 25 Poets, that Verses were not to be compos'd by them, but already made in them. Some may object, That this Argument is trivial, because, whatever is shew'd, 'tis known still to be but a Play ; but such may as well excuse an ill Scene, that is not naturally painted, because they 30 know 'tis only a Scene, and not really a City or Country.

But there is yet another thing which makes Verse upon the Stage appear more unnatural ; that is, when a Piece of a Verse is made up by one that knew not what the other meant to say, and the former Verse answered as perfectly in Sound as the last is suppli'd in Measure; so that the smartness of a Reply, which has it's beauty by coming from sudden Thoughts, seems lost by that which rather looks like a Design of two than the Answer of one. It may be said, That Rhime is such a confinement to a quick 5 and luxuriant Phansie, that it gives a stop to its speed, till slow Judgment comes in to assist it; but this is no Argument for the Question in hand; for the dispute is not which way a Man may write best in, but which is most proper for the Subject he writes upon; and if this were let pass, the 10 Argument is yet unsolv'd in it self, for he that wants Judgment in the liberty of his Phancy may as well shew the defect of it in its Confinement; and to say truth, he that has Judgment will avoid the errors, and he that wants it will commit them both. It may be objected, 'Tis improbable that any 15 should speak *ex tempore* as well as *Beaumont* and *Fletcher* makes them, though in Blank Verse; I do not only acknowledg that, but that 'tis also improbable any will write so well that way; but if that may be allow'd improbable, I believe it may be concluded impossible that any should speak as 20 good Verses in Rhime as the best Poets have writ, and therefore that which seems neerest to what it intends is ever to be prefer'd : Nor is great Thoughts more adorned by Verse than Verse unbeautifi'd by mean ones; so that Verse seems not only unfit in the best use of it, but much 25 more in the worse, when a Servant is call'd or a Door bid to be shut in Rhime. Verses (I mean good ones) do in their height of Phancy declare the labour that brought them forth, like Majesty that grows with care; and Nature, that made the Poet capable, seems to retire and leave its 30 offers to be made perfect by Pains and Judgment. Against this I can raise no Argument but my Lord of *Orory*'s Writings, in whose Verse the greatness of the Majesty seems unsullied with the Cares, and his unimitable Phancy descends to us in such easie Expressions that they seem 35

as if neither had ever been added to the other, but both together flowing from a height, like Birds got so high, that use no labouring Wings, but only with an easie care preserve a steadiness in motion : But this particular
5 Happiness, among those multitudes which that excellent Person is Owner of, does not convince my Reason, but employ my Wonder : Yet I am glad such Verse has been writ for our Stage, since it has so happily exceeded those whom we seem'd to imitate. But while I give these Argu-
10 ments against Verse, I may seem faulty that I have not only writ ill ones, but writ any ; but since it was the fashion, I was resolv'd, as in all indifferent things, not to appear singular, the danger of the vanity being greater than the error ; and therefore I follow'd it as a Fashion, though
15 very far off.

For the *Italian* Plays I have seen some of them which have been given me as the best, but they are so inconsider-able that the Particulars of them are not at all worthy to entertain the Reader ; but as much as they are short of
20 others in this, they exceed in their other performances on the Stage,—I mean their *Opera*'s, which consisting of Musique and Painting, there's none but will believe it is much harder to equal them in that way than 'tis to excel them in the other.

25 The *Spanish* Plays pretend to more, but indeed are not much, being nothing but so many Novels put into Acts and Scenes, without the least attempt or design of making the Reader more concern'd than a well-told Tale might do ; whereas a Poet that endeavours not to heighten the
30 Accidents which Fortune seems to scatter in a well-knit Design had better have told his tale by a Fire-side than presented it on a Stage.

For these Times wherein we write, I admire to hear the Poets so often cry out upon and wittily (as they believe)
35 threaten their Judges, since the effects of their Mercy has

so much exceeded their Justice, that others with me cannot but remember how many favourable Audiences some of our ill Plays have had ; and when I consider how severe the former Age has been to some of the best of *M*ʳ *Johnson*'s never to be equal'd Comedies, I cannot but 5 wonder why any Poet should speak of former Times, but rather acknowledg that the want of Abilities in this Age are largely supply'd with the Mercys of it.   I deny not but there are some who resolve to like nothing ; and such perhaps are not unwise, since by that general resolution 10 they may be certainly in the right sometimes, which perhaps they would seldom be if they should venture their Understandings in different Censures ; and being forc'd to a general liking or disliking, lest they should discover too much their own weakness, 'tis to be expected 15 they would rather chuse to pretend to Judgment than good Nature, though I wish they could find better ways to shew either.

But I forget my self, not considering, That while I enter- tain the Reader in the Entrance with what a good Play 20 should be, when he is come beyond the Entrance he must be treated with what ill Plays are : But in this I resemble the greatest part of the World, that better know how to talk of things than to perform them, and live short of their own Discourses.   25

And now I seem like an eager Hunter that has long pursu'd a Chase after an inconsiderable Quarry, and gives over weary, as I do.

II. PREFACE TO *THE GREAT FAVOURITE, OR THE DUKE OF LERMA*

1668

To the
READER.

I CANNOT plead the usual excuse for publishing this trifle, which is commonly the Subject of most Prefaces, by charging it upon the importunity of friends, for, I confess, I was my selfe willing at the first desire of Mr. *Herringman*
5 to print it, not for any great opinion that I had entertain'd, but for the opinion that others were pleas'd to express: which being told me by some friends, I was concern'd to let the World judge what subject matter of offence was contain'd in it; some were pleas'd to believe little of it
10 mine: but they are both obliging to me, though perhaps not intentionally; the last, by thinking there was any thing in it that was worth so ill design'd an Envy as to place it to another Author; the others, perhaps the best bred Informers, by continuing their displeasure towards
15 me, since I most gratefully acknowledge to have received some advantage in the opinion of the sober part of the World by the loss of theirs.

For the Subject, I came accidentally to write upon it, for a Gentleman brought a Play to the Kings Company,
20 call'd *The Duke of* Lerma, and by them I was desir'd to peruse it and return my opinion whether I thought it fit for the Stage; after I had read it, I acquainted them that in my judgement it would not be of much use for such a design, since the contrivance scarce would merit the
25 name of a plot; and some of that, assisted by a disguise; and it ended abruptly: and on the Person of *Philip* the 3. there was fixt such a mean Character, and on the Daughter of the Duke of *Lerma* such a vitious one, that I cou'd not

but judge it unfit to be presented by any that had a respect,
not only of Princes, but indeed to either Man or Woman;
and about that time, being to go into the Countrey, I was
persuaded by Mr. *Hart* to make it my diversion there that
so great a hint might not be lost, as the Duke of *Lerma* 5
saving himself in his last extremity by his unexpected
disguise, which is as well in the true story as the old
Play; and besides that and the Names, my altering the
most part of the Characters, and the whole design, made
me uncapable to use much more, though perhaps written 10
with higher Stile and Thoughts than I cou'd attain to.

I intend not to trouble myself nor the World any more
in such Subjects, but take my leave of these my too long
acquaintances, since that little fancy and liberty I once
enjoy'd is now fetter'd in business of more unpleasant 15
Natures; yet were I free to apply my thoughts as my own
choice directed them, I should hardly again venter into the
Civil Wars of Censures.

Ubi—Nullos habitura Triumphos.

In the next place, I must ingeniously confess that the 20
manner of Plays which now are in most esteem is beyond
my pow'r to perform; nor do I condemn in the least any
thing of what Nature soever that pleases, since nothing
cou'd appear to me a ruder folly than to censure the
satisfaction of others; I rather blame the unnecessary 25
understanding of some that have labour'd to give strict
rules to things that are not Mathematical, and with such
eagerness persuing their own seeming reasons that at last
we are to apprehend such Argumentative Poets will grow
as strict as *Sancho Pancos* Doctor was to our very 30
Appetites; for in the difference of *Tragedy* and *Comedy*,
and of *Fars* it self, there can be no determination but by
the Taste; nor in the manner of their Composure; and
who ever wou'd endeavour to like or dislike by the Rules

of others, he will be as unsuccessful as if he should try to be perswaded into a power of believing, not what he must, but what others direct him to believe.

But I confess, 'tis not necessary for Poets to study strict reason, since they are so us'd to a greater Latitude then is allow'd by that severe Inquisition, that they must infringe their own Jurisdiction to profess themselves oblig'd to argue well. I will not therefore pretend to say why I writ this Play, some Scenes in blank Verse, others in Rhime; since I have no better a reason to give then Chance, which waited upon my present Fancy, and I expect no better a reason from any ingenious person then his Fancy for which he best relishes.

I cannot therefore but beg leave of the Reader to take a little notice of the great pains the Author of an Essay of Dramatick Poesie has taken to prove Rhime as natural in a serious Play, and more effectual then blank Verse : thus he states the question, but persues that which he calls Natural in a wrong Application ; for 'tis not the question whether Rhime or not Rhime be best or most Natural for a grave and serious Subject, but what is neerest the nature of that which it presents. Now, after all the endeavours of that ingenious Person, a Play will still be supposed to be a Composition of several Persons speaking *ex tempore*, and 'tis as certain that good Verses are the hardest things that can be imagin'd to be so spoken ; so that if any will be pleas'd to impose the rule of measuring things to be the best by being neerest Nature, it is granted, by consequence, that which is most remote from the thing supposed must needs be most improper ; and therefore I may justly say that both I and the question were equally mistaken, for I do own I had rather read good Verses then either blank Verse or Prose ; and therefore the Author did himself injury, if he like Verse so well in Plays, to lay down rules to raise Arguments only unanswerable against himself.

But the same Author, being fill'd with the presidents of the Antients writing their Plays in Verse, commends the thing, and assures us that our Language is Noble, Full, and Significant, charging all defects upon the ill placing of words, and proves it by quoting *Seneca* loftily expressing such an ordinary thing as shutting a door :

Reserate Clusos Regii postes Laris.

I suppose he was himself highly affected with the sound of these words ; but to have Compleated his Dictates together with his Arguments, he should have oblig'd us by charming our Eares with such an Art of placing words, as in an English Verse to express so loftily the shutting of a Door, that we might have been as much affected with the sound of his words ; this, in stead of being an argument upon the question rightly stated, is an attempt to prove that nothing may seeme something by the help of a Verse, which I easily grant to be the ill-fortune of it ; and therefore the question being so much mistaken, I wonder to see that Author trouble himself twice about it, with such an absolute triumph declared by his own imagination. But I have heard that a Gentleman in Parliament going to speak twice, and being interrupted by another Member as against the Orders of the House, he was excused by a third assuring the House he had not yet spoken to the Question.

But if we examine the general rules laid down for Playes by strict Reason, we shall find the errors equally gross ; for the great foundation that is laid to build upon is nothing, as it is generally stated, which will appear upon the examination of the particulars.

First, We are told the Plot should not be so rediculously contriv'd as to crowd two several Countries into one stage ; secondly, to cramp the Accidents of many years or dayes into the representation of two houres and a halfe : And Lastly, a Conclusion drawn, that the only remaining dispute is concerning time, whether it should be contain'd in twelve or four and twenty hours, and the place to be limited to the spot of ground, either in Town or City, where the Play is suppos'd to begin : And this is call'd neerest to Nature ; For that is concluded most natural which is most probable and neerest to that which it presents.

I am so well pleas'd with any ingenuous offers, as all these are, that I should not examine this strictly, did not the confidence of others force me to it,—there being not any thing more unreasonable to my Judgment then the attempt to infringe the Liberty of Opinion by Rules so little demonstrative.

To shew therefore upon what ill grounds they dictate Lawes for *Dramatick Poesie*, I shall endeavour to make it evident that there's no such thing as what they all pretend ; for, if strictly and duely weigh'd, 'tis as impossible for one stage to present two Houses or two Roomes truely as two Countreys or Kingdomes, and as impossible that five houres, or four and twenty houres should be two houres and a halfe as that a thousand houres or yeares should be less then what they are, or the greatest part of time to be comprehended in the less ; for all being impossible, they are none of them nearest the truth or nature of what they present, for Impossibilities are all equal, and admit no degrees ; and then if all those Poets that have so fervently labour'd to give Rules as Maximes would but be pleased to abreviate, or endure to hear their Reasons reduc't into one strict definition, it must be that there are degrees in impossibilities, and that many things which are not possible may yet be more or less impossible, and from this proceed to give rules to observe the least absurdity in things which are not at all.

I suppose I need not trouble the Reader with so impertinent a delay to attempt a farther Confutation of such ill-grounded reasons then thus by opening the true state of the Case, nor do I design to make any farther use of it then from hence to draw this modest Conclusion, That I would have all attempts of this nature be submitted to the fancy of others, and bear the name of Propositions, not of Confident Lawes, or Rules made by Demonstration; and then I shall not discommend any Poet that dresses his Play in such a fashion as his fancy best approves, and fairly leave it for others to follow, if it appears to them most convenient and fullest of ornament.

But writing this Epistle in so much haste, I had almost forgot one Argument or Observation which that Author has most good fortune in : It is in his *Epistle Dedicatory* before his *Essay* of *Dramaticke Poesie*, where, speaking of Rhyme in Playes, he desires it may be observ'd, That none are violent against it but such as have not attempted it, or who have succeeded ill in the attempt,—which as to my self and him I easily acknowledge ; for I confess none has written in that way better then himself, nor few worse than I. Yet I hope he is so ingenuous that he would not wish this Argument should extend further then to him and me ; for if it should be received as a good one, all *Divines* and *Philosophers* would find a readier way of Confutation then they yet have done of any that should oppose the least Thesis or Definition, by saying they were denied by none but such as never attempted to write or succeeded ill in the attempt.

Thus as I am one that am extreamly well pleas'd with most of the *Propositions* which are ingeniously laid down in that Essay for regulating the Stage, so I am also alwayes Concern'd for the true honour of reason, and would have no spurious issue Father'd upon her. Fancy may be allow'd her wantonness ; but reason is always pure and chast ; and as it resembles the Sun in making all things clear, it also resembles it in its several positions :

when it shines in full height and directly ascendant over any Subject, it leaves but little shaddow ; But when descended and grown low, its oblique shining renders the shadow larger then the substance, and gives the deceiv'd
5 person a wrong measure of his own proportion.

Thus begging the *Readers* Excuse for this seeming Impertinency, I submit what I have written to the liberty of his unconfin'd Opinion, which is all the favour I ask of others to afford to me.

THOMAS SPRAT

I. FROM *THE HISTORY OF THE ROYAL-SOCIETY OF LONDON*

1667

I

⟨The First Part,⟩ Sect. XX. *A proposal for erecting an English Academy.* I HOPE now it will not be thought a vain digression, if I step a little aside to recommend the forming of such an *Assembly* to the Gentlemen of our Nation. I know indeed that the *English Genius* is not so airy and discoursive as that of some of our neighbors, but that we generally love to 5 have Reason set out in plain, undeceiving expressions, as much as they to have it deliver'd with colour and beauty. And besides this, I understand well enough that they have one great assistance to the growth of Oratory which to us is wanting ; that is, that their Nobility live commonly close 10 together in their Cities, and ours for the most part scattered in their Country Houses. For the same reason, why our streets are not so well built as theirs will hold also for their exceeding us in the Arts of Speech. They prefer the Pleasures of the Town, we, those of the field ; 15 whereas it is from the frequent conversations in Cities that the Humour and Wit and Variety and Elegance of Language are chiefly to be fetch'd. But yet, notwithstanding these discouragements, I shall not stick to say that such a project is now seasonable to be set on foot, and 20 may make a great Reformation in the manner of our Speaking and Writing. First, the thing itself is no way contemptible. For the purity of Speech and greatness of

Empire have in all Countries still met together. The *Greeks* spoke best when they were in their glory of conquest. The *Romans* made those times the Standard of their Wit, when they subdu'd and gave Laws to the World. 5 And from thence, by degrees, they declin'd to corruption, as their valour, their prudence, and the honor of their Arms did decay, and at last did even meet the *Northern Nations* half way in *Barbarism*, a little before they were overrun by their Armies.

10   But besides, if we observe well the *English Language*, we shall find that it seems at this time more than others to require some such aid to bring it to its last perfection. The Truth is, it has been hitherto a little too carelessly handled, and, I think, has had less labor spent about its 15 polishing then it deserves. Till the time of *King Henry* the *Eighth*, there was scarce any man regarded it but *Chaucer*, and nothing was written in it which one would be willing to read twice but some of his *Poetry*. But then it began to raise it self a little, and to sound tolerably well. 20 From that Age down to the beginning of our late *Civil Wars*, it was still fashioning and beautifying it self.   In the Wars themselves (which is a time wherein all Languages use, if ever, to increase by extraordinary degrees, for in such busie and active times there arise more new thoughts 25 of men which must be signifi'd and varied by new expressions), then, I say, it receiv'd many fantastical terms, which were introduc'd by our *Religious Sects*, and many outlandish phrases, which several *Writers* and *Translators* in that great hurry brought in and made free as they pleas'd, 30 and with all it was inlarg'd by many sound and necessary Forms and Idioms which it before wanted. And now, when mens minds are somewhat settled, their Passions allai'd, and the peace of our Country gives us the opportunity of such diversions, if some sober and judicious Men 35 would take the whole Mass of our Language into their

hands as they find it, and would set a mark on the ill
Words, correct those which are to be retain'd, admit and
establish the good, and make some emendations in the
Accent and Grammar, I dare pronounce that our *Speech*
would quickly arrive at as much plenty as it is capable to 5
receive, and at the greatest smoothness which its derivation
from the rough *German* will allow it.

Nor would I have this new *English Academy* confin'd
only to the weighing Words and Letters.   But there may
be also greater Works found out for it.   By many signs 10
we may ghess that the Wits of our Nation are not inferior
to any other, and that they have an excellent mixture of
the Spirit of the *French* and the *Spaniard*; and I am confident that we only want a few more standing Examples,
and a little more familiarity with the Antients, to excel all 15
the Moderns.   Now the best means that can be devis'd to
bring that about is to settle a fixt and *Impartial Court* of
Eloquence, according to whose Censure all Books or Authors
should either stand or fall.   And above all, there might be
recommended to them one Principal Work in which we 20
are yet defective, and that is the compiling of a *History* of
our late *Civil Wars*.   Of all the labors of mens Wit and
Industry, I scarce know any that can be more useful to the
World then *Civil History*, if it were written with that
sincerity and majesty, as it ought to be, as a faithful Idea 25
of humane Actions.   And it is observable that almost in all
civiliz'd Countries it has been the last thing that has come
to perfection.   I may now say that the *English* can already
shew many industrious and worthy Pieces in this kind.
But yet I have some Prophetical imagination in my 30
thoughts, that there is still behind something Greater then
any we have yet seen reserv'd for the Glory of this Age.
One Reason of this my strong persuasion is a comparison
that I make between the condition of our *State* and that of
the *Romans*.   They at first writ in this way not much 35

better then our *Moncks*, onely Registring in an undigested
manner some few naked Breviaries of their Wars, and
Leagues, and Acts of their City Magistrates. And indeed
they advanc'd forward by very slow degrees. For I remember that *Tully* somewhere complains in these Words :
Historia nondum latinis literis illustrata. But it was in the
peaceful reign of *Augustus*, after the conclusion of their long
Civil Wars, that most of their perfect *Historians* appear'd.
And it seems to me that we may expect the same progress
amongst us. There lye now ready in Bank the most
memorable Actions of Twenty years, a Subject of as great
Dignity and Variety as ever pass'd under any Mans hands ;
the peace which we injoy gives leisure and incouragement
enough. The effects of such a Work would be wonderfully advantageous to the safety of our Country and to *His
Majesties* Interest, for there can be no better means to
preserve his Subjects in obedience for the future than to
give them a full view of the miseries that attended
rebellion. There are onely therefore wanting, for the
finishing of so brave an undertaking, the united indeavors
of some publick minds who are conversant both in Letters
and business ; and if it were appointed to be the labor of
one or two men to compose it, and of such an *Assembly* to
revise and correct it, it might certainly challenge all the
Writings of past or present Times.

But I see I have already transgress'd. For I know it
will be thought unadvisedly done, while I was inforcing a
weightier Design, to start and to follow another of less
moment. I shall therefore let it pass as an extravagant
conceit . only I shall affirm that the *Royal Society* is so far
from being like to put a stop to such a business, that I know
many of its Members, who are as able as any others, to
assist in the bringing it into practice.

II

〈The
Second
Part,〉
Sect. XX.
*Their
manner of
Discourse.*

Thus they have directed, judg'd, conjectur'd upon, and improved *Experiments*. But lastly, in these and all other businesses that have come under their care, there is one thing more about which the *Society* has been most sollicitous, and that is the manner of their *Discourse*, which, unless they had been very watchful to keep in due temper, the whole spirit and vigour of their *Design* had been soon eaten out by the luxury and redundance of *speech*. The ill effects of this superfluity of talking have already overwhelm'd most other *Arts* and *Professions*, insomuch that when I consider the means of *happy living* and the causes of their corruption, I can hardly forbear recanting what I said before, and concluding that *eloquence* ought to be banish'd out of all *civil Societies*, as a thing fatal to Peace and good Manners. To this opinion I should wholly incline, if I did not find that it is a Weapon which may be as easily procur'd by *bad* men as *good*, and that, if these should onely cast it away, and those retain it, the *naked Innocence* of vertue would be upon all occasions expos'd to the *armed Malice* of the wicked. This is the chief reason that should now keep up the Ornaments of speaking in any request, since they are so much degenerated from their original usefulness. They were at first, no doubt, an admirable Instrument in the hands of *Wise Men*, when they were onely employ'd to describe *Goodness, Honesty, Obedience*, in larger, fairer and more moving Images; to represent *Truth*, cloth'd with Bodies; and to bring *Knowledg* back again to our very senses, from whence it was at first deriv'd to our understandings. But now they are generally chang'd to worse uses: They make the *Fancy* disgust the best things, if they come sound and unadorn'd; they are in open defiance against *Reason*, professing not to hold much correspondence with that, but with its Slaves,

the Passions; they give the mind a motion too changeable
and bewitching to consist with *right practice*. Who can
behold without indignation how many mists and uncertainties these specious *Tropes* and *Figures* have brought on
our knowledg? How many rewards which are due to
more profitable and difficult *Arts* have been still snatch'd
away by the easie vanity of *fine speaking*? For now I am
warm'd with this just Anger, I cannot with-hold my self
from betraying the shallowness of all these seeming
Mysteries upon which *we Writers* and *Speakers* look so
bigg. And, in few words, I dare say that, of all the Studies
of men, nothing may be sooner obtain'd than this vicious
abundance of *Phrase*, this trick of *Metaphors*, this volubility
of *Tongue*, which makes so great a noise in the World.
But I spend words in vain, for the evil is now so inveterate
that it is hard to know whom to *blame*, or where to begin
to *reform*. We all value one another so much upon this
beautiful deceipt, and labour so long after it in the years of
our education, that we cannot but ever after think kinder
of it than it deserves. And indeed, in most other parts of
Learning, I look on it to be a thing almost utterly desperate in its cure, and I think it may be plac'd amongst
those *general mischiefs*, such as the *dissention* of Christian
Princes, the *want of practice* in Religion, and the like,
which have been so long spoken against that men are
become insensible about them, every one shifting off the
fault from himself to others, and so they are only made
bare common places of complaint. It will suffice my
present purpose to point out what has been done by the
Royal Society towards the correcting of its excesses in
Natural Philosophy, to which it is, of all others, a most
profest enemy.

They have therefore been most rigorous in putting in
execution the only Remedy that can be found for this
extravagance, and that has been a constant Resolution to

reject all amplifications, digressions, and swellings of style ;
to return back to the primitive purity and shortness, when
men deliver'd so many *things* almost in an equal number
of *words*. They have exacted from all their members a
close, naked, natural way of speaking, positive expressions, 5
clear senses, a native easiness, bringing all things as near
the Mathematical plainness as they can, and preferring the
language of Artizans, Countrymen, and Merchants, before
that of Wits or Scholars.

And here there is one thing not to be pass'd by, which 10
will render this establish'd custom of the *Society* well nigh
everlasting, and that is the general constitution of the minds
of the *English*. I have already often insisted on some of the
prerogatives of *England*, whereby it may justly lay claim
to be the Head of a *Philosophical league* above all other 1
Countries in *Europe*. I have urg'd its scituation, its
present Genius, and the disposition of its Merchants ; and
many more such *arguments* to incourage us still remain to
be us'd. But of all others, this which I am now alledging
is of the most weighty and important consideration. If 2
there can be a true character given of the *Universal Temper*
of any Nation under Heaven, then certainly this must be
ascrib'd to our Countrymen, that they have commonly an
unaffected sincerity, that they love to deliver their minds
with a sound simplicity, that they have the middle qualities 2
between the reserv'd, subtle southern and the rough,
unhewn Northern people, that they are not extreamly
prone to speak, that they are more concern'd what others
will think of the strength than of the fineness of what they
say, and that an universal modesty possesses them. These 3
qualities are so conspicuous and proper to the Soil that we
often hear them objected to us by some of our neighbour
Satyrists in more disgraceful expressions. For they are
wont to revile the *English* with a want of familiarity, with
a melancholy dumpishness, with slowness, silence, and 3

with the unrefin'd sullenness of their behaviour. But these are only the reproaches of partiality or ignorance; for they ought rather to be commended for an honourable integrity, for a neglect of circumstances and flourishes, for regarding things of *greater* moment more than *less*, for a scorn to deceive as well as to be deceiv'd, which are all the best indowments that can enter into a *Philosophical Mind.* So that even the position of our climate, the air, the influence of the heaven, the composition of the English blood, as well as the embraces of the Ocean, seem to joyn with the labours of the *Royal Society* to render our Country a Land of *Experimental knowledge.* And it is a good sign that Nature will reveal more of its secrets to the English than to others, because it has already furnish'd them with a Genius so well proportion'd for the receiving and retaining its mysteries.

II. *AN ACCOUNT OF THE LIFE AND WRITINGS OF MR. ABRAHAM COWLEY: WRITTEN TO MR. M. CLIFFORD.*

1668

SIR,

MR. *Cowley* in his Will recommended to my care the revising of all his Works that were formerly printed, and the collecting of those Papers which he had design'd for the Press. And he did it with this particular Obligation, *That I should be sure to let nothing pass that might seem the least offence to Religion or good Manners.* A caution which you will judge to have been altogether needless. For certainly, in all Ancient or Modern Times, there can scarce any Authour be found, that has handled so many different Matters in such various sorts of Style, who less wants the correction of his Friends, or has less reason to fear the severity of Strangers.

According to his desire and his own intention, I have now set forth his Latin and English Writings, each in a Volume apart; and to that which was before extant in both Languages, I have added all that I could find in his Closet, which he had brought to any manner of perfection. I have thus, Sir, performed the Will of the Dead. But I doubt I shall not satisfie the expectation of the Living, unless some Account be here premis'd concerning this excellent Man. I know very well that he has given the World the best Image of his own mind in these immortal Monuments of his Wit. Yet there is still room enough left for one of his familiar acquaintance to say many things of his Poems, and chiefly of his life, that may serve for the information of his Readers, if not for the encrease of his Fame, which, without any such helps, is already sufficiently establish'd.

This, Sir, were an argument most proper for you to manage, in respect of your great abilities, and the long friendship you maintain'd with him. But you have an obstinate aversion from publishing any of your Writings. I guess what pretence you have for it, and that you are confirm'd in this resolution by the prodigious multitude and imperfections of us Writers of this Age. I will not now dispute whether you are in the right, though I am confident you would contribute more to our reformation by your example than reproofs. But, however, seeing you persist in your purpose, and have refus'd to adorn even this very subject which you love so well, I beg your assistance while I my self undertake it. This I do with the greater willingness, because I believe there is no man who speaks of Mr. *Cowley* that can want either matter or words. I only therefore intreat you to give me leave to make you a party in this Relation, by using your Name and Testimony. For by this means, though the memory of our Friend shall not be delivered to posterity with the advantage of your Wit, which were most to be desir'd, yet his praise will be strengthen'd by the consent of your judgment and the authority of your approbation.

Mr. *A. Cowley* was born in the City of *London*, in the Year One thousand six hundred and eighteen. His Parents were Citizens of a virtuous life and sufficient Estate, and so the condition of his Fortune was equal to the temper of his mind, which was always content with moderate things. The first years of his youth were spent in *Westminster* School, where he soon obtain'd and increas'd the noble Genius peculiar to that place. The occasion of his first inclination to Poetry was his casual lighting on *Spencer's Fairy Queen*, when he was but just able to read. That indeed is a Poem fitter for the examination of men than the consideration of a Child. But in him it met with a Fancy whose strength was not to be judged by the number of his years.

In the thirteenth year of his age there came forth a little Book under his Name, in which there were many things that might well become the vigour and force of a manly Wit. The first beginning of his Studies was a familiarity with the most solid and unaffected Authors of Antiquity, which he fully digested not only in his memory but his judgment. By this advantage he learnt nothing while a Boy that he needed to forget or forsake when he came to be a man. His mind was rightly season'd at first, and he had nothing to do but still to proceed on the same Foundation on which he began.

He was wont to relate that he had this defect in his memory at that time, that his Teachers could never bring it to retain the ordinary Rules of Grammar. However, he supply'd that want, by conversing with the Books themselves from whence those Rules had been drawn. That no doubt was a better way, though much more difficult, and he afterwards found this benefit by it, that having got the Greek and Roman Languages, as he had done his own, not by precept but use, he practis'd them not as a Scholar but a Native.

With these extraordinary hopes he was remov'd to *Trinity* Colledge in *Cambridge*, where by the progress and continuance of his Wit, it appear'd that two things were join'd in it which seldom meet together, that it was both early-ripe and lasting. This brought him into the love and esteem of the most eminent members of that famous Society, and principally of your Uncle Mr. *Fotherby*, whose favours he since abundantly acknowledg'd, when his Benefactor had quite forgot the obligation. His Exercises of all kinds are still remembred in that University with great applause, and with this particular praise, that they were not only fit for the obscurity of an Academical life, but to have been shown on the true Theater of the World. There it was that before the twentieth year of his Age, he laid the design of divers of his most Masculine Works that he finish'd long after. In which I know not whether I should most commend that a mind so young should conceive such great things, or that it should be able to perfect them with such felicity.

The first occasion of his entring into business was the Elegy that he writ on Mr. *Herveys* Death, wherein he described the highest Characters of Religion, Knowledge, and Friendship, in an Age when most other men scarce begin to learn them. This brought him into the acquaintance of Mr. *John Hervey*, the Brother of his deceased Friend, from whom he received many Offices of kindness through the whole course of his life, and principally this, that by his means he came into the service of my Lord St. *Albans*.

When the Civil War broke out, his affection to the Kings Cause drew him to *Oxford*, as soon as it began to be the chief seat of the Royal Party. In that University he prosecuted the same Studies with a like success. Nor in

the mean time was he wanting to his duty in the War
it self, for he was present and in service in several of the
Kings Journeys and Expeditions.   By these occasions and
the report of his high deserts, he speedily grew familiar to
5 the chief men of the Court and the Gown, whom the Fortune
of the War had drawn together.   And particularly, though
he was then very young, he had the entire friendship of my
Lord *Falkland*, one of the Principal Secretaries of State.
That affection was contracted by the agreement of their
10 Learning and Manners.   For you may remember, Sir,
we have often heard Mr. *Cowley* admire him, not only for
the profoundness of his Knowledge, which was applauded
by all the world, but more especially for those qualities
which he himself more regarded, for his generosity of mind
15 and his neglect of the vain pomp of humane greatness.

During the heat of the Civil War, he was setled in
my Lord St. *Albans* Family, and attended her Majesty the
Queen-Mother, when by the unjust persecution of her
Subjects she was forc'd to retire into *France*.   Upon this
20 wandring condition of the most vigorous part of his life, he
was wont to reflect, as the cause of the long interruption of
his Studies.   Yet we have no reason to think that he lost
so great a space of Time, if we consider in what business he
employ'd his banishment.   He was absent from his native
25 Country above twelve years, which were wholly spent
either in bearing a share in the distresses of the Royal
Family or in labouring in their Affairs.   To this purpose
he performed several dangerous journeys into *Jersey*,
Scotland, *Flanders*, *Holland*, or wherever else the Kings
30 Troubles requir'd his attendance.   But the chief Testimony
of his Fidelity was the laborious service he underwent
in maintaining the constant correspondence between the
late King and the Queen his Wife.   In that weighty Trust
he behaved himself with indefatigable integrity and un-
35 suspected secrecy.   For he cypher'd and decypher'd with

his own hand the greatest part of all the Letters that passed between their Majesties, and managed a vast Intelligence in many other parts : which for some years together took up all his days, and two or three nights every week.

At length upon his present Majesties removal out of *France*, and the Queen-Mothers staying behind, the business of that nature passed of course into other hands.   Then it was thought fit by those on whom he depended, that he should come over into *England*, and under pretence of privacy and retirement, should take occasion of giving notice of the posture of things in this Nation.   Upon his return he found his Country groaning under the oppression of an unjust Usurpation.   And he soon felt the effects of it. For while he lay hid in *London*, he was seiz'd on by a mistake, the search having been intended after another Gentleman, of considerable note in the Kings Party. Being made a Prisoner, he was often examined before the Usurpers, who tryed all imaginable ways to make him serviceable to their ends.   That course not prevailing, he was committed to a severe restraint ; and scarce at last obtained his liberty upon the hard terms of a Thousand pound Bail, which burden Dr. *Scarborough* very honourably took upon himself.   Under these Bonds he continued till the general redemption.   Yet taking the opportunity of the Confusions that followed upon *Cromwels* death, he ventured back into *France*, and there remained in the same Station as before, till neer the time of the Kings return.

This certainly, Sir, is abundantly sufficient to justifie his Loyalty to all the world, though some have indeavoured to bring it in question, upon occasion of a few lines in the Preface to one of his Books.   The Objection I must not pass by in silence, because it was the only part of his life that was lyable to mis-interpretation, even by the confession of those that envyed his Fame.

In this case perhaps it were enough to alledge for him to men of moderate minds, that what he there said was published before a Book of Poetry, and so ought rather to be esteemed as a Probleme of his Fancy and Invention
5 than as the real Image of his Judgment. But his defence in this matter may be laid on a surer Foundation. This is the true reason that is to be given of his delivering that opinion. Upon his coming over he found the state of the Royal Party very desperate. He perceived
10 the strength of their Enemies so united, that till it should begin to break within it self, all endeavours against it were like to prove unsuccessful. On the other side he beheld their zeal for his Majesties Cause to be still so active, that it often hurryed them into inevitable ruine. He saw this
15 with much grief. And though he approv'd their constancy as much as any man living, yet he found their unseasonable shewing it did only disable themselves, and give their Adversaries great advantages of riches and strength by their defeats. He therefore believed that it would be a
20 meritorious service to the King, if any man who was known to have followed his interest could insinuate into the Usurpers minds, that men of his Principles were now willing to be quiet, and could perswade the poor oppressed Royalists to conceal their affections for better
25 occasions. And as for his own particular, he was a close Prisoner, when he writ that against which the exception is made ; so that he saw it was impossible for him to pursue the ends for which he came hither, if he did not make some kind of declaration of his peaceable intentions. This
30 was then his opinion. And the success of things seems to prove that it was not very ill grounded. For certainly it was one of the greatest helps to the Kings Affairs, about the latter end of that Tyranny, that many of his best Friends dissembled their Counsels, and acted the same
35 Designs, under the Disguises and Names of other Parties.

This, Sir, you can testifie to have been the innocent occasion of these words on which so much clamour was rais'd. Yet seeing his good intentions were so ill interpreted, he told me, the last time that ever I saw him, that he would have them omitted in the next Impression : of which his 5 Friend Mr. *Cook* is a witness. However, if we should take them in the worst sense of which they are capable, yet methinks for his maintaining one false Tenent in the Political Philosophy, he made a sufficient atonement by a continual service of twenty years, by the perpetual loyalty 10 of his Discourse, and by many of his other Writings, wherein he has largely defended and adorned the Royal Cause. And to speak of him not as our Friend, but according to the common Laws of Humanity, certainly that life must needs be very unblamable, which had been tryed in 15 business of the highest consequence, and practis'd in the hazardous secrets of Courts and Cabinets, and yet there can nothing disgraceful be produc'd against it, but only the errour of one Paragraph and a single Metaphor.

But to return to my Narration which this Digression 20 has interrupted : Upon the Kings happy Restauration Mr. *Cowley* was past the fortieth year of his Age, of which the greatest part had been spent in a various and tempestuous condition. He now thought he had sacrificed enough of his life to his curiosity and experience. He had enjoyed 25 many excellent occasions of observation. He had been present in many great revolutions, which in that tumultuous time disturb'd the peace of all our Neighbour-States as well as our own. He had neerly beheld all the splendour of the highest part of mankind. He had lived in the 30 presence of Princes, and familiarly convert with greatness in all its degrees, which was necessary for one that would contemn it aright ; for to scorn the pomp of the World before a man knows it does commonly proceed rather from ill Manners than a true Magnanimity.

35

He was now weary of the vexations and formalities of an active condition. He had been perplexed with a long compliance to Foreign Manners. He was satiated with the Arts of Court, which sort of life, though his virtu had
5 made innocent to him, yet nothing could make it quiet. These were the reasons that moved him to forego all Public Employments, and to follow the violent inclination of his own mind, which in the greatest throng of his former business had still called upon him, and represented to him
10 the true delights of solitary Studies, of temperate Pleasures, and of a moderate Revenue, below the malice and flatteries of Fortune.

At first he was but slenderly provided for such a retire-ment, by reason of his Travels and the Affliction of the
15 Party to which he adhered, which had put him quite out of all the rodes of gain. Yet, notwithstanding the narrow-ness of his Income, he remained fixed to his resolution, upon his confidence in the temper of his own mind, which he knew had contracted its desires into so small a compass that
20 a very few things would supply them all. But upon the setlement of the Peace of our Nation, this hinderance of his design was soon remov'd; for he then obtain'd a plentiful Estate by the favour of my Lord St. *Albans* and the bounty of my Lord Duke of *Buckingham*, to whom he
25 was always most dear, and whom he ever respected as his principal Patrons. The last of which great men, you know, Sir, it is my duty to mention, not only for Mr. *Cowleys* sake, but my own; though I cannot do it without being asham'd, that having the same Encourager of my Studies, I should
30 deserve his Patronage so much less.

Thus he was sufficiently furnished for his retreat. And immediately he gave over all pursuit of Honour and Riches, in a time when, if any ambitious or covetous thoughts had remain'd in his mind, he might justly have expected to have
35 them readily satisfied. In his last seven or eight years he

was conceal'd in his beloved obscurity, and possess'd that Solitude which from his very childhood he had always most passionately desired. Though he had frequent invitations to return into business, yet he never gave ear to any per- swasions of Profit or Preferment. His visits to the City 5 and Court were very few: his stays in Town were only as a Passenger, not an Inhabitant. The Places that he chose for the Seats of his declining life were two or three Villages on the Bank of the *Thames*. During this recess his mind was rather exercised on what was to come than what was 10 pass'd; he suffer'd no more business nor cares of life to come neer him than what were enough to keep his Soul awake, but not to disturb it. Some few Friends and Books, a cheerful heart, and innocent conscience were his constant Companions. His Poetry indeed he took with him, but he 15 made that an Anchorite as well as himself: he only dedi- cated it to the service of his Maker, to describe the great images of Religion and Virtue wherewith his mind abounded. And he employed his Musick to no other use than as his own *David* did towards *Saul*, by singing the 20 Praises of God and of Nature, to drive the evil Spirit out of mens minds.

Of his Works that are Publish'd it is hard to give one general Character, because of the difference of their subjects and the various forms and distant times of their writing. 25 Yet this is true of them all, that in all the several shapes of his Style there is still very much of the likeness and impression of the same mind: the same unaffected modesty, and natural freedom, and easie vigour, and chearful passions, and innocent mirth, which appear'd in all his 30 Manners. We have many things that he writ in two very un- like conditions, in the University and the Court. But in his Poetry as well as his Life, he mingled with excellent skill what was good in both states. In his life he join'd the innocence and sincerity of the Scholar with the humanity 35

and good behaviour of the Courtier. In his Poems he
united the Solidity and Art of the one with the Gentility
and Gracefulness of the other.

If any shall think that he was not wonderfully curious in
5 the choice and elegance of all his words, I will affirm with
more truth on the other side, that he had no manner of
affectation in them : he took them as he found them made
to his hands ; he neither went before nor came after the
use of the Age. He forsook the Conversation, but never
10 the Language, of the City and Court. He understood
exceeding well all the variety and power of Poetical
Numbers, and practis'd all sorts with great happiness. If
his Verses in some places seem not as soft and flowing as
some would have them, it was his choice, not his fault.
15 He knew that in diverting mens minds there should be the
same variety observ'd as in the prospects of their Eyes,
where a Rock, a Precipice, or a rising Wave is often more
delightful than a smooth, even ground or a calm Sea.
Where the matter required it, he was as gentle as any man.
20 But where higher Virtues were chiefly to be regarded, an
exact numerosity was not then his main care. This may
serve to answer those who upbraid some of his Pieces with
roughness, and with more contractions than they are willing
to allow. But these Admirers of gentlenesse without sinews
25 should know that different Arguments must have different
Colours of Speech : that there is a kind of variety of Sexes
in Poetry as well as in Mankind : that as the peculiar
excellence of the Feminine Kind is smoothnesse and beauty,
so strength is the chief praise of the Masculine.

30 He had a perfect mastery in both the Languages in
which he writ. But each of them kept a just distance from
the other : neither did his Latin make his English too old,
nor his English make his Latin too modern. He excelled
both in Prose and Verse ; and both together have that per-
35 fection which is commended by some of the Antients above

all others, that they are very obvious to the conception, but most difficult in the imitation.

His Fancy flow'd with great speed, and therefore it was very fortunate to him that his Judgment was equal to manage it. He never runs his Reader nor his Argument 5 out of Breath. He perfectly practises the hardest secret of good Writing, to know when he has done enough. He always leaves off in such a manner that it appears it was in his power to have said much more. In the particular expressions there is still much to be Applauded, but more 10 in the disposition and order of the whole. From thence there springs a new comliness, besides the feature of each part. His Invention is powerful and large as can be desir'd. But it seems all to arise out of the Nature of the subject, and to be just fitted for the thing of which he speaks. 15 If ever he goes far for it, he dissembles his pains admirably well.

The variety of Arguments that he has manag'd is so large that there is scarce any particular of all the passions of Men or works of Nature and Providence which he has 20 pass'd by undescrib'd. Yet he still observes the rules of Decence with so much care, that whether he inflames his Reader with the softer Affections, or delights him with inoffensive Raillery, or teaches the familiar manners of Life, or adorns the discoveries of Philosophy, or inspires him 25 with the Heroick Characters of Charity and Religion : To all these matters that are so wide asunder, he still proportions a due figure of Speech and a proper measure of Wit. This indeed is most remarkable, that a Man who was so constant and fix'd in the Moral Ideas of his mind should 30 yet be so changeable in his Intellectual, and in both to the highest degree of Excellence.

If there needed any excuse to be made that his Love-Verses should take up so great a share in his Works, it may be alledg'd that they were compos'd when he was very 35

young. But it is a vain thing to make any kind of Apology for that sort of Writings. If Devout or Virtuous Men will superciliously forbid the minds of the young to adorn those subjects about which they are most conversant: They would
5 put them out of all capacity of performing graver matters, when they come to them. For the exercises of all Mens Wits must be always proper for their Age, and never too much above it: And by practice and use in lighter Arguments, they grow up at last to excel in the most weighty.
10 I am not therefore asham'd to commend Mr. *Cowley's* Mistress. I only except one or two Expressions, which I wish I could have prevail'd with those that had the right of the other Edition to have left out. But of all the rest I dare boldly pronounce, that never yet so much was written
15 on a subject so Delicate, that can less offend the severest rules of Morality. The whole Passion of Love is inimitably describ'd, with all its mighty Train of Hopes, and Joys, and Disquiets. Besides this amorous tenderness, I know not how in every Copy there is something of more useful
20 Knowledge very naturally and gracefully insinuated, and every where there may be something found to inform the minds of wise Men as well as to move the hearts of young Men or Women.

The occasion of his falling on the Pindaric way of
25 Writing was his accidental meeting with *Pindars* Works in a place where he had no other Books to direct him. Having then considered at leisure the height of his Invention and the Majesty of his Style, he try'd immediately to imitate it in *English*. And he perform'd it without the
30 danger that *Horace* presag'd to the Man who should dare to attempt it.

If any are displeas'd at the boldness of his Metaphors and length of his Digressions they contend not against Mr. *Cowley*, but *Pindar* himself, who was so much reverenc'd
35 by all Antiquity that the place of his Birth was preserv'd as

Sacred, when his Native City was twice destroy'd by the
fury of two Conquerours.   If the irregularity of the number
disgust them, they may observe that this very thing makes
that kind of Poesie fit for all manner of subjects : For the
Pleasant, the Grave, the Amorous, the Heroic, the Philo- 5
sophical, the Moral, the Divine.   Besides this they will find
that the frequent alteration of the Rhythm and Feet affects
the mind with a more various delight, while it is soon apt
to be tyr'd by the setled pace of any one constant measure.
But that for which I think this inequality of number is 10
chiefly to be preferr'd is its near affinity with Prose : From
which all other kinds of *English* Verse are so far distant
that it is very seldom found that the same Man excels in
both ways.   But now this loose and unconfin'd measure
has all the Grace and Harmony of the most Confin'd. 15
And withal it is so large and free, that the practice of it will
only exalt, not corrupt our Prose, which is certainly the
most useful kind of Writing of all others, for it is the style
of all business and conversation.

Besides this imitating of *Pindar*, which may perhaps be 20
thought rather a new sort of Writing than a restoring of an
Ancient, he has also been wonderfully happy in Translating
many difficult parts of the Noblest Poets of Antiquity.   To
perform this according to the Dignity of the attempt, he had,
as it was necessary he should have, not only the Elegance 25
of both the Languages, but the true spirit of both the
Poetries.   This way of leaving Verbal Translations, and
chiefly regarding the Sense and Genius of the Author, was
scarce heard of in *England* before this present Age.   I will
not presume to say that Mr. *Cowley* was the absolute 30
Inventor of it.   Nay, I know that others had the good
luck to recommend it first in Print.   Yet I appeal to you,
Sir, whether he did not conceive it, and discourse of it, and
practise it, as soon as any Man.

His *Davideis* was wholly written in so young an Age, 35

that if we shall reflect on the vastness of the Argument,
and his manner of handling it, he may seem like one of the
Miracles that he there adorns, like a Boy attempting
Goliah. I have often heard you declare that he had
5 finish'd the greatest part of it while he was yet a young
Student at *Cambridge*. This perhaps may be the reason
that in some few places there is more youthfulness and
redundance of Fancy than his riper judgment would have
allow'd. I know, Sir, you will give me leave to use this
10 liberty of censure; for I do not here pretend to a profess'd
Panegyrick, but rather to give a just opinion concerning
him. But for the main of it, I will affirm, that it is a better
instance and beginning of a Divine Poem than I ever yet
saw in any Language. The contrivance is perfectly antient,
15 which is certainly the true form of Heroic Poetry, and such
as was never yet outdone by any new Devices of Modern
Wits. The subject was truly Divine, even according to
Gods own heart: The matter of his invention, all the
Treasures of Knowledge and Histories in the Bible. The
20 model of it comprehended all the Learning of the East:
The Characters, lofty and various; The Numbers, firm
and powerful; The Digressions, beautiful and proportionable; The Design, to submit mortal Wit to heavenly
Truths: in all there is an admirable mixture of humane
25 Virtues and Passions with religious Raptures.

The truth is, Sir, methinks in other matters his Wit
excell'd most other mens; but in his Moral and Divine
Works it outdid it self. And no doubt it proceeded from
this Cause, that in other lighter kinds of Poetry he chiefly
30 represented the humours and affections of others; but in
these he sat to himself and drew the figure of his own
mind. I know it has been objected against him by some
morose Zealots, that he has done an injury to the Scripture
by sprinkling all his Works with many Allusions and
35 Similitudes that he took out of the Bible. But to these

men it were a sufficient reply to compare their own Practise with his in this particular. They make use of Scripture Phrases and Quotations in all their common Discourse. They employ the words of Holy Writ to countenance the extravagance of their own opinions and 5 affections. And why then might not he take the liberty to fetch from thence some ornament for the innocent Passions, and natural Truths, and moral Virtues which he describes?

This is confutation enough to that sort of men. As to 10 the thing itself, it is so far from being a debasing of Divinity to make some parts of it the subjects of our Fancy, that it is a sure way to establish it familiarly on the hearts of the people, and to give it a durable impression on the minds of wise men. Of this we have a powerful instance 15 amongst the Antients. For their Wit has lasted much longer than the Practise of any of their Religions. And the very memory of most of their Divine Worship had perished, if it had not been expressed and preserved by their Poets. But Mr. *Cowley* himself did of all men living 20 abhor the abuse of Scripture by licentious Raillery, which ought not only to be esteemed the meanest kind of Wit, but the worst sort of ill Manners. This perhaps some men would be loth to hear proved, who practise it under the false title of a Gentile Quality: But the truth of it is 25 unquestionable. For the ordinary ill breeding is only an indecence and offence against some particular Custom, or Gesture, or Behaviour in use. But this prophaneness is a violation of the very support of humane Society, and a rudeness against the best Manners that all mankind can 30 practise, which is a just reverence of the Supreme Power of all the World.

In his Latin Poems he has expressed to admiration all the Numbers of Verse and Figures of Poesie that are scattered up and down amongst the Antients. There is 35 hardly to be found in them all any good fashion of Speech, or colour of Measure, but he has comprehended it, and given instances of it, according as his several Arguments required either a Majestick Spirit, or a passionate, or a

5 pleasant. This is the more extraordinary in that it was never yet performed by any single Poet of the Antient Romans themselves. They had the Language natural to them, and so might easily have moulded it into what form or humour they pleas'd : Yet it was their constant Custom

10 to confine all their thoughts and practice to one or two ways of Writing, as despairing ever to compass all together. This is evident in those that excelled in Odes and Songs, in the Comical, Tragical, Epical, Elegiacal, or Satyrical way. And this perhaps occasioned the first distinction and

15 number of the Muses. For they thought the task too hard for any one of them, though they fancied them to be Goddesses. And therefore they divided it amongst them all, and only recommended to each of them the care of a distinct Character of Poetry and Musick.

20 The occasion of his chusing the subject of his six Books of Plants was this : when he returned into *England,* he was advised to dissemble the main intention of his coming over under the disguise of applying himself to some setled Profession. And that of Physic was thought most proper.

25 To this purpose, after many Anatomical Dissections, he proceeded to the consideration of Simples ; and having furnish'd himself with Books of that Nature, he retir'd into a fruitful part of *Kent,* where every Field and Wood might shew him the real Figures of those Plants of which he

30 read. Thus he speedily Master'd that part of the Art of Medicine. But then, as one of the Antients did before him in the study of Law, instead of employing his Skill for practice and profit, he presently digested it into that form which we behold.

35 The two first Books Treat of Herbs, in a style resembling

the Elegies of *Ovid* and *Tibullus* in the sweetness and freedom of the Verse: But excelling them in the strength of the Fancy and vigour of the Sense.   The third and fourth discourse of Flowers in all the variety of *Catullus* and *Horaces* Numbers: For the last of which Authors he had a peculiar Reverence, and imitated him, not only in the stately and numerous pace of his *Odes* and *Epodes*, but in the familiar easiness of his Epistles and Speeches. The two last speak of Trees, in the way of *Virgils Georgics.* Of these the sixth Book is wholly Dedicated to the Honour of his Country.   For making the *British* Oak to preside in the Assembly of the Forrest Trees, upon that occasion he enlarges on the History of our late Troubles, the Kings Affliction and Return, and the beginning of the *Dutch* War; and Manages all in a style that (to say all in a word) is equal to the Greatness and Valour of the *English* Nation.

I told you, Sir, that he was very happy in the way of *Horaces* Speeches.   But of this there are but two Instances preserv'd: that part of an Epistle to Mr. *Creswel* with which he concludes his Preface to his Book of Plants, and that Copy which is written to your self.   I confess I heartily wish he had left more Examples behind him of this kind, because I esteem it to be one of the best and most difficult of all those that Antiquity has taught us.   It is certainly the very Original of true Raillery, and differs as much from some of the other Latin *Satyrs*, as the pleasant reproofs of a Gentleman from the severity of a School-master.   I know some Men dis-approve it, because the Verse seems to be loose, and near to the plainness of common Discourse.   But that which was admir'd by the Court of *Augustus* never ought to be esteem'd flat or vulgar.   And the same judgment should be made of Mens styles as of their behaviour and carriage: wherein that is most courtly and hardest to be imitated, which consists of a Natural easiness and unaffected Grace, where nothing seems to be studied, yet everything is extraordinary.

This familiar way of Verse puts me in mind of one kind of Prose wherein Mr. *Cowley* was excellent, and that is his Letters to his private Friends. In these he always express'd the Native tenderness and Innocent gayety of his Mind. I think, Sir, you and I have the greatest Collection of this sort. But I know you agree with me that nothing of this Nature should be publish'd: And herein you have always consented to approve of the modest Judgment of our Country-men above the practice of some of our Neighbours, and chiefly of the *French*. I make no manner of question but the *English* at this time are infinitely improv'd in this way above the skill of former Ages, nay, of all Countries round about us that pretend to greater Eloquence. Yet they have been always judiciously sparing in Printing such composures, while some other Witty Nations have tyr'd all their Presses and Readers with them. The truth is, the Letters that pass between particular Friends, if they are written as they ought to be, can scarce ever be fit to see the light. They should not consist of fulsom Complements, or tedious Politicks, or elaborate Elegancies, or general Fancies. But they should have a Native clearness and shortness, a Domestical plaines, and a peculiar kind of Familiarity, which can only affect the humour of those to whom they were intended. The very same passages which make Writings of this Nature delightful amongst Friends will lose all manner of taste when they come to be read by those that are in-different. In such Letters the Souls of Men should appear undress'd: And in that negligent habit they may be fit to be seen by one or two in a Chamber, but not to go abroad into the Streets.

The last Pieces that we have from his hands are Dis-courses, by way of Essays, upon some of the gravest subjects that concern the Contentment of a Virtuous Mind. These he intended as a real Character of his own thoughts upon the point of his Retirement. And accordingly you may observe that in the Prose of them there is little Curiosity of Ornament, but they are written in a lower and 5 humbler style than the rest, and as an unfeigned Image of his Soul should be drawn without Flattery. I do not speak this to their disadvantage. For the true perfection of Wit is to be plyable to all occasions, to walk or flye, according to the Nature of every subject. And there is no doubt as 10 much Art to have only plain Conceptions on some Arguments as there is in others to have extraordinary Flights.

To these that he has here left scarce finish'd, it was his design to have added many others. And a little before his death he communicated to me his resolutions to have 15 dedicated them all to my Lord St. *Albans,* as a testimony of his entire respects to him, and a kind of Apology for having left humane Affairs, in the strength of his Age, while he might still have been serviceable to his Country. But though he was prevented in this purpose by his death, 20 yet it becomes the Office of a Friend to make good his intentions. I therefore here presume to make a Present of them to his Lordship. I doubt not but according to his usual humanity, he will accept this imperfect Legacy of the man whom he long honoured with his domestic conversation. 25 And I am confident his Lordship will believe it to be no injury to his Fame that in these Papers my Lord St. *Albans* and Mr. *Cowleys* name shall be read together by posterity.

I might, Sir, have made a longer Discourse of his Writings, but that I think it fit to direct my Speech 30 concerning him by the same rule by which he was wont to judge of others. In his esteem of other men, he constantly prefer'd the good temper of their minds and honesty of their Actions above all the excellencies of their Eloquence or Knowledge. The same course I will take in his praise, 35 which chiefly ought to be fixed on his life. For that he deserves more applause from the most virtuous men than for his other abilities he ever obtained from the Learned.

He had indeed a perfect natural goodness, which neither
5 the uncertainties of his condition nor the largeness of his wit could pervert. He had a firmness and strength of mind that was of proof against the Art of Poetry it self. Nothing vain or fantastical, nothing flattering or insolent appeared in his humour. He had a great integrity and plainness of
10 Manners, which he preserv'd to the last, though much of his time was spent in a Nation, and way of life, that is not very famous for sincerity. But the truth of his heart was above the corruption of ill examples : And therefore the sight of them rather confirm'd him in the contrary Virtues.
15 There was nothing affected or singular in his habit, or person, or gesture. He understood the forms of good breeding enough to practise them without burdening him-self or others. He never opprest any mans parts, nor ever put any man out of countenance. He never had any
20 emulation for Fame or contention for Profit with any man. When he was in business he suffer'd others importunities with much easiness : When he was out of it he was never importunate himself. His modesty and humility were so great, that if he had not had many other equal Virtues, they
25 might have been thought dissimulation.

His Conversation was certainly of the most excellent kind, for it was such as was rather admired by his familiar Friends than by Strangers at first sight. He surpriz'd no man at first with any extraordinary appearance : he never
30 thrust himself violently into the good opinion of his company. He was content to be known by leisure and by degrees ; and so the esteem that was conceiv'd of him was better grounded and more lasting.

In his Speech, neither the pleasantness excluded gravity,
35 nor was the sobriety of it inconsistent with delight. No

man parted willingly from his Discourse; for he so ordered it that every man was satisfied that he had his share. He govern'd his Passions with great moderation. His Virtues were never troublesome or uneasy to any. Whatever he disliked in others, he only corrected it by the silent reproof 5 of a better practise.

His Wit was so temper'd that no man had ever reason to wish it had been less: he prevented other mens severity upon it by his own : he never willingly recited any of his Writings. None but his intimate friends ever discovered 10 he was a great Poet by his discourse. His Learning was large and profound, well compos'd of all Antient and Modern Knowledge. But it sat exceeding close and handsomly upon him : it was not imbossed on his mind, but enamelled. 15

He never guided his life by the whispers or opinions of the World. Yet he had a great reverence for a good reputation. He hearkened to Fame when it was a just Censurer : But not when an extravagant Babler. He was a passionate lover of Liberty and Freedom from restraint 20 both in Actions and Words. But what honesty others receive from the direction of Laws, he had by native Inclination : And he was not beholding to other mens wills but to his own for his Innocence.

He perform'd all his Natural and Civil Duties with 25 admirable tenderness. Having been Born after his Fathers Death and bred up under the Discipline of his Mother, he gratefully acknowledg'd her care of his Education to her Death, which was in the Eightieth year of her Age. For his three Brothers he always maintain'd a 30 constant affection. And having surviv'd the two first, he made the third his Heir. In his long dependance on my Lord St. *Albans*, there never happened any manner of difference between them, except a little at last, because he would leave his service : which only shewed the innocence 35 of the Servant and the kindness of the Master. His Friendships were inviolable. The same men with whom he was familiar in his Youth were his neerest acquaintance at the day of his Death. If the private Course of his last 5 years made him contract his Conversation to a few, yet he only withdrew, not broke off, from any of the others.

His thoughts were never above nor below his condition. He never wished his Estate much larger. Yet he enjoyed what he had with all innocent Freedom; he never made 10 his present life uncomfortable by undue expectations of future things. Whatever disappointments he met with, they only made him understand Fortune better, not repine at her the more: His Muse indeed once complain'd, but never his Mind. He was accomplish'd with all manner of 15 Abilities for the greatest business, If he would but have thought so himself.

If any thing ought to have been chang'd in his Temper and Disposition, It was his earnest Affection for Obscurity and Retirement. This, Sir, give me leave to condemn, 20 even to you, who I know agreed with him in the same humour. I acknowledge he chose that state of Life, not out of any Poetical Rapture, but upon a steady and sober experience of Humane things. But however I cannot applaud it in him. It is certainly a great disparagement to 25 Virtue and Learning it self, that those very things which only make Men useful in the World should encline them to leave it. This ought never to be allow'd to good Men, unless the bad had the same moderation, and were willing to follow them into the Wilderness. But if the one shall 30 contend to get out of Employment while the other strive to get into it, the affairs of Mankind are like to be in so ill a posture, that even the good Men themselves will hardly be able to enjoy their very retreats in security.

Yet I confess, if any deserv'd to have this priviledge, it 35 ought to have been granted to him as soon as any Man living, upon consideration of the manner in which he spent the Liberty that he got. For he withdrew himself out of the crowd with desires of enlightning and instructing the minds of those that remain'd in it. It was his resolution in that Station to search into the Secrets of Divine and Humane Knowledge, and to communicate what he should observe. He always profess'd that he went out of the world as it was mans, into the same World as it was Natures and as it was Gods. The whole compass of the Creation, and all the wonderful effects of the Divine Wisdom, were the constant Prospect of his Senses and his Thoughts. And indeed he enter'd with great advantage on the studies of Nature, even as the first great Men of Antiquity did, who were generally both Poets and Philosophers. He betook himself to its Contemplation, as well furnish'd with sound Judgment and diligent Observation and good Method to discover its Mysteries, as with Abilities to set it forth in all its Ornaments.

This labour about Natural Science was the perpetual and uninterrupted task of that obscure part of his life. Besides this, we had perswaded him to look back into his former Studies and to publish a Discourse concerning Style. In this he had design'd to give an account of the proper sorts of writing that were fit for all manner of Arguments, to compare the perfections and imperfections of the Authors of Antiquity with those of this present Age, and to deduce all down to the particular use of the English Genius and Language. This subject he was very fit to perform : It being most proper for him to be the Judge who had been the best Practiser. But he scarce liv'd to draw the first lines of it. All the footsteps that I can find remaining of it are only some indigested Characters of Antient and Modern Authors. And now for the future I almost despair ever to see it well accomplished, unless you, Sir, would give me leave to name the man that should undertake it.

But his last and principal Design was that which ought to be the principal to every wise man, the establishing his mind in the Faith he professed. He was in his practise exactly obedient to the Use and Precepts of our Church.
5 Nor was he inclined to any uncertainty and doubt, as abhorring all contention in indifferent things, and much more in sacred. But he beheld the Divisions of Christendom: he saw how many controversies had been introduced by zeal or ignorance, and continued by Faction. He had
10 therefore an earnest intention of taking a Review of the Original Principles of the Primitive Church, believing that every true Christian had no better means to settle his spirit than that which was proposed to *Æneas* and his Followers to be the end of their wanderings, *Antiquam*
15 *exquirite Matrem.*

This examination he purposed should reach to our Saviours and the Apostles lives, and their immediate Successors, for four or five Centuries, till Interest and Policy prevailed over Devotion. He hoped to have
20 absolutely compassed it in three or four years, and when that was done, there to have fixed for ever, without any shaking or alteration in his judgment. Indeed it was a great damage to our Church that he lived not to perform it. For very much of the Primitive Light might have been
25 expected from a mind that was endued with the primitive meekness and innocence. And besides, such a Work, coming from one that was no Divine, might have been very useful for this age, wherein it is one of the principal Cavils against Religion that it is only a matter of interest, and
30 only supported for the gain of a particular Profession.

But alas! while he was framing these great things in his thoughts, they were unfortunately cut off together with his life. His Solitude from the very beginning had never agreed so well with the constitution of his Body as of his
35 Mind. The chief cause of it was that out of hast to be

gone away from the Tumult and Noyse of the City, he had
not prepar'd so healthful a situation in the Country as he
might have done if he had made a more leasurable choice.
Of this he soon began to find the inconvenience at *Barn
Elms*, where he was afflicted with a dangerous and lingring 5
Fever. After that he scarce ever recover'd his former
Health, though his Mind was restor'd to its perfect Vigour;
as may be seen by his two last Books of Plants, that were
written since that time, and may at least be compar'd with
the best of his other Works. Shortly after his removal to 10
Chertsea, he fell into another consuming Disease. Having
languish'd under this for some months, he seem'd to be
pretty well cured of its ill Symptomes. But in the heat of
the last Summer, by staying too long amongst his Laborers
in the Medows, he was taken with a violent Defluxion and 15
Stoppage in his Breast and Throat. This he at first
neglected as an ordinary Cold, and refus'd to send for his
usual Physicians till it was past all remedies; and so in
the end, after a fortnight sickness, it prov'd mortal to him.

Who can here, Sir, forbear exclaiming on the weak 20
hopes and frail condition of humane Nature? For as
long as Mr. *Cowley* was pursuing the course of Ambition
in an active life, which he scarce esteem'd his true life, he
never wanted a constant health and strength of body. But
as soon as ever he had found an opportunity of beginning 25
indeed to live, and to enjoy himself in security, his contentment was first broken by Sickness, and at last his death
was occasion'd by his very delight in the Country and the
Fields, which he had long fancied above all other Pleasures.
But let us not grieve at this fatal accident upon his account, 30
lest we should seem to repine at the happy change of his
condition, and not to know that the loss of a few years,
which he might longer have liv'd, will be recompenc'd by
an immortal Memory. If we complain, let it only be for
our own sakes,—that in him we are at once depriv'd of the 35

greatest natural and improv'd abilities, of the usefullest conversation, of the faithfullest Friendship, of a mind that practis'd the best Virtues it self, and a Wit that was best able to recommend them to others.

5 His Body was attended to *Westminster Abby* by a great number of Persons of the most eminent quality, and follow'd with the praises of all good and Learned Men. It lies near the Ashes of *Chaucer* and *Spencer*, the two most Famous *English* Poets of former times. But whoever
10 would do him right should not only equal him to the Principal Ancient Writers of our own Nation, but should also rank his name amongst the Authors of the true Antiquity, the best of the *Greeks* and *Romans*. In that place there is a Monument design'd for him by my Lord
15 Duke of *Buckingham* in Testimony of his Affection. And the King himself was pleas'd to bestow on him the best Epitaph, when upon the news of his Death his Majesty declar'd, *That Mr.* Cowley *had not left a better Man behind him in* England.

20 This, Sir, is the account that I thought fit to present the World concerning him. Perhaps it may be judged that I have spent too many words on a private man and a Scholar, whose life was not remarkable for such a variety of Events as are wont to be the Ornaments of this kind of
25 Relations. I know it is the custom of the World to prefer the pompous Histories of great Men, before the greatest Virtues of others whose lives have been led in a course less illustrious. This indeed is the general humour. But I believe it to be an errour in mens judgments. For
30 certainly that is a more profitable instruction which may be taken from the eminent goodness of men of lower rank, than that which we learn from the splendid representations of the Battels, and Victories, and Buildings, and Sayings of great Commanders and Princes. Such specious matters,
35 as they are seldom delivered with fidelity, so they serve but

for the imitation of a very few, and rather make for the ostentation than the true information of humane life : Whereas it is from the practice of men equal to our selves that we are more naturally taught how to command our Passions, to direct our Knowledge, and to govern our Actions.

For this reason I have some hope that a Character of Mr. *Cowley* may be of good advantage to our Nation. For what he wanted in Titles of Honour and the Gifts of Fortune was plentifully supplyed by many other Excellencies, which make perhaps less noise, but are more beneficial for Example. This, Sir, was the principal end of this long Discourse. Besides this, I had another design in it, that only concerns our selves ; that having this Picture of his life set before us, we may still keep him alive in our memories, and by this means we may have some small reparation for our inexpressible loss by his death.

Sir, I am

Your most humble, and most

affectionate Servant,

T. SPRAT.

THOMAS SHADWELL

I. PREFACE TO *THE SULLEN LOVERS, OR THE IMPERTINENTS, A COMEDY*

1668

Reader,

THE success of this Play, as it was much more then
it deserv'd, so was much more than I expected :
Especially in this very Critical age, when every man
pretends to be a Judge, and some that never read Three
5 Playes in their lives, and never understood one, are as
positive in their Judgement of Playes as if they were all
Johnsons.   But had I been us'd with all the severity
imaginable, I should patiently have submitted to my Fate ;
not like the rejected Authors of our time, who, when their
10 Playes are damn'd, will strut, and huff it out, and laugh at
the Ignorance of the Age : Or like some other of our
Modern Fopps, that declare they are resolv'd to justifie
their Playes with their Swords, though perhaps their
Courage is as little as their Wit,—such as peep through
15 their loop-holes in the Theatre to see who looks glum
upon their Playes, and if they spy a Gentle Squire making
Faces, he, poor soul, must be *Hector'd* till he likes 'em,
while the more stubborn *Bully-Rock* damm's and is safe :
Such is their discretion in the Choice of their men.   Such
20 Gentlemen as these I must confess had need pretend they
cannot erre.   These will huffe and look big upon the
success of an ill Play stuff'd full of Songs and Dances,
which have that constraint upon 'em, too, that they seldome
seem to come in willingly : When in such Playes the
25 Composer and the Dancing-Master are the best Poets, and

yet the unmerciful Scribler would rob them of all the Honour.

I am so far from valuing my self (as the phrase is) upon this Play, that perhaps no man is a severer Judge of it then my self; yet if anything could have made me proud of it, It would have been the great Favour and Countenance it receiv'd from His Majesty and their Royal Highnesses.

But I could not perswade my self that they were so favourable to the Play for the Merit of it, but out of a Princely Generosity, to encourage a young-beginner that did what he could to please them, and that other wise might have been baulk'd for ever: 'Tis to this I owe the success of the Play, and am as far from presumption of my own merits in it as one ought to be who receives an Alms.

The first hint I receiv'd was from the report of a Play of *Molieres* of three Acts, called *Les Fascheux*, upon which I wrote a great part of this before I read that; and after it came to my hands, I found so little for my use (having before upon that hint design'd the fittest Characters I could for my purpose) that I have made use of but two short Scenes, *Viz.*, the first Scene in the Second Act between *Stanford* and *Roger*, and *Molier's* story of Piquette, which I have translated into Back-gammon, both of them so vary'd you would not know them. But I freely confess my Theft, and am asham'd on 't, though I have the example of some that never yet wrote Play without stealing most of it; And (like Men that lye so long, till they believe themselves) at length, by continual Thieving, reckon their stolne goods their own, too: which is so ignoble a thing, that I cannot but believe that he that makes a common practice of stealing other mens Witt, would, if he could with the same safety, steale any thing else.

I have in this Play, as neer as I could, observed the three Unities of Time, Place, and Action. The time of

the Drama does not exceed six houres; the place is in
a very narrow Compass; and the Main-Action of the Play,
upon which all the rest depend, is the Sullen-Love betwixt
Stanford and *Emilia*, which kind of love is onely proper to
5 their Characters.   I have here, as often as I could naturally,
kept the Scenes unbroken, which, though it be not so
much practised or so well understood by the *English*, yet
among the French-Poets is accompted a great Beauty; but
after these frivolous excuses, the want of design in the
10 Play has been objected against me; which fault, though
I may endeavour a little to extenuate, I dare not absolutely
deny.   I conceive, with all submission to better Judgments,
that no man ought to expect such Intrigues in the little
actions of Comedy as are requir'd in Playes of a higher
15 Nature; but in Playes of Humour, where there are so
many Characters as there are in this, there is yet less
design to be expected; for, if after I had form'd three or
four forward prating Fopps in the Play, I had made it full
of Plott and Business, at the latter end, where the turnes
20 ought to be many, and suddenly following one another,
I must have let fall the humour, which I thought wou'd be
pleasanter then Intrigues could have been without it; and
it would have been easier to me to have made a Plott then
to hold up the Humour.

25   Another objection that has been made by some is that
there is the same thing over and over: which I do not
apprehend, unless they blame the unity of the action; yet
Horace de Arte Poetica sayes,

> *Sit quod vis, simplex duntaxat, & unum;*

30 Or whether it be the carrying on of the humours to the
last, which the same Author directs me to doe:

> *Si quid inexpertum Scenæ committis, & audes*
> *Personam formare novam, Servetur ad Imum*
> *Qualis ab incepto processerit, & sibi constet.*

I have endeavour'd to represent variety of Humours, most of the persons of the *Play* differing in their Characters from one another, which was the practise of *Ben Johnson*, whom I think all Drammatick *Poets* ought to imitate, though none are like to come near; he being the onely 5 person that appears to me to have made perfect Representations of Humane Life; most other Authors that I ever read either have wilde Romantick *Tales*, wherein they strein Love and Honour to that Ridiculous height that it becomes Burlesque, or in their lower Comœdies 10 content themselves with one or two Humours at most, and those not near so perfect Characters as the admirable *Johnson* alwayes made, who never wrote Comedy without seven or eight considerable Humours. I never saw one except that of *Falstaffe* that was in my judgment comparable 15 to any of *Johnson*'s considerable Humours. You will pardon this digression when I tell you he is the man of all the World I most passionately admire for his Excellency in Drammatick-*Poetry*.

Though I have known some of late so Insolent to say 20 that *Ben Johnson* wrote his best *Playes* without Wit,— imagining that all the Wit in Playes consisted in bringing two persons upon the Stage to break Jests, and to bob one another, which they call Repartie, not considering that there is more wit and invention requir'd in the finding out 25 good Humor, and Matter proper for it, then in all their smart reparties. For, in the Writing of a Humor, a Man is confin'd not to swerve from the Character, and oblig'd to say nothing but what is proper to it: but in the *Playes* which have been wrote of late, there is no such thing as 30 perfect Character, but the two chief persons are most commonly a Swearing, Drinking, Whoring Ruffian for a Lover, and an impudent, ill-bred *tomrig* for a Mistress, and these are the fine people of the *Play*; and there is that Latitude in this, that almost any thing is proper for 35

them to say ; but their chief Subject is bawdy and profaness, which they call *brisk writing*, when the most dissolute of Men, that rellish those things well enough in private, are *chok'd* at e'm in publick ; and, methinks, if there were
5 nothing but the ill Manners of it, it should make Poets avoid that Indecent way of Writing.

But perhaps you may think me as impertinent as any one I represent, that having so many faults of my own, shou'd take the liberty to Judge of others, to impeach my
10 fellow Criminalls.   I must confess it is very ungenerous to accuse those that modestly confess their own Errors ; but positive men, that Justifie all their faults, are Common Enemies that no man ought to spare, prejudicial to all Societies they live in, destructive to all Communication,
15 always indeavouring Magisterially to Impose upon our understandings against the Freedome of Mankind : These ought no more to be suffer'd amongst us then wild beasts, for no corrections that can be laid upon e'm are of power to reforme e'm ; and certainly it was a positive Foole that
20 *Salomon* spoke of, when he said, *bray him in a Mortar, and yet he will retain his folly.*

But I have troubled you too long with this Discourse, and am to aske your pardon for it and the many faults you will find in the *Play*, and beg you will believe that whatever
25 I have said of it was intended not in Justification, but Excuse of it.   Look upon it as it really was, wrote in haste by a Young Writer, and you will easily pardon it, especially when you know that the best of our Drammatick Writers have wrote very ill *Playes* at first,—nay, some of
30 e'm have wrote several before they could get one to be Acted, and their best *Playes* were made with great expence of labour and time.   Nor can you expect a very Correct *Play*, under a Years pains at the least, from the Wittiest man of the Nation : It is so difficult a thing to write well
35 in this kind.   Men of quality that write for their pleasure

will not trouble themselves with exactness in their *Playes*; and those that write for profit would find too little incouragement for so much paines as a correct *Play* would require.

Vale.   5

II. PREFACE TO *THE HUMORISTS, A COMEDY*

1671

THis Play, besides the Errors in the writing of it, came upon the Stage with all the disadvantages imaginable. First, I was forced, after I had finish'd it, to blot out the main design of it, finding that, contrary to my intention, it had given offence. The second disadvantage was 10 that notwithstanding I had (to the great prejudice of the Play) given satisfaction to all the exceptions made against it, it met with the clamorous opposition of a numerous party bandied against it, and resolved as much as they could to damn it, right or wrong, before they had 15 heard or seen a word on't. The last, and not the least, was that the *Actors* (though since they have done me some right) at first were extreamly imperfect in the Action of it. The least of these had been enough to have spoil'd a very good Comedy, much more such a one as mine. The last 20 (*viz.*, imperfect Action) had like to have destroyd *She would if she could*, which I think (and I have the Authority of some of the best Judges in *England* for 't) is the best Comedy that has been written since the Restauration of the Stage: And even that, for the imperfect representa- 25 tion of it at first, received such prejudice that, had it not been for the favour of the *Court*, in all probability it had never got up again; and it suffers for it in a great measure

to this very day.   This of mine, after all these blows, had
fallen beyond redemption, had it not been revived after the
second day by her kindness (which I can never enough
acknowledge) who for days together beautified it with
the most excellent *Dancings* that ever has been seen
upon the Stage.   This drew my enemies as well as friends,
till it was something better acted, understood, and liked
than at first.   By this means the poor Play's life was
prolonged, and, I hope, will live in spight of Malice, if not
upon the Stage, at least in Print.

Yet do not think I will defend all the faults of it.   Before
it was alter'd, I could better have answer'd for it ; yet, as it
is, I hope it will not wholly displease you in the reading.
I should not say so much for it, if I did not find so much
undeserved malice against it.

My design was in it to reprehend some of the Vices and
Follies of the Age, which I take to be the most proper and
most useful way of writing Comedy.   If I do not perform
this well enough, let not my endeavors be blam'd.

Here I must take leave to Dissent from those who seem
to insinuate that the ultimate end of a Poet is to delight,
without correction or instruction.   Methinks a Poet should
never acknowledge this, for it makes him of as little use to
Mankind as a Fidler or Dancing Master, who delights
the fancy onely, without improving the Judgement.

Horace, the best judge of Poetry, found other business
for a Poet.

> *Pectus præceptis format amicis,*
> *Asperitatis & Invidiæ corrector & Iræ,*
> *Recte facta refert, orientia tempora notis*
> *Instruit Exemplis.*

I confess a Poet ought to do all that he can decently
to please, that so he may instruct : To adorn his Images of
Vertue so delightfully to affect people with a secret
veneration of it in others, and an emulation to practice

it in themselves : And to render their Figures of *Vice* and *Folly* so ugly and detestable, to make people hate and despise them, not onely in others, but (if it be possible) in their dear selves. And in this latter I think Comedy more useful than Tragedy ; because the Vices and Follies in *Courts*, as they are two tender to be touch'd, so they concern but a few, whereas the Cheats, Villanies, and troublesome Follies in the common conversation of the World are of concernment to all the Body of Mankind.

And a Poet can no more justly be censured for ill nature, in detesting such *Knaveries* and troublesome impertinencies as are an imposition on all good men and a disturbance of Societies in general, than the most vigilant of our Judges can be thought so for detesting Robbers and High-way-men, who are hanged, not for the sake of the money they take (for of what value can that be to the life of a man ?) but for interrupting common communication and disturbing Society in general. For the sake of good men, ill should be punished ; and 'tis ill nature to the first, not to punish the last. A man cannot truly love a good man, that does not hate a bad one ; nor a Wiseman, that does not hate a Fool : this love and hatred are correlatives, and the one necessarily implies the other. I must confess it were ill nature, and below a man, to fall upon the natural imperfections of men, as of Lunaticks, Ideots, or men born monstrous. But these can never be made the proper subject of a Satyr ; but the affected vanities and artificial fopperies of men, which (sometimes even contrary to their natures) they take pains to acquire, are the proper subject of a Satyr.

And for the reformation of Fopps and Knaves I think Comedy most useful, because to render Vices and Fopperies very ridiculous is much a greater punishment than Tragedy can inflict upon 'em. There we do but subject 'em to hatred, or at worst to death ; here we make them live to be despised and laugh'd at, which certainly makes more impression upon men than even death can do.

Again, I confess a Poet ought to endeavour to please, and by this way of writing may please as well as by any way whatsoever, if he writes it well, when he does

Simul & Jucunda & idonea dicere vitæ.

Men of Wit and Honour, and the best Judges, and such as cannot be touch'd by Satyr, are extreamly delighted with it ; and for the rest,

Odi profanum vulgus, & Arceo.

The rabble of little people are more pleas'd with *Jacob Puddings* being soundly kick'd, or having a Custard handsomely thrown in his face, than with all the wit in Plays ; and the higher sort of Rabble (as there may be a rabble of very fine people in this illiterate age) are more pleased with the extravagant and unnatural actions, the trifles and fripperies of a Play, or the trappings and ornaments of Nonsense, than with all the wit in the world.

This is one reason why we put our Fopps into extravagant and unnatural habits ; it being a cheap way of conforming to the understanding of those brisk, gay Sparks that judge of Wit or Folly by the Habit ; that being indeed the onely measure they can take in judging of Mankind, who are Criticks in nothing but a Dress.

Extraordinary pleasure was taken of old in the Habits of the Actors, without reference to sense, which *Horace* observes and reprehends in his Epistle to *Augustus :*

Garganum mugire putes nemus aut Mare Tuscum,
Tanto cum strepitu ludi spectantur, & Artes,
Divitiæque peregrinæ, quibus oblitus actor
Cum stetit in scæna, concurrit dextera Lævæ,
Dixit adhuc aliquid ? nil sane : quid placet ergo ?

But for a Poet to think, without wit or good humour, under

such á Habit to please men of sense is a presumption inexcusable. If I be guilty of this, it is an error of my understanding, not of my will. But I challenge the most clamorous and violent of my Enemies (who would have the Town believe that every thing I write is too nearly reflecting upon persons) to accuse me, with truth, of representing the real actions or using the peculiar, affected phrases or manner of speech of any particular Man or Woman living.

I cannot indeed create a new Language; but the Phantastick Phrases used in any Play of mine are not appropriate to any one *Fop*, but applicable to many.

Good men, and men of sence, can never be represented but to their advantage, nor can the Characters of Fools, Knaves, Whores, or Cowards (who are the people I deal most with in Comedies) concern any that are not eminently so: Nor will any apply to themselves what I write in this kind, that have but the wit or honesty to think tolerably well of themselves.

But it has been objected that good men, and men of sence enough, may have blind-sides that are liable to reprehension, and that such men should be represented upon a Stage is intollerable.

'Tis true, excellent men may have errors, but they are not known by them, but by their excellencies; their prudence overcomes all gross follies, or conceals the less vanities that are unavoidable Concomitants of humane nature; or if some little errors do escape 'em and are known, they are the least part of those men, and they are not distinguished in the world by them, but by their perfections; so that, if such blind-sides or errors be represented, they do not reflect upon them, but upon such on whom these are predominant, and that receive such a Bias from 'em that it turns 'em wholly from the wayes of Wisdom or Morality.

And even this representation does not reflect upon any

particular man, but upon very many of the same kind : For if a man should bring such a humor upon the Stage (if there be such a humor in the world) as onely belongs to one or two persons, it would not be understood by 5 the Audience, but would be thought, for the singularity of it, wholly unnatural, and would be no jest to them neither.

But I have had the fortune to have had a general humor in a Play of mine applied to three or four men, whose persons I never saw, or humors ever heard of, till the Play 10 was acted.

As long as men wrest the Writings of Poets to their own corrupted sense, and with their Clamors prevail too, you must never look for a good Comedy of Humor; for a humor, being the representation of some extravagance 15 of Mankind, cannot but in some thing resemble some man or other, or it is monstrous and unnatural.

After this restraint upon Poets, there is little scope left, unless we retrieve the exploded Barbarismes of Fool, Devil, Giant, or Monster, or translate French Farces, which, with 20 all the wit of the English added to them, can scarce be made tollerable.

Mr. *Johnson*, I believe, was very unjustly taxed for personating particular men, but it will ever be the fate of them that write the humors of the *Town*, especially in a 25 foolish and vicious Age. Pardon me, *Reader*, that I name him in the same page with my self, who pretend to nothing more than to joyn with all men of sense and learning in admiration of him ; which, I think, I do not out of a true understanding of him, and for this I cannot but value 30 my self. Yet, by extolling his way of writing, I would not insinuate to you that I can practise it, though I would if I could a thousand times sooner than any mans.

And here I must make a little digression, and take liberty to dissent from my particular friend, for whom I 35 have a very great respect, and whose Writings I extreamly admire; and though I will not say his is the best way of writing, yet I am sure his manner of writing it is much the best that ever was. And I may say of him, as was said of a Celebrated Poet, *Cui unquam Poetarum magis proprium fuit subito œstro incalescere? Quis, ubi incaluit,* 5 *fortius, & fœlicius debacchatur.* His Verse is smoother and deeper, his thoughts more quick and surprising, his raptures more mettled and higher, and he has more of that in his writing which *Plato* calls σώφρονα μανίαν, than any other Heroick Poet. And those who shall go about to imitate him 10 will be found to flutter and make a noise, but never rise. Yet, after all this, I cannot think it impudence in him or any man to endeavour to imitate Mr. *Johnson*, whom he confesses to have fewer failings than all the English Poets, which implies he was the most perfect and best 15 Poet; and why should not we endeavour to imitate him? because we cannot arrive at his excellence? 'Tis true, we cannot; but this is no more an argument than for a Soldier, who considers with himself he cannot be so great a one as *Julius Cæsar*, to run from his Colours, and be 20 none; or to speak of a less thing, why should any man study *Mathematicks* after *Archimedes, &c.?* This Principle would be an obstruction to the progress of all learning and knowledge in the world. Men of all Professions ought certainly to follow the best in theirs; and let not their 25 endeavours be blamed, if they go as far as they can in the right way, though they be unsuccessful and attain not their ends. If Mr. *Johnson* be the most faultless Poet, I am so far from thinking it impudence to endeavour to imitate him that it would rather, in my opinion, seem impudence in 30 me not to do it.

I cannot be of their opinion who think he wanted wit; I am sure, if he did, he was so far from being the most faultless, that he was the most faulty Poet of his time: but it may be answered that his Writings were correct, though 35

he wanted fire ; but I think flat and dull things are as
incorrect, and shew as little Judgment in the Author, nay,
less, than sprightly and mettled Nonsense does. But I
think he had more true wit than any of his Contemporaries :
5 that other men had sometimes things that seemed more
fiery than his, was because they were placed with so many
sordid and mean things about them that they made a
greater show.

> *Inter quæ verbum emicuit si fortè decorum,*
> 10 *Si versus paulo concinn⟨i⟩or unus & alter,*
> *Injuste totum ducit, venditque Poema.*

Nor can I think, to the writing of his humors, which
were not onely the follies but vices and subtleties of men,
that wit was not required, but judgment ; where, by
15 the way, they speak as if judgment were a less thing than
wit. But certainly it was meant otherwise by nature, who
subjected wit to the government of judgment, which is the
noblest faculty of the mind. Fancy rough-draws, but judgement smooths and finishes ; nay, judgment does in deed
20 comprehend wit, for no man can have that who has not wit.
In fancy mad men equal if not excel all others ; and
one may as well say that one of those mad men is as good
a man as a temperate wiseman, as that one of the very
fancyful Plays, admired most by Women, can be so
25 good a Play as one of *Johnson's* correct and well-govern'd
Comedies.

The reason given by some why *Johnson* needed not wit
in writing humor is because humor is the effect of
observation, and observation the effect of judgment ; but
30 observation is as much necessary in all other Plays as
in Comedies of humour : For, first, even in the highest
Tragedies, where the scene lies in Courts, the Poet must
have observed the Customs of Courts and the manner
of conversing there, or he will commit many indecencies,
35 and make his Persons too rough and ill-bred for a Court.

Besides, Characters in Plays being representations of the Vertues and Vices, Passions or Affections of Mankind, since there are no more new Vertues or Vices, Passions or Affections, the Idea's of these can no other way be received into the imagination of a Poet, but either from the Conversation or Writings of men. After a Poet has formed a Character (as suppose of an Ambitious Man) his design is certainly to write it naturally, and he has no other rule to guid him in this, but to compare him with other men of that kind, that either he has heard of or conversed with in the world, or read of in Books (and even this reading of Books is conversing with men); nay, more; besides judging of his Character, the Poet can fancy nothing of it but what must spring from the Observation he has made of Men or Books.

If this argument that the enemies of humor use be meant in this sense, that a Poet, in the writing of a Fools Character, needs but have a man sit to him, and have his words and actions taken, in this case there is no need of wit. But 'tis most certain that if we should do so, no one fool, though the best about the Town, could appear pleasantly upon the Stage: he would be there too dull a Fool, and must be helped out with a great deal of wit in the Author. I scruple not to call it so, first, because 'tis not your down-right Fool that is a fit Character for a Play, but like Sir *John Dawe* and Sir *Amorous la Foole*, your witty, brisk, aiery *Fopps*, that are *Entreprennants*. Besides, wit in the Writer, I think, without any Authority for it, may be said to be the invention of remote and pleasant thoughts of what kind soever; and there is as much occasion for such imaginations in the writing of a Curious Coxcomb's part as in writing the greatest Hero's; and that which may be folly in the Speaker may be so remote and pleasant to require a great deal of wit in the Writer. The most

Excellent *Johnson* put wit into the mouths of the meanest of his people, and, which is infinitely difficult, made it proper for 'em. And I once heard a Person of the greatest Wit and Judgement of the Age say that *Bartholomew Fair*,
5 which consists most of low persons, is one of the Wittiest Plays in the World. If there be no wit required in the rendering Folly ridiculous or Vice odious, we must accuse *Juvenal*, the best Satyrist and wittiest Man of all the Latine Writers, for want of it.

10 I should not say so much of Mr. *Johnson*, whose Merit sufficiently justifies him to all Men of Sense, but that I think my self a little obliged to vindicate the Opinion I publickly declared in my *Epilogue* to this *Play*, which I did upon mature consideration, and with a full satisfaction
15 in my Judgement, and not out of a bare affected vanity in being thought his Admirer.

I have only one word more to trouble you with concerning this Trifle of my own, which is, that, as it is at present, it is wholly my own, without borrowing a tittle
20 from any man; which I confess is too bold an attempt for so young a Writer; for let it seem what it will, a Comedy of humor that is not borrowed is the hardest thing to write well, and a way of writing of which a man can never be certain.

25 *Creditur, ex medio quia res accessit, habere*
Sudoris minimum, sed habet comœdia tanto
Plus oneris, quanto veniœ minus.

That which (besides judging truly of Mankind) makes Comedy more difficult is that the faults are naked and bare
30 to most people, but the wit of it understood or valued but by few. Wonder not then if a man of ten times my parts miscarries in the Attempt.

I shall say no more of this of mine, but that the Humors are new (how well chosen I leave to you to judge), and
35 all the words and actions of the Persons in the Play

are alwayes sutable to the Characters I have given of them; and in all the Play I have gone according to that definition of humor which I have given you in my *Epilogue*, in these words :

> *A Humor is the Biasse of the Mind,*   5
> *By which, with violence, 'tis one way inclin'd ;*
> *It makes our actions lean on one side still,*
> *And, in all Changes, that way bends the Will.*

Vale.

THOMAS RYMER

I. PREFACE TO THE TRANSLATION OF RAPIN'S *REFLECTIONS ON ARISTOTLE'S TREATISE OF POESIE*

1674

THE

PREFACE

OF THE

TRANSLATOR.

THE Artist would not take pains to polish a Diamond, if none besides himself were quick-sighted enough to discern the flaw: And Poets would grow negligent, if the Criticks had not a strict eye over their miscarriages. Yet
5 it often happens that this eye is so distorted by envy or ill nature that it sees nothing aright. Some Criticks are like Wasps, that rather annoy the Bees than terrifie the Drones.

For this sort of Learning our Neighbour Nations have got
10 far the start of us; in the last *Century Italy* swarm'd with Criticks, where, amongst many of less note, *Castelvetro* opposed all comers, and the famous Academy *La Crusca* was allways impeaching some or other of the best Authors. *Spain* in those dayes bred great Wits, but, I think, was
15 never so crowded that they needed to fall out and quarrel amongst themselves. But from *Italy France* took the Cudgels; and though some light strokes passed in the dayes of *Marot, Baif,* &c., yet they fell not to it in earnest, nor was any noble Contest amongst them till the *Royal*
20 *Academy* was founded, and Cardinal *Richlieu* encouraged

and rallied all the scattered Wits under his Banner. Then *Malherb* reform'd their ancient licentious *Poetry* ; and *Corneille's Cid* rais'd many Factions amongst them. At this time with us many great Wits flourished, but *Ben Johnson*, I think, had all the Critical learning to himself ; 5 and till of late years *England* was as free from Criticks as it is from *Wolves*, that a harmless well-meaning Book might pass without any danger. But now this priviledge, whatever extraordinary Talent it requires, is usurped by the most ignorant ; and they who are least acquainted with the 10 game are aptest to bark at every thing that comes in their way. Our fortune is, *Aristotle*, on whom our Author makes these *Reflections*, came to this great work better accomplished. He who Criticis'd on the ancient and his contemporary Philosophers, on *Pythagoras, Democritus, Empe-* 15 *docles, Heraclitus, Epicharmus, Parmenides, Xenophanes, Melissus, Anaxagoras, Protagoras, Eudoxus, Solon, Anaximander, Anaximenes, Plato, Speusippus ;* who examin'd and censur'd the *Laws* and *Polities* of *Minos, Lycurgus, Solon, Hippodamus, Phaleas,* and all the other Common- 20 wealths ; 'tis he, I say, that undertakes this Province, to pass a judgment on the *Poets* and their Works ; and him Antiquity first honoured with the name of *Critick*.

It is indeed suspected that he dealt not alwayes fairly with the Philosophers, misreciting sometimes, and mis- 25 interpreting their opinions. But I find him not tax'd of that injustice to the *Poets*, in whose favour he is so ingenious, that to the disadvantage of his own profession he declares, *That Tragedy more conduces to the instruction of Mankind than even Philosophy it self.* And however cryed 30 down in the Schools, and vilified by some modern Philosophers ; since Men have had a taste for *good sense*, and could discern the beauties of correct writing, he is prefer'd in the *politest* Courts of *Europe*, and by the *Poets* held in great veneration. Not that these can servilely yield to his 35

Authority, who, of all men living, affect liberty.   The truth
is, what *Aristotle* writes on this Subject are not the dictates
of his own magisterial will or dry deductions of his
Metaphysicks :   But the Poets were his Masters, and what
5 was their practice he reduced to principles.   Nor would
the *modern Poets* blindly resign to this practice of the
Ancients, were not the Reasons convincing and clear as
any demonstration in *Mathematicks*.   'Tis only needful that
we understand them for our consent to the truth of them.
10 The *Arabians*, 'tis confess'd, who glory in their *Poets* and
Poetry more than all the world besides, and who, I suppose,
first brought the art of *Riming* into *Europe*, observe but
little these Laws of *Aristotle* : yet *Averroie* rather chooses On *Arist*
to blame the practice of his Countreymen as vicious than to *de Poet.*
15 allow any imputation on the doctrine of this *Philosopher* as
imperfect.   *Fancy* with them is predominant, is wild, vast,
and unbridled, o're which their *judgment* has little command
or authority : hence their conceptions are monstrous, and
have nothing of exactness, nothing of resemblance or pro-
20 portion.

   The Author of these *Reflections* is as well known amongst
the *Criticks* as *Aristotle* to the *Philosophers* : never man
gave his judgment so generally, and never was judgment
more free and impartial.   He might be thought an enemy
25 to the *Spaniards*, were he not as sharp on the *Italians* ;
and he might be suspected to envy the *Italians*, were he
not as severe on his own Countreymen.   These Nations
make it a Problem whether a *Dutchman* or *German* may
be a *Wit* or no ; and our Author finds none worthy of his
30 censure amongst them, except *Heinsius* and *Grotius.*
Amongst us he gives *Buchanan* a particular Character :
but for such as writ in the *English* Tongue, he has not,
I presume, understood the language so well to pass a
judgment on them ; onely in general he confesses that we
35 have a *Genius* for *Tragedy* above all other people ; one

reason he gives we cannot allow of, *viz. The disposition of our Nation, which,* he saith, *is delighted with cruel things.* 'Tis ordinary to judge of Peoples manners and inclinations by their publick diversions ; and Travellers, who see some of our *Tragedies,* may conclude us certainly the cruellest 5 minded people in *Christendom.*

In another place this Author sayes of us, *That we are men in an Island, divided from the rest of the world, and that we love blood in our sports.* And perhaps it may be true that on our Stage are more Murders than on all the Thea- 10 tres in *Europe.* And they who have not time to learn our Language or be acquainted with our Conversation may there in three hours time behold so much bloodshed as may affright them from the inhospitable shore, as from the Cyclops Den. Let our Tragedy-makers consider this, and 15 examine whether it be the disposition of the People or their own *Caprice* that brings this Censure on the best natur'd Nation under the Sun.

His other Reason is our Language, *which,* he sayes, *is proper for great expressions.* The *Spanish* is big and 20 fastuous, proper only for *Rodomontades,* and compar'd with other Languages is like the Kettle-drum to Musick.

The *Italian* is fittest for *Burlesque,* and better becomes the mouth of *Petrolin* and *Arloquin* in their *Farces* than any *Heroick* character. The perpetual termination in 25 vowels is childish, and themselves confess, rather sweet than grave.

The *French* wants sinews for great and heroick Subjects, *Mesnardire* and even in Love-matters, by their own confession, is a *& al.* very Infant; the *Italians* call it the *Kitchin-language,* it 30 *Lingua di* *Masseritie.* being so copious and flowing on those occasions.

The *German* still continues rude and unpolisht, not yet filed and civiliz'd by the commerce and intermixture with strangers to that smoothness and humanity which the *English* may boast of. 35

The dissyllable Rimes force the *Italians* and *Spaniards* on the *Stanza* in *Heroicks*; which, besides many other disadvantages, renders the Language unfit for *Tragedy*.

The *French* now onely use the long *Alexandrins*, and
5 would make up in length what they want in strength and substance; yet are they too faint and languishing, and attain not that *numerosity* which the dignity of Heroick Verse requires, and which is ordinary in an *English* Verse of *ten syllables*. But I shall not here examine the weight,
10 the fulness, the vigour, force, gravity, and the fitness of the *English* for *Heroick Poesie* above all other Languages; the world expecting these matters learnedly and largely *Shering-* discussed in a particular Treatise on that Subject. *ham.*

But from our Language proceed to our Writers, and
15 with the freedom of this Author, examine how unhappy the greatest *English* Poets have been through their igno- rance or negligence of these fundamental Rules and Laws of *Aristotle*. I shall leave the Author of the *Romance of Bellay.* the Rose (whom *Sir Richard Baker* makes an *Englishman*) *Pasquier prefers*
20 for the *French* to boast of, because he writ in their *him to the* Language. Nor shall I speak of *Chaucer*, in whose time *best of Italy.* our Language, I presume, was not capable of any Heroick Character. Nor indeed was the most polite Wit of *Europe* in that Age sufficient for a great *design*. That was the
25 Age of *Tales*, *Ballads*, and *Roundelays*. *Petrarch* in those days attempted the *Epick* strain in his *Africa*; but though most happy in his *Sonnets* and *Madrigals*, was far too feeble for a work of that weight and importance.

Spencer, I think, may be reckon'd the first of our *Heroick*
30 *Poets*; he had a large spirit, a sharp judgment, and a *Genius* for *Heroic Poesie*, perhaps above any that ever writ since *Virgil*. But our misfortune is, he wanted a true *Idea*, and lost himself by following an unfaithful guide. Though besides *Homer* and *Virgil* he had read *Tasso*, yet
35 he rather suffer'd himself to be misled by *Ariosto*; with

whom blindly rambling on *marvellous* Adventures, he
makes no Conscience of *Probability.* All is fanciful and
chimerical, without any uniformity, without any foundation
in truth ; his Poem is perfect *Fairy-land.*

They who can love *Ariosto* will be ravish'd with *Spencer,* 5
whilst men of juster thoughts lament that such great Wits
have miscarried in their Travels for want of direction to
set them in the right way. But the truth is, in *Spencer's*
time, *Italy* it self was not well satisfied with *Tasso* ; and
few amongst them would then allow that he had excell'd 10
their *divine Ariosto.* And it was the vice of those Times
to affect superstitiously the *Allegory* ; and nothing would
then be currant without a mystical meaning. We must
blame the *Italians* for debauching great *Spencer's* judgment ;
and they cast him on the unlucky choice of the *stanza,* 15
which in no wise is proper for our Language.

The next for *Epick Poesie* is Sir *William D'avenant* ; his
Wit is well known, and in the Preface to his *Gondibert*
appear some strokes of an extraordinary judgment. He
is for *unbeaten tracks,* and *new wayes of thinking* : but 20
certainly in his *untry'd Seas* he is no great discoverer.

Et Pater
Æneas
& Avun-
culus
excitat
Hector.

One design of the *Epick Poets* before him was to adorn
their own Countrey, there finding their *Heroes* and
patterns of Virtue, whose example (as they thought) would
have greatest influence and power over Posterity ; but 25
this Poet steers a different course : his *Heroes* are all
Forreigners. He cultivates a Countrey that is nothing
akin to him ; 'tis *Lombardy* that reaps the honour of all.

Other Poets chose some *Action* or *Heroe* so illustrious,
that the name of the Poem prepared the Reader, and made 30
way for its reception ; but in this Poem none can divine
what *great action* he intended to celebrate, nor is the
Reader obliged to know whether the *Heroe* be *Turk* or
Christian. Nor do the first lines give any light or prospect
into his *design.* Methinks, though his Religion could not 35

dispense with an *Invocation,* he needed not have scrupled
at the *Proposition* ; yet he rather chooses to enter in at
the top of an house, because the mortals of *mean* and
satisfied minds go in at the door.   And I believe the
5 Reader is not well pleas'd to find his Poem begin with the
praises of *Aribert,* when the Title had promised a *Gondibert.*
But before he falls on any other business, he presents the
Reader with a description of each particular *Heroe,* not
trusting their *actions* to speak for them, as former Poets
10 had done.   Their practice was fine and artificial ; his (he
tells us) is a *new way.*   Many of his *Characters* have but
little of the *Heroick* in them : *Dalga* is a Jilt, proper onely
for *Comedy* ; *Birtha,* for a *Pastoral* ; and *Astragon,* in the
manner here described, yields no very great ornament to
15 an *Heroick Poem* : nor are his Battels less liable to censure
than those of *Homer.*

He dares not, as other *Heroick Poets,* heighten the *action*
by making Heaven and Hell interess'd, for fear of offending
against *probability* ; and yet he tells of

20   —— *Threads by patient* Parcæ *slowly spun.*

And for being dead, his phrase is,

Heaven call'd him, where peacefully he rules a Star.

And the *Emerald* he gives to *Birtha* has a stronger *tang* of
the Old Woman, and is a greater *improbability* than all
25 the enchantments in *Tasso.*   A just *medium* reconciles the
farthest extremes, and due preparation may give credit to
the most unlikely Fiction.   In *Marino, Adonis* is presented
with a *Diamond Ring,* where indeed the stone is much-
what of the same nature ; but this Present is made by
30 *Venus,* and from a *Goddess* could not be expected a gift
of ordinary virtue.

Although a Poet is oblig'd to know all Arts and Sciences,
yet he ought discreetly to manage this knowledge.   He

must have judgment to select what is noble or beautiful, and proper for his occasion. He must by a particular Chymistry extract the essence of things, without soiling his Wit with the gross and trumpery. But some Poets labour to appear skilful with that wretched affectation, they dote on the very terms and *jargon*; exposing themselves rather to be laught at by the Apprentices than to be admir'd by Philosophers: But whether *D'Avenant* be one of those, I leave others to examine.

The sort of Verse he makes choice of might, I suppose, contribute much to the vitiating of his stile; for thereby he obliges himself to stretch every period to the end of four lines. Thus the sense is broken perpetually with *parentheses*, the words jumbl'd in confusion, and a darkness spread over all, that the sense is either not discern'd or found not sufficient for one just Verse, which is sprinkl'd on the whole *tetrastick*.

In the *Italian* and *Spanish*, where all the *Rimes* are dissyllable, and the percussion stronger, this kind of Verse may be necessary; and yet to temper that grave march, they repeat the same Rime over again, and then they close the *Stanza* with a *Couplet* further to sweeten the severity. But in *French* and *English*, where we rime generally with onely one syllable, the *Stanza* is not allow'd, much less the *alternate* Rime in long Verse; for the sound of the monosyllable Rime is either lost ere we come to its correspondent, or we are in pain by the so long expectation and suspense.

This alternate Rime, and the downright Morality throughout whole *Canto's* together, shew him better acquainted with the *quatrains of Pybrach*, which he speaks of, than with any true Models of *Epick Poesie*.

After all, he is said to have a particular Talent for the *Manners*: his thoughts are great, and there appears something *roughly Noble* throughout this fragment, which, had he been pleased to finish it, would doubtless not have been left so open to the attack of Criticks.

A more happy *Genius* for *Heroick Poesie* appears in *Cowley*. He understood the *purity*, the *perspicuity*, the 5 *majesty* of stile and the vertue of *numbers*. He could discerne what was beautiful and pleasant in Nature, and could express his Thoughts without the least difficulty or constraint. He understood to dispose of the matters, and to manage his Digressions. In short, he understood *Homer* 10 and *Virgil*, and as prudently made his advantage of them.

Yet as it may be lamented that he carried not on the work so far as he design'd, so it might be wish'd that he had lived to revise what he did leave us. I think the *Troubles of David* is neither title nor matter proper for an 15 *Heroick* Poem, seeing it is rather the *actions* than his sufferings that make an *Heroe*; nor can it be defended by *Homer's Odysseis*, since *Ulysse's* sufferings conclude with one *great* and *perfect* action.

After all the heavy Censures that jointly from all Criticks 20 have fall'n on *Lucan*, I do a little wonder that this Author should choose *History* for the Subject of his Poem, and a History where he is so strictly ty'd up to the Truth. *Aristotle* tells us, *That Poetry is something more excellent and more philosophical than History*, and does not inform us 25 what has been done, but teaches what may and what ought to be done. And since many particulars in Sacred Story are neither *Heroick* nor indeed consistent with the common principles of Morality, but of a singular, extraordinary, and unaccountable dispensation; and since in the principal 30 actions all is carried on by *Machine*; how can these examples be propos'd for great persons to imitate? or what foundation for their hopes in *impossibilities*? *Poetry* has no life, nor can have any operation, without *probability*; it may indeed amuse the People, but moves not the *Wise*, ἀείσω 35 for whom alone (according to *Pythagoras*) it is ordain'd. συνετοῖς, &c. Stob.

Instead of one *illustrious* and *perfect action*, which properly is the subject of an *Epick* Poem, *Cowley* proposes to adorn some several particulars of *David's* life ; and these particulars have no necessary relation to the end, nor in any wise lead to the great revolution : *David* is made King, 5 but this is the work of Heaven, not any atchievement of his own.   He neither did, nor ought to lift a finger for gaining the Crown ; he is amongst the *Amalekites*, whilst his work is done without him.   This ill choice of a Subject forces the Poet (how excellent otherwise soever) per- 10 petually on digressions ; and *David* is the least part of the Poem.

Some, perhaps, may object, *That he begins not his Poem with all the art and address as might be desired.*   *Homer* would make us believe the drawing of *Achilles*, adorn'd 15 with all his glorious actions, a design too vast and impossible ; and therefore only proposes his *resentment* of the affront given him by *Agamemnon*, as if any one particular of his life were sufficient to employ the greatest humane Wit with all its *Muses* and divine assistance.   *Achilles* 20 could not be *angry*, but Heaven and Earth are engaged, and just matter given for an *Heroick* Poem.   Thus whilst he *proposes* but one passage, we conceive a greater *Idea* of the rest than any words could express ; and whilst he promises so little, his performances are the more admirable 25 and surprising.   But in the *Davideis* we have all the *Heroe* at the first : in the Proposition, he is the *best Poet* and the *best King*; now, all the Author could do afterwards is onely to make good his word, and make us conceive of his *Heroe* the same *Idea* at the end of the Poem which was 30 given us in the beginning ; whereas *Homer* calls the man he designs to celebrate barely *Achilles, son of Peleus*, and recording his actions, leaves others to conclude from them what a great *Captain, Prince,* and *Heroe* this *Achilles* was.

Tasso left the *Episode* of *Sophonia* out of his Poem, 35

because it was *Troppo Lyrico*. Yet Mr. *Cowley* is not content to mix *matters* that are purely *lyrical* in this *Heroick*
Poem, but employs the *measures* also.

Yet, notwithstanding what has been said, we cannot now
approve the reason (which Sir *Philip Sidney* gives) why
Poets are less esteem'd in *England* than in the other
famous Nations, to be *want of merit*; nor be of their
opinion, who say that *Wit* and *Wine* are not of the growth
of our Countrey. Valour they allow us; but what we gain
by our Arms, we lose by the weakness of our Heads: our
good *Ale* and English *Beef*, they say, may make us *Soldiers*,
but are no very good Friends to *Speculation*. Were it
proper here to handle this Argument, and to make comparisons with our Neighbors, it might easily by our *Poetry*
be evinced that our *Wit* was never inferior to theirs, though
perhaps our *honesty* made us worse Polititians. Wit and
Valor have always gone together, and *Poetry* been the
companion of Camps. The *Heroe* and *Poet* were inspired
with the same Enthusiasm, acted with the same heat, and
both were crown'd with the same *laurel*. Had our Tongue
been as generally known, and those who felt our blows
understood our Language, they would confess that our
Poets had likewise done their part, and that our Pens had
been as successful as our Swords. And certainly if Sir
Philip Sidney had seen the Poets who succeeded him, he
would not have judg'd the *English* less deserving than
their Neighbors. In the *Davideis* (fragment and imperfect
as it is) there shines something of a more fine, more free,
more new, and more noble *air* than appears in the *Hieru-*
salem of *Tasso*, which for all his care is scarce perfectly
purg'd from *Pedantry*. But in the *Lyrick* way, however,
Cowley far exceeds him and all the rest of the *Italians*,
though *Lyrick Poesie* is their principal glory, and Pope
Urban VIII. had the honour a little before him to enrich
modern *Poesie* with the *Pindarick* strains. Many the

greatest Wits of *France* have attempted the Epick, but their performance answer'd not expectation; our fragments are more worth than their finish'd pieces. And though, perhaps, want of encouragement has hinder'd our labours in the *Epic*, yet for the *Drama* the World has nothing to 5 be compared with us. But a debate of this importance is not the work of a Preface: I shall only here on the behalf of our *English Poetry* give one single instance, and leave the Reader to judge of *Hercules* by his *foot*.

Amongst the common places, by which *Scaliger*, and 10 before him *Macrobius, Agellius*, and the other Criticks have compared the Poets and examin'd their worth, none has been more generally and more happily handled, and in none have the Noblest wits both *ancient* and *modern* more contended with each other for victory, than in the 15 *description of the night*. Yet in this the *English* has the advantage, and has even outdone them where they have outdone themselves. The first I meet with who had the *lucky hit* is *Apollonius* in his *Argonautiques*:

Νὺξ μὲν ἔπειτ' ἐπὶ γαῖαν ἄγεν κνέφας· οἱ δ' ἐνὶ πόντῳ   20
Ναῦται εἰς Ἑλίκην τε καὶ ἀστέρας Ὠρίωνος
Ἔδρακον ἐκ νηῶν· ὕπνοιο δὲ καί τις ὁδίτης
Ἤδη καὶ πυλαωρὸς ἐέλδετο· καί τινα παίδων
Μητέρα τεθνεώτων ἀδινὸν περὶ κῶμ' ἐκάλυπτεν·
Οὐδὲ κυνῶν ὑλακὴ ἔτ' ἀνὰ πτόλιν, οὐ θρόος ἦεν   25
Ἠχήεις· σιγὴ δὲ μελαινομένην ἔχεν ὄρφνην.
Ἀλλὰ μάλ' οὐ Μήδειαν ἐπὶ γλυκερὸς λάβεν ὕπνος.

Here we have variety of matter, yet rather *many* than *choice* thoughts. He gives us the face of things both by Land and Sea, City and Countrey, the Mariner, the 30 Traveller, the Door-keeper, the Mistress of the Family, her Child and Dog; but loses himself amongst his particulars, and seems to forget for what occasion he mentions them. He would say that all the world is fast asleep but onely *Medea*; and then his Mariners, who are gazing from 35

their ships on *Helice* and *Orion*, can serve but little for his purpose, unless they may be supposed to sleep with their eyes open. Neither dares he say that the *Traveller* and *Porter* are yet taking a Nap, but onely that they have a
5 good mind to 't. And after all, we find none but the good Woman who had lost her Child (and she indeed is fast) asleep, unless the Dogs may likewise be supposed so, because they had left off barking: And these, methinks, were scarce worthy to be taken notice of in an *Heroick*
10 *Poem*, except we may believe that in the *old time*, or that in *Greek*, they bark Heroically! *Scaliger*, as his manner is to prefer *Virgil*, calls this description *mean* and *vulgar*. *Virgil* well saw the levity and trifling of the *Greeks*, and from him we may expect something better digested.

15   *Nox erat, & placidum carpebant fessa soporem*
   Corpora per terras, sylvæque & sæva quierant
   Æquora ; cum Medio volvuntur sydera lapsu,
   Cum tacet omnis ager, pecudes pictæque volucres,
   Quæque lacus late liquidos, quæque aspera dumis
20   *Rura tenent, somno positæ sub nocte silenti,*
   Lenibant curas, & corda oblita laborum. (*Æn.* l. 4.)

Against this may be objected, That sleep being of such a soft and gentle nature that 'tis said to steal upon our senses, the word *carpebant* suits but ill with it : this word
25 seeming to imply a force, and might rather express the violence of Robbers than the slieness of a Thief. Nor can it be pretended that *sopor* signifies a kind of violent and snoring sleep, for here we have it *placidum soporem.* Instead of *Woods* and *Seas*, *Tasso* rather chooses to join
30 *Winds* and *Seas*, as of a nearer relation, and going more naturally together ; the Commentators being certainly mistaken, who would have a *Metonymie* in this place. The third Verse I can scarce believe legitimate: the *words* speak nothing but motion, and the *numbers* are so ratling
35 that nothing can be more repugnant to the general repose

and silence which the Poet describes; or, if any Copies might favour the conjecture, I should rather read,

—— *cum medio librantur sydera cursu.*

For nothing can be more Poetical, than to suppose the Stars rest (as it were poiz'd) in their Meridian; and this 5 would not only express it to be Midnight, but heighten the Poets design, which by the common reading is absolutely destroy'd. The fifth line seems to bear a doubtful face, and looks not unlike something of equivocation: an ordinary *Grammarian* would seek no further than the 10 *antecedent, volucres,* to refer these *relatives* to; and might construe Wild ducks and Woodcocks, what the Poet intended for *Fish* in the Sea and the *wild Beasts* of the Forest.

Besides this, I find none amongst the *Latins* that deserves 15 to be brought into comparison. In the *Italian, Ariosto* (whose every description is said to be a *master-piece*) in this is not over-fortunate; he is easie and smooth, but produces nothing of his own invention. He only enlarges on a thought of *Virgils,* which yet he leaves without that 20 *turn* which might give it perfection. What, I think, is more considerable is this of *Tasso*:

> *Era la notte all' hor, ch' alto riposo*
> *Han l' onde e i venti, e parea muto il mondo:*
> *Gli animai lassi, e quei, che 'l mar ondoso,*   25
> *O de' liquidi laghi alberga il fondo,*
> *E chi si giace in tana, o in mandra ascoso,*
> *E i pinti augelli ne l' oblio profondo,*
> *Sotto il silentio de' secreti horrori,*
> *Sopian gli affanni, e raddolciano i cori.*   30

Tasso, when he reform'd his Poem, could mend nothing in this description, but repeats it entire in his *Hierusalem liberata,* without any alteration. 'Tis well nigh word for word taken out of *Virgil,* and (to give it its due) is a most

excellent Translation. He most judiciously leaves out
that *Hemistick, volvuntur sydera lapsu,* the place whereof is
(perhaps from *Statius*) supply'd with *parea muto il mondo.*
Yet on the other hand, here seems to be some superfluity
5 of Fish : *those in the Sea and those at the bottom of the Lakes*
are more by half than *Virgil,* or perhaps than *Tasso,* had
occasion for in this place.

Achillei-
dos, l. 1 :
mutumque
ample-
ctitur
orbem.

But that we may have something *new* from the *Italians*
on this Subject, *Marino* has taken care in his *Adonis,*
10 *Canto* 13 :

> *Notte era, allhor che dal diurno moto*
> *Ha requie ogni pensier, tregua ogni duolo ;*
> *L'onde giacean, tacean zepiro e Noto,*
> *E cedeva il quadrante a l'horiuolo,*
> 15 *Sopra l' huom la fatica, il pesce il nuoto,*
> *La fera il Corso, e l' augelletto il volo,*
> *Aspettando il tornar del novo lume*
> *Tra l' alghe, o tra rami, o su le piume.*

In these we have more of the *fancy* than of the *judgment,*
20 variety of matter rather than exquisite sense. *Marino* is
perfectly himself throughout ; the *thoughts diurnal motion,*
I fear, will scarce pass for a very pathetical expression,
nor will it satisfie that he makes *Zephyrus* and the *South-
wind silent* ; if he particularize these, he should also name
25 the rest, otherwise the *East-wind* and *Boreas* have leave to
bluster. But, above all, he tells us that the *Clocks* have
got the better of the *Sun-dials.* A thought purely New
and strangely Heroick ! What could come more sudden
or surprising ? In the latter part of the *Stanza* we have
30 some strokes of *Ariosto,* but far more lame and imperfect
than the original. Neither ought he in this place to speak
of any expecting the return of the light ; *omnia noctis erant.*

But I hasten to the *French,* amongst whom none more
eminent than *Chapelain,* nor was ever a Poem of greater
35 expectation. His description is thus :

> *Cependant la nuit vole & sous son aile obscure*
> *Invite a sommeiller l'agissante Nature.*
> *Dans les plaines des airs tient les vents en repos,*
> *Et sur les champs salez fait reposer les flots.*
> *A tout ce qui se meut, à tout ce qui respire,*   5
> *Dans les prés, dans les bois le repos elle inspire ;*
> *Elle suspend par tout les travaux & les bruits,*
> *Et par tout dans les cœurs assoupit les ennuis.*
> *Charles seul esveillé—*

This description is perfect *French*. There is scarce any 10
coming at a little sense, 'tis so encompassed about with
words. What *Virgil* or *Tasso* would have dispatch'd in
half a Verse, here fills out the measures of two whole
Alexandrins.

Some Caviller would object, That since the *Night flies*, 15
there is little sleep to be got under *her wing*, unless for
such as can walk in their sleep. And that the *Night* might
have spared this *invitation*, seeing those she *invites* are
asleep already : *Charles alone is awake*, and for that reason
was the onely thing fit to be invited ; and doubtless the 20
Night was as free of her *invitation* to him as to any others ;
'twas his fault that he had no stomack to 't. And here is
much power given to the *Night* which she has no claim or
title to : 'tis not the *Night* that makes the *Waves and*
Winds and all the things that *move and breath in Meads* 25
and Woods to *repose*. She onely invites them to sleep, and
it is sleep that makes them rest. In the space of four
lines, we meet with *repos, reposer, repos*, which argue the
language very barren, or else the Poet extremely negligent,
and a lover of repose. He tells us that the Night *inspires* 30
repose. But certainly motion is a more likely thing to be
inspired than rest, as more properly the effect of breath.

But without examining this further, let us try if *Le Moyne*
(whom our Critick prefers before all others of the *French*
Epick Poets) be more fortunate :
                                           35

Cependant le soleil se couche dans son lit,
Que luymesme de pourpre & de laque embellit :
Et la nuit qui survient aussi triste que sombre,
De toutes les couleurs ne fait qu' une grand'ombre.
5 *Aveque le sommeil le silence la suit,*
L'un amy du repos, l'autre ennemy du bruit :
Et quoique sous leur pas la tempeste se taise,
Quoique le vent s'endorme & que l'onde s'appaise.
(St. Louys.)

10 Here again are words in abundance. He cannot tell us
that 'tis Midnight till he first have informed us that *the Sun
is gone to Bed,* to a fine Bed of *his own trimming*; and this
is matter enough for the first two Verses. Then we are
told that the *Night of all Colours makes but one great shade,*
15 and this suffices for the second *Couplet. Aussi triste que
sombre* is an expression the *French* are so delighted with,
they can scarce name any thing of Night without it. The
third *Couplet* is much-what as in a *Bill* of fare :

Item—Beef and Mustard,
20 *That Friend to th' Stomach, this a Foe to th' Nose—*

The second line in both being alike impertinent.

Any further *Reflections,* or more examples, would be
superfluous. What has been noted rather concerns the
Niceties of *Poetry* than any the little trifles of *Grammar.*
25 We have seen what the noblest Wits, both ancient and
modern, have done in other languages, and observ'd that
in their very Master-pieces they sometimes trip, or are
however liable to Cavils. It now remains that our *English*
be expos'd to the like impartial Censure.

30 *All things are hush'd, as Nature's self lay dead :*
The Mountains seem to Nod their drowsie head,
The little Birds in dreams their Songs repeat,
And sleeping flowers beneath the Night-dew sweat :
Even Lust and Envy sleep.
35 (In the Conquest of *Mexico.*)

In this description, four lines yield greater variety of

matter and more choice thoughts than twice the number
of any other Language.   Here is something more *fortunate*
than the boldest fancy has yet reached, and something
more *just* than the severest reason has observed.   Here
are the *flights of Statius* and *Marino* temper'd with a more 5
discerning judgment, and the *judgment* of *Virgil* and *Tasso*
animated with a more sprightly Wit.   Nothing has been
said so expressive and so home in any other Language as
the first Verse in this description.   The second is *Statius*
improv'd.   10

     Et simulant fessos curvata cacumina somnos,

Saith *Statius*, where *simulant* is a bold word in comparison of our *English* word *seem*, being of an active signification ; and *cacumina* may as well be taken for the tops
of Trees as the tops of Mountains, which doubtful meaning 15
does not so well content the Reader as the certainty.

In the *third* Verse, 'tis not said that the Birds sleep, but
what is more new and more Poetical, their sleep is imply'd
by their dreams.   Somewhat like to the *Fourth* we have in
Marino :   20

    —— *E languidetti i fiori*
  Giaceano a l' herba genitrice in seno.
                    (Adonis, Canto 20.)

Which is a pretty image, but has not so near a resemblance with truth, nor can so generally be apply'd to 25
all flowers.   Our Author here dares not say directly that
the flowers sleep, which might sound a little harsh, but
slurs it over in the *participle* as taken for granted, and
affirms only that they *sweat*, which the *Night-dew* makes
very easie.   30

In the last Half-verse, we may see how far our Author
has out-done *Apollonius*.   'Twas no such strange thing in
the sorrowful Woman, when she had spent her tears, for
sleep to close her eyes ; but here we have the most raging
and watchful passions, *Lust* and *Envy*.   And these, too, 35

instead of the lustful and the envious, for the greater force
and emphasis in the *abstract*.

Some may object, That the *third* Verse does contradict
the *first*. How can *all things be hush'd, if Birds in dreams*
5 *repeat their Songs*? Is not this like the indiscretion of
Marino, who says, *That the Winds and all things are husht,
and the Seas so fast asleep that they snore.* (Canto 20.)

It may be answer'd, That in this place 'tis not the Poet
that speaks, but another person; and that the Poet here
10 truly represents the nature of man, whose first thoughts
break out in bold and more general terms, which by the
second thoughts are more correct and limited. As if one
should say all things are silent or asleep; however, if there
is any noise, 'tis still but the effect of sleep, as the dreams
15 of Birds, &c. This comparison might be much further
improved to our advantage, and more observations made,
which are left to the Readers ingenuity.

II. FROM *THE TRAGEDIES OF THE LAST AGE
CONSIDER'D AND EXAMIN'D BY THE PRAC-
TICE OF THE ANCIENTS AND BY THE
COMMON SENSE OF ALL AGES*

1678

TO

Fleetwood Shepheard, Esq;

HAving several mornings, and early, travell'd to
St. *James's*, with the only design of being with you,
20 and missing you as often, I became so mortifi'd with the
misfortune that I resolv'd to come into the Town no more
till assur'd of your return from *Copt-Hall*; but because I
meant not altogether to kill my self, for my entertainment

I provided me some of those *Master-pieces* of Wit, so renown'd every-where and so edifying to the *Stage*,—I mean the choicest and most applauded *English Tragedies* of this last age, as *Rollo, A King and no King*, the *Maids Tragedy* by *Beaumont* and *Fletcher, Othello* and *Julius Caesar* 5 by *Shakespear*, and *Cataline* by Worthy *Ben*.

These I perus'd with some attention, and some reflections I made, in which how far I mistake your sense, that is, how far I am mistaken, I desire to be inform'd.

I had heard that the *Theater* was wont to be call'd the 10 *School* of *Vertue*, and *Tragedy* a *Poem* for *Kings*: That they who first brought Tragedy to perfection were made *Vice-Roys* and Governors of *Islands*, were honoured every-where with Statues of Marble and Statues of Brass, were stil'd the *Wise Sophocles*, the *Wise Euripides* by God and 15 Man, by Oracles and Philosophers: That for teaching Morality *Crantor* and *Chrysippus* were no-body to 'em (This latter transcrib'd the whole *Medea* of *Euripides* into his works): That so refin'd a People and so frugal a *Common-wealth* as *Athens* did tax and assess themselves, 20 and laid out more of their publick Exchequer upon the representation of these Plays than all their Wars stood them in, though sometimes both Seas and Land were cover'd with Pagan Enemies that invaded them. And not *Athens* only, but (who hated *Athens*) so austere and glum 25 a generation as those of *Sparta*, by the care of *Lycurgus*, agreed the same honour to these *Athenian Poets*.

These things coming into my mind, surely (thought I) mens brains lye not in the same place as formerly, or else Poetry is not now the same thing it was in those days of 30 yore.

I therefore made enquiry what *difference* might be in our *Philosophy* and *Manners*. I found that our *Philosophers* agreed well enough with theirs in the *main*; however, that our Poets have forc'd another way to the *wood*,—a *by-* 35

road that runs directly cross to that of *Nature, Man-*
ners, and *Philosophy*, which gain'd the *Ancients* so great
veneration.

I would not examin the *proportions*, the *unities* and *out-*
5 *ward* regularities, the *mechanical part* of Tragedies; there is
no talking of Beauties when there wants Essentials; 'tis
not necessary for a man to have a nose on his face, nor to
have two legs: he may be a *true* man, though aukward and
unsightly as the *Monster* in the *Tempest*.

10   Nor have I much troubl'd their phrase and expression;
I have not vex'd their language with the *doubts*, the *remarks*
and eternal triflings of the *French Grammaticasters*;
much less have I cast about for Jests, and gone a quibble-
catching.

15   1 have chiefly consider'd the *Fable* or *Plot*, which all
conclude to be the *Soul* of a *Tragedy*; which with the
Ancients is always found to be a *reasonable Soul*, but *with*
us for the most part a *brutish* and often worse than *brutish*.

And certainly there is not requir'd much Learning, or
20 that a man must be some *Aristotle*, and *Doctor* of *Subtilties*,
to form a right judgment in this particular: common sense
suffices; and rarely have I known the *Women-judges*
mistake in these points, when they have the patience to
think, and, left to their own heads, they decide with their
25 own sense.   But if people are prepossest, if they will judg
of *Rollo* by *Othello*, and one *crooked line* by another, we can
never have a certainty.

Amongst those who will be objecting against the doctrin
I lay down, may peradventure appear a sort of men who
30 have remember'd *so* and *so*, and value themselves upon
their *experience*.   I may write by the *Book* (say they) what
I have a mind, but they *know* what will *please*.   These are
a kind of *Stage-quacks* and *Empericks* in Poetry, who have
got a *Receit* to *please*: And no *Collegiate* like 'em for *purging*
35 the Passions.

These say, for instance, a *King* and no *King pleases.* I say the *Comical* part *pleases.*

I say that Mr. *Hart pleases*; most of the business falls to his share, and what he *delivers* every one takes upon *content*; their *eyes* are prepossest and charm'd by his *action* before 5 ought of the *Poets* can approach their *ears*, and to the most wretched of *Characters* he gives a lustre and *brillant* which dazles the *sight*, that the *deformities* in the Poetry cannot be perceiv'd.

Therefore a distinction is to be made between what 10 *pleases naturally* in it self, and what *pleases* upon the account of *Machines, Actors, Dances*, and circumstances which are meerly *accidental* to the *Tragedy.*

Aristotle observes that in his time some who, wanting the talent to *write* what might *please*, made it their care that the 15 *Actors* should help out where the *Muses* faild.

These objectors urge that there is also another great *accident*, which is that *Athens* and *London* have not the same *Meridian.*

Certain it is that *Nature* is the same, and *Man* is the 20 same: he *loves, grieves, hates, envies*, has the same *affections* and *passions*, in both places, and the same *springs* that give them *motion.* What mov'd *pity* there will *here* also produce the same effect.

This must be confest, unless they will in effect say that 25 we have not that *delicate tast* of things; we are not so *refin'd* nor so *vertuous*; that *Athens* was more *civiliz'd* by their *Philosophers* than we with both our *Philosophers* and *twelve Apostles.*

But were it to be suppos'd that *Nature* with us is a *corrupt* 30 and deprav'd *Nature*, that we are *Barbarians*, and *humanity* dwells not amongst us, shall our *Poet* therefore pamper this *corrupt* nature and indulge our barbarity? Shall he not rather *purge* away the corruption, and reform our *manners*? Shall he not with *Orpheus* rather choose to draw 35 the *Brutes* after him than be himself a *follower* of the *Herd*? Was it thus that the *ancient* Poets by the best *Philosophers* became stil'd the *Fathers* of Knowledg and *Interpreters* of the Gods?

5   Lastly, though *Tragedy* is a Poem chiefly for *men* of *sense*, yet I cannot be perswaded that the people are so very mad of *Acorns* but that they could be well content to eat the *Bread* of civil persons.

Say others, *Poetry* and *Reason*, how come these to be
10 Cater-cousins? Poetry is the *Child* of *Fancy*, and is never to be school'd and *disciplin'd* by *Reason*; Poetry, say they, is *blind* inspiration, is pure *enthusiasm*, is *rapture* and *rage* all over.

But *Fancy*, I think, in Poetry, is like *Faith* in Religion:
15 it makes far discoveries, and soars above reason, but never clashes or runs against it. *Fancy* leaps and frisks, and away she's gone, whilst *reason* rattles the chains and follows after. *Reason* must consent and ratify what-ever by *fancy* is attempted in its absence, or else 'tis all *null* and void in law.
20 However, in the contrivance and *œconomy* of a Play, *reason* is always principally to be consulted. Those who object against reason are the *Fanaticks* in Poetry, and are never to be sav'd by their good works.

Others imagin that these rules and restraints on the *Plot*
25 and *Argument* of Tragedy wou'd hinder much good *intrigue*, wou'd clog invention, and make all *Plays* alike and *uniform*.

But certainly *Nature* affords plenty and variety enough of *Beauties*, that no man need complain if the *deform'd* are
30 cloyster'd up and shut from him. Such a Painter has been who could draw nothing but a *Rose*, yet other Painters can design one and the same good face in a thousand several figures: it may be remember'd that there are but five vowels, or be consider'd, from *seven* Planets and their
35 several positions how *many fates* and fortunes the

Astrologer distributes to the people. And has not a Poet
more *vertues* and *vices* within his *circle*, cannot he observe
them and their influences in their several *situations*, in
their *oppositions* and *conjunctions*, in their *altitudes* and
depressions,—and he shall sooner find his *ink* than the *stores* 5
of Nature exhausted ?

Other objections may be answer'd as they fall in the
way. I would only have you before hand advertiz'd that
you will find me ty'd to no certain *stile*, nor laying my
reasons together in *form* and *method*. You will find me 10
sometimes reasoning, sometimes declaiming, sometimes
citing authority for common sense, sometimes *uttering* as
my *own* what may be had at any *Bookshop* in the Nation ;
sometimes doubting when I might be positive, and sometimes confident out of season ; sometimes turning *Tragedy* 15
into what is *light* and comical, and sporting when I should
be serious. This variety made the travel more easy. And
you know I am not cut out for writing a *Treatise*, nor have
a *genius* to *pen* any thing *exactly* ; so long as I am *true*
to the *main sense* before me, you will pardon me in the 20
rest.

Nor will it, I hope, give offence that I handle these
Tragedies with the same liberty that I formerly had taken
in examining the *Epick Poems* of *Spencer*, *Cowley*, and such
names as will ever be *sacred* to me. *Rapin* tells us, for 25
his own *Countreymen*, that none of them had writ a good
Tragedy, nor was ever like to write one. And an eminent
Italian confesses that the best of theirs exceeded not a
mediocrity[1] ; and yet their *Divine Tasso* had then writ a
Tragedy, and *Torrismo⟨n⟩do* strutted it in *buskins*. 30

But I have elsewhere declar'd my opinion that the *English*
want neither *genius* nor *language* for so great a work. And,
certainly, had our Authors began with Tragedy as *Sophocles*

---

[1] *O sia stata la loro poca fortuna, ò l'imperfezione della nostra
lingua nelle cose gravi. A. Tassone.*

and *Euripides* left it, had they either built on the same
foundation or after their *model*, we might e're this day have
seen Poetry in greater perfection, and boasted such
Monuments of wit as *Greece* or *Rome* never knew in all
5 their *glory*.

ACCORDING to the best account I can gather from
old Authors, Tragedy was originally with the Ancients
a piece of *Religious* worship, a part of their *Liturgy*.   The
Priests sung an Anthem to their god *Dionysus*, whilst the
10 *Goat* [1] stood at his Altar to be *sacrific'd*.   And this was
call'd the *Goat-song*, or *Tragedy*.

These Priests were call'd the *Chorus*, and now the whole
Ceremony was perform'd by them, till *Thespis* introduced
the *Episode* and brought an *Actor* on the Stage.
15   Which *Episode* the Priests at first mutini'd against as an
Innovation ; they listen'd a long while, thought it ran off
from the Text, and wonder'd how it wou'd be appli'd, till
at last their patience could hold no longer, and they roar'd
out, [2] *Nothing to* Dionisus, *nothing to* Dionysus, which gave
20 beginning to the Proverb.

But the *Poet*, gaining upon them by little and little,
enlarged the *Episod* till it grew the *main part*, the *part*
which only is by us call'd the *Tragedy*.   And to make
amends to *Dionysus*, the *Theaters* were all consecrated to
25 him, and the Plays acted *there* call'd *Dionysus*'s *Plays*.

After much new-modelling, many changes and alterations,
Æschylus came with a *second* Actor on the stage, and
lessen'd the business of the *Chorus* proportionably.   But
Sophocles, adding a *third* Actor and *painted* Scenes, gave
30 (in *Aristotle*'s opinion) the utmost *perfection* to Tragedy.

---

[1] *Would therefore read in* Horace, Vilem certavit ad hircum,
as Rhetor dicturus ad aras,—*not being satisfied in Antiquity
with what the Commentators devise when they read,* Vilem certavit
ob hircum.
[2] Οὐδὲν πρὸς Διόνυσον.

And now it was that (the *men* of *sense* grown weary with discoursing of *Atoms* and *empty Space*, and the *humour* of *Mechanical* Philosophy near spent) *Socrates* set up for *Morality*, and all the buz in *Athens* was now about vertue and good life.   5

Camerades with him, and Confederates in his worthy design, were our *Sophocles* and *Euripides* : But these took a different method.

He instructed in a pleasant, facetious manner, by witty *questions, allusions*, and *parables*.   10

These were for teaching by *examples*, in a graver way, yet extremely *pleasant* and *delightful*. And finding in History the same *end* happen to the *righteous* and to the *unjust, vertue* often opprest, and *wickedness* on the Throne, they saw these particular *yesterday-truths* were imperfect and unproper to   15 illustrate the *universal* and *eternal truths* by them intended. Finding also that this *unequal* distribution of rewards and punishments did perplex the *wisest*, and by the *Atheist* was made a scandal to the *Divine Providence*, They concluded that a *Poet* must of necessity see *justice* exactly administred,   20 if he intended to please. For, said they, if the World can scarce be satisfi'd with God Almighty, whose holy will and purposes are not to be *comprehended*, a *Poet*, in these matters, shall never be pardon'd, who, they are sure, is not *incomprehensible*, whose *ways* and *walks* may without *impiety*   25 be penetrated and examin'd. They knew, indeed, that many things naturally unpleasant to the World in *themselves*, yet gave *delight* when well *imitated*.[1] These they consider'd as the picture of some *deform'd* old Woman, that might cause *laughter* or some light, superficial, and   30 *comical* pleasure, but never to be endur'd on serious occasions, where the attention of the mind and where the heart was engaged.

We have pictures that yield another sort of pleasure, as

[1] Aristotle, *Poet.*

the *last Judgment* of *Mich. Angelo*, the *Massacre* of the *Innocents*, the *Baptist*'s head, *&c.*

'Tis true ; but if they yield any pleasure besides what proceeds from the art and what rests in eye, 'Tis by the ₅ History, to which the picture serves only as an *Index*.

For till our memory goes back to the History, the *head* of the *Baptist* can say no more to us than the *head* of *Goliah*. But the Ancients in their Tragedies rested not on History. They found that *History*, grosly taken, was neither ₁₀ proper to *instruct* nor apt to *please* ; and therefore they would not trust History for their examples, but refin'd upon the History, and thence contriv'd something[1] more *philosophical* and more *accurate* than *History*. But whether our *English* Authors of Tragedy lay their foundations so ₁₅ deep, whether they had any *design* in their *designs*, and whether it was to *prudence* or to *chance* that they sacrific'd, is the business of this present enquiry.

.   .   .   .

The business of the *Maids Tragedy* is this :

A MINTOR, *contracted to* Aspatia, Callianax's *Daughter, by the King's command marries* Evadne, *Sister to* ₁₀ Melanthius, *and expects to lye with her* ; *but the Bride, mincing nothing, flatly tells him that he is but taken for a Cloak, that She indeed is a Bedfellow only for the King. The good man is perswaded to dissemble all, till his friend,* Melanthius, *extorts from him the secret, and thereupon hectors his Sister,* ₅ Evadne, *into repentance, and makes her promise to murder the King. Which she effects* ; *in the mean time, by vexing* Callianax, Melanthius *prevails with him to deliver up the Fort wherein consisted the strength of the Kingdom, and so provides for his own security.* Lysimachus, *Brother to the*

---

[1] Σπουδαιότερον καὶ φιλοσοφικότερον.

murder'd King, succeeds on the Throne, and pardons all.
Evadne *would now go to bed with her Husband, he refuses,
she kills her self.*   Aspatia *in mans habit kicks her Sweetheart,*
Amintor, *duels him, and is kill'd ; and now* Amintor *kills
himself to follow her : at which sight his friend,* Melanthius, 5
would also take the same course, but is prevented.

Here we find *Amintor* false to his Mistress ; and this
fault is the source of all the revolutions in this Tragedy.

Amintor therefore should have named the Tragedy, and
some additional title should have hinted the Poet's design. 1

But seeing the *Maid* comes in at the latter end, only, to
be kill'd for company, and seeing the King is the person of
greatest importance, is the greatest loser and concern'd in
the action of the Play more than enough : And seeing that
the new King, *Lysimachus,* in the close of the Tragedy 1
makes this sober conclusion, says he :

> *May this a fair example be to me,*
> *To rule with temper ; for on lustful Kings*
> *Unlookt-for sudden deaths from heaven are. sent ;*
> *But curst is he that is their instrument,—*   2

From these considerations we might gather that the
Poets intent was to show the dismal consequences of *forni-
cation* : And if so, then the Title of the Tragedy should
have related to the King.

Whil'st thus we are uncertain what ought to be the *title,* 2
we may suspect that the *Action* of the Tragedy is *double* ;
where there seem two centers, neither can be right, and
the lines leading towards them must all be false and confus'd;
the *preparation,* I mean, and conduct must be all at random,
since not directed to any one certain end.   3

But what ever the Poet design'd, nothing in *History* was
ever so *unnatural,* nothing in *Nature* was ever so *improbable,*
as we find the whole conduct of this Tragedy,—so far are
we from any thing accurate and Philosophical as Poetry
requires.   3.

This will appear as we examin the particular actions and Characters apart.

Our Poet here gives to the great Comical *Booby, Callianax*, the honour of a long name with a King at th' end on't, yet lets the King himself go without. But since he must be nameless, we may treat him with the greater freedom ; and to tell my mind, certainly God never made a King with so little wit, nor the devil with so little grace, as is this King *Anonymus*.

A King of History might marry his Concubine to another man for a Maid, might deter that man from the enjoyment : But would not then turn them into the bed-chamber to be all night together, nor would come in the morning to interrogate and question him, and torture the soul of him, as we find in this Tragedy, nor would impose it on a husband thus affronted, whom he calls *honest* and *valiant*, to be the pimp to his bride. To have taken *Amintors* head off had been clemency in comparison of these outrages without any cause or colour. And how wise the King was in all this may be judg'd from his own mouth ; finding the husband contented and all quiet, the King, jealous that *Evadne* had not observ'd covenants, thus taxes her :

> *Do not I know the uncontrolled thoughts*
> *That youth brings with him, when his blood is high*
> *With expectation and desire of that*
> *He long had waited for ? is not his spirit,*
> *Though he be temperate, of a valiant strain*
> *As this our age has known ? what could he do,*
> *If such a sudden speech had met his blood,*
> *But ruine thee for ever, if he had not kill'd thee ?*
> *He could not bear it thus ; he is as we,*
> *Or any other wronged man.*

As if he had said : you have, *Evadne*, you have broken Articles with me ; it cannot be otherwise ; for had you kept them, flesh and blood could not endure the affront, and he is such a man as would have cut us all to pieces in revenge. The danger being so cleer and certain, and a thousand safe courses before his nose, why should he stumble on this?—never was a King of History so errant a fool and madman!

In framing a Character for Tragedy, a Poet is not to leave his reason, and blindly abandon himself to follow fancy, for then his fancy might be monstrous, might be singular, and please no body's *maggot* but his own; but reason is to be his guide, reason is common to all people, and can never carry him from what is Natural.

Many are apt to mistake *use* for *nature*, but a Poet is not to be an Historiographer, but a Philosopher; he is not to take *Nature* at the *second hand*, soyl'd and deform'd as it passes in the customes of the unthinking vulgar.

The [1] *Phedra* in *Euripides* told us truly that it is *not Natural to do evil when we know good.* Therefore vice can never please unless it be painted and dress'd up in the colours and disguise of vertue; and should any man knowingly and with open eyes prefer what is evil, he must be reckon'd the greatest of Monsters [2], and in no wise be lookt on as any image of what is Natural, or what is suitable with humane kind.

What is there of the *Heroe*, of Man, or of Nature in these Kings of our Poets framing? And for *Evadne*'s part, did Hell ever give reception to such a Monster, or *Cerberus* ever wag his tayl at an impudence so *sacred*?

On the Wedding night the Bridegroom is cajol'd by her in no better terms than—

> Evad. *A mayden-head*, Amintor, *at my years!—*
> *Alas*, Amintor, *thinkest thou I forbear*
> *To sleep with thee, because I have put on*

---

[1] Καί μοι δοκοῦσιν οὐ κατὰ γνώμης φύσιν
πράσσειν κάκιον.

[2] —— *majus est monstro nefas*
Nam monstra fato, moribus scelera imputes. Sen.

> *A Mayden strictness? look upon these cheeks,*
> *And thou shalt find the hot and rising blood*
> *Unapt for such a vow; no, in this heart*
> *There dwells as much desire, and as much will*
> 5 *To put that wish't act in practice, as ever yet*
> *Was known to woman, and they have been shown*
> *Both; but it was the folly of thy youth*
> *To think this beauty, to what land so e're*
> *It shall be call'd, shall stoop to any second.*
> 10 *I do enjoy the best, and in that height*
> *Have sworn to stand or dye.*

Soon after she tells him:

> *Alas, I must have one*
> *To Father Children, and to bear the name*
> 15 *Of husband to me, that my sin may be*
> *More honourable.*

Hitherto she is bashful; after this the *Scene* is to be *wrought* up, and the next Scene presents her impudence *triumphant*; but I shall trace her duty towards her husband 20 no farther.

Had *Evadne* been the injur'd *Lady's* sister, and had marry'd *Amintor* out of revenge, or had their been any foundation from circumstances for this sort of carriage, the Character then might have been contriv'd plausible enough; 25 but both the Kings behaviour and hers, uncircumstanc'd as we have them, are every way so harsh and against Nature that every thing said by them strikes like a dagger to the souls of any reasonable *audience*.

Whatever persons enter upon the Stage, the Poetry 30 would be gross enough if the audience could not by the *manners* distinguish in what Country the *Scene* lay, whether in *England, Italy,* or *Turky*; more gross would it be if the manners would not discover which were men and which the women.

35 Now Nature knows nothing in the *manners* which so properly and particularly distinguishes woman as doth her

modesty; consonant therefore to our principles, and Poetical, is what some writers of Natural History have reported,—that women when drowned swim with their faces downwards, though men on the contrary.

Tragedy cannot represent a woman without modesty as natural and essential to her.

If a woman has got any accidental historical impudence, if, documented in the School of *Nanna* or *Heloisa*, she is furnish'd with some stock of acquired impudence, she is no longer to stalk in Tragedy on her high shoes, but must rub off and pack down with the Carriers into the *Provence* of Comedy, there to be kickt about and expos'd to laughter.

There are degrees of modesty. *Evadne* and every person feign'd ought to be represented with more modesty then *Phedra* or *Semiramis*, because the History makes it credible that these had less of modesty then Naturally is inherent to the Sex, yet ought these also to show more of modesty then is ordinarily seen in men, that the Characters might still be distinguish'd.

But, of all, the Kings murder is attended with those circumstances, with such a knot of absurdity and injustice, that I well know not where to begin to unravel it.

This King indeed is born a Monster, a Monster of great hopes, and what might we not have expected from him? yet certainly the Poet cuts him off e're ripe for punishment.

And by such unproper means that to remove one guilty person he makes an hundred, and commits the *deadly* sins to punish a *venial* one.

If *Amintors* falshood and its fatal consequences are to be noted, what occasion have we for a King in this Tragedy? cannot *Corydon* deceive his *Amarillis* (for such is *Aspatia*) but the King must know of it, the King must be murder'd for't?

To vex this false man, a Groom might have done the job, and have been the Poets Cuckold-maker to all intents and purposes every jot as well.

If it be said that the King was accessary to the falshood, I question whether in Poetry a King can be an accessary to a crime ; if the King commanded *Amintor, Amintor* should have begg'd the Kings pardon, should have suffer'd
5 all the racks and tortures a Tyrant could inflict, and from *Perillus*'s Bull should have still bellowed out that eternal truth, that his *Promise was to be kept,* that he is true to *Aspatia,* that he dies for his Mistress ; then would his memory have been precious and sweet to after-ages, and
10 the Midsummer-Maydens would have *offer'd* their Garlands all at his grave.

And thus the King might kill *Amintor,* but *Amintor* could not pretend that the King or Fortune had made him false.

> ——*nec si miserum fortuna Sinonem*
15 *Finxit, vanum etiam mendacemque improba finget.*

Therefore, I say, the King was not to blame, or however not so far, as in any wise to render his life obnoxious.

But if the Poet intended to make an example of this King, and that the King right or wrong must be kill'd,
20 *Amintor* only felt the highest provocations, and he alone should have been drawn out for the wicked instrument, for *Melantius* had no reason to be angry at any but at his Sister, *Evadne,* nor could she have any pretence to exercise her hands, unless it were against her self.

25 If I mistake not, in Poetry no woman is to kill a man, except her quality gives her the advantage above him, nor is a Servant to kill the Master, nor a Private Man, much less a Subject, to kill a King, nor on the contrary.

Poetical decency will not suffer death to be dealt to each
30 other by such persons whom the Laws of Duel allow not to enter the lists together.

There may be circumstances that alter the case, as when there is a sufficient ground of partiality in an *Audience,* either upon the account of *Religion* (as *Rinaldo* or *Riccardo,*

in *Tasso,* might kill *Soliman,* or any other *Turkish* King
or great *Sultan*) or else in favour of our *Country,* for then
a private *English Heroe* might overcome a King of some
Rival Nation.

But grant that *Evadne* lies under none of all these im- 5
pediments ; suppose her duly qualifi'd, and let the King
wave his priviledges.   Is there in History any president
of a *Magdalen* sinner that meerly from a fit of repentance
fell foul on her *Gallant* at this horrid rate ?   Indeed,
amongst 'em, they call him *lustful Thief, Devil-King,* 10
shameless Villain, &c.   The *Athenian* Servants were
better bred :

> [1] ὦ μῶρος, εἰ χρὴ δεσπότας εἰπεῖν τόδε.
> *Ah, fool,—if we may term our Masters so!*
> ὄλοιτο μὲν μή· δεσπότης γάρ ἐστ' ἐμός.   15
> *Death take him!   no, he is my Master.*

But, I say, what reason is there for all this outcry ?
What can she lay to the King's charge ?

> *Thou kept'st me brave at Court, and Whor'd me ;*
> *Thou marri'd me to a young noble Gentleman,*   20
> *And whor'd me still.*

The *noble Gentleman* indeed is wrong'd ; but, good
Madam, what reason is there for you to complain ? did
any force or philter overcome you ? was not you as
forward ? did not you freely and heartily consent ? do not 25
we remember your *hot, rising blood,*

> *—Your much desire, and as much will*
> *To put that wish'd act in practise, as ever yet*
> *Was known to Woman?*

Has the King cast you off, or broken articles ? no ; but 30
you repent ? then repent at home ; you may make bold
with your own body, and there let fly your rage and
violence.   For to kill your Lover is no effect or operation

[1] *Euripides.*

of repentance, nor has any ground in nature or reason;
'tis worse than brutish.

But indeed most of our Murderers hitherto have been
no better; they are the Poets Ban-dogs, let loose to worry
5 those the Poet had mark'd out for slaughter, and never
shew more reason or consideration; and consequently can
in no wise occasion either pitty or terror to cause that
delight expected from Tragedy.

In *Epick Poetry* enemies are kill'd; and *Mezentius* must
10 be a wicked Tyrant, the better to set off *Æneas*'s piety.
In Tragedy all the clashing is amongst friends; no *panegyrick*
is design'd, nor ought intended but pitty and terror; and
consequently no shadow of sense can be pretended for
bringing any wicked persons on the Stage. And yet, in
15 that *Mezentius* of *Virgil*, we find more vertue than in all
the characters I have yet examind, and greater occasion
for pitty. We forget all his cruelties when we see that
trouble and infinite passion for his Son *Lausus* (who was
slain in his defence and whom he would not survive) which
20 is so admirably exprest:

> ——*Æstuat ingens,*
> *Imo in corde pudor, mistoque insania luctu,*
> *Et furiis agitatus amor, & conscia virtus, &c.*

Which lines *Tasso*, who translates the whole passage
25 under the names of *Solimano* and *Amiralto* into his
Gerusalemme, thus renders in more words, but not with
more advantage:

> *Ferue in mezzo del cor lo sdegno e l'onta,*
> *E co'l lutto la rabbia e mista insieme,*
> 30 *E da le furie l'agitato amore,*
> *E noto a se medesmo l'empio valore.*

But to return, what yet makes this fact of *Evadne* more
unlikely is that she should be hector'd into a repentance
so pernicious by her Brother, *Melantius*, who is said to be
35 *noble* and *brave*; but from his own mouth we may judg

him a *Heroe*, like those we met with formerly; all his
words are brags; no *Dangerfield* nor Captain *Thundergun*
could sit neer him. And for his manners, after one King
was murder'd by his contrivance, he stands on his guard,
and takes up the next King thus roundly: 5

> Mel. *The short is this,*
> *'Tis no ambition to lift up my self*
> *Urges me thus; I do desire again*
> *To be a Subject, so I may be freed;*
> *If not, I know my strength, and will unbuild* 10
> *This goodly Town; be speedy and be wise*
> *In a reply.*

And now this new King, Brother to the former, as
heroickly throws him a *blank*, and bids him make his own
terms. His words are these: 15

> Lis. Melanthius, *write in that thy choice;*
> *My seal is at it.*

And more to the purpose we find not, in the Tragedy,
of this second King, save only when he concludes the
Play, and tells us that he, for his part, will take warning 20
how ever he meddles with a Woman, as before has been
cited.

Callianax is an old humorous Lord, neither *wise* nor
valiant, as himself confesses, and yet is entrusted with the
strength and keys of the Kingdom, whereas in Comedy he 25
would scarce pass for a good Yeoman of the Cellar.

His Daughter, *Aspatia*, that gives name to this Tragedy,
makes also here a very simple *figure*. Never did *Amintas*
or *Pastor fido* know any thing so tender, nor were the
Arcadian Hills ever water'd with the tears of a creature 30
so innocent. Pretty Lamb! how mournfully it bleats! it
needs no *articulate* voice to move our compassion; it seeks
no shades but under the *dismal Yew*, and browses only on
Willow-garlands; yet it can speak for a kiss or so:

Asp. *I'll trouble you no more, yet I will take*
A parting kiss, and will not be deny'd.
You'l come, my Lord, and with the Virgins weep
When I am laid in earth, though you your self
Can know no pitty. Thus I wind my self
Into this Willow-garland, &c.

At this rate of tattle she runs on, and never knows when she has said enough.

This *Aspatia* is a Lord's Daughter, and bred at Court, yet is in the presence, and in the Bed-chamber, of the Lady that supplants her, and amongst the Bride-maids, where she acts her part, and fawns upon the perjur'd man that forsakes her. And now cannot I be perswaded that there is ought of nature or probability in all this? Much less would I think this a Woman to handle a Sword, and kick *Amintor*, as we see her do soon after. Nor can I conceive wherein consists that *blessing*, as she calls it, which she propos'd to her self, in being kill'd by his hands. This may be *Romance*, but not *Nature*.

And certainly, of all the characters, this of *Amintor* is the most unreasonable. No reason appears why he was contracted to *Aspatia*, and less why he forsook her for *Evadne*; and least of all for his dissembling and bearing so patiently the greatest of provocations that could possibly be given. Certainly no spectacle can be more displeasing than to see a man ty'd to a post, and another buffeting him with an immoderate tongue. Certainly nothing can please a generous mind better than that of *Virgil*,—

Parcere subjectis, & debellare superbos.

Poetry will allow no provocation or injury where it allows no revenge. And what pleasure can there be in seeing a King threaten and hector without cause, when none may be suffer'd to make return? Poetry will not permit an affront where there can be no reparation. But well was it for us all that *Amintor* was by the Poet, his *maker*, endu'd with a restraining grace, and had his hands ty'd.

The King should first have kill'd his own Mother to have made him mad enough and fitted him for such a monstrous provocation. And *Amintor*, too, should have been guilty of some enormous crime (as he is indeed) that drew this curse upon him, and prepar'd him to receive so horrid an out-rage. Both should have been ripe for punishment, which this occasion pulls down upon them, by making them kill each other. Then *Poetical Justice* might have had its course, though no way could pitty be due to either of them.

But surely this character of *Amintor* is [1] inconsistent, and is contradiction all over. He is a man of *Honour*, yet breaks his Faith with his Mistress, bears the greatest of affronts from his Wife that ever was given, and dissembles it. 'Tis true, once or twice he is for singing a *Catch*, for the Fiddle and Dancing, but his countenance is not always set after that copy; he does not always dissemble *scurvily*, for sometimes we have him looking so pleas'd that Comedy would almost be asham'd of such a Cuckold.

He is also honest, and of unshaken loyalty, yet sometimes has such devillish *throws* as would afright any true *liege* people from sitting at a Coffee-house near him.

And all the *passions* in him work so aukwardly, as if he had *suck'd a Sow*. Thus he threatens:

> Am.—*Come to my bed! or by those hairs*
> (*Which, if thou hadst a Soul like to thy locks,*
> *Were threads for Kings to wear about their arms—*
> Evad. *Why, so perhaps they are.*)
> Am. *I'l drag thee to my bed.—*

[1]   —— *Servetur ad imum*
Qualis ab incepto processerit, & sibi constet.

Should not he rather have kick'd her out of doors? And did ever man huff with such a *parenthesis*?

As the *Scene* and provocations work higher, what *Aspatia* might have said to him he whines to *Evadne*:

5   Am. *What a strange thing am I!*
    Evad. *A miserable one, one that my self am sorry for.*
    Am. *Why, shew it then in this:*
    If thou hast pitty, though thy love is none,
    Kill me ; and all true Lovers that shall live
0   *In after-ages crost in their desires,*
    Shall bless thy memory, and call thee good,
    Because such mercy in thy heart was found,
    To rid a lingring Wretch.

Amintor lov'd *Aspatia*, and marri'd *Evadne* only because
5 the King commanded him. We heard nothing of his love to *Evadne* till now, that he is turn'd the amorous *Owf*, when he ought to be all rage and indignation.

When he should be silenc'd, he falls a preaching:

  Am. *Oh, thou hast nam'd a word that wipes away*
20   *All thoughts revengeful! in that sacred name,*
    The King, there lies a terror ; what frail man
    Dares lift his hand against it? let the gods
    Speak to him when they please ; till then, let us suffer
    and wait.

25 This is loyal breath; but presently comes a puff that drives us back to the North of *Scotland*:

  Am.—*And it is some ease*
    To me in these extremes, that I knew this
    Before I touch't thee ; else, had all the sins
30   *Of mankind stood betwixt me and the King,*
    I had gone through 'em to his heart and thine.

Oh, says he, 'tis well its no worse, for had I lain with thee, I should have been all fire and fury; I would not have valu'd twenty Kings, but have kill'd 'em all. Well,
35 *Amintor, de gustibus non est disputandum*, there is difference

betwixt men and men ; some one, peradventure, of a grosser
sense, might have been as cool and well content if he had
been permitted the honour to *touch* for once where his
Majesty had toucht before.   But now the storm is over,
and he proceeds :

>   5
> Am.—*Give me thy hand ;*
> *Be careful of thy credit, and sin close,*
> *'Tis all I wish ; upon my Chamber-floor*
> *I'le rest to night, that morning visiters*
> *May think we did as married people use ;*   10
> *And prithee smile upon me when they come,*
> *And seem to toy, as if thou hadst been pleas'd*
> *With what we did.* Evad. *Fear not, I will do this.*
> Am. *Come, let us practise ; and as wantonly*
> *As ever loving Bride and Bridegroom met,*   15
> *Let's laugh and enter here.* Evad. *I am content.*
> Am. *Down all the swellings of my troubled heart!*
> *When we walk thus entwin'd, let all eyes see*
> *If ever Lovers better did agree.*

See how he concludes, too, to the eternal disgrace of 20
Rhime.   One might think that a man in his *predicament*
should scarce be in a mood to be so very particular, and
enlarge thus upon the subject, unless he were well pleas'd
with the occasion.   Besides, we find here, *Lovers, entic'd,
laugh, Bridegroom, Bride, loving, wantonly, pleas'd, toy,* 25
prethee, did as married people use,—so many pleasant words
and pretty got together, *Longinus* would swear that no
man could be angry at heart with all these in his mouth ;
they ought none of them to be nam'd on the same day with
Evadne and the transactions in this *Tragedy.*   What I have 30
cited is only from the *first Scene* wherein *Amintor* has
business ; nor would I follow him farther, but that, in the
third *Act*, betwixt him and *Melantius* we find the first
occasion for a Tragical passion that yet, I think, these
Plays have afforded us, which arises from the conduct of 35
an Husband who discovers the secret of his Wives
dishonour to his Friend, her Brother.   *Melantius* im-

portunes *Amintor* to tell the cause of his trouble.   When
the matter comes to be broken, they proceed thus :

> Mel. *What is it ?*
> Am. *Why, 'tis this—it is too big*
> *To get out ; let my tears make way awhile.*

Here, I suppose, *Amintor* might better have wept,
without telling it to *Melantius.*

> Mel. *Punish me strangely, Heaven, if he escape,*
> *Of life or fame, that brought this Youth to this !*
> Am. *Your sister—*
> Mel. *Well said.*
> Am. *You'l wish't unknown when you have heard it.*
> Mel. *No.*
> Am. *Is much to blame,*
> *And to the King has given her Honour up—*

This line at the full length is surely enough ; his care is
so to mince that matter as not to offend the Brother. Some
broken speeches, as *your Sister, the King, her honour,* or
the like, with now and then a sprinkling of his tears, might
have suffic'd ; and the Brother should have been left to
guess and paraphrase the broad meaning.   But *Amintor*
harps upon the same string out of time himself.   What
follows is plainly to upbraid and affront his Friend by words,
though he intended nothing less ; for he goes on :

> Am. *And lives in whoredom with him.*

And what yet is more silly, in the next he adds :

> Am. *She's wanton ; I am loath to say, a whore,*
> *Though it be true.*

This provokes *Melantius* to draw his Sword, and he is
for fighting *Amintor ;* yet I am apt to be of *Amintors* mind,
which he thus expresses :

> Am.—*It was base in you*
> *To urge a weighty secret from your Friend,*
> *And then rage at it.*

Yet *Melantius* persists, till *Amintor* is provoked to draw his Sword, and then *Melantius* puts up. *Harlequin* and *Scaramouttio* might do these things. Tragedy suffers 'em not; here is no place for Cowards, nor for giddy fellows and Bullies with their squabbles. When a Sword is once 5 drawn in Tragedy, the Scabbard may be thrown away; there is no leaving what is once design'd till it be thoroughly effected. *Iphigenia Taurica* went to sacrifice *Orestes*, and she desisted; why? she discover'd him to be her Brother. None here are such Fools as by words to begin a quarrel, 10 nor of so little resolution to be talkt agen from it without some new emergent cause that diverts them. No[1] simple alteration of mind ought to produce or hinder any action in a Tragedy.

Yet far more faulty is what follows; the *counter-turn* 15 has no shadow of sense or sobriety. *Melantius* has swaggered away his fury, and now *Amintor* is all agog to be afighting; for what? but to get his secret back again.

> Am.—*Give it me again,*
> *Or I will find it wheresoe're it lies,*   20
> *Hid in the mortall'st part; invent a way to get it back.*

Thou art mad, *Amintor*, Bedlam is the only place for thee; if thou comest here with thy madness, Tragedy expects [2] *ut cum ratione insanias.*

Hercules was mad, and kill'd his Wife and Children, yet 25 there was reason in his madness; a mist was cast before his eyes, he mistook them for their enemies, and believ'd he was revenging their quarrel whilst he beat their brains out. That was a madness might move pity; but this of *Amintor* is meerly bruitish, and can move nothing but 30 our aversion. Here is a bluster begun without provocation, and ended without any thing of satisfaction.

But that I may never find a fault without shewing some-

---

[1] *Arist.*   [2] *Terence.*

thing better,—For a quarrel betwixt two friends, with the *turn* and *counter-turn*, let me commend that Scene in the *Iphigenia* in *Aulide* : Where *Agamemnon* having consented that his Daughter should be sacrific'd, and (that her Mother might let her come the more willingly) sent for her with a pretence that she was to be marri'd to *Achilles*, yet in a fit of Fatherly tenderness he privately despatches Letters to hinder her coming. *Menelaus* meets the Messenger going from *Agamemnon*, suspects the business, takes the Letters from him before *Agamemnon*'s face, and read⟨s⟩ them; and now arose the contest: *Menelaus* was zealous for the publick good, the more because it agreed so much with his own interest, and *Agamemnon* had cause enough to stand up for his Daughter ; but yet, at length, with weeping eyes and shame for his weakness and partiality, he yielded up the cause. But *Menelaus* now seeing the conflict of *Agamemnon*, the tears rowling down his cheeks, and his repentance, this sight melted the heart of him, and now he turns Advocate for *Iphigenia* : He will have *Hellen* and the concerns of *Greece* left to the mercy of Heaven rather than that his Brother, *Agamemnon*, should do so much violence to himself, and that so vertuous a young Princess be trapan'd to lose her life.

Here all the motions arise from occasions great and just, and this is matter for a *Scene* truly passionate and Tragical.

We may remember (how-ever we find this Scene of *Melanthius* and *Amintor* written in the Book) that at the *Theater* we have a good Scene Acted ; there is work cut out, and both our *Æsopus* and *Roscius* are on the Stage together. Whatever defect may be in *Amintor* and *Melanthius*, Mr. *Hart* and Mr. *Mohun* are wanting in nothing. To these we owe for what is pleasing in the Scene ; and to this Scene we may impute the success of the *Maids Tragedy*.

The *Drolls* in this *Play* make not so much noise as in the two former, but are less excusable here. In the former they keep some distance, and make a sort of *interlude*; but here they thrust into the principal places, when we should give our full attention to what is Tragedy. When we would listen to a *Lute*, our ears are rapt with the *tintamar* and twang of the *Tongs* and *Jewstrumps*. A man may be free to make a jest of his own misfortunes, but surely 'tis unnatural and barbarous to laugh when we see another on the Scaffold. Some would laugh to find me mentioning *Sacrifices*, *Oracles*, and *Goddesses*: old Superstitions, say they, not practicable, but more than ridiculous on our Stage. These have not observ'd with what Art *Virgil* has manag'd the Gods of *Homer*, nor with what judgment *Tasso* and *Cowley* employ the heavenly powers in a Christian Poem. The like hints from *Sophocles* and *Euripides* might also be improv'd by modern Tragedians, and something thence devis'd suitable to our Faith and Customes. 'Tis the general reason I contend for: Nor would I more have Oracles or Goddesses on the Stage then hear the persons speak *Greek*; they are Apes and not men that imitate with so little discretion.

Some would blame me for insisting and examining only what is apt to *please*, without a word of what might profit.

1. I believe the end of all Poetry is to *please*.

2. Some sorts of Poetry please without profiting.

3. I am confident whoever writes a Tragedy cannot please but must also profit; 'tis the Physick of the mind that he makes palatable.

And besides the *purging* of the *passions*, something must stick by observing that constant order, that harmony and beauty of Providence, that necessary relation and chain, whereby the causes and the effects, the vertues and rewards, the vices and their punishments are proportion'd and link'd together, how deep and dark soever are laid the Springs and however intricate and involv'd are their operations.

But these enquiries I leave to men of more flegm and consideration.

5 *Othello* comes next to hand, but laying my Papers together without more scribling I find a volumn, and a greater burthen then I dare well obtrude upon you.

If I blindly wander in erroneous paths, 'tis more then time, Mr. *Shepheard*, that you set me right; and if I am
10 not so much out of the way, then most of the main faults in these other Tragedies cannot be far from our view, if we tread not on their skirts already.

I will wait your direction e're I advance farther, and be sure of your pardon for what is past. Many seeming
15 contradictions I rather chose to slip over then to be ever casting in your way some *parenthesis* or some *distinction*.

Many other slips and mistakes too you meet withall, but *the fortune of* Greece *depends not on them.*

Nor, I know, could you, that read Hebrew without the
20 pricks, be at a loss for the sense, where you found not a period truly pointed.

If the Characters I have examin'd are the same I take them for, I send you Monsters enough for one *Bartholmew-fair*; but what would vex a Christian, these are shown us
25 for our own likenesses, these are the *Duch* Pictures of humane kind.

I have thought our Poetry of the last Age as rude as our Architecture; one cause thereof might be that *Aristotle*'s *treatise of Poetry* has been so little studied amongst us; it
30 was perhaps Commented upon by all the great men in *Italy* before we well knew, on this side of the *Alps*, that there was such a Book in being. And though *Horace* comprizes all in that small Epistle of his, yet few will think long enough together to be Masters, and to under-
35 stand the reason, of what is deliver'd so in short.

With the remaining *Tragedies* I shall also send you some reflections on that *Paradise lost* of *Miltons* which some are pleas'd to call a Poem, and assert *Rime* against the slender Sophistry wherewith he attacques it; and also a Narrative of *Petrarch's* Coronation in the *Capitol*, with 5 all the *Pontificalibus* on that occasion, which seems wanting in *Selden* where he treats on that subject. Let me only anticipate a little in behalf of the *Cataline*, and now tell my thoughts, that though the contrivance and œconomy is faulty enough, yet we there find (besides what is borrow'd 10 from others) more of Poetry and of good thought, more of Nature and of Tragedy, then peradventure can be scrap't together from all those other *Plays*.

Nor can I be displeas'd with honest *Ben*, when he rather chooses to borrow a *Melon* of his Neighbour than to treat 15 us with a *Pumpion* of his own growth.

But all is submitted to you Men of better sense by,

SIR,

Your most obliged,
humble Servant, 20
T. Rymer.

III. FROM *A SHORT VIEW OF TRAGEDY, ITS
ORIGINAL, EXCELLENCY, AND CORRUPTION,
WITH SOME REFLECTIONS ON SHAKESPEAR
AND OTHER PRACTITIONERS FOR THE
STAGE*

1693

CHAP. I

The Contents.

The Chorus *keeps the Poet to Rules. A* show *to the Spectators.
Two* Senses *to be pleased. The* Eye, *by the* Show *and by the*
Action. *Plays Acted without Words. Words often better out
of the way. Instances in* Shakespear. Ben Johnson *and* 25
Seneca *Noted. To the* Ear, Pronunciation *is all in all. The*

W HAT Reformation may not we expect, now that in
    France they see the necessity of a *Chorus* to their
Tragedies? *Boyer* and *Racine*, both of the Royal Academy,
15 have led the Dance; they have tried the success in the
last Plays that were Presented by them.

The *Chorus* was the root and original, and is certainly
always the most necessary part, of Tragedy.

The *Spectators* thereby are secured that their Poet shall
20 not juggle, or put upon them in the matter of *Place* and *Time*
other than is just and reasonable for the representation.

And the *Poet* has this benefit: the *Chorus* is a goodly
Show, so that he need not ramble from his Subject, out of
his Wits for some foreign Toy or Hobby-horse to humor
25 the Multitude.

[1]*Aristotle* tells us of *Two Senses* that must be pleas'd, our
Sight and our *Ears*. And it is in vain for a *Poet*, with
Bays in the Rehearsal, to complain of Injustice and the
wrong Judgment in his *Audience*, unless these *Two senses*
30 be gratified.

The worst on it is that most People are wholly led by
these *Two senses*, and follow them upon content, without
ever troubling their Noddle farther.

How many Plays owe all their success to a rare *Show*?
35 Even in the days of *Horace*, enter on the Stage a Person

---

[1] Poetica.

in a *Costly strange Habit*, Lord! *What Clapping, what Noise*
and Thunder, as Heaven and Earth were coming together!
yet not one word spoken.

> *Dixit adhuc aliquid? nil sane: quid placet Ergo?*
> *Lana Tarentino violas imitata veneno.* 5

Was there ought said? troth, no! What then did touch ye?
Some Prince of *Bantham*, or a *Mamamouche*.

It matters not whether there be any *Plot*, any *Characters*,
any *Sense*, or a wise *Word* from one end to the other,
provided in our Play we have the *Senate* of *Rome*, the 10
Venetian Senate in their Pontificalibus, or a *Blackamoor*
Ruffian, or *Tom Dove*, or other Four-leg'd Hero of the
Bear-Garden.

The *Eye* is a quick sense, will be in with our Fancy, and
prepossess the Head strangely. Another means whereby 15
the *Eye* misleads our Judgment is the *Action*. We go to
see a Play *Acted*; in Tragedy is represented a Memorable
Action; so the Spectators are always pleas'd to see *Action*,
and are not often so ill-natur'd to pry into and examine
whether it be Proper, Just, Natural, in season or out of 20
season. *Bays* in the Rehearsal well knew this secret.
The *Two Kings* are at their *Coranto*; nay, the *Moon and
the Earth* dance the *Hey*; any thing in Nature or against
Nature, rather than allow the *Serious Councel* or other dull
business to interrupt or obstruct *Action*. 25

This thing of *Action* finds the blindside of humane-kind
an hundred ways. We laugh and weep with those that
laugh or weep; we gape, stretch, and are very *dotterels* by
example.

Action is speaking to the Eyes; and all *Europe* over, 30
Plays have been represented with great applause in a
Tongue unknown, and sometimes without any Language
at all.

Many, peradventure, of the Tragical Scenes in *Shakespear*,

cry'd up for the *Action*, might do yet better without words. Words are a sort of heavy baggage that were better out of the way at the push of Action, especially in his *bombast Circumstance*, where the Words and Action are seldom akin, generally are inconsistent, at cross purposes, embarrass or destroy each other; yet to those who take not the words distinctly, there may be something in the buz and sound, that, like a drone to a Bagpipe, may serve to set off the *Action*. For an instance of the former, Would not a rap at the door better express *Jago*'s meaning than

> —— *Call aloud.*
> Jago. *Do, with like timerous accent and dire yel*
> *As when, by night and negligence, the fire*
> *Is spied in populous Cities?*

For, What Ship? Who is Arrived? The Answer Is:

> *'Tis one* Jago, *Auncient to the General.*
> *He has had most Favourable and Happy speed;*
> *Tempests themselves, high Seas, and houling Winds,*
> *The guttered Rocks, and congregated Sands,*
> *Traytors ensteep'd to clog the guiltless Keel,*
> *As having sense of Beauty, do omit*
> *Their common Natures, letting go safely by*
> *The divine* Desdemona.

Is this the Language of the Exchange or the Ensuring-Office? Once in a man's life, he might be content at *Bedlam* to hear such a rapture. In a Play one should speak like a man of business; his speech must be Πολιτικός, which the *French* render *Agissante*, the *Italians*, *Negotiosa* and *Operativa*; but by this Gentleman's talk one may well guess he has nothing to do. And he has many Companions that are

> —— *Hey day!*
> *I know not what to do nor what to say.*[1]

It was then a strange imagination in *Ben. Johnson*, to go stuff out a Play with *Tully's* Orations: And in *Seneca*, to

---

[1] Rehearsal.

think his dry Morals and a tedious strain of Sentences might do feats or have any wonderful operation in the *Drama*.

Some go to *see*, others to *hear* a Play. The Poet should please both ; but be sure that the *Spectators* be satisfied, 5 whatever Entertainment he give his Audience.

But if neither the *Show* nor the *Action* cheats us, there remains still a notable vehicle to carry off nonsense, which is the *Pronunciation*.

> *By the loud Trumpet which our Courage aids,* 10
> *We learn, That sound as well as sense perswades.*[1]

Demosthenes[2] had a good stock of Sense, was a great Master of Words, could turn a period, and draw up his tropes in a line of Battel ; and fain would he have seen some effect of his Orations : no body was mov'd, no body 15 minded him. He goes to the Playhouse, bargains with an Actor, and learn'd of him to speak Roundly and Gracefully. From that time, Who but *Demosthenes* ? Never such a leading man ! whenever he spake, no division, not a vote to the contrary, the whole House were with him, *Nemine* 20 *Contradicente*. This change observ'd, a Friend went to him for the secret. Tell me, says he, your *Nostrum*, tell me your Receipt : What is the main Ingredient that makes an Orator ? *Demosthenes* answered, *Pronunciation*. What then the next thing ? *Pronunciation*. Pray, then, What 25 the Third ? Still the answer was *Pronunciation*.

Now this was at *Athens*, where want of Wit was never an objection against them. So that it is not in *Song* only that a *good voice* diverts us from the Wit and Sense. From the Stage, the Bar, or the Pulpit, a *good voice* will 30 prepossess our ears, and, having seized that Pass, is in a fair way to surprise our Judgment.

Considering then what power the *Show*, the *Action*, and

---

[1] Waller. [2] Plutarch, *Demosthen.*

the *Pronunciation* have over us, it is no wonder that wise men often mistake, and give an hasty Judgment, which upon a review is justly set aside.

Horace divides the *Judges* into *Majores Numero* and the
5 few or *better sort* ; and these for the most part were of different Judgments. The like distinction may hold in all other Nations ; only at *Athens* there was a third sort, who were Judges upon [1] Oath, Judges in Commission, by the Government sworn to do right, and determine the Merits
10 of a Play without favour or affection.

But amongst the Moderns never was a Cause canvass'd with so much heat between the Play-Judges as that in *France* about *Corneille*'s Tragedy of the Cid. The *Majority* were so fond of it that with them it became a Proverb,[2] *Cela*
15 *est plus beau que le Cid.* On the other side, Cardinal *Richelieu* damn'd it, and said, *All the pudder about it was only between the ignorant people and the men of judgment.*

Yet this Cardinal with so nice a taste had not many years before been several times to see acted the Tragedy
20 of Sir *Thomas Moor*, and as often wept at the Representation. Never were known so many people crowded to death as at that Play.[3] Yet was it the Manufacture of *Jehan de Serre*, one about the form of our *Flekno* or *Thomas Jordan* : The same *de Serre* that dedicated a Book of
25 Meditations to K. *Charles* I. and went home with Pockets full of Medals and Reward.

By this Instance we see a man the most sharp and of the greatest penetration was imposed upon by these cheating Sences, the Eyes and the Ears, which greedily took in
30 the impression from the *Show*, the *Action*, and from the Emphasis and *Pronunciation*, tho there was no great matter of *Fable*, no *Manners*, no fine *Thoughts*, no *Language* ; that is, nothing of a Tragedy, nothing of a Poet all the while.

---

[1] Plutarch, *Cimon.*   [2] Pelisson, *Hist. Acad.*
[3] *Parnasse Reform.*

Horace was very angry with these empty *Shows* and Vanity, which the Gentlemen of his time ran like mad after.

—— *Insanos oculos, et gaudia vana.*

What would he have said to the *French Opera*, of late so much in vogue ? There it is for you to bewitch your *eyes* [5] and to charm your *ears*. There is a Cup of Enchantment, there is Musick and Machine ; *Circe* and *Calipso* in conspiracy against Nature and good Sense. 'Tis a Debauch the most insinuating and the most pernicious ; none would think an *Opera* and Civil Reason should be the growth of [10] one and the same Climate. But shall we wonder at any thing for a Sacrifice to the *Grand Monarch* ? such Worship, such Idol ! All flattery to him is insipid unless it be prodigious. Nothing reasonable or within compass can come near the Matter. All must be monstrous, enormous, and [15] outragious to Nature, to be like him, or give any Eccho on his Appetite.

Were *Rabelais* alive again, he would look on his *Garagantua* as but a Pygmy.

[1] *The Heroes Race excels the Poets Thought.* [20]

The Academy Royal may pack up their Modes and Methods, *& pensees ingenieuses* ; the *Racines* and the *Corneilles* must all now dance to the Tune of *Baptista*. Here is the *Opera* ; here is *Machine* and *Baptista*, farewell *Apollo* and the Muses ! [25]

Away with your *Opera* from the Theatre ; better had they become the *Heathen* Temples, for the *Corybantian Priests* and (*Semiviros Gallos*) the old *Capons* of *Gaul*, than a People that pretend from *Charlemayn* or descend from the undoubted Loyns of *Germain* and *Norman* Conquerors. [30]

In the *French*, not many years before, was observed the like vicious appetite and immoderate Passion for *vers Burlesque.*

[1] Waller.

They were currant in *Italy* an hundred years ere they passed to this side the *Alps*. But when once they had their turn in *France*, so right to their humour, they over-ran all ;[1] nothing wise or sober might stand in their way.
5 All were possessed with the Spirit of *Burlesk*, from *Doll* in the Dairy to the Matrons at Court and Maids of Honour. Nay, so far went the Frenzy, that no Bookseller wou'd meddle on any terms without *Burlesk* ; insomuch that *Ann.* 1649 was at *Paris* printed a serious Treatise with
10 this Title :

—*La Passion de Nostre Seigneur, En vers Burlesques.*

If we cannot rise to the Perfection of intreigue in *Sophocles*, let us sit down with the honesty and simplicity of the first beginners in Tragedy. As for example :
15 One of the most simple now extant is the *Persians* by *Aeschylus*.

Some ten years after that Darius *had been beaten by the* Greeks, Xerxes (*his Father* Darius *being dead*) *brought against them such Forces by Sea and Land, the like never*
20 *known in History ;* Xerxes *went also in person, with all the* Maison de Roy, Satrapie, and Gendarmery : *all were routed.* Some forty years afterwards the Poet takes hence his subject for a Tragedy.

The Place *is by* Darius's *Tomb, in the Metropolis of* Persia.
25 *The* Time *is the Night, an hour or two before day-break.*

First, on the Stage are seen 15 *Persons in Robes proper for the Satrapa, or Chief Princes in* Persia. *Suppose they met so early at the Tomb, then sacred, and ordinarily resorted to by people troubled in mind, on the accounts of Dreams or*
30 *any thing not boding good. They talk of the state of Affairs : Of* Greece, *and of the Expedition : After some time take upon them to be the* Chorus.

[1] Pelisson, *Histor. Acad.*

The next on the Stage comes Atossa, *the Queen Mother of* Persia ; *she cou'd not lie in Bed for a Dream that troubled her, so in a fit of Devotion comes to her Husband's Tomb, there luckily meets with so many Wise-men and Counsellors to ease her Mind by interpreting her Dream. This, with the* Chorus, *makes the Second Act.*

After this, their Disorder, Lamentation, and Wailing is such that Darius *is disturbed in his Tomb, so his Ghost appears, and belike stays with them till Day-break.* Then the Chorus concludes the Act.

In the Fourth Act come the Messengers with sad Tidings, which, with the reflections and troubles thereupon and the Chorus, *fill out this Act.*

In the Last, Xerxes *himself arrives, which gives occasion of condoling, houling, and distraction enough, to the end of the Tragedy.*

One may imagine how a *Grecian* Audience that lov'd their Countrey, and glory'd in the Vertue of their Ancestors, wou'd be affected by this Representation.

Never appeared on the Stage a Ghost of greater conse- quence. The *Grand Monarch Darius,* who had been so shamefully beaten by those petty Provinces of the United *Grecians,* could not now lye quiet in his Grave for them, but must be raised from the dead again, to be witness of his Son's Disgrace and of their Triumph.

Were a Tragedy after this Model to be drawn for our Stage, *Greece* and *Persia* are too far from us. The Scene must be laid nearer home : As at the *Louvre* ; and instead of *Xerxes* we might take *John,* King of *France,* and the Battel of *Poictiers.* So if the *Germans* or *Spaniards* were to compose a Play on the Battel of *Pavia,* and King *Francis* there taken Prisoner, the Scene shou'd not be laid at *Vienna* or at *Madrid,* but at the *Louvre.* For there the Tragedy wou'd principally operate, and there all the Lines most naturally centre.

But perhaps the memorable Adventure of the *Spaniards*
in 88 against *England* may better resemble that of *Xerxes*.
Suppose, then, a Tragedy call'd The *Invincible Armado*.

The Place, *then, for the Action may be at* Madrid, *by some*
Tomb *or solemn place of resort ; or if we prefer a Turn in it*
from good to bad Fortune, then some Drawing-Room *in the*
Palace near the King's Bed-chamber.

The Time *to begin, Twelve at Night.*

The Scene opening presents 15 *Grandees of* Spain, *with*
their most solemn Beards and Accoutrements, met there
(*suppose*) *after some Ball or other publick occasion. They*
talk of the state of Affairs, the greatness of their Power, the
vastness of their Dominions, and prospect to be infallibly, ere
long, Lords of all. With this prosperity and goodly thoughts
transported, they at last form themselves into the Chorus, *and*
walk such measures, with Musick, as may become the gravity
of such a Chorus.

Then enter two or three of the Cabinet Councel, who now
have leave to tell the Secret, That the Preparations and the
Invincible Armado was to conquer England. *These, with*
part of the Chorus, *may communicate all the Particulars, the*
Provisions, and the Strength by Sea and Land, the certainty
of success, the Advantages by that accession, and the many
Tun of Tar-Barrels for the Hereticks. These Topicks may
afford matter enough, with the Chorus, *for the Second Act.*

In the Third Act, these Gentlemen of the Cabinet cannot
agree about sharing the Preferments of England, *and a*
mighty broil there is amongst them. One will not be content
unless he is King of Man ; *another will be Duke of* Lancaster.
One, that had seen a Coronation in England, *will by all means*
be Duke of Aquitayn, *or else Duke of* Normandy. (And on
this occasion two Competitors have a juster occasion to
work up and shew the Muscles of their Passion then
Shakespear's Cassius and Brutus.) *After, the* Chorus.

The Fourth Act may, instead of Atossa, *present some old*

Dames of the Court, us'd to dream Dreams and to see Sprights, in their Night-Rails and Forhead-Cloaths, to alarm our Gentlemen with new apprehensions, which make distraction and disorders sufficient to furnish out this Act.

In the last Act the King enters, and wisely discourses 5 *against Dreams and Hobgoblins, to quiet their minds. And the more to satisfie them and take off their fright, he lets them to know that St.* Loyala *had appeared to him and assured him that all is well. This said, comes a Messenger of the ill News ; his Account is lame, suspected, he sent to Prison. A* 10 *second Messenger, that came away long after but had a speedier Passage, his account is distinct, and all their loss credited. So, in fine, one of the* Chorus *concludes with that of* Euripides: Thus you see the Gods bring things to pass often otherwise than was by man proposed. 15

In this Draught we see the Fable, and the Characters or Manners of *Spaniards*, and room for fine Thoughts and noble Expressions, as much as the Poet can afford.

The First Act gives a Review or Ostentation of their
    Strength in Battel-array. 20

In the Second, they are in motion for the Attack, and we
    see where the Action falls.

In the Third, they quarrel about dividing the Spoil.

In the Fourth, They meet with a Repulse, are beaten off
    by a Van-Guard of Dreams, Goblins, and Terrors of 25
    the Night.

In the Fifth, They rally under their King in Person, and
    make good their Ground, till overpowered by fresh
    Troops of Conviction, and mighty Truth prevails.

For the First Act, a Painter would draw *Spain* hovering 30
    and ready to strike at the Universe.

In the Second, just taking *England* in her Pounces.

But it must not be forgotten, in the Second Act, that there be some *Spanish-Fryar* or *Jesuit*, as St. *Xaviere* (for he may drop in by miracle any where), to ring in their ears *the* 35

Northern Heresie, like *Jago* in *Shakespear,—Put Money in
thy Purse,* I say, *Put Money in thy Purse.* So often may
he repeat *the Northern Heresie.* Away with your Secular
Advantages ; *I say, the Northern Heresie* ; there is Roast-
5 meat for the Church ; *Voto a Christo, the Northern Heresie.*

If Mr. *Dryden* might try his Pen on this Subject,
doubtless, to an Audience that heartily love their Countrey
and glory in the Vertue of their Ancestors, his imitation of
Aeschylus would have better success, and would *Pit, Box,*
10 and *Gallery,* far beyond any thing now in possession of the
Stage, however wrought up by the unimitable *Shakespear.*

CHAP. V⟨II⟩.

Othello. *More of a piece. In Tragedy, four parts.* Fable, *the
Poets part.* Cinthio's *Novels.* Othello altered *for the worse.
Marriage, absurd, forbidden by* Horace. *Fable of* Othello.
15 *Use and application.* Othello's *Love-powder. High-German
Doctor. Venetians odd taste of things. Their Women fools.
Employ Strangers. Hate the Moors.* Characters. *Nothing of
the Moor in* Othello, *of a Venetian in* Desdemona. *Of a
Souldier in* Jago. *The Souldiers Character by* Horace. *What*
20 *by* Shakespear. Agamemnon. *Venetians no sense of Jealousie.*
Thoughts *in* Othello, *in a Horse or Mastiff more sensibly
exprest. Ill Manners. Outragious to a Nobleman, to Humanity.
Address in telling bad news. In Princes Courts. In* Aristo-
phanes. *In* Rabelais. *Venetian Senate. Their Wisdom.*

25 FROM all the Tragedies acted on our English Stage,
Othello is said to bear the Bell away. The *Subject* is
more of a piece, and there is indeed something like, there
is, at it were, some phantom of a *Fable.* The *Fable* is
always accounted the *Soul* of Tragedy. And it is the
30 *Fable* which is properly the *Poets* part. Because the other
three parts of Tragedy, to wit, the *Characters* are taken
from the Moral Philosopher ; the *thoughts,* or sence, from

them that teach *Rhetorick* : And the last part, which is the *expression*, we learn from the Grammarians.

This Fable is drawn from a Novel compos'd in Italian by *Giraldi Cinthio*, who also was a Writer of Tragedies : And to that use employ'd such of his Tales as he judged 5 proper for the Stage. But with this of the *Moor* he meddl'd no farther.

Shakespear alters it from the Original in several particulars, but always, unfortunately, for the worse. He bestows a name on his *Moor*, and styles him the Moor of 10 *Venice*,—a Note of pre-eminence which neither History nor Heraldry can allow him. *Cinthio*, who knew him best, and whose creature he was, calls him simply a *Moor*. We say the Piper of *Strasburgh*, the Jew of *Florence* : And, if you please, the Pindar of *Wakefield* ;—all upon Record, and 15 memorable in their Places. But we see no such Cause for the *Moors* preferment to that dignity. And it is an affront to all Chroniclers and Antiquaries to top upon 'um a *Moor*, with that mark of renown, who yet had never faln within the Sphere of their Cognisance. 20

Then is the Moors *Wife*, from a simple Citizen in *Cinthio*, dress'd up with her Top knots, and rais'd to be *Desdemona*, a Senators Daughter. All this is very strange ; And therefore pleases such as reflect not on the improbability. This match might well be without the Parents 25 Consent. Old *Horace* long ago forbad the Banes :

> *Sed non ut placidis Coeant immitia, non ut*
> *Serpentes avibus geminentur, tigribus agni.*

The Fable.

Othello, *a Blackmoor Captain, by talking of his Prowess and Feats of War, makes* Desdemona, *a* 30 *Senators Daughter, to be in love with him, and to be married to him without her Parents knowledge ; And having preferred*

Cassio *to be his Lieutenant, a place which his Ensign,* Jago, *sued for,* Jago *in revenge works the Moor into a Jealousy that* Cassio *Cuckolds him,—which he effects by stealing and conveying a certain Handkerchief which had at the Wedding been*
5 *by the Moor presented to his Bride. Hereupon* Othello *and* Jago *plot the Deaths of* Desdemona *and* Cassio. Othello *Murders her, and soon after is convinced of her Innocence. And as he is about to be carried to Prison in order to be punish'd for the Murder, He kills himself.*

10 What ever rubs or difficulty may stick on the Bark, the Moral, sure, of this Fable is very instructive.

First, This may be a caution to all Maidens of Quality how, without their Parents consent, they run away with Blackamoors.

15 *Di non si accompagnare con huomo cui la natura & il cielo & il modo della vita disgiunge da noi.*—Cinthio.

Secondly, This may be a warning to all good Wives that they look well to their Linnen.

Thirdly, This may be a lesson to Husbands that before
20 their Jealousie be Tragical the proofs may be Mathematical.

Cinthio affirms that *She was not overcome by a Womanish Appetite, but by the Vertue of the Moor.* It must be a good-natur'd Reader that takes *Cinthio*'s word in this case, tho'
25 in a Novel. *Shakespear,* who is accountable both to the *Eyes* and to the *Ears,* And to convince the very heart of an Audience, shews that *Desdemona* was won by hearing *Othello* talk.

Othello.—*I spake of most disastrous chances,*
30 *Of Moving accidents by flood and field,*
Of hair-breadth scapes i' th' imminent deadly breach,
Of being taken by the insolent foe,
And sold to slavery, of my redemption thence,
And portents in my Travels History;
35 *Wherein of Antars vast and Desarts idle,*
Rough Quarries, Rocks, and Hills whose heads touch Heaven,

> *It was my hint to speak,—such was my process;*
> *And of the* Cannibals *that each others eat,*
> *The* Anthropophagi, *and men whose heads*
> *Do grow beneath their shoulders.—*

This was the Charm, this was the philtre, the love-powder, 5
that took the Daughter of this Noble Venetian. This was
sufficient to make the Black-amoor White, and reconcile
all, tho' there had been a Cloven-foot into the bargain.

A meaner woman might be as soon taken by *Aqua
Tetrachymagogon*. 10

Nodes, Cataracts, Tumours, Chilblains, Carnosity,
Shankers, or any *Cant* in the Bill of an High-German
Doctor is as good *fustian Circumstance*, and as likely
to charm a Senators Daughter. But, it seems, the noble
Venetians have an other sence of things. The *Doge* him- 15
self tells us:

> Doge. *I think this Tale wou'd win my Daughter too.*

Horace tells us:

> *Intererit Multum* ————
> *Colchus an Assyrius, Thebis nutritus an Argis.* 20

Shakespear in this Play calls 'em the *supersubtle Venetians*.
Yet examine throughout the Tragedy, there is nothing in
the noble *Desdemona* that is not below any Countrey
Chamber-maid with us.

And the account he gives of their Noblemen and Senate 25
can only be calculated for the latitude of *Gotham*.

The Character of that State is to employ strangers in
their Wars: But shall a Poet thence fancy that they will
set a Negro to be their General, or trust a *Moor* to defend
them against the *Turk*? With us a Black-amoor might 30
rise to be a Trumpeter; but *Shakespear* would not have
him less than a Lieutenant-General. With us a *Moor*
might marry some little drab or Small-coal Wench; *Shakespear* would provide him the Daughter and Heir of some

great Lord or Privy-Councellor : And all the Town should reckon it a very suitable match.   Yet the English are not bred up with that hatred and aversion to the *Moors* as are the Venetians, who suffer by a perpetual Hostility from
5 them,—

Littora littoribus contraria.

Nothing is more odious in Nature than an improbable lye ; And certainly never was any Play fraught like this of *Othello* with improbabilities.

10   The *Characters* or Manners, which are the second part in a Tragedy, are not less unnatural and improper than the Fable was improbable and absurd.

Othello is made a Venetian General.   We see nothing done by him nor related concerning him that comports
15 with the condition of a General, or indeed of a Man, unless the killing himself to avoid a death the Law was about to inflict upon him.   When his Jealousy had wrought him up to a resolution of 's taking revenge for the suppos'd injury, He sets *Jago* to the fighting part to kill *Cassio* ;   And
20 chuses himself to murder the silly Woman his Wife, that was like to make no resistance.

His Love and his Jealousie are no part of a Souldiers Character, unless for Comedy.

But what is most intolerable is *Jago*.   He is no Black-
25 amoor Souldier, so we may be sure he should be like other Souldiers of our acquaintance ; yet never in Tragedy, nor in Comedy, nor in Nature, was a Souldier with his Character ; take it in the Authors own words :

Em. —— *some Eternal Villain,*
30   *Some busie and insinuating Rogue,*
   Some cogging, couzening Slave, to get some Office.

Horace Describes a Souldier otherwise :

Impiger, iracundus, inexorabilis, acer.

Shakespear knew his Character of *Jago* was inconsistent. In this very Play he pronounces :

> *If thou dost deliver more or less than Truth,*
> *Thou art no Souldier.*

This he knew ; but to entertain the Audience with some- thing new and surprising, against common sense and Nature he would pass upon us a close, dissembling, false, insinuating rascal instead of an open-hearted, frank, plain-dealing Souldier, a character constantly worn by them for some thousands of years in the World.

[1] *Tiberius Caesar* had a Poet Arraign'd for his Life, because *Agamemnon* was brought on the Stage by him with a character unbecoming a Souldier.

Our *Ensigns* and Subalterns, when disgusted by the Captain, throw up their Commissions, bluster, and are bare-fac'd. *Jago*, I hope, is not brought on the Stage in a Red-Coat. I know not what Livery the Venetians wear, but am sure they hold not these conditions to be *alla soldatesca*.

Non sia egli per far la vendetta con insidie, ma con la spada in mano. Cinthio.

Nor is our Poet more discreet in his *Desdemona*. He had chosen a Souldier for his Knave ; And a Venetian Lady is to be the Fool.

This Senators Daughter runs away to a Carriers Inn, the *Sagittary*, with a Black-amoor ; is no sooner wedded to him, but the very night she Beds him is importuning and teizing him for a young smock-fac'd Lieutenant, *Cassio*. And tho' she perceives the *Moor* Jealous of *Cassio*, yet will she not forbear, but still rings *Cassio, Cassio*, in both his Ears.

Roderigo is the Cully of *Jago*, brought in to be murder'd by *Jago*, that *Jago's* hands might be the more in Blood,

---

[1] *Sueton.* in Tib.

and be yet the more abominable Villain : who without that was too wicked on all Conscience ; And had more to answer for than any Tragedy or Furies could inflict upon him. So there can be nothing in the *characters*, either for
5 the profit or to delight an Audience.

The third thing to be consider'd is the *Thoughts*. But from such *Characters* we need not expect many that are either true, or fine, or noble.

And without these, that is, without sense or meaning,
10 the fourth part of Tragedy, which is the *expression*, can hardly deserve to be treated on distinctly. The verse rumbling in our Ears are of good use to help off the action.

In the *Neighing* of an Horse, or in the *growling* of a
15 Mastiff, there is a meaning, there is as lively expression, and, may I say, more humanity, than many times in the Tragical flights of *Shakespear*.

Step then amongst the Scenes to observe the Conduct in this Tragedy.
20 The first we see are *Jago* and *Roderigo*, by Night in the Streets of *Venice*. After growling a long time together, they resolve to tell *Brabantio* that his Daughter is run away with the Black-a-moor. *Jago* and *Roderigo* were not of quality to be familiar with *Brabantio*, nor had any
25 provocation from him to deserve a rude thing at their hands. *Brabantio* was a Noble Venetian, one of the Sovereign Lords and principal persons in the Government, Peer to the most Serene *Doge*, one attended with more state, ceremony, and punctillio than any English Duke or
30 Nobleman in the Government will pretend to. This misfortune in his Daughter is so prodigious, so tender a point, as might puzzle the finest Wit of the most *supersubtle* Venetian to touch upon it, or break the discovery to her Father. See then how delicately *Shakespear* minces the
35 matter :

Rod. *What ho*, Brabantio, *Signior* Brabantio, *ho*!
Jago. *Awake! what ho*, Brabantio! *Thieves, thieves,*
thieves!
Look to your House, your Daughter, and your Bags.
Thieves, thieves!   5

Brabantio at a Window.

Bra. *What is the reason of this terrible summons?*
What is the matter there?
Rod. *Signior, is all your Family within?*
Jago. *Are your Doors lockt?*   10
Bra. *Why, wherefore ask you this?*
Jago. *Sir, you are robb'd; for shame, put on your*
Gown;
Your Heart is burst, you have lost half your Soul;
Even now, very now, an old black Ram   15
Is tupping your white Ewe: arise, arise,
Awake the snorting Citizens with the Bell,
Or else the Devil will make a Grandsire of you: arise,
I say.

Nor have they yet done; amongst other ribaldry, they 20
tell him:

Jago. *Sir, you are one of those that will not serve God,*
if the Devil bid you; because we come to do you service,
you think us Ruffians, you 'le have your Daughter covered
with a Barbary Stallion. You 'le have your Nephews neigh 25
to you; you 'le have Coursers for Cousins, and Gennets for
Germans.
Bra. *What prophane wretch art thou?*
Jago. *I am one, Sir, that come to tell you, your Daughter*
and the Moor are now making the Beast with two backs.   30

In former days there wont to be kept at the Courts of
Princes some body in a Fools Coat, that in pure simplicity
might let slip something which made way for the ill news,
and blunted the shock, which otherwise might have come
too violent upon the party.   35

Aristophanes puts *Nicias* and *Demosthenes* in the disguise
of Servants, that they might, without indecency, be Drunk;
And Drunk he must make them that they might without

reserve lay open the *Arcana* of State, And the Knavery
of their *Ministers*.

After King *Francis* had been taken Prisoner at *Pavia*,
Rabelais tells of a Drunken bout between *Gargantua* and
5 Fryer *John*, where the valiant Fryer, bragging over his
Cups, amongst his other flights, says he, *Had I liv'd in the
days of Jesus Christ, I would ha' guarded* Mount Olivet *that
the Jews should never ha' tane him. The Devil fetch me, if I
would not have ham string'd those Mr. Apostles, that after*
10 *their good Supper ran away so scurvily and left their Master
to shift for himself. I hate a Man should run away, when he
should play at sharps. Pox on 't, that I shou'd not be King
of* France *for an hundred years or two. I wou'd curtail all
our French Dogs that ran away at* Pavia.

15 This is address, this is truly Satyr, where the preparation
is such that the thing principally design'd falls in as it only
were of course.

But *Shakespear* shews us another sort of address; his
manners and good breeding must not be like the rest of the
20 Civil World. *Brabantio* was not in Masquerade, was not
incognito ; *Jago* well knew his rank and dignity.

> Jago. The Magnifico *is much beloved,*
> *And hath in his effect a voice potential*
> *As double as the Duke.*——

25 But besides the Manners to a *Magnifico*, humanity cannot
bear that an old Gentleman in his misfortune should be
insulted over with such a rabble of Skoundrel language,
when no cause or provocation. Yet thus it is on our
Stage; this is our School of good manners, and the
30 *Speculum Vitæ*.

But our *Magnifico* is here in the dark, nor are yet his
Robes on : attend him to the Senate house, and there see
the difference, see the effects of Purple.

So, by and by, we find the Duke of *Venice*, with his
35 Senators in Councel, at Midnight, upon advice that the

Turks, or Ottamites, or both together, were ready in transport Ships, put to Sea, in order to make a Descent upon
Cyprus.   This is the posture when we see *Brabantio* and
Othello join them.   By their Conduct and manner of talk,
a body must strain hard to fancy the Scene at *Venice*; And 5
not rather in some of our Cinq-ports, where the Baily and
his Fisher-men are knocking their heads together on
account of some Whale, or some terrible broil upon the
Coast.   But to shew them true Venetians, the Maritime
affairs stick not long on their hand; the publick may sink 10
or swim.   They will sit up all night to hear a Doctors
Commons, Matrimonial Cause: And have the Merits of
the Cause at large laid open to 'em, that they may decide
it before they Stir.   What can be pleaded to keep awake
their attention so wonderfully?   15

Never, sure, was *form* of *pleading* so tedious and so
heavy as this whole Scene and midnight entertainment.
Take his own words; says the *Respondent*:

> Oth. *Most potent, grave, and reverend Signiors,*
> *My very noble and approv'd good Masters :*   20
> *That I have tane away this old mans Daughter,*
> *It is most true ; true, I have Married her ;*
> *The very front and head of my offending*
> *Hath this extent, no more : rude I am in my speech,*
> *And little blest with the set phrase of peace ;*   25
> *For since these Arms of mine had seven years pith,*
> *Till now some nine Moons wasted, they have us'd*
> *Their dearest action in the Tented Field ;*
> *And little of this great World can I speak*
> *More than pertains to Broils and Battail ;*   30
> *And therefore little shall I grace my Cause*
> *In speaking of my self ; yet by your gracious patience,*
> *I would a round unravish'd Tale deliver,*
> *Of my whole course of love, what drags, what charms,*
> *What Conjuration, and what mighty Magick,*   35
> *(for such proceedings am I charg'd withal)*
> *I won his Daughter.*

All this is but *Preamble* to tell the Court that He wants words. This was the Eloquence which kept them up all Night, and drew their attention in the midst of their alarms.

5   One might rather think the novelty and strangeness of the case prevail'd upon them : no, the Senators do not reckon it strange at all. Instead of starting at the Prodigy, every one is familiar with *Desdemona* as he were her own natural Father, rejoice in her good fortune, and wish their own several Daughters as hopefully married. Should the Poet have provided such a Husband for an only Daughter of any noble Peer in *England*, the Black-amoor must have chang'd his Skin to look our House of Lords in the Face.

Æschylus is noted in *Aristophanes* for letting *Niobe* be two or three *Acts* on the Stage before she speaks. Our Noble Venetian, sure, is in the other more unnatural extreme. His words flow in abundance ; no Butter-Quean can be more lavish. Nay, he is for talking of State-Affairs, too, above any body :

    Bra. *Please it your Grace, on to the state Affairs.—*

Yet is this *Brabantio* sensible of his affliction ; before the end of the Play his Heart breaks, he dies.

    Gra. *Poor* Desdemona, *I am glad thy Father's dead ;*
    Thy match was mortal to him, and pure grief
    Shore his old thread in twain.——

A third part in a Tragedy is the *Thoughts*: from Venetians, Noblemen, and Senators we may expect fine *Thoughts*. Here is a tryal of skill : for a parting blow, the *Duke* and *Brabantio* Cap *sentences*. Where then shall we seek for the *Thoughts*, if we let slip this occasion ? says the Duke :

    Duk. *Let me speak like your self, and lay a* Sentence
    Which, like a greese or step, may help these lovers
    Into your favour.

When remedies are past, the grief is ended
By seeing the worst, which late on hopes depended.
To mourn a mischief that is past and gone
Is the next way to draw more mischief on;
What cannot be preserv'd when Fortune takes,   5
Patience her injury a Mocker makes.
The rob'd that smiles steals something from a Thief;
He robs himself that spends an hopeless grief.
    Bra. *So let the Turk of* Cyprus *us beguile;*
We lose it not so long as we can smile.   10
He bears the sentence well, that nothing bears
But the free comfort which from thence he hears;
But he bears both the sentence and the sorrow,
That to pay grief must of poor patience borrow:
These Sentences, *to Sugar or to Gall,*   15
Being strong on both sides, are equivocal.
But words are words; I never yet did hear
That the bruis'd Heart was pierced through the Ear.
Beseech you, now to the affairs of State.

How far wou'd the Queen of *Sheba* have travell'd to hear 20
the Wisdom of our Noble Venetians? or is not our [1]*Brent-*
ford a *Venetian* Colony, for methinks their talk is the very
same?

What says Prince *Volscius*?

    Volscius. *What shall I do, what conduct shall I find* 25
To lead me through this twy light of my mind?

What says *Amaryllis*?

    Ama. *I hope its slow beginning will portend*
A forward exit *to all future end.*

What says Prince *Pretty-man*?   30

    Pre. *Was ever Son yet brought to this distress,*
To be, for being a Son, made Fatherless?
Ah, you just Gods, rob me not of a Father,
The being of a Son take from me rather.

Panurge, sadly perplexed, and trying all the means in 35

---

[1] Rehearsal.

the World to be well advised in that knotty point *whether
he should Marry or no,* Amongst the rest consults *Raminigrobis,* an old Poet, as one belonging to *Apollo,* And from
whom he might expect something like an Oracle.   And he
5 was not disappointed.   From *Raminigrobis* he had this
Answer :

> *Prenez la, ne la prenez pas.*
> *Si vous la prenez, c'est bien faict.*
> *Si ne la prenez en effect,*
> 10 *Ce sera œuuré par compas.*
> *Guallopez, mais allez le pas.*
> *Recullez, entrez y de faict.*
> > *Prenez-la, ne.*
>
> *Take, or not take her, off or on :*
> 15 *Handy dandy is your Lot.*
> *When her name you write, you blot.*
> *'Tis undone when all is done,*
> *Ended ere it is begun.*
> *Never Gallop whilst you Trot;*
> 20 *Set not forward when you run,*
> *Nor be single, tho' alone.*
> *Take, or not take her, off or on.*

What provocation or cause of malice our Poet might
have to Libel the most *Serene Republick* I cannot tell ; but
25 certainly there can be no wit in this representation.

For the *second Act,* our Poet, having dispatcht his affairs
at *Venice,* shews the Action next (I know not how many
leagues off) in the Island of *Cyprus.*   The Audience must
be there too :   And yet our *Bays* had it never in his head
30 to make any provision of Transport Ships for them.

In the days that the *Old Testament* was Acted in *Clerken-
well* by the *Parish Clerks* of *London,* the Israelites might
pass through the *Red sea* ; but alas, at this time, we have
no *Moses* to bid the Waters *make way* and to Usher us
35 along.   Well, the absurdities of this kind break no Bones.
They may make Fools of us, but do not hurt our Morals.

Come a shoar then, and observe the Countenance of the

People, after the dreadful Storm, and their apprehensions from an Invasion by the Ottomites, their succour and friends scatter'd and tost, no body knew whither. The first that came to Land was *Cassio*; his first Salutation to the Governour, *Montanio*, is: 5

> Cas. *Thanks to the valiant of this Isle,*
> *That so approve the Moor, and let the Heavens*
> *Give him defence against their Elements,*
> *For I have lost him on the dangerous Sea.*

To him the Governour speaks, indeed, like a Man in his 10 wits.

> Mont. *Is he well Shipt?*

The Lieutenant answers thus:

> Cas. *His Bark is stoutly Tymber'd, and his Pilot*
> *Of very expert and approv'd allowance;*   15
> *Therefore my hopes (not surfeited to death)*
> *Stand in bold care.*

The Governours first question was very proper; his next question, in this posture of affairs, is:

> Mont. *But, good Lieutenant, is our general Wiv'd?* 20

A question so remote, so impertinent and absurd, so odd and surprising never entered *Bayes's Pericranium*. Only the answer may Tally with it:

> Cas. *Most fortunately, he hath atcheiv'd a Maid,*
> *That Parragons description and wild fame:*   25
> *One that excels the quirks of blasoning Pens,*
> *And in the essential vesture of Creation,*
> *Does bear an excellency.* ——

They who like this Authors writing will not be offended to find so much repeated from him. I pretend not here to 30 tax either the *Sense* or the *Language*; those *Circumstances* had their proper place in the Venetian Senate. What I now cite is to shew how probable, how natural, how reasonable the Conduct is all along.

I thought it enough that *Cassio* should be acquainted
with a Virgin of that rank and consideration in *Venice* as
Desdemona. I wondred that in the Senate-house every one
should know her so familiarly; yet here also at *Cyprus*,
5 every body is in a rapture at the name of *Desdemona*, except
only *Montanio*, who must be ignorant, that *Cassio*, who has
an excellent cut in shaping an Answer, may give him the
satisfaction:

  Mont. *What is she?*
10 Cas. *She that I spoke of, our Captains Captain,*
Left in the Conduct of the bold Jago ;
Whose footing here anticipates our thoughts
A Sennets speed: great Jove, Othello *guard,*
And swell his Sail with thine own powerful breath,
15 *That he may bless this Bay with his Tall Ship,*
And swiftly come to Desdemona's *Arms,*
Give renewed fire to our extincted Spirits,
And bring all Cyprus *comfort.*

   Enter Desdemona, &c.
   O behold,
20 *The riches of the Ship is come on shoar!*
Ye men of Cyprus, *let her have your Knees.*
Hail to the Lady! and the Grace of Heaven,
Before, behind thee, and on every hand,
Enwheel the round!

25 In the name of phrenzy, what means this Souldier? or
would he talk thus, if he meant any thing at all? Who can
say *Shakespear* is to blame in his *Character* of a Souldier?
Has he not here done him reason? When cou'd our
Tramontains talk at this rate? but our *Jarsey* and *Garnsey*
30 Captains must not speak so fine things, nor compare with
the Mediterranean, or Garisons in *Rhodes* and *Cyprus*.

 The next thing our Officer does is to salute *Jago's* Wife,
with this *Conge* to the Husband:

  Cas. *Good Ancient, you are welcome; welcome, Mistriss:*
35 *Let it not Gall your Patience, good* Jago,

That I extend my Manners; 'tis my Breeding
That gives me this bold shew of Curtesy.
   Jago. *Sir, would she give you so much of her lips,*
As of her tongue she has bestow'd on me,
You'd have enough.   5
   Des. *Alass! she has no speech.*

Now follows a long rabble of Jack-pudden farce between
Jago and *Desdemona*, that runs on with all the little plays,
jingle, and trash below the patience of any Countrey
Kitchin-maid with her Sweet-heart.   The Venetian *Donna* 10
is hard put to 't for pastime !   And this is all when they
are newly got on shoar from a dismal Tempest, and when
every moment she might expect to hear her Lord (as she
calls him), that she runs so mad after, is arriv'd or lost :
And moreover,   15

            —In a Town of War,
      —The peoples Hearts brimful of fear.

Never in the World had any Pagan Poet his Brains turn'd
at this Monstrous rate.   But the ground of all this Bedlam-
Buffoonery we saw in the case of the French *Strolers*; the 20
Company for Acting *Christs Passion* or the *Old Testament*
were Carpenters, Coblers, and illiterate fellows, who found
that the Drolls and Fooleries interlarded by them brought
in the rabble and lengthened their tune, so they got Money
by the bargain.   25
   Our *Shakespear*, doubtless, was a great Master in this
craft.   These Carpenters and Coblers were the guides he
followed.   And it is then no wonder that we find so much
farce and *Apocryphal Matter* in his Tragedies :   Thereby
un-hallowing the Theatre, profaning the name of Tragedy; 30
And instead of representing Men and Manners, turning all
Morality, good sence, and humanity into mockery and
derision.
   But pass we to something of a more serious air and
Complexion.   *Othello* and his Bride are the first Night no 35

sooner warm in Bed together, but a Drunken Quarrel
happening in the Garison, two Souldiers Fight, And the
General rises to part the Fray.   He swears :

    Othel. *Now, by Heaven,*
5 *My blood begins my safer guides to rule,*
And passion, having my best judgment cool'd,
Assays to lead the way ; if once I stir,
Or do but lift this arm, the best of you
Shall sink in my rebuke : give me to know
10 *How this foul rout began, who set it on,*
And he that is approv'd in this offence,
Tho' he had twin'd with me, both at a birth,
Should lose me : what, in a Town of War,
Yet wild, the peoples Hearts brimful of fear,
15 *To manage private and domestick quarrels,*
In Night, and on the Court and guard of safety,
'Tis Monstrous ; Jago, *who began ?*

In the days of yore Souldiers did not swear in this
fashion.   What should a Souldier say farther when he
20 swears, unless he blaspheme ? action shou'd speak the
rest.   What follows must be *ex ore gladii* :   He is to rap
out an Oath, not Wire-draw and Spin it out : by the style
one might judge that *Shakespears* Souldiers were never
bred in a Camp, but rather had belong'd to some Affidavit-
25 Office.   Consider also, throughout this whole Scene, how
the Moorish General proceeds in examining into this
Rout : No Justice *Clod-pate* could go on with more Phlegm
and deliberation.   The very first night that he lyes with
the *Divine Desdemona* to be thus interrupted might provoke
30 a Mans Christian Patience to swear in another style.   But
a Negro General is a Man of strange Mettle.   Only his
Venetian Bride is a match for him.   She understands that
the Souldiers in the Garison are by th' ears together : And
presently she, at midnight, is in amongst them.

35   Desd. *What's the matter there ?*
    Othel. *All's well now, Sweeting.*
Come away to Bed.

In the beginning of this *second Act*, before they had lain together, *Desdemona* was said to be *our Captains Captain*. Now they are no sooner in Bed together, but *Jago* is advising *Cassio* in these words :

> Jago. —— *Our Generals Wife is now the General ; I* *may say so in this respect, for that he hath devoted and given up himself to the contemplation, mark, and devotement of her parts and graces. Confess your self freely to her, importune her ; she'll help to put you in your place again : she is so free, so kind, so apt, so blessed a disposition, that she holds it a vice in her goodness not to do more than she is requested. This broken joint between you and her Husband, intreat her to splinter.*——

And he says afterwards :

> Jago. —— *'Tis most easie*
> *The inclining* Desdemona *to subdue*
> *In any honest suit. She's fram'd as fruitful*
> *As the free Elements : And then for her*
> *To win the Moor, were 't to renounce his Baptism,*
> *All seals and symbols of redeemed sin,*
> *His soul is so enfetter'd to her love*
> *That she may make, unmake, do what she list ;*
> *Even as her appetite shall play the God*
> *With his weak function.*——

This kind of discourse implies an experience and long conversation, the Honey-Moon over, and a Marriage of some standing. Would any man in his wits talk thus of a Bridegroom and Bride the first night of their coming together ?

Yet this is necessary for our Poet ; it would not otherwise serve his turn. This is the source, the foundation of his Plot, hence is the spring and occasion for all the Jealousie and bluster that ensues.

Nor are we in better circumstances for *Roderigo*. The last thing said by him in the former *Act* was :

> Rod. —— *I'll go sell all my Land.*

A fair Estate is sold to *put money in his Purse* for this adventure.   And lo, here, the next day :

> Rod. *I do follow here in the Chace, not like a Hound*
> *that hunts, but one that fills up the cry.   My Money is*
> *almost spent.   I have been tonight exceedingly well cudgell'd.*
> *I think the issue will be, I shall have so much experience for*
> *my pains, and so no Money at all, and with a little more*
> *wit return to* Venice.

The Venetian squire had a good riddance for his Acres. The Poet allows him just time to be once drunk, a very conscionable reckoning !

In this *Second Act*, the face of affairs could in truth be no other than

> ———*In a Town of War,*
> *Yet wild, the peoples Hearts brim ful of fear.*

But nothing, either in this *Act* or in the rest that follow, shew any colour or complexion, any resemblance or proportion to that face and posture it ought to bear.   Should a Painter draw any one *Scene* of this Play, and write over it, *This is a Town of War*, would any body believe that the Man were in his senses ?   would not a *Goose* or *Dromedary* for it be a name as just and suitable?   And what in Painting would be absurd can never pass upon the World for Poetry.

Cassio, having escaped the Storm, comes on shoar at *Cyprus*, that night gets Drunk, Fights, is turn'd out from his Command, grows sober again, takes advice how to be restor'd, is all Repentance and Mortification ; yet, before he sleeps, is in the Morning at his Generals door with a noise of Fiddles, and a Droll to introduce him to a little Mouth-speech with the Bride.

> Cassio. *Give me advantage of some brief discourse*
> *With* Desdemona *alone.*
> Em. *Pray you come in ;*
> *I will bestow you where you shall have time*
> *To speak your bosom freely.*

So they are put together. And when he had gone on a good while *speaking his bosom, Desdemona* answers him :

> **Des.** *Do not doubt that, before* Emilia *here,*
> *I give thee warrant of thy place ; assure thee,*
> *If I do vow a friendship, I'll perform it*   5
> *To the last article.——*

Then, after a ribble rabble of fulsome impertinence, She is at her Husband slap dash :

> Desd. —— *Good love, call him back.*
> Othel. *Not now, sweet* Desdemona, *some other time.* 10
> Desd. *But shall 't ⟨be⟩ shortly ?*
> Othel. *The sooner, sweet, for you.*
> Desd. *Shall 't be to-night at Supper ?*
> Othel. *No, not to-night.*
> Desd. *To-Morrow Dinner then ?*   15
> Othel. *I shall not dine at home ;*
> *I meet the Captains at the Citadel.*
> Desd. *Why, then to morrow night, or Tuesday morn,*
> *Or night, or Wednesday morn ?*

After forty lines more at this rate, they part ; and then 20
comes the wonderful scene where *Jago*, by shrugs, half words, and ambiguous reflections, works *Othello* up to be Jealous. One might think, after what we have seen, that there needs no great cunning, no great poetry and address to make the *Moor* Jealous. Such impatience, such a rout 25
for a handsome young fellow the very morning after her Marriage, must make him either to be jealous or to take her for a *Changeling* below his Jealousie. After this *Scene* it might strain the Poets skill to reconcile the couple and allay the Jealousie. *Jago* now can only *actum agere*, and 30
vex the audience with a nauseous repetition.

Whence comes it, then, that this is the top scene, the Scene that raises *Othello* above all other Tragedies on our Theatres ? It is purely from the *Action* : from the Mops and the Mows, the Grimace, the Grins and Gesticulation. 35

Such scenes as this have made all the World run after *Harlequin* and *Scaramuccio*.

The several degrees of *Action* were amongst the Ancients distinguish'd by the *Cothurnus*, the *Soccus*, and by the *Planipes*.

Had this scene been represented at old *Rome*, *Othello* and *Jago* must have quitted their Buskins; They must have played *barefoot*: the spectators would not have been content without seeing their Podometry, And the Jealousie work at the very Toes of 'em. Words, be they Spanish, or Polish, or any inarticulate sound, have the same effect; they can only serve to distinguish, and, as it were, beat time to the *Action*. But here we see a known Language does wofully encumber and clog the operation, as either forc'd, or heavy, or trifling, or incoherent, or improper, or most what improbable. When no words interpose to spoil the conceipt, every one interprets as he likes best. So in that memorable dispute betwixt *Panurge* and our English Philosopher in *Rabelais*, perform'd without a word speaking: The Theologians, Physicians, and Surgeons made one inference; the Lawyers, Civilians, and Canonists drew another conclusion more to their mind.

Othello, the night of his arrival at *Cyprus*, is to consummate with *Desdemona*; they go to Bed. Both are rais'd and run into the Town amidst the Souldiers that were a fighting, then go to Bed again; that morning he sees *Cassio* with her: She importunes him to restore *Cassio*. *Othello* shews nothing of the Souldiers Mettle; but, like a tedious, drawling, tame Goose, is gaping after any paultrey insinuation, labouring to be jealous, And catching at every blown surmize.

> Jago. *My Lord, I see you are moved.*
> Oth. *No, not much moved.*
> *Do not think but* Desdemona *is honest.*
> Jag. *Long live she so, and long live you to think so!*

Oth. *And yet how Nature erring from it self——*
Jag. *I, There's the point: as, to be bold with you,*
Not to affect many proposed Matches
Of her own clime, complexion, and degree,
Wherein we see, in all things, Nature tends,   5
Fye, we may smell in such a will most rank,
Foul disproportion, thoughts unnatural.——

The Poet here is certainly in the right, and by consequence the foundation of the Play must be concluded to be
Monstrous, And the constitution, all over, to be   10

> *most rank,*
> *Foul disproportion, thoughts unnatural:*

Which, instead of moving pity or any passion Tragical
and Reasonable, can produce nothing but horror and
aversion and what is odious and grievous to an Audience. 15
After this fair Mornings work, the Bride enters, drops a
Cursey:

Desd. *How now, my dear* Othello.
Your Dinner, and the generous Islanders
By you invited, do attend your presence.   20
Oth. *I am to blame.*
Desd. *Why is your speech so faint? Are you not well?*
Oth. *I have a pain upon my Fore-head, dear.*

Michael Cassio came not from *Venice* in the Ship with
Desdemona, nor till this Morning could be suspected of an 25
opportunity with her.   And 'tis now but Dinner time; yet
the *Moor* complains of his Fore-head.   He might have set
a Guard on *Cassio,* or have lockt up *Desdemona,* or have
observ'd their carriage a day or two longer.   He is on
other occasions phlegmatick enough; this is very hasty. 30
But after Dinner we have a wonderful flight:

Othel. *What sense had I of her stoln hours of lust?*
I saw 't not, thought it not, it harm'd not me:
I slept the next night well, was free and merry;
I found not Cassio's *kisses on her lips.——*   35

A little after this, says he :

> Oth. *Give me a living reason that she's disloyal.*
> Jago. ——*I lay with* Cassio *lately,*
> *And being troubled with a raging Tooth, I could not sleep.*
> 5 *There are a kind of men so loose of Soul,*
> *That in their sleeps will mutter their affairs :*
> *One of this kind is* Cassio.
> *In sleep I heard him say : sweet* Desdemona,
> *Let us be wary, let us hide our loves :*
> 10 *And then, Sir, wou'd he gripe and wring my hand,*
> *Cry out, sweet Creature! and then kiss me hard,*
> *As if he pluckt up kisses by the roots,*
> *That grew upon my Lips ; then laid his Leg*
> *Over my Thigh, and sigh'd and kiss'd, and then*
> 15 *Cry'd : cursed fate that gave thee to the Moor!*

By the Rapture of *Othello* one might think that he raves, is not of sound Memory, forgets that he has not yet been two nights in the Matrimonial Bed with his *Desdemona*. But we find *Jago*, who should have a better memory, forging 20 his lies after the very same Model. The very night of their Marriage at *Venice*, the Moor and also *Cassio* were sent away to *Cyprus*. In the *Second Act*, *Othello* and his Bride go the first time to Bed : The *Third Act* opens the next morning. The parties have been in view to this moment. 25 We saw the opportunity which was given for *Cassio* to *speak his bosom* to her : *once*, indeed, might go a great way with a Venetian. But *once* will not do the Poets business. The *Audience* must suppose a great many bouts to make the plot operate. They must deny their senses to reconcile 30 it to common sense, or make it any way consistent and hang together.

Nor, for the most part, are the single thoughts more consistent than is the œconomy. The Indians do as they ought in painting the Devil White ; but says *Othello* :

> 35 Oth. ——*Her name, that was as fresh*
> *As* Dian's *Visage, is now begrim'd and black*
> *As mine own face.*——

There is not a Monky but understands Nature better, not a Pug in *Barbary* that has not a truer taste of things.

> Othel. ——*O now for ever*
> *Farewel the tranquil mind! farewel content!*
> *Farewel the plumed troop and the big Wars*　　　5
> *That make Ambition Vertue! O farewel,*
> *Farewel the neighing Steed and the shrill Trump,*
> *The spirit stirring Drum, th' ear-piercing Fife,*
> *The royal Banner, and all quality,*
> *Pride, Pomp, and Circumstance of glorious War!*　　10
> *And O ye Mortal Engines, whose wide throats*
> *Th' immortal Joves great clamours counterfeit,*
> *Farewel!* Othello's *occupation's gone!*

These lines are recited here, not for any thing Poetical in them, besides the sound, that pleases. Yet this sort of 15 imagery and amplification is extreamly taking where it is just and natural: As in *Gorboduck*, when a young Princess, on whose fancy the personal gallantry of the Kings Son, then slain, had made a strong impression, thus, out of the abundance of her imagination, pours forth her grief:　　20

> Marcella.——*Ah, noble Prince, how oft have I beheld*
> *Thee mounted on thy fierce and trampling Steed,*
> *Shining in Armour bright before the Tilt,*
> *Wearing thy Mistress sleeve ty'd on thy helm,*
> *Then charge thy staff to please thy Ladies Eye,*　　25
> *That bow'd the head piece of thy friendly Foe!*
> *How oft in arms, on Horse, to bend the Mace,*
> *How oft in arms, on foot, to break the Spear,*
> *Which never now these Eyes may see agen!*

Notwithstanding that this Scene had proceeded with 30 fury and bluster sufficient to make the whole Isle ring of his Jealousy, yet is *Desdemona* diverting her self with a paultry buffoon and only solicitous in quest of *Cassio*:

> Desd. *Seek him, bid him come hither, tell him*——
> *Where shou'd I lose that Handkerchief,* Emilia?　　35
> *Believe me, I had rather lose my Purse*

Full of Crusado's : And, but my noble Moor
Is true of mind and made of no such baseness
As Jealous Creatures are, it were enough
To put him to ill thinking.
  5 Em. *Is he not Jealous ?*
     Desd. *Who, he ? I think the Sun, where he was born,*
Drew all such humours from him.

By this manner of speech one wou'd gather the couple
had been yoak'd together a competent while ; what might
10 she say more, had they cohabited and had been Man and
Wife seven years ?

She spies the Moor.

     Desd. *I will not leave him now,*
Till Cassio *is recall'd,*
15 *I have sent to bid* Cassio *come speak with you.*
     Othel. ——*Lend me thy Handkerchief.*
     Desd.——*This is a trick to put me from my suit.*
I pray let Cassio *be receiv'd agen.*
     Em.——*Is not this man Jealous ?*
20 ——*'Tis not a year or two shews us a man.*——

As if for the first year or two *Othello* had not been
jealous ! This *third Act* begins in the morning, at noon she
drops the Handkerchief, after dinner she misses it, and
then follows all this outrage and horrible clutter about it.
25 If we believe a small Damosel in the last *Scene* of this *Act*,
this day is effectually seven days.

     Bianca.——*What, keep a week away ? seven days,*
          seven nights ?
Eightscore eight hours ? and lovers absent hours,
30 *More tedious than the Dial eightscore times ?*
Oh weary reckoning !

Our poet is at this plunge, that whether this *Act* contains
the compass of one day, of seven days, or of seven years,
or of all together, the repugnance and absurdity would be
35 the same.   For *Othello* all the while has nothing to say or
to do but what loudly proclaim him jealous: her friend and

confident, *Emilia*, again and again rounds her in the Ear
that *the Man* is Jealous: yet this Venetian dame is neither
to see, nor to hear, nor to have any sense or understanding,
nor to strike any other note but *Cassio, Cassio.*

The Scotchman, hearing *trut Scot, trut Scot*, when he saw 5
it came from a Bird, checkt his Choler, and put up his
Swerd again, with a *Braad O God, G. if thaa 'dst ben a
Maan, as th' art ane Green Geuse, I sud ha stuck tha' to thin
heart.* *Desdemona* and that Parrot might pass for Birds of
a Feather; and if *Sauney* had not been more generous 10
that *Othello*, but continued to insult the poor Creature after
this beastly example, he would have given our Poet as
good stuff to work upon: And his *Tragedy of the Green
Geuse* might have deserv'd a better audience than this of
Desdemona, or *The Moor of Venice.* 15

ACT IV.

Enter Jago *and* Othello.

Jago. *Will you think so?*
Othel. *Think so*, Jago!
Jago. *What, to kiss in private?*
Othel. *An unauthorised kiss.*
Jago. *Or to be naked with her friend a-bed* 20
An hour or more, not meaning any harm?
Othel. *Naked a-bed*, Jago, *and not mean harm!*——

At this gross rate of trifling, our General and his Auncient
March on most heroically, till the Jealous Booby has his
Brains turn'd, and falls in a Trance. Would any imagine 25
this to be the Language of Venetians, of Souldiers and
mighty Captains? no *Bartholomew* Droll cou'd subsist
upon such trash. But lo, a Stratagem never presented in
Tragedy:

Jago. *Stand you ⟨a⟩ while a part*—— 30
——*Incave your self,*
And mark the Jeers, the Gibes, and notable scorns,

That dwell in every region of his face ;
For I will make him tell the tale a new,
Where, how, how oft, how long ago, and when
He has and is again to Cope your Wife :
5 *I say, but mark his gesture.*——

With this device *Othello* withdraws.   Says *Jago* aside :

Jago. *Now will I question* Cassio *of* Bianca,
A Huswife——
That doats on Cassio.——
10 *He, when he hears of her, cannot refrain*
From the excess of Laughter.——
As he shall smile, Othello *shall go mad ;*
And his unbookish jealousy must conster
Poor Cassio's *smiles, gesture, and light behaviour,*
15 *Quite in the wrong.*——

So to work they go : And *Othello* is as wise a commentator, and makes his applications pat, as heart cou'd wish —but I wou'd not expect to find this Scene acted nearer than in *Southwark* Fair ! But the *Handkerchief* is brought
20 in at last, to stop all holes and close the evidence.   So now being satisfied with the proof, they come to a resolution that the offenders shall be murdered.

Othel.——*But yet the pity of it,* Jago ! *ah, the pity !*
Jago. *If you be so fond over her iniquity, give her*
25 *Patent to offend.   For if it touches not you, it comes near*
no Body.—
Do it not with poison, strangle her in her Bed ; Even the
Bed she has contaminated.
Oth. *Good, good ; the Justice of it pleases ; very good.*
30 Jago. *And for* Cassio, *let me be his undertaker.*—

Jago had some pretence to be discontent with *Othello* and *Cassio* : And what passed hitherto was the operation of revenge.   *Desdemona* had never done him harm, always kind to him and to his Wife, was his Country-woman,
35 a Dame of quality : for him to abet her Murder shews nothing of a Souldier, nothing of a Man, nothing of Nature

in it. The *Ordinary* of *New-gate* never had the like Monster to pass under his examination. Can it be any diversion to see a Rogue beyond what the Devil ever finish'd ? Or wou'd it be any instruction to an Audience ? *Jago* cou'd desire no better than to set *Cassio* and *Othello*, his two Enemies, by the Ears together, so he might have been reveng'd on them both at once : And chusing for his own share the Murder of *Desdemona*, he had the opportunity to play booty, and save the poor harmless wretch. But the Poet must do every thing by contraries, to surprize the Audience still with something horrible and prodigious beyond any human imagination. At this rate he must out-do the Devil to be a Poet in the rank with *Shakespear*.

Soon after this, arrives from *Venice Ludovico*, a noble Cousin of *Desdemona* ; presently she is at him also on the behalf of *Cassio*.

> Desd. *Cousin, there's fallen between him and my Lord*
> *An unkind breach ; but you shall make all well.*
> Lud. *Is there division 'twixt my Lord and* Cassio ?
> Desd. *A most unhappy one ; I wou'd do much*
> *To attone them, for the love I bear to* Cassio.

By this time we are to believe the couple have been a week or two Married : And *Othello*'s Jealousie, that had rag'd so loudly and had been so uneasie to himself, must have reach'd her knowledge. The *Audience* have all heard him more plain with her than was needful to a Venetian capacity : And yet she must still be impertinent in her suit for *Cassio*. Well, this *Magnifico* comes from the *Doge* and Senators to displace *Othello*.

> Lud. ——*Deputing* Cassio *in his Government.*
> Desd. *Trust me, I am glad on't.*
> Oth. *Indeed!*
> Desd. *My Lord!*
> Oth. *I am glad to see you mad.*
> Desd. *How, sweet* Othello ?
> Oth. *Devil!*

Desd. *I have not deserved this.*
Oth. *O Devil, Devil!—*
Out of my sight.
Desd. *I will not stay to offend you.*
5   Lud. *Truly, an obedient Lady.*
I do beseech your Lordship call her back.
Oth. *Mistress!*
Desd. *My Lord?*
Oth. *What would you with her, Sir?*
10   Lud. *Who, I, my Lord?*
Oth. *I, you did wish that I wou'd make her turn:*
Sir, she can turn, and turn, and yet go on,
And turn agen; and she can weep, Sir, weep;
And she is obedient, as you say, obedient,
15 *Very obedient.—*
Lud. *What, strike your Wife!*

Of what flesh and blood does our Poet make these noble
Venetians,—the men without Gall, the Women without
either Brains or Sense? A Senators Daughter runs away
20 with this Black-amoor; the Government employs this
Moor to defend them against the Turks, so resent not the
Moors Marriage at present; but the danger over, her
Father gets the Moor Cashier'd, sends his Kinsman,
Seignior *Ludovico*, to *Cyprus* with the Commission for
25 a new General; who, at his arrival, finds the Moor calling
the Lady, his Kinswoman, Whore and Strumpet, and
kicking her: what says the *Magnifico?*

Lud. *My Lord, this would not be believ'd in* Venice,
Tho' I shou'd swear I saw't; 'tis very much;
30 *Make her amends: she weeps.*

The Moor has no body to take his part, no body of his
Colour; *Ludovico* has the new Governour, *Cassio*, and all
his Countrymen Venetians about him. What Poet wou'd
give a villanous Black-amoor this Ascendant? What
35 Tramontain could fancy the Venetians so low, so de-
spicable, or so patient? this outrage to an injur'd Lady, the
Divine Desdemona, might in a colder Climate have provoked

some body to be her Champion ; but the Italians may well conclude we have a strange Genius for Poetry. In the next Scene *Othello* is examining the supposed Bawd ; then follows another storm of horrour and outrage against the poor Chicken, his Wife. Some Drayman or drunken 5 Tinker might possibly treat his drab at this sort of rate and mean no harm by it ; but for his excellency, a My lord General, to Serenade a Senator's Daughter with such a volly of scoundrel filthy Language is sure the most absurd Maggot that ever bred from any Poets addle Brain. 10
And she is in the right, who tells us,

> Emil.——*A Begger in his Drink*
> *Cou'd not have laid such terms upon his Callet.*

This is not to describe passion. *Seneca* had another notion in the Case :   15

> *Parvæ loquuntur curæ, ingentes stupent.*

And so had the Painter who drew *Agamemnon* with his Face covered. Yet to make all worse, her Murder, and the manner of it, had before been resolv'd upon and concerted. But nothing is to provoke a Venetian ; she takes 20 all in good part ; had the Scene lain in *Russia*, what cou'd we have expected more ? With us a Tinkers Trull wou'd be Nettled, wou'd repartee with more spirit, and not appear so void of spleen :

> Desd. *O good* Jago,   25
> *What shall I do to win my Lord agen ?*

No woman bred out of a Pig-stye cou'd talk so meanly. After this she is call'd to Supper with *Othello, Ludovico,* &c. ; after that comes a filthy sort of Pastoral Scene, where the *Wedding Sheets*, and Song of *Willow,* and her 30 Mothers Maid, poor *Barbara,* are not the least moving things in this entertainment. But that we may not be kept too long in the dumps, nor the melancholy Scenes lye too heavy undigested on our Stomach, this *Act* gives us for a farewell the *salsa, O picante*, some quibbles and smart touches, as *Ovid* had Prophecied:

Est & in obscœnos deflexa Tragœdia risus.

5 The last *Act* begins with *Jago* and *Roderigo* : Who a little before had been upon the huff :

> Rod. *I say it is not very well. I will make my self known to* Desdemona : *if she will return me my Jewels, I will give over my suit and repent my unlawful sollicitation ;*
> 10 *if not, assure your self I'll seek satisfaction of you.*

Roderigo, a Noble Venetian, had sought *Desdemona* in Marriage, is troubled to find the Moor had got her from him, advises with *Jago*, who wheadles him to sell his Estate and go over the Sea to *Cyprus* in expectation to 15 Cuckold *Othello* ; there having cheated *Roderigo* of all his Money and Jewels on pretence of presenting them to *Desdemona*, our Gallant grows angry, and would have satisfaction from *Jago*, who sets all right by telling him *Cassio* is to be Governour, *Othello* is going with *Desdemona* 20 into *Mauritania* ; to prevent this, you are to murder *Cassio*, and then all may be well.

> Jago. *He goes into* Mauritania, *and takes with him the fair* Desdemona, *unless his abode be lingred here by some accident, wherein none can be so determinate as the removing* 25 *of* Cassio.

Had *Roderigo* been one of the *Banditi*, he might not much stick at the Murder. But why *Roderigo* should take this for payment, and risque his person where the prospect of advantage is so very uncertain and remote, no body can 30 imagine. It had need be a *super-subtle* Venetian that this Plot will pass upon. Then, after a little spurt of villany and Murder, we are brought to the most lamentable that ever appear'd on any Stage. A noble Venetian Lady is to be murdered by our Poet,—in sober sadness, purely for being a Fool. No Pagan Poet but wou'd have found some *Machine* for her deliverance. *Pegasus* wou'd have strain'd hard to have brought old *Perseus* on his back, time enough to rescue this *Andromeda* from so foul a Monster. Has our Christian Poetry no generosity, nor 5 bowels? Ha, Sir *Lancelot*! ha, St. *George*! will no Ghost leave the shades for us in extremity to save a distressed Damosel?

But for our comfort, however felonious is the Heart, hear with what soft language he does approach her, with 10 a Candle in his Hand:

> Oth. *Put out the light, and then put out the light:*
> *If I quench thee, thou flaming Minister,*
> *I can again thy former light restore.—*

Who would call him Barbarian, Monster, Savage? Is 15 this a Black-amoor?

> *Soles occidere & redire possunt—*

The very Soul and Quintessence of Sir *George Etheridge*!

One might think the General should not glory much in this action, but make an hasty work on't, and have turn'd 20 his Eyes away from so unsouldierly an Execution; yet is he all pause and deliberation, handles her as calmly and is as careful of her Souls health as it had been her *Father Confessor*. *Have you prayed to Night,* Desdemona? But the suspence is necessary that he might have a convenient 25 while so to *roul his Eyes*, and so to *gnaw* his *nether lip* to the spectators. Besides the greater cruelty—*sub tam lentis maxillis.*

But hark, a most tragical thing laid to her charge!

> Oth. *That Handkerchief, that I so lov'd and gave thee,* 30
> *Thou gav'st to Cassio.*
> Desd. *No, by my Life and Soul!*
> *Send for the man, and ask him.*
> Oth. *By Heaven, I saw my Hankerchief in his hand.—*
> ——*I saw the Handkerchief.* 35

So much ado, so much stress, so much passion and repetition about an Handkerchief! Why was not this call'd the *Tragedy of the Handkerchief*? What can be more absurd than (as *Quintilian* expresses it) *in parvis litibus*
5 *has Tragœdias movere*? We have heard of *Fortunatus his Purse* and of the *Invisible Cloak*, long ago worn threadbare and stow'd up in the Wardrobe of obsolete Romances: one might think that were a fitter place for this Handkerchief than that it, at this time of day, be worn on the Stage,
10 to raise every where all this clutter and turmoil. Had it been *Desdemona*'s Garter, the Sagacious Moor might have smelt a Rat; but the Handkerchief is so remote a trifle, no Booby on this side *Mauritania* cou'd make any consequence from it.
15 We may learn here that a Woman never loses her Tongue, even tho' after she is stifl'd:

    Desd. *O falsly, falsly murder'd!*
    Em. *Sweet* Desdemona, *O sweet Mistress, speak!*
    Desd. *A guiltless death I dye.*
20   Em. *O who has done the deed?*
    Desd. *No body; I my self; farewel:*
   Commend me to my kind Lord; O farewel!

This *Desdemona* is a black swan, or an old Black-amoor is a bewitching Bed-fellow. If this be Nature, it is a *laschete*
25 below what the English Language can express.

For *Lardella* to *make love like an Humble Bee* was, in the Rehearsal, thought a fancy odd enough.

But hark what follows:

    Oth. ——*O heavy hour!*
30 *Methinks it shou'd be now a huge Eclipse*
Of Sun and Moon, and that the affrighted globe
Shou'd yawn at Alteration.

This is wonderful! Here is Poetry to *elevate* and *amuse*. Here is sound All-sufficient. It wou'd be uncivil to ask
35 *Flamstead* if the Sun and Moon can both together be so

hugely eclipsed in any *heavy hour* whatsoever.   Nor must
the Spectators consult *Gresham* Colledge whether a body
is naturally *frighted* till he *Yawn* agen.   The Fortune of
Greece is not concern'd with these Matters.   These are
Physical circumstances a Poet may be ignorant in, without 5
any harm to the publick.   These slips have no influence
on our Manners and good Life, which are the Poets
Province.

Rather may we ask here what unnatural crime *Desdemona*
or her Parents had committed, to bring this Judgment 10
down upon her : to Wed a Black-amoor, and innocent to
be thus cruelly murder'd by him.   What instruction can
we make out of this Catastrophe ? Or whither must our
reflection lead us ? Is not this to envenome and sour our
spirits, to make us repine and grumble at Providence and 15
the government of the World ? If this be our end, what
boots it to be Vertuous ?

Desdemona dropt the Handkerchief, and missed it that
very day after her Marriage ; it might have been rumpl'd
up with her Wedding sheets : And this Night that she lay 20
in her wedding sheets, the *Fairey* Napkin (whilst *Othello*
was stifling her) might have started up to disarm his fury
and stop his ungracious mouth.   Then might she (in
a Traunce for fear) have lain as dead.   Then might he,
believing her dead, touch'd with remorse, have honestly 25
cut his own Throat, by the good leave and with the
applause of all the Spectators : Who might thereupon have
gone home with a quiet mind, admiring the beauty of
Providence, fairly and truly represented on the Theatre.

Oth. —— *Why, how shou'd she be murdered?*   30
Em. *Alas, who knows?*
Oth. *You heard her say her self, it was not I.*
Em. *She did so ; I must needs report a truth.*
Oth. *She's like a liar gone to burn in Hell.*
  'Twas I that did it.   35
Em. *O, the more Angel she,*

And you the blacker Devil!
   Oth. *She turn'd to folly, and she was an Whore.*
   Em. *Thou dost belye her, and thou art a Devil.*
   Oth. *She was false as Water.*
   Em. *Thou art rash as Fire,*
To say that she was false: O, she was heavenly true.

In this kind of Dialogue they continue for forty lines
farther, before she bethinks her self to cry Murder.

   Em. ——*Help, help, O help!*
The Moor has kill'd my Mistress! murder, Murder!

But from this Scene to the end of the Play we meet with
nothing but blood and butchery, described much-what to
the style of *the last Speeches and Confessions of the persons
executed at Tyburn*; with this difference, that there we
have the *fact* and the due course of Justice, whereas our
Poet, against all Justice and Reason, against all Law,
Humanity, and Nature, in a barbarous, arbitrary way,
executes and makes havock of his subjects, *Hab-nab*, as
they come to hand. *Desdemona* dropt her Handkerchief;
therefore she must be stifl'd. *Othello*, by law to be broken
on the Wheel, by the Poets cunning escapes with cutting
his own Throat. *Cassio*, for I know not what, comes off
with a broken shin. *Jago* murders his Benefactor *Roderigo*,
as this were poetical gratitude. *Jago* is not yet kill'd,
because there yet never was such a villain alive. The
Devil, if once he brings a man to be dipt in a deadly sin,
lets him alone to take his course; and now when the *Foul
Fiend* has done with him, our wise Authors take the sinner
into their poetical service, there to accomplish him and do
the Devils drudgery.

Philosophy tells us it is a principle in the Nature of Man
to be grateful.

History may tell us that *John an Oaks, John a Stiles,*
or *Jago* were ungrateful. *Poetry* is to follow Nature;
Philosophy must be his guide: history and *fact* in particular

cases of *John an Oaks* or *John of Styles* are no warrant or direction for a Poet. Therefore *Aristotle* is always telling us that Poetry is σπουδαιότερον καὶ φιλοσοφώτερον, is more general and abstracted, is led more by the Philosophy, the reason and nature of things than History, which only records things higlety piglety, right or wrong, as they happen. History might without any preamble or difficulty say that *Jago* was ungrateful. Philosophy then calls him unnatural. But the Poet is not without huge labour and preparation to expose the Monster, and after shew the Divine Vengeance executed upon him. The Poet is not to add wilful Murder to his ingratitude : he has not antidote enough for the Poison : his Hell and Furies are not punishment sufficient for one single crime of that bulk and aggravation.

> Em. *O thou dull Moor, that Handkerchief thou*
>   *speakest on*
> *I found by Fortune and did give my Husband ;*
> *For often with a solemn earnestness,*
> *More than indeed belong'd to such a trifle,*
> *He beg'd of me to steal it.*

Here we see the meanest woman in the Play takes this *Handkerchief* for a *trifle* below her Husband to trouble his head about it. Yet we find it entered into our Poets head to make a Tragedy of this *Trifle.*

Then, for the *unraveling of the Plot*, as they call it, never was old deputy Recorder in a Country Town, with his spectacles, in summoning up the evidence, at such a puzzle, so blunder'd and be-doultefied, as is our Poet to have a good riddance, And get the *Catastrophe* off his hands.

What can remain with the Audience to carry home with them from this sort of Poetry for their use and edification ? how can it work, unless (instead of settling the mind and purging our passions) to delude our senses, disorder our thoughts, addle our brain, pervert our affections, hair our imaginations, corrupt our appetite, and fill our head with vanity, confusion, *Tintamarre*, and Jingle-jangle, beyond what all the Parish Clarks of *London* with their *old Testament* farces and interludes, in *Richard* the seconds time, cou'd ever pretend to? Our only hopes for the good of their Souls can be that these people go to the Playhouse as they do to Church, to sit still, look on one another, make no reflection, nor mind the Play more than they would a Sermon.

There is in this Play some burlesk, some humour and ramble of Comical Wit, some shew and some *Mimickry* to divert the spectators; but the tragical part is plainly none other than a Bloody Farce, without salt or savour.

EDWARD PHILLIPS

PREFACE TO *THEATRUM POETARUM, OR A COMPLEAT COLLECTION OF THE POETS*

1675

The Preface

To the most Learned, Vertuous, and by Me most
honour'd Pair of Friends, THOMAS STANLY, of
Cumberlo Green in *Hertfordshire*, and EDWARD
SHERBURN, Clerk of His *Majesties* Ordinance in
the *Tower* of *London*, Esq^s.

A S oft as I seriously consider with My self, most worthy
Associates in Learning and Vertue, and My most
honour'd Friends, what a vast difference there is, or at
least seems to be, between one part of Mankind and the
other,—how near the Intelligence of Angels the one, how 5
beneath the Ingenuity and Industry of many Brute
Animals the other ; how aspiring to the Perfection of knowledge the one, how immers't in swinish sloth and ignorance
the other,—I am apt to wonder how it could possibly be
imagin'd that the same rationality of Soul should inform 10
alike, as we are oblig'd to beleive by the authority of Sacred
Scriptures and the Doctrine of the Souls Immortality, the
whole mass & frame of Human Nature, and not rather that
there should be a gradation of notion from the lowest brute
up to the Angelic Region : But that calling to mind the 15
common maxim of Philosophy, that the perfection of Soul
is the same in the Infant as in the ripe of age, only acting

more or less vigorously, according to the capacity of the
Organs, I thence collect that there is also a different
capacity of the Organs, whence ariseth a different Spirit
and Constitution, or some intervening cause, by which it
5 either acts or lies dormant even in Persons of the same
age : the first is that *Melior Natura* which the Poet speaks
of, with which whoever is amply indued, take that Man
from his Infancy, throw him into the Deserts of *Arabia*,
there let him converse some years with Tygers and
10 Leopards, and at last bring him where civil society &
conversation abides, and ye shall see how on a sudden, the
scales and dross of his barbarity purging off by degrees, he
will start up a Prince or Legislator, or some such illustrious
Peroon : the other is that noble thing call'd *Education*, this
15 is, that Harp of *Orpheus*, that lute of *Amphion*, so elegantly
figur'd by the Poets to have wrought such Miracles among
irrational and insensible Creatures, which raiseth beauty
even out of deformity, order and regularity out of Chaos
and confusion, and which, if throughly and rightly prose-
20 cuted, would be able to civilize the most savage natures, &
root out barbarism and ignorance from off the face of the
Earth : those who have either of these qualifications singly
may justly be tearm'd *Men* ; those who have both united in
a happy conjunction, *more* than *Men* ; those who have
25 neither of them in any competent measure, certainly, in
the conduct of their lives, *less* then *Men* ; and of this last
sort is compos'd that greatest part by far of *our* habitable
world (for what the Nature and distinction is of the
Inhabitants of other orbs is to us utterly unknown, though
30 not any where circumscrib'd, but diffused alike through the
4 quarters), commonly call'd the vulgar or Multitude,—
I mean not altogether those of the lowest birth or Fortune,
but those of what degree or quality so ever, who live
Sardinapalian lives, τῶν ἀνδραπόδων τρόπῳ, as the Philo-
35 sopher has it, not caring to understand ought beyond to *eat*,

drink, and *play*; and no wonder if the memories of such Persons as these sink with their Bodys into the earth, and lie buried in profound obscurity and oblivion, when even among those that tread the paths of Glory and Honour, those who have signaliz'd themselves either by great actions in the field or by Noble Arts of Peace or by the Monuments of their written Works more lasting sometimes than Brass or Marble, very many, but especially of the writing party, have fallen short of their deserved immortality of Name, and lie under a total eclipse, or at least cast but a faint and glimmering light, like those innumerable seeds of Stars in the *Galaxie*, not distinctly to be discern'd by any telescope; and indeed there is an exact resemblance between the fate of writers & the common fate of Mankind; for as in human affairs some Men, never so vertuously, never so bravely acting, are pass't by unvalew'd, unrewarded, or at least not deserving ill fall by unhappy lot into unreasonable hands and miseries far worse then death, others for no desert are hoisted up to honours which of right belong not to them, or being guilty of things worthy utmost shame or punishments, yet scape the stroak of Justice, and oft times with hoary heads go down to the grave in peace; some deserving well meet with rewards suitable to their merits, others with contempt due to their no deserts, or if criminal, with punishments proportionable to their crimes; so in the State of Learning, among the Writers of all Ages, some deserve Fame & have it, others neither have nor deserve it, some have it, not deserving, others though deserving yet totally miss it, or have it not equall to their deserts; & these are the Men who require our most peculiar consideration, and for whose sake chiefly it is that this design hath been undertaken; for though the personal calamities of poor wretched mortals are the highest object of human pity, yet methinks there is some thing of compassion due to extinguisht vertue, and the loss of many ingenuous, elaborate, and useful Works,

and even the very names of some, who having perhaps
been comparable to *Homer* for Heroic Poesy, or to
Euripides for Tragedy, yet nevertheless sleep inglorious
in the croud of the forgotten vulgar; and for as many of
5 those Names of Writers, whether more or less Eminent,
as have been preserv'd from utter oblivion, together with
an account for the most part of what they writ, all Learned
Men, especially such as are curious of antiquity, are oblig'd
to those generous Registers who have been studious to
10 keep alive the memories of Famous Men, of whom it is at
least some satisfaction to understand that there were once
such Men or Writings in being. However, since their
Works having by what ever casualty perisht, their Names,
though thus recorded, yet as being dispeirc't in several
15 Authors, and some of those not of the most conspicuous
note, are scarce known to the generality even of the
Learned themselves ; and since of later Ages the memories
of many whose works have been once made public and in
general esteem have, nevertheless, through tract of time
20 and the succession of new Generations, fallen to decay and
dwindled almost to nothing, I judged it a Work in some
sort not unconducing to a public benefit, and to many not
ungratefull, to muster up together in a body, though under
their several Classes, as many of those that have imploy'd
25 their fancies or inventions in all the several Arts and
Sciences, as I could either collect out of the several Authors
that have mention'd them in part, or by any other ways
could come to the knowledge of; but finding this too
various and manifold a task to be manag'd at once, I pitcht
30 upon one Faculty first, which, not more by chance than
inclination, falls out to be that of the Poets, a Science
certainly of all others the most noble and exalted, and
not unworthily tearmed *Divine*, since the heighth of Poetical rapture hath ever been accounted little less then
35 *Divine Inspiration*.   Pardon me, therefore, most Honour'd

Friends, if having undertaken a Province more weighty
and difficult then the account of any other Art and Science,
and which beyond all others exerciseth the utmost nicety
and sagacity of judgement, I ambitiously make address to
the Patronage of Persons of so fair a reputation, as well in 5
Poetry as other parts of Learning, and who are your selves
partys not obscurely or without just merit concerned,
whom against what ever may happen either of deserv'd or
undeserv'd Censure, I crave leave in the first case to have
recourse to as Advocates, in the next to appeal to as 10
Judges, it being studiously my desire to anticipate as
much as possibly in me lies all that can be said of prejudice or exception, which, if I fore-see aright, will amount
only in the main to one grand objection, namely, the
omission of some that ought to have been mention'd and 15
the mentioning of others that might without injury have
been omitted ; as to the first part of this objection I have
nothing to do, but humbly to beg the pardon of the Persons
so neglected if alive, or otherwise of the concerned Reader
in their behalf, not that I think my self oblig'd to receive 20
prescriptions from any but whom I think competent to
judge who are and who are not worthy, but as being not
altogether unconscious to my self, and conceiving it no
disparagement to acknowledge, that for hast and want of
that profound leasure and other advantages which are 25
requisite for the bringing of all endeavours to maturity
(though I question whether ever any human work was
ever yet so perfect as might not admit either of addition or
diminution) many things may possibly have been omitted,
some things also mistaken, though I dare confidently 30
avouch that of very conspicuous note there have been forgotten very few if any ; and for those who, pretending and
perhaps not without reason to Poetical fancy or judgement
equal to many that have written with applause, yet nevertheless have contented themselves to be wise, ingenuous, 35

or judicious only to themselves, not caring to transmit any memorials to posterity, certainly those Men, though able to contend with *Apollo* himself, cannot in reason challenge to themselves a place among the Poetical Writers, except
5 upon the testimony of some very authentic Author ; what shall we say of these who, studying no doubt public benefit above privat fame, for so in charity we ought to believe, have forborn to set their names to what they have written, which if by any kind of intelligence they could be
10 recovered, it would be a most unmannerly thing to divulge his name to the World who thinks fit himself to have it conceal'd ; sorry I am I cannot pay a due respect to Mr. *Anonymus*, but he is the Author of so many Books that to make but a Catalogue of them would require a Volume
15 sufficient of itself ; others there are who vouchsafe but the two first letters of their Names, and these, it is to be supposed, desire to be known onely to some Friends, that understand the Interpretation of those letters, or some cunning Men in the Art of Divination ; now, as to the
20 last part of the objection, I have so much the more confidence to stand upon my own justification, by how much I rely upon this Maxim, that it is less injustice to admit of 20 that deserve no notice or mention then to omit one that really deserves ; and here, methinks, there seems to arise
25 a large feild of examination and distinction, between those that are in truth of no valew or desert and those that are generally reputed so ; it is to be observed that some have been once of great esteem and have afterwards grown out of date, others have never arriv'd to any esteem, and
30 possibly in both cases the merits of the cause may have been various on either side ; yet I am apt to beleive that as it is a more frequent thing to over then undervalew, so a universal contempt is a shrew'd, not infallible, sign of a universal indesert ; the reason is plain, for though no doubt
35 the number of judicious and knowing is as great if not

greater then ever, yet most confessedly not so great as that of the ignorant or only superficially knowing, there are many that think, few only that judge ; therefore things of the most transcendent excellence are for the most part only valew'd by Persons of transcendent judgment, whereas the indifferent and plausible are received with general and vulgar applause. So that those Works which, being advantageously publisht, nevertheless obtain no Fame, may be justly suspected of little or no worth ; since, had they been excellent, they might, falling into the hands of the few that judge, have been buoy'd up by their authority ; had they been plausible, they would have been cry'd up by the many that think. And shall such very Ignote and con- temptible pretenders be allow'd a place among the most renowned of Poetic Writers, among so many Laureated heads, with the triumphant wreath of *Parnassus* ? I beg your favourable attentions, yours in the first place, most equal Judges, yours in the next, most Curteous *Readers*; let me plead a little for the well meaners only, as something Sympathising with those for whom I plead ; Vertue will plead for it self, and needs no Advocate; first let it ⟨be⟩ consider'd that no Man designs to writ ill, every one either writes well or would write well; it is not in the power of mortal Man to discover that Wit, Judgment, Fancy, or Industry, with which he never was endow'd, and without most of which, if not all, a good Poem cannot be written : It is his hard fate, therefore, who void of all becomes a dabler in Poetry ; we are not all born *Heroic* Poets, nor Writers of sublime Tragedy ; however, there is no Poeti- cal Volume, be it never so small, but it requires some pains to bring it forth, or else a notable fluent knack of Riming or Versifying ; and how small a matter is it for never so trivial a Work, before it comes to be condemn'd to the drudgery of the *Chandler* or *Tobacco Man*, after the double expence of Brain to bring it forth and of purse to

publish it to the World, to have this small Memorial, *Such
a one wrote such a thing*; besides that it will easily be
imagin'd in Works of this nature, that we write as well to
the Inquisitive as the Judicious, to the Curious as the
Critic, there are many buisy inquirers after Books, not
good Books, but Books, what hath been written on such or
such a subject; for these Men who would grudge the
slight mention of a Book and its Author, yet not so far as
to condescend to the taking notice of every single-sheeted
Pie-corner Poet, who comes squirting out with an Elegy in
mourning for every Great Person that dies? As for the
Antiquated & fallen into obscurity from their former credit
& reputation, they are for the most part those that have
written beyond the verge of the present Age; for let us
look back as far as about 30 or 40 years, and we shall find
a profound silence of the Poets beyond that time, except
of some few Dramatics, of whose real worth the Interest
of the now flourishing Stage cannot but be sensible. Is
Antiquity then a crime? no, certainly, it ought to be rather
had in veneration; but nothing, it seems, relishes so well
as what is written in the smooth style of our present Language, taken to be of late so much refined. True it is that
the style of Poetry till *Henry* the 8th's time, and partly
also within his Reign, may very well appear uncouth,
strange, and unpleasant to those that are affected only with
what is familiar and accustom'd to them, not but there
were even before those times some that had their Poetical
excellencies, if well examin'd, and chiefly among the rest
Chaucer, who through all the neglect of former ag'd Poets
still keeps a name, being by some few admir'd for his real
worth, to others not unpleasing for his facetious way,
which joyn'd with his old *English* intertains them with a
kind of Drollery; however, from Qu. *Elizabeth's* Reign
the Language hath been not so unpolisht as to render the
Poetry of that time ungratefull to such as at this day will

take the paines to examin it well; besides, if no Poetry should Pleas but what is calculated to every refinement of a Language, of how ill consequence this would be for the future let him consider and make it his own case, who, being now in fair repute & promising to himself a lasting 5 Fame, shall two or three Ages hence, when the Language comes to be double refin'd, understand (if Souls have any intelligence, after their departure hence, what is done on Earth) that his Works are become obsolete and thrown aside. If then their Antiquated style be no sufficient 1 reason why the Poets of former Ages should be rejected, much less the pretence of their antiquated mode or fashion of Poetry, which, whether it be altered for the better or not, I cannot but look upon it as a very pleasant humour, that we should be so complyant with the *French* custom as 1 to follow set fashions, not only in Garments, but also in Music (wherein the *Lydian* Mood is now most in request) and Poetry : for Cloths, I leave them to the discretion of the Modish, whether of our own or the *French* Nation ; Breeches and Doublet will not fall under a Metaphysical 2 consideration : but in Arts and Sciences, as well as in Moral Notions, I shall not scruple to maintain that what was *verum & bonum* once continues to be so always ; now, whether the Trunck-Hose Fancy of Queen *Elizabeth*'s days or the Pantaloon Genius of ours be best, I shall not 2 be hasty to determin, not presuming to call in question the judgment of the present Age ; only thus much I must needs see, that Custom & Opinion oft times take so deep a root that Judgment hath not free power to act. To the Antient Greecs and Latins, the Modern Poets of all Nations and 3 for several Ages have acknowledged themselves beholding for those, both Precepts and examples, which have been thought conducing to the perfection of Poetry ; for the manner of its Garb and dress, which is Vers, we in parti- cular to the *Italians*, the first of the Moderns that have 35

been eminently Famous in this Faculty, the measure of
the Greec and Latin Verse being no way suitable to the
Modern Languages; & truly, so far as I have observed,
the Italian *Stanza* in Heroic Poem, and the Sonnet,
5 Canzon, and Madrigal in the Lyric, as they have been
formerly more frequently made use of by the *English* than
by any, so except their own proper Language they become
none better then ours; and therefore having been used
with so good success, I see no reason why they should be
10 utterly rejected; there is certainly a decency in one sort
of Verse more then another, which custom cannot really
alter, only by familiarity make it seem better; how much
more stately and Majestic in Epic Poems, especially of
Heroic Argument, *Spencer's Stanza*, which I take to be
15 but an Improvement upon *Tasso's Ottava Rima*, or the
Ottava Rima it self, used by many of our once esteemed
Poets, is above the way either of Couplet or Alternation of
four Verses only, I am perswaded, were it revived, would
soon be acknowledg'd; and in like manner the *Italian*
20 Sonnet and Canzon above *Pindaric* Ode, which, whatever
the name pretends, comes not so near in resemblance to
the Odes of *Pindarus* as the Canzon, which, though it
answers not so exactly as to consist of *Stroph*, *Antistroph*,
and *Epod*, yet the Verses, which in the first *Stroph* of the
25 Canzon were tied to no fixt number, order, or measure,
nevertheless in the following Strophs return in the same
number, order, & measure as were observ'd in the first;
whereas that which we call the *Pindaric* hath a nearer
affinity with the *Monostrophic*, or *Apolelymenon*, used in
30 the Chorus's of *Æschylus* his Tragedies: one thing more
is to be observ'd between the *Italian* Verse and ours,
namely, that the Dissyllable, which in that Language is the
only way of Riming, is also in ours very applicable to
Rime, and hath been very much used formerly,—I was
35 going to say with as much grace sometimes, if not more,

then the Monosyllable, but that I am loath to appear too
singularly addicted to that which is now so utterly exploded,
especially since there are other things of much greater
consequence then the Verse, though it cannot be deny'd
but that a Poetical fancy is much seen in the choise of 5
Verse proper to the chosen subject ; yet, however, let the
fashion of the Vers be what it will, according to the different humour of the Writer, if the Style be elegant and
suitable, the Verse, whatever it is, may be the better
dispenc't with ; and the truth is the use of Measure alone 10
without any Rime at all would give far more ample Scope
and liberty both to Style and fancy then can possibly be
observed in Rime, as evidently appears from an *English*
Heroic poem which came forth not many years ago, and
from the Style of *Virgil, Horace, Ovid*, and others of the 15
Latins, which is so pure and proper that it could not
possibly have been better in Prose : another thing yet
more considerable is conduct and design in whatever kind
of Poetry, whether the *Epic*, the *Dramatic*, the *Lyric*, the
Elegiac, the *Epænetic*, the *Bucolic*, or the *Epigram*, under 20
one of which all the whole circuit of Poetic design is one
way or other included ; so that whoever should desire to
introduce some new kind of Poem, of different fashion
from any known to the Antients, would do no more then
he that should study to bring a new Order into *Architecture*, 25
altogether different both from the *Doric, Ionic, Corinthian,
Tuscan*, and *Composite*. *Epigram* is, as it were, the fag
end of *Poetry*, and indeed consists rather of conceit and
acumen of Wit then of Poetical invention, yet it is more
commendable to be a *Martial* in *Epigram* then *Juvenal*'s 30
Codrus in *Heroic Poetry*. The *Epænetic* comprehends
the *Hymn*, the *Epithalamium*, the *Genethliacon*, or what else
tends to the praise or congratulation of Divine or on
Earth Eminent Persons ; the *Bucolic*, or *Eclogue*, pretends
only the familiar discourse of Sheapheards about their 35

Loves or such like concernments, yet under that umbrage
treats oft times of higher matters, thought convenient to
be spoken of rather mysteriously and obscurely then in
plain tearms ; the *Elegiac* seems intended at first for com-
5 plaint of crosses in Love or other calamitous accidents,
but became applicable afterwards to all manner of subjects
and various occasions ; the *Lyric* consists of Songs or
Airs of Love, or other the most soft and delightfull subject,
in verse most apt for Musical Composition, such as the
10 *Italian* Sonnet, but most especially Canzon and Madrigal
before mentioned, and the *English* Ode heretofore much
after the same manner ; the *Dramatic* comprehends *Satyr*
and her two Daughters, *Tragedy* and *Comedy* ; the *Epic* is
of the largest extent, and includes all that is narrative
15 either of things or Persons, the hig⟨he⟩st degree whereof
is the *Heroic*, as *Tragedy* of the *Dramatic*, both which
consist in the greatness of the *Argument* and this is that
which makes up the Perfection of a *Poet* ; in other *Arguments* a Man may appear a good *Poet*, in the right
20 management of this alone a great *Poet* ; for if Invention be
the grand part of a *Poet* or *Maker*, and Verse the least,
then certainly the more sublime the *Argument*, the nobler
the Invention, and by consequence the greater the *Poet* ;
and therefore it is not a meer Historical relation, spic't
25 over with a little slight fiction, now and then a personated
vertue or vice rising out of the ground and uttering a
speech, which makes a *Heroic Poem* ; but it must be
rather a brief, obscure, or remote Tradition, but of some
remarkable piece of story, in which the Poet hath an ample
30 feild to inlarge by feigning of probable circumstances, in
which, and in proper Allegorie, Invention (the well
management whereof is indeed no other then *decorum*)
principally consisteth, and wherein there is a kind of truth
even in the midst of Fiction ; for what ever is pertinently
35 said by way of *Allegorie* is Morally though not Historically

true ; and circumstances, the more they have of verisimi-
lity, the more they keep up the reputation of the Poet,
whose business it is to deliver feign'd things as like to
truth as may be, that is to say, not too much exceeding
apprehension or the beleif of what is possible or likely, or 5
positively contradictory to the truth of History. So that
it would be absurd in a *Poet* to set his Hero upon Roman-
tic actions (let his courage be what it will) exceeding
Human strength and power, as to fight singly against whole
Armies and come off unhurt, at least if a mortal Man, and 10
not a Deity or armed with Power Divine ; in like manner
to transgress so far the compute of time as to bring together those that liv'd several Ages asunder, as if
Alexander the *Great* should be brought to fight a single
Duel with *Julius Cæsar*, would either argue a shamefull 15
ignorance in Chronologie or an irregular and boundless
licence in Poetical fiction, which I reckon is allow'd the
Poet chiefly upon this consideration, because being
supposed as he ought to understand the ways of Heroic
vertue & Magnanimity from better principles then those of 20
common and implicite opinion, he hath the advantage of
representing and setting forth greater *Idea*'s and more
noble *Examples* then probably can be drawn from known
History ; and indeed there is no ingenuous or excellent
quality, either native or acquired, wherewith he should 25
not be fully acquainted, no part of Learning in which he
ought not to be exactly instructed ; since, as a curious
piece of History-painting, which is the highest perfection in the Art of Picture, is the result of several other
Arts, as *Perspective, Proportion,* the knowledge of 30
History, Morality, the passions of the mind, &c., so
Heroic Poesie ought to be the result of all that can be
contrived of profit, delight, or ornament, either from
experience in human affairs or from the knowledge of all
Arts and *Sciences*, it being but requisite that the same 35

Work which sets forth the highest Acts of Kings and
Heroes should be made fit to allure the inclinations of
such like Persons to a studious delight in reading of those
things which they are desired to imitate.

5   They likewise very much erre from probability of circumstance who go about to describe antient things after a
modern Model, which is an untruth even in Poetry it self,
and so against all *Decorum* that it shows no otherwise then
as if a Man should read the Antient History of the
10 *Persians* or *Egyptians* to inform himself of the customs
and manners of the modern *Italians* and *Spaniards*;
besides that our Author should avoid, as much as might
be, the making such descriptions as should any way
betray his ignorance in antient customs, or any other
15 knowledge in which he ought industriously to shew himself accomplish't.

There is also a *Decorum* to be observ'd in the style of
the H. Poem, that is, that it be not inflate or gingling
with an empty noise of Words, nor creepingly low and
20 insipid, but of a Majesty suitable to the Grandeur of the
subject,—not nice or ashamed of vulgarly unknown or
unusual words, if either tearms of Art well chosen or
proper to the occasion, for fear of frighting the Ladies
from reading, as if it were not more reasonable that Ladies
25 who will read Heroic Poem should be qualified accordingly, then that the Poet should check his fancy for such,
either Men or Ladys, whose capacities will not ascend
above *Argalus* and *Parthenia*.   Next to the *Heroic Poem*
(if not, as some think, equal) is *Tragedy*, in conduct very
30 different, in heighth of Argument alike, as treating only of
the actions and concernments of the most Illustrious
Persons, whereas *Comedy* sets before us the humours,
converse, and designs of the more ordinary sort of People :
the chief parts thereof are the ἦθος & πάθος, by which latter
35 is meant that moving and Pathetical manner of expression,

which in some respect is to exceed the highest that can be delivered in Heroic Poesie, as being occasioned upon representing to the very life the unbridled passions of Love, Rage, and Ambition, the violent ends or down falls of great Princes, the subversion of Kingdoms and Estates, 5 or what ever else can ⟨be⟩ imagined of funest or Tragical, all which will require a style not ramping, but passionately sedate & moving ; as for the *Ethos*, waving farther large Discourses, as intending a Preface only, not Poetical System, I shall only leave it to consideration whether the 10 use of the *Chorus* and the observation of the ancient Law of Tragedy, particularly as to limitation of time, would not rather, by reviving the pristine glory of the *Tragicall*, advance then diminish the present, adding moreover this caution that the same *Indecorums* are to be avoided in 15 *Tragedy* as have already been intimated in Heroic Poem, besides one incident to *Tragedy* alone, as namely that *Linsie-woolsie* intermixture of *Comic* mirth with Tragic seriousness, which being so frequently in use, no wonder if the name of Play be apply'd without distinction as well 20 to *Tragedy* as *Comedy* ; and for the Verse, if it must needs be Rime, I am clearly of opinion that way of Versifying, which bears the name of *Pindaric*, and which hath no necessity of being divided into *Strophs* or *Stanzas*, would be much more suitable for *Tragedy* then the continued 25 *Rhapsodie* of Riming Couplets, which whoever shall mark it well will find it appear too stiff and of too much constraint for the liberty of conversation and the interlocu- tion of several Persons : and now before ⟨I⟩ conclude, I cannot but call to mind something that may be yet alledged 30 against some very noted Writers, either Philosophers, Historians, Mathematicians, or the like, here mentioned, who for what they are said to have written in Poetry, being perhaps but small or inconsiderable, will scarce be thought worthy a place among the *Poets* ; It is true, indeed, they 35

do not shine here as in their proper *Sphear* of *Fame*;
nevertheless, since it is not ungrateful to many to know
all that hath been written by famous Men, as well in the
Arts they least as those they most profess, and since the
Register of one Science only may well take the greater
Scope within that circuit, I judged it not impertinent to
mention, as well those Famous men in other Faculties who
have also writ Poetically, as the most Famous of Poetical
Writers, considering especially how largely the Name of
Poet is generally taken; for if it were once brought to a
strict Scrutinie who are the right genuine and true born
Poets, I fear me our number would fall short, and there
are many that have a Fame deservedly for what they have
writ even in Poetry it self, who, if they came to the test,
I question how well they would endure to hold open their
Eagle eys against the Sun : Wit, Ingenuity, and Learning
in Verse, even Elegancy it self, though that comes neerest,
are one thing, true Native *Poetry* is another; in which
there is a certain Air and Spirit which perhaps the most
Learned and judicious in other Arts do not perfectly
apprehend, much less is it attainable by any Study or
Industry; nay, though all the Laws of *Heroic Poem*, all
the Laws of *Tragedy* were exactly observed, yet still this
tour entrejeant, this Poetic *Energie*, if I may so call it,
would be required to give life to all the rest, which shines
through the roughest, most unpolish't, and antiquated
Language, and may happly be wanting in the most polite
and reformed ; let us observe *Spencer*, with all his Rustie,
obsolete words, with all his rough-hewn, clowterly Verses,
yet take him throughout, and we shall find in him a grace-
full and Poetic Majesty; in like manner *Shakespear*, in
spight of all his unfiled expressions, his rambling and
indigested Fancys, the laughter of the *Critical*, yet must be
confess't a *Poet* above many that go beyond him in
Literature some degrees.   All this while it would be very

unreasonable that those who have but attempted well, much more those who have been learned, judicious, or Ingenuous in Verse, should be forgotten, and left out of the circuit of *Poets* in the larger acceptation.

Thus, most *Worthy Arbiters*, I have layd before you the reason and occasion of this design, have Apologized for what I judg'd most obnoxious to Censure or Objection, have lastly deliver'd my own sentiment in some things relating to Poetry, wherein, if I have differ'd ought from the received opinion, I can safely aver that I have not done it out of affectation of singularity, but from a different apprehension, which a strict inquiry into the truth of things (for there is also a Right and a Wrong, a Best and a Worst, as well in Poetical as other Assertions) hath suggested to my reason, perswading my self, that no right judgement can be given or distinction made in the Writings of This or That Author, in whatever Art or Science, but, without taking ought upon trust, by an unbiass'd and, from the knowledge of ancient Authors, judicious examination of each; being also sufficiently assur'd of the concurrence with me in this matter of all impartial Readers,—of yours especially, my most honoured Friends, whom I wish that fate which I am concern'd in for all deserving Writers, a lasting Fame, equal to the merit to what you have so advantagiously publisht to the World.

JOSEPH GLANVILL

FROM *AN ESSAY CONCERNING PREACHING,*
WRITTEN FOR THE DIRECTION OF A YOUNG
DIVINE, AND USEFUL ALSO FOR THE PEOPLE
IN ORDER TO PROFITABLE HEARING

1678

PLAINNESS is a Character of great latitude, and
stands in opposition, First, to *hard words*; Secondly,
to *deep* and *mysterious notions*; Thirdly, to *affected Rhetori
cations*; and Fourthly, to *Phantastical Phrases*.

1. The Preacher should use *plain words*: so the end,
Edification, requires. He that affects hard ones speaks in
an unknown tongue, and is a *Barbarian* to his Auditors;
they hear the sound, but are not edified: of all the vanities
of Speech, there is none more contemptible than this, and
none is more exploded among the wise, not only in preaching, but in all matters of solemn discourse and ordinary
conversation. It is commonly the Error of the Youth, and
may be pardon'd to such, in Moral and Philosophical
subjects; but in *Men* set apart to instruct the people in
things of spiritual and eternal concernment, 'tis not ⟨to⟩ be
indured. If you here ask me, *What I mean by hard words?*
I will presume that you cannot think I intend to condemn
all that are borrow'd from the *Greek, Latin*, or other more
modern languages. No, the *English* is a mixt speech,
made up of divers tongues, and we cannot speak without
using forreign words: So that those that talk of *pure
English*, if they mean *unmixt* by it, dream of Chimæra's:
our Language hath in all Ages been inlarging by the

Introduction of borrow'd words, which when they are once brought into common use, they may be spoken without blame of affectation ; yea, there is sometimes vanity and affectation in avoiding them. You know a great instance of this in a late Writer, who, to shun the Latinisms of 5 *immensity, eternity, penetrability,* &c., useth these—*all-place-ness, all-timeness, thorow-fareness,* and abundance such like. This *English* is far more unintelligible than that *Latin* which custom of speech hath made easie and familiar. I therefore blame not all forreign words, provided common 10 usage hath made them free of our language, and when we have not native ones that do as well express what we would say ; but to affect outlandish words that have not yet receiv'd the publick stamp, and especially to do it when the ordinary *English* will represent the thing as well,— 15 These are the hard words I condemn, and this is a vanity I think extreamly reprehensible in a Preacher. Besides which, I note by way of further limitation, and for more clearness, that I blame not all words that are not understood by the meer vulgar : every Art, every Profession, every 20 Subject hath proper terms which are of hard and harsh sound to those that understand not those matters respect-ively, but are easie and familiar to such as know them. And in Divinity there are frequent occasions of using reasons and illustrations taken from the Philosophy and 25 nature of things, as particularly in the discourses concern-ing the *Being* and *Attributes* of *God,* the *Immortality* of the *Soul,* and a future life, about *Enthusiasm* and *Fanatical* pretences to the *Spirit.* These and divers other main subjects of Religion, that are fit and necessary to be spoken 30 to, sometimes, especially among hearers of more advanced understandings, cannot be treated of without using words which the meer common sort cannot comprehend ; and yet as long as they are such as are known and frequently used in those subjects, 'twere humour and ignorance to interdict 35

them. But then I would caution here that the Preacher
should not employ more terms of art than need : Yea, he
should always avoid them when they are not necessary,
that is, when more generally known expressions will explain
the thing as well. And this further I would advise, that
you deal not much on such arguments among common
hearers. These are strong meat ; babes must have milk
and simpler diet.

To this head of hard words I may refer another vanity,
which is an affected use of scraps of *Greek* and *Latin*,
things of no Service to the vulgar, by whom they are not
understood ; and by the wise they are now generally
despised. I suppose I need not caution you, in more
words, against this antiquated pedantry, which is worn out
every where, except in some remote and dark corners,
where mean spirits seek the admiration of the ignorant by
such low and little devices. Indeed, in solemn assemblies of
knowing and learn'd men, the Authority of the ancients
may properly be cited in their own words, when they serve
to confirm or illustrate some doubted truth ; but to do it
frequently in common and vulgar matters, among ordinary
hearers, is affected folly, that signifieth nothing but the
weakness and vanity of him that doth it.

2. Preaching should be plain, in opposition to deep and
mysterious notions. We should not trouble our pulpits
with Hypotheses of Philosophy or the heights of speculative
Theology. The generality are not capable of much
Theory ; those are matters fit for the schools of learning
and the thoughts of deep, considering men. Much mischief
is faln on Religion by reason of the transgression of this
Rule ; mysterious, notional preaching hath put many conceited people upon medling with what they can never well
understand, and so hath fill'd them with air and vanity, and
made them proud, phantastical, and troublesome, disobedient to their Governours and contemptuous to their

betters.   True knowledge indeed humbleth ; but the conceited image of it, knowledge *falsly so call'd*, puffeth up,
and is an instrument of mischief.

3. Plainness may be opposed to affected Rhetorick ; and
in this sense, too, Preaching should be plain : *Not in the
inticing words of mans wisdome* or *excellency of speech* (as
the Apostle speaks), *viz.* not like the Orators and Rhetoricians of those times, who coveted the glory of being
accounted eloquent, and when they were praised they had
their reward ; but our ends are far greater and nobler, and
so we should speak, *not as pleasing men, but God*, with that
seriousness and gravity as becomes those that design
to *persuade men* in the matters that relate to the glory of
God and their own present and future well-being ; for which
purposes a manly unaffectedness and simplicity of speech
is most proper.   There is a bastard kind of eloquence that
is crept into the Pulpit, which consists in affectations of wit
and finery, flourishes, metaphors, and cadencies.   This
may be pardon'd to young men in their first Essays of
Preaching, but is by no means to be used by an exercised
and constant Preacher, for the meer common sort heed
not those things and the wise despise them, so that all the
praise that is aim'd at is lost, except it be among some
phantastical and unjudicious hearers, and on those they
have usually no other effect but that they entertain and tickle
their phancies for the present, without making any impression upon their minds or affections : And this is a very low
End for a Minister of God, who is to *beseech men in* Christ's
stead.   If we would acquit our selves as such, we must not
debase our great and important message by those vanities
of conceited speech : plainness is for ever the best eloquence,
and 'tis the most forcible ; so that our study should be to
represent what we have to deliver in proper and easie
expressions, neglecting and despising all starchedness of set
and affected speaking.

4. Plainness of preaching implies also the avoiding of phantastical phrases. There are some that place the power and spirituality of Preaching in these, and reckon that there is something of extraordinary grace and force in 5 them ; so that if a man represents the truths of the Gospel in simplicity and plainness, that shall go for dull morality ; but the same things set off by conceited, fashionable phrases shall be most rare and spiritual Divinity. Thus if you teach men to believe *Christ*'s Doctrines, to obey his Laws, 10 to trust to his promises, and to conform to his Example, these shall be counted dull, dry, and unedifying things that no-ways affect or move ; but if you tell the people that they must roll upon *Christ*, close with *Christ*, get into *Christ*, get a saving interest in the Lord *Christ*, O, this is savoury, 15 this precious, this is spiritual teaching indeed ; whereas if any thing more be meant by those phrases than what the other plain expressions intend, it is either falshood or non-sense. If therefore you would be a taking popular Preacher, here is your way ; but if you would (as I hope you design) 20 be a solid and honest one, you must avoid such odd and foolish affectations. For by the use and delight in such, ignorant people are blown up into an apprehension of their extraordinary knowledge and acquaintedness with the mysteries of the Gospel, when as indeed they know 25 nothing ; and when they hear such phrases, they are pleased with their sound, but have no meaning or know-ledge of any thing convey'd by them ; and though this be vulgarly accounted plain preaching, yet in truth it is the most difficult, and for the most part neither teachers 30 nor hearers understand it.

Thus I have described to you the first Rule and Charac-ter of Preaching : it should be PLAIN.

SAMUEL BUTLER

UPON CRITICS WHO JUDGE OF MODERN PLAYS PRECISELY BY THE RULES OF THE ANTIENTS

1678 ?

WHO ever wil Regard Poetique Fury,
    When it is once found Idiot by a Jury;
And evry Peart & Arbitrary Fool
Can all Poetique Licence over-Rule;
Assume a Barbrous Tyranny to Handle   5
The Muses worse then Ostro-goth or vandal;
Make 'em submit to verdict & Report,
And stand or Fall to th' orders of a Court?
Much lesse Be sentenc'd by the Arbitrary
Proceedings of a Witles Plagiary,   10
That forges old Records & Ordinances
Against the Right & Property of Fancys,
More False & Nice then weighing of the weather
To th' Hundredth Atom of the lightest Feather,
Or measuring of Aire upon Pernassus   15
With Cilinders of Torricellian Glasses;
Reduce all Tragedy by Rules of Art
Back to its Antique Theater, a Cart,
And make em henceforth keep the beaten Roades
Of Reverend Choruses & Episodes;   20
Reforme & Regulate a Puppet-Play,
According to the tru & antient way,
That not an Actor shal Presume to Squeek
Unless he hav a Licence for 't in Greek,

Nor Whittington Henceforward sel his Cat in
Plaine vulgar English, without Mewing Latin ;
No Pudding shalbe sufferd to be witty,
Vnless it be to terrify or Pitty ;
5   Nor Devil in the Puppet Play b' allowd
To Rore & Spit fire but to fright the Crowd,
Vnless some God or Dev'l chance t' have Piques
Against an Antient Family of Greeks ;
Others may have Leave to tremble & take warning
10   How such a Fatal Progeny th' are Born in ;
For none but such for Tragedy are fitted,
That have been Ruin'd only to be Pittyd ;
And only those held Proper to Deterre
Wh' have had th' Il Luck against their wils to erre ;
15   Whence only such as are of Midling Sizes,
Between Morality & venial vices,
Are Qualifyd to be Destroyd by Fate,
For other Mortals to take warning at ;
As if the Antique Laws of Tragedy
20   Did with our own Municipall agree ;
And serv'd like Cobwebs, but t' insnare the weake,
And give Diversion to the Great to break,
To make a lesse Delinquent to be brought
To Answer for a Greater Persons Fault,
25   And suffer all the worst, the worst Approver
Can, to excuse & save himself, Discover.
No longer shal Dramatiques be confind
To Draw tru Images of al Mankinde,
To Punish in Effigie Criminals,
30   Reprieve the Innocent, & hang the False ;
But a Club-Law ⟨to⟩ execute & kill,
For nothing, whom so ere they Please, at will,
To terrify Spectators from committing
The Crimes they did, & sufferd for, unwitting.
35   These are the Reformations of the Stage,

Like other Reformations of the Age,
On Purpose to Destroy all wit & sense,
As th' other did all Law & Conscience;
No Better then the Laws of British Plays,
Confirm'd in th' Antient good king Howels Days, 5
Who made a Gen'ral Councel Regulate
Mens catching women by the—you know what;
And set down in the Rubrick, at what time
It should be counted Legal, when a Crime,
Declare when twas, & when 'twas not a sin, 10
And on what days it went out, or came in.
An English Poet should be tryd b' his Peres
And not by Pedants & Philosophers,
Incompetent to Judge Poetique Fury,
As Butchers are forbid to b' of a Jury; 15
Beside the most Intollerable wrong,
To try their matters in a Forrain Tongue,
By Forrain Jury men, like Sophocles,
Or Tales falser then Euripides;
When not an English Native dares appear, 20
To be a witnes for the Prisoner;
When all the Laws they use t' Arraigne & try
The Innocent & wrongd Delinquent by,
Were made b' a Farraine Laweyer & his Pupils,
To Put an End to all Poetique Scruples; 25
And by th' Advice of virtuosi-Tuscans,
Determind al the Doubts of Socks & Buskins;
Gave Judgment on all Past & Future Plays,
As is Apparent by Speronys Case,
Which Lope Vega first began to steale, 30
And after him the French Filew, Corniele;
And since our English Plagiarys Nim
And steal Their farfet Criticismes from him,
And by an Action falsly layd of Trover,
The Lumber for their Proper Goods Recover; 35

Enough to furnish al the Lewd Impeachers
Of witty Beumonts Poetry, & Fletchers,
Who, for a few Misprisions of wit,
Are chargd by those who tentimes worse commit;
And for Misjudging some vnhappy scenes,
Are censurd for't with more vnlucky sense;
When all their worst miscarriages Delight
And please more then the Best that Pedants write.

JOHN WILMOT
EARL OF ROCHESTER

AN ALLUSION TO THE TENTH SATYR OF THE
FIRST BOOK OF HORACE

1677–79?

An allusion to *Horace.*
The 10th *Satyr of the* 1st *Book.*
Nempe incomposito dixi pede, &c.

WELL, Sir, 'tis granted, I said *Dryden's* Rhimes
    Were stoln, unequal, nay, dull many times :   5
What foolish Patron is there found of his,
So blindly partial, to deny me this ?
But that his Plays, embroider'd up and down
With Wit and Learning, justly pleas'd the Town,
In the same paper I as freely own.   10
Yet having this allow'd, the heavy Mass
That stuffs up his loose *Volumns* must not pass ;
For by that Rule, I might aswel admit
Crown's tedious Sense for Poetry and Wit.
'Tis therefore not enough when your false sense   15
Hits the false Judgment of an Audience
Of clapping Fools assembled, a vast crowd,
Till the throng'd Play-house crack with the dull load ;
Though ev'n that Talent merits, in some sort,
That can divert the City and the Court ;   20
Which blundring *Settle* never cou'd attain,
And puzling *Otway* labours at in vain.
But, within due proportions, circumscribe

What e're you write, that with a flowing Tide
The Style may rise: yet in its rise forbear
With useless words t' oppress the weary'd Ear.
Here be your Language lofty, there more light,
5 Your Rethorick with your Poetry unite;
For Elegance sake, sometimes allay the force
Of *Epithets*, 'twill soften the discourse;
A jeast in scorn points out and hits the thing
More home than the *Morosest* Satyrs sting.
10 *Shake-spear* and *Johnson* did herein excell,
And might in this be imitated well;
Whom refin'd *Etherege* coppy's not at all,
But is himself a sheer Original.
Nor that slow Drudge in swift *Pindarick* strains,
15 *Flatman*, who *Cowley* imitates with pains,
And rides a jaded *Muse*, whipt, with loose Rains.
When *Lee* makes temp'rate *Scipio* fret and rave,
And *Hannibal* a whining, Amorous Slave,
I laugh, and wish the hot-brain'd Fustian Fool
20 In *Busby's* Hands, to be well lasht at School.
Of all our Modern Wits, none seems to me
Once to have toucht upon true Comedy,
But hasty *Shadwell*, and slow *Wycherley*.
Shadwell's unfinish'd works do yet impart
25 Great proofs of force of Nature, none of Art;
With just bold strokes he dashes here and there,
Shewing great Mastery, with little Care;
And scorns to varnish his good touches o're,
To make the Fools and Women praise 'em more.
30 But *Wycherley* earns hard what e're he gains;
He wants no judgment, nor he spares no pains
He frequently excells, and, at the least,
Makes fewer faults than any of the best.
Waller, by nature for the *Bays* design'd,
35 With force and Fire and fancy unconfin'd,

In *Panegyricks* does excell Mankind.
He best can turn, enforce, and soften things,
To praise great Conquerors or to flatter Kings.
    For pointed Satyrs I wou'd *Buckhurst* choose,
The best good Man with the worst natur'd Muse.   5
For Songs and Verses mannerly obscene,
That can stir Nature up by spring unseen,
And, without forcing blushes, please the Queen;
Sidley has that prevailing gentle Art,
That can with a resistless Charm impart   10
The loosest wishes to the chastest Heart;
Praise such a conflict, kindle such a Fire
Betwixt declining Vertue and Desire,
Till the poor vanquish't Maid dissolves away,
In Dreams all Night, in Sighs and Tears all day.   15
Dryden in vain try'd this nice way of wit;
For he, to be a tearing *Blade*, thought fit
To give the Ladies a dry Bawdy bob,
And thus he got the name of Poet *Squab*.
But to be just, 'twill to his praise be found,   20
His Excellencies more than faults abound;
Nor dare I from his sacred Temples tear
That Lawrel which he best deserves to wear.
But does not *Dryden* find ev'n *Johnson* dull?
Fletcher and *Beaumont* uncorrect, and full   25
Of lewd Lines, as he calls 'em? *Shake-spear's* stile
Stiff and affected; to his own the while
Allowing all the justness that his Pride
So arrogantly had to these deny'd?
And may not I have leave impartially   30
To search and censure *Dryden's* Works, and try
If those gross faults his choice Pen does commit
Proceed from want of Judgment or of Wit;
Or if his lumpish fancy does refuse
Spirit and Grace to his loose slattern Muse?   35

Five hundred Verses ev'ry Morning writ,
Proves you no more a Poet than a Wit:
Such scribling Authors have been seen before:
Mustapha, the *English Princess*, forty more,
5 Were things perhaps compos'd in half an hour.
To write what may securely stand the *Test*
Of being well read over thrice at least,
Compare each Phrase, examine ev'ry Line,
Weigh ev'ry Word, and ev'ry thought refine;
10 Scorn all Applause the vile Rout can bestow,
And be content to please those few who know.
Canst thou be such a vain mistaken thing,
To wish thy *Works* might make a Play-house ring
With the unthinking Laughter and poor praise
15 Of Fops and Ladies, Factious for thy Plays?
Then send a cunning Friend, to learn thy doom
From the shrewd Judges of the drawing Room.
I've no Ambition on that idle score,
But say with *Betty Morice* heretofore,
20 When a great Woman call'd her Bawdy Whore:
I please one Man of Wit, am proud on 't too,
Let all the Coxcombs dance to Bed to you.
Shou'd I be troubled when the Pur-blind Knight,
Who squints more in his Judgment than his sight,
25 Picks silly faults, and censures what I write?
Or when the poor-fed Poets of the Town
For Scraps and Coach-room cry my Verses down?
I loath the rabble; 'tis enough for me
If *Sidley, Shadwell, Shephard, Wycherley,*
30 *Godolphin, Butler, Buckhurst, Buckingham,*
And some few more whom I omit to name,
Approve my sense: I count their censure Fame.

JOHN SHEFFIELD

EARL OF MULGRAVE, DUKE OF BUCKING-HAMSHIRE

AN ESSAY UPON POETRY

1682

OF Things in which Mankind does most excell,
 Nature's chief Master-piece is writing well ;
And of all sorts of Writing none there are
That can the least with *Poetry* compare ;
No kind of work requires so nice a touch,   5
And if well done, there 's nothing shines so much ;
But Heav'n forbid we should be so prophane,
To grace the vulgar with that sacred name ;
'Tis not a Flash of Fancy which sometimes
Dasling our Minds, sets off the slightest Rimes,   10
Bright as a blaze, but in a moment done ;
True Wit is everlasting, like the Sun,
Which though sometimes beneath a cloud retir'd,
Breaks out again, and is by all admir'd.
Number, and Rime, and that harmonious sound,   15
Which never does the Ear with harshness wound,
Are necessary, yet but vulgar Arts,
For all in vain these superficial parts
Contribute to the structure of the whole
Without a Genius too, for that 's the Soul,—   20
A Spirit which inspires the work throughout,
As that of Nature moves this World about :
A heat that glows in every word that 's writ,
That 's something of Divine, and more than Wit ;

It self unseen, yet all things by it shown
Describing all men, but describ'd by none:
Where dost thou dwell? what caverns of the Brain
Can such a vast and mighty thing contain?
5 When I at idle hours in vain thy absence mourn,
O where dost thou retire? and why dost thou return,
Sometimes with powerful charms to hurry me away
From pleasures of the night and business of the day?
Ev'n now, too far transported, I am fain
10 To check thy course, and use the needfull rein:
As all is dullness, when the Fancy's bad,
So without Judgment, Fancy is but mad;
And Judgment has a boundless influence,
Not upon words alone, or only sence,
15 But on the world, of manners, and of men:
Fancy is but the Feather of the Pen;
Reason is that substantial, useful part,
Which gains the Head, while t' other wins the Heart.

Here I should all the differing kinds reherse
20 Of *Poetry* with various sorts of Verse;
But who that task can after *Horace* do,
That mighty Master and Example too?
Ecchoes at best, all we can say is vain,
Dull the design, and fruitless were the pain.
25 'Tis true, the Ancients we may rob with ease,
But who with that sad shift himself can please,
Without an Actor's pride? A Players Art
Is more than his who writes the borrow'd part.
Yet modern Laws are made for later Faults,
30 And new Absurdities inspire new thoughts;
What need has *Satyr* then to live on theft,
When so much fresh occasion still is left?
Folly abounds, nay, flourishes at Court,
Where on its sphere it finds a kind support;

But hold, *White-Hall* has nothing now to fear,
'Tis Wit and Sence that is the Subject here.
Defects of witty Men deserve a Cure,
And those who are so will the worst endure.

 First then of *Songs*, that now so much abound : 5
Without his Song no Fop is to be found,
A most offensive Weapon which he draws
On all he meets, against *Apollo's* Laws :
Though nothing seems more easy, yet no part
Of Poetry requires a nicer Art ; 10
For as in rows of richest Pearl there lyes
Many a blemish that escapes our Eyes,
The least of which Defects is plainly shewn
In some small Ring, and brings the value down ;
So Songs should be to just perfection wrought ; 15
Yet where can we see one without a fault,
Exact propriety of words and thought ?
Th' expression easy, and the fancy high,
Yet that not seem to creep, nor this to fly ;
No words transpos'd, but in such just cadance, 20
As, though hard wrought, may seem the effect of chance ;
Here, as in all things else, is most unfit
Bawdry barefac'd, that poor pretence to Wit,—
Such nauseous Songs as the late Convert made,
Which justly call this censure on his Shade ; 25
Not that warm thoughts of the transporting joy
Can shock the Chastest or the Nicest cloy,
But obscene words, too gross to move desire,
Like heaps of Fuel do but choak the Fire.
That Author's Name has undeserved praise, 30
Who pall'd the appetite he meant to raise.

 Next, *Elegie*, of sweet but solemn voice,
And of a Subject grave, exacts the choice,
The Praise of Beauty, Valour, Wit contains,

And there too oft despairing Love complains ;
In vain, alas, for who by Wit is moved ?
That Phoenix-she deserves to be beloved ;
But Noisy Nonsence, and such Fops as vex
5 Mankind, take most with that fantastick Sex :
This to the praise of those who better knew,
The many raise the value of the few.
But here, as I too oft, alas, have tryed,
Women have drawn my wandering thoughts aside.
10 Their greatest fault, who in this kind have writ,
Is neither want of words, nor dearth of wit ;
But though this Muse harmonious numbers yield,
And every Couplet be with fancy fill'd,
If yet a just coherence be not made
15 Between each thought, and the whole model layed
So right that every step may higher rise,
As in a Ladder, till it reach the Skies ;
Trifles like these perhaps of late have past,
And may be lik'd awhile, but never last ;
20 'Tis Epigram, 'tis Point, 'tis what you will,
But not an Elegie, nor writ with skill,
No *Panegyrick*[1], nor a *Coopers-Hill*.

[1] Wallers.

A higher flight, and of a happier force,
Are *Odes*, the Muses most unruly Horse,
25 That bounds so fierce the Rider has no rest,
But foams at mouth, and speaks like one possest
The Poet here must be indeed Inspired,
And not with fancy, but with fury fired.
Cowley might boast to have perform'd this part,
30 Had he with Nature joyn'd the rules of Art ;
But ill expression gives too great Allay
To that rich Fancy which can ne're decay.
Though all appears in heat and fury done,
The Language still must soft and easy run

These Laws may seem a little too severe,
But Judgment yields, and Fancy governs there,
Which, though extravagant, this Muse allows,
And makes the work much easier than it shews.

Of all the ways that Wisest Men could find   5
To mend the Age, and mortify Mankind,
Satyr well writ has most successful prov'd,
And cures because the remedy is lov'd.
'Tis hard to write on such a Subject more,
Without repeating things said oft before.   10
Some vulgar Errors only Lets remove,
That stain this Beauty, which we chiefly love.
Of well-chose words some take not care enough,
And think they may be, as the Subject, rough.
This great work must be more exactly made,   15
And sharpest thoughts in smoothest words convey'd :
Some think if sharp enough, they cannot fail,
As if their only business was to rail ;
But 'tis mens *Foibles* nicely to unfold,
Which makes a Satyr different from a Scold.   20
Rage you must hide, and prejudice lay down :
A Satyr's Smile is sharper than his Frown.
So while you seem to scorn some Rival Youth,
Malice it self may pass sometimes for Truth.
The Laureat here may justly claim our praise,   25
Crown'd by *Mac-Fleckno* with immortal Bays ;
Though prais'd and punish'd for another's Rimes,
His own deserve that glorious fate sometimes,
Were he not forc'd to carry now dead weight,
Rid by some Lumpish Minister of State.   30

Here rest, my Muse, suspend thy cares awhile,
A greater Enterprize attends thy toil ;
And as some Eagle that intends to fly
A long and tedious Journy through the Sky,

Considers first the perils of her case,
Over what Lands and Seas she is to pass,
Doubts her own strength so far, and justly fears
That lofty Road of Airy Travellers ;
5 But yet incited by some great design,
That does her hopes beyond her fears incline,
Prunes every feather, views her self with care,
Then on a sudden flounces in the Air ;
Away she flies so strong, so high, so fast,
10 She lessens to us, and is lost at last :
So greater things my Muse prepares to sing,
Things that will Malice, and may Envy bring ;
Yet why should Truth offend, when only told
T' inform the Ignorant, and warn the Bold ?
15 On then, my Muse, adventrously engage
To give Instructions that concern the Stage.
The *Unities* of Action, Time, and Place,
Which, if observed, give Plays so great a grace,
Are, though but little practis'd, too well known
20 To be taught here, where we pretend alone
From nicer faults to purge the present Age,
Less obvious Errors of the *English* Stage.

First then, *Soliloquies* had need be few,
Extreamly short, and spoke in passion too.
25 Our Lovers talking to themselves, for want
Of others, make the Pit their Confidant ;
Nor is the matter mended much, if thus
They trust a friend only to tell it us.
Th' occasion should as naturally fall,
30 As when *Bellario* confesses all.

Figures of *Speech*, which Poets think so fine,
Art's needless Varnish to make Nature shine,
Are all but Paint upon a beauteous Face,
And in Descriptions only claim a place.

But to make Rage declame, and Grief discourse,
From Lovers in despair fine things to force,
Must needs succeed, for who can chuse but pity
To see poor Hero's miserably witty?
But O the Dialogues, where jest and mock   5
Is held up like a rest at Shittle-cock!
Or else like Bells eternally they Chime,
Men dye in Simile, and live in Rime.
What things are these who would be Poets thought,
By Nature not inspir'd, nor Learning taught?   10
Some Wit they have, and therefore may deserve
A better way than this by which they starve:
But to write Plays? why, 'tis a bold pretence
To Language, Breeding, Fancy, and good Sense;
Nay, more, for they must look within to find   15
Those secret turns of Nature in the mind;
Without this part in vain would be the whole,
And but a Body all without a Soul.
All this together yet is but a part
Of Dialogue, that great and powerful Art,   20
Now almost lost, which the old *Grecians* knew,
From whence the *Romans* fainter Copies drew,
Scarce comprehended since by but a few.
Plato and *Lucian* are the best Remains
Of all the wonders which this art contains;   25
Yet to our selves we Justice must allow,
Shakespear and *Fletcher* are the wonders now:
Consider them, and read them o're and o're,
Go see them play'd, then read them as before.
For though in many things they grosly fail,   30
Over our Passions still they so prevail,
That our own grief by theirs is rockt asleep,
The dull are forc'd to feel, the wise to weep.
Their Beauties Imitate, avoid their faults;
First on a Plot employ thy carefull thoughts,   35

Turn it with time a thousand several waies,
This oft alone has given success to Plays.
Reject that vulgar error which appears
So fair, of making perfect characters ;
5 There's no such thing in Nature, and you'l draw
A faultless Monster which the world ne're saw ;
Some faults must be, that his misfortunes drew,
But such as may deserve compassion too.
Besides the main Design, composed with Art,
10 Each moving Scene must be a Plot a part ;
Contrive each little turn, mark every place,
As Painters first chalk out the future face,
Yet be not fondly your own slave for this,
But change hereafter what appears amiss.
15 Think not so much where shining thoughts to place,
As what a man would say in such a case.
Neither in Comedy will this suffice ;
The Actor too must be before your eyes ;
And though 'tis Drudgery to stoop so low,
20 To him you must your utmost meaning show.
Expose no single Fop, but lay the load
More equally, and spread the Folly broad ;
The other way's too common : oft we see
A fool derided by as bad as he ;
25 Hawks fly at nobler game, but in his way,
A very *Owl* may prove a Bird of prey ;
Some *Poets* so will one poor Fop devour ;
But to Collect, like Bees from every flower,
Ingredients to compose that precious juice,
30 Which serves the world for pleasure and for use,
In spite of faction this will favour get,
But *Falstaff* seems unimitable yet.

Another fault which often does befall,
Is when the wit of some great *Poet* shall

So overflow, that is, be none at all,
That all his fools speak sence, as if possest,
And each by Inspiration breaks his jest ;
If once the Justness of each part be lost,
Well may we laugh, but at the *Poets* cost.   5
That silly thing men call sheer Wit avoid,
With which our Age so nauseously is cloy'd ;
Humour is all, and 'tis the top of wit
T' express agreeably a thing that 's fit.
But since the *Poets* we of late have known   10
Shine in no dress so well as in their own,
The better by example to convince,
Lets cast a view on this wrong side of sence.

  First, a Soliloquie is calmly made,
Where every reason is most nicely weigh'd ;   15
At the end of which most opportunely comes
Some Hero frighted at the noise of Drums,
For her dear sake whom at first sight he loves,
And all in Metaphor his passion proves ;
But some sad accident, that 's yet unknown,   20
Parting this pair, to leave the man alone,
He 's Jealous presently, we know not why,
Then, to oblige his Rival needs must dy ;
But first he makes a Speech, wherein he tells
The absent Nymph how much his flame excells,   25
And yet bequeaths her generously now
To that dear Rival whom he does not know,
Who, coming in, sent sure by Fate's command,
Too late alas withholds his hasty hand,
Which now has given that most lamented stroke,   30
At which this very Stranger's heart is broke ;
Who, more to his new friend than Mistress kind,
Mourns the sad Fate of being left behind,
Most naturally prefers those dying Charms

To Love and living in his Ladyes Arms.
How shamefull and what monstrous things are these !
And then they rail at th' Age they cannot please,
Conclude us only partial for the dead,
5 And grudge the Sign of old *Ben. Johnson's* head ;
When the Intrinsick value of the Stage
Can scarce be judg'd but by the following Age ;
For Dances, Flutes, *Italian* Songs, and rime
May keep up sinking Nonsence for a time ;
0 But that will fail which now so much o're rules,
And sence no longer will submit to fools.

By painfull steps we are at last got up
Pernassus hill, upon whose Airy top
The *Epick* Poets so divinely show,
15 And with just pride behold the rest below.
Heroick Poems have a just pretence
To be the chief effort of humane sence,
A work of such inestimable worth,
There are but two the world has yet brought forth,
20 *Homer* and *Virgil* : with what awfull sound
Each of those names the trembling Air does wound !
Just as a Changeling seems below the rest
Of men, or rather is a two legg'd beast,
So those Gigantick souls, amaz'd, we find
25 As much above the rest of humane kind.
Nature's whole strength united ! endless fame,
And universal shouts attend their name !
Read Homer once, and you can read no more,
For all things else will seem so dull and poor,
30 You'l wish 't unread ; but oft upon him look,
And you will hardly need another book.
Had *Bossu* never writ, the world had still
Like *Indians* view'd this wondrous piece of Skill ;
As something of Divine the work admired,

Hoped not to be Instructed, but Inspired;
Till he, disclosing sacred Mysteries,
Has shewn where all the mighty Magick lyes,
Describ'd the Seeds, and in what order sown,
That have to such a vast proportion grown.   5
Sure from some Angel he the secret knew,
Who through this Labyrinth has given the clue!
But what, alas, avails it poor Mankind
To see this promised Land, yet stay behind?
The way is shewn, but who has strength to go?   10
Who can all Sciences exactly know?
Whose fancy flyes beyond weak reason's sight,
And yet has Judgment to direct it right?
Whose nice distinction, *Virgil*-like, is such,
Never to say too little nor too much?   15
Let such a man begin without delay;
But he must do much more than I can say,
Must above *Cowley*, nay, and *Milton* too prevail,
Succeed where great *Torquato*, and our greater *Spencer* fail.

WENTWORTH DILLON

EARL OF ROSCOMMON

AN ESSAY ON TRANSLATED VERSE

1684

HAPPY that Author whose correct Essay
 Repairs so well our Old *Horatian* way,
And happy you, who, by propitious fate,
On great *Apollo*'s sacred Standard wait,
5 And with strict discipline instructed right,
 Have learn'd to *use* your arms before you *fight*.
But since the *Press*, the *Pulpit*, and the *Stage*
Conspire to censure and expose our Age,
Provok'd too far, we resolutely must
10 To the few Vertus that we have be just.
 For who have long'd, or who have labour'd more
To search the Treasures of the *Roman* store,
Or dig in *Grecian Mines* for *purer Oar*?
The noblest Fruits, Transplanted, in our Isle
15 With early Hope and fragrant Blossoms smile.
Familiar *Ovid* tender thoughts inspires,
And *Nature* seconds all his soft *Desires*;
Theocritus do's now to *Vs* belong,
And *Albion*'s *Rocks* repeat his *Rural Song*.
20 Who has not heard how *Italy* was blest,
Above the *Medes*, above the wealthy *East*?
Or *Gallus* Song so tender, and so true,
As evn *Lycoris* might with pity view!
When *Mourning Nymphs* attend their *Daphni's Herse*,

Who do's not *Weep* that *Reads* the *moving Verse*?
But hear, oh hear, in what exalted streins
Sicilian Muses through these happy Plains
Proclaim *Saturnian* Times, our own *Apollo* Reigns.

When *France* had breath'd, after intestine Broils,   5
And Peace and Conquest crown'd her forreign Toils,
There, cultivated by a Royal Hand,
Learning grew fast, and spread, and blest the Land;
The choicest Books that *Rome* or *Greece* have known,
Her excellent *Translators* made her own;   10
And *Europe* still considerably gains,
Both by their good *Example* and their *Pains*.
From hence our gen'rous Emulation came,
We undertook, and we perform'd the same.
But now *We* shew the world a nobler way,   15
And in *Translated Verse* do more than *They*.
Serene and clear, Harmonious *Horace* flows,
With sweetness not to be exprest in *Prose*;
Degrading *Prose* explains his meaning ill,
And shews the *Stuff*, but not the Workman's skill;   20
I, who have serv'd him more than twenty years,
Scarce know my Master as he there appears.
Vain are our *Neighbours Hopes*, and *Vain* their *Cares*,
The *Fault* is more their *Languages* than theirs:
'Tis courtly, florid, and abounds in words,   25
Of softer sound than ours perhaps affords;
But who did ever in *French Authors see*
The comprehensive *English Energy*?
The weighty *Bullion* of *One Sterling Line*,
Drawn to *French Wire*, would thro' whole *Pages* shine.   30
I speak my *private* but *impartial sense*,
With *Freedom*, and (I hope) without *offence*;
For I'le Recant, when *France* can shew me *Wit*,
As strong as *Ours*, and as *succinctly Writ*.

'Tis true, *Composing* is the *Nobler* Part,
But good *Translation* is no *easie* Art ;
For tho *Materials* have long since been found,
Yet both your *fancy* and your *Hands* are *bound*;
5 And by *Improving* what was writ *Before*,
Invention Labours *Less*, but *Judgment more.*

The Soil intended for *Pierian seeds*
Must be well *purg'd* from *rank Pedantick Weeds.*
Apollo starts, and all *Parnassus* shakes,
10 At the rude Rumbling *Baralipton* makes.
For none have been with *Admiration* read,
But who, beside their *Learning,* were *Well-bred.*

The first great work (a Task perform'd by few)
Is that *your self* may to *your self* be *True* :
15 No *Masque,* no *Tricks,* no *Favour,* no *Reserve* ;
Dissect your Mind, examine ev'ry *Nerve.*
Whoever *Vainly* on his *strength* depends,
Begins like *Virgil,* but like *Mævius Ends* :
That wretch, in spight of his forgotten Rhymes,
20 Condemn'd to Live to all succeeding Times,
With *pompous Nonsense* and a *bellowing sound*
Sung *lofty Ilium Tumbling* to the *Ground.*
And, if my Muse can through past Ages see,
That *Noisy, Nauseous, Gaping Fool* was *He* ;
25 Exploded, when, with universal scorn,
The *Mountains Labour'd* and a *Mouse* was *Born.*

Learn, learn, *Crotona's* brawny Wrestler cryes,
Audacious Mortals, and be *Timely* Wise !
'Tis I that call, remember *Milo's End,*
30 *Wedgd* in that Timber which he strove to *Rend.*

Each Poet with a *different Talent* writes,
One *Praises,* One *Instructs,* Another *Bites* ;

Horace did ne're aspire to *Epick Bays*,
Nor lofty *Maro* stoop to *Lyrick Lays*.
Examine how your *Humour* is inclin'd,
And which the *Ruling Passion* of your Mind ;
Then seek a *Poet* who *your* way do's bend,   5
And chuse an *Author* as you chuse a *Friend* :
United by this *Sympathetick Bond*,
You grow *Familiar, Intimate,* and *Fond* ;
Your *thoughts,* your *Words,* your *Stiles,* your *Souls* agree,
No Longer his *Interpreter,* but *He.*   10

With how much ease is a *young Muse Betray'd,*
How *nice* the *Reputation* of the *Maid* !
Your *early, kind, paternal* care appears,
By *chast Instruction* of her *Tender Years.*
The *first Impression* in her *Infant* Breast   15
Will be the *deepest* and should be the best.
Let no Austerity breed servile *Fear,*
No *wanton* Sound offend her *Virgin-Ear.*
Secure from *foolish Pride's affected state,*
And *specious Flattery's more pernicious Bait,*   20
Habitual Innocence adorns her *Thoughts,*
But your neglect must answer for her *Faults.*

Immodest words admit of no defence,
For want of *Decency* is want of *Sense.*
What mod'rate *Fop* would rake the *Park* or *Stews,*   25
Who among Troops of *faultless Nymphs* may chuse ?
Variety of *such* is to be found ;
Take then a Subject *proper* to expound :
But *Moral, Great,* and worth a *Poet's Voice,*
For Men of *sense despise a trivial Choice* :   30
And such *applause* it must expect to meet,
As wou'd some Painter, busie in a Street,
To copy *Bulls* and *Bears,* and ev'ry *Sign*
That calls the *staring Sots* to *nasty Wine.*

Yet 'tis not all to have a Subject *Good*;
It must *Delight* us when 'tis *understood*.
He that brings *fulsome Objects* to my view
(As many *Old* have done, and many *New*)
5 With *nauseous Images* my Fancy fills,
And all goes down like *Oxymel* of *Squils*.
Instruct the list'ning world how *Maro* sings
Of *useful subjects* and of *lofty Things* :
These will such true, such bright *Idea*'s raise,
10 As merit *Gratitude* as well as *Praise* ;
But *foul Descriptions* are *offensive* still,
Either for being *Like* or being *Ill*.
For who, without a *Qualm*, hath ever lookt
On *Holy Garbage*, tho by *Homer Cookt*,
15 Whose *Rayling Hero's* and whose *wounded Gods*
Make some suspect He *Snores* as well as *Nods* ?
But I offend——*Virgil* begins to *frown*,
And *Horace* looks with *Indignation* down ;
My blushing Muse with *Conscious fear* retires,
20 And whom *They like Implicitely Admires*.

On *sure Foundations* let your *Fabrick Rise*,
And with attractive *Majesty* surprise,
Not by affected, *meritricious Arts*,
But strict *harmonious Symetry* of *Parts*,
25 Which through the *Whole* insensibly must pass,
With vital Heat to animate the Mass,—
A *pure*, an *Active*, an *Auspicious flame*,
And *bright* as *Heav'n* from whence the *Blessing* came.
But few, oh few Souls, præordain'd by *Fate*,
30 The Race of *Gods* have reach'd that *envy'd Height* ;
No *Rebel-Titan's sacrilegious Crime*,
By heaping Hills on Hills can *thither climb*.
The grizly *Ferry-man of Hell* deny'd
Æneas entrance, till he knew his *Guid* ;

How justly then will impious Mortals fall,
Whose *Pride* would soar to *Heav'n* without a *Call*!

   Pride, of all others the most *dangerous* Fau't,
Proceeds from want of *Sense* or want of *Thought*.
The Men who *labour* and *digest* things *most*   5
Will be much apter to *despond* than *boast*.
For if your Author be *profoundly good*,
'Twill cost you *dear* before he's *understood*.
How many Ages since has *Virgil* writ!
How few are they who understand him *yet*!   10
Approach his Altars with *religious Fear*,
No *vulgar Deity* inhabits *there*:
Heav'n shakes not more at *Jove's imperial Nod*
Then *Poets* shou'd before their *Mantuan God*.
Hail, mighty MARO! may that Sacred Name   15
Kindle *my Breast* with *thy celestial Flame*,
Sublime Ideas and *apt Words* infuse;
The *Muse* instruct *my Voice*, and *Thou* inspire the *Muse*!

   What I have instanced only in the *best*
Is in proportion true of All the *rest*.   20
Take pains the *genuine* Meaning to explore,
There *Sweat*, there *Strain*, tug the laborious *Oar*.
Search *ev'ry Comment* that your Care can find,
Some here, some there may hit the Poets *Mind*.
Yet be not blindly guided by the *Throng*;   25
The Multitude is alwayes in the *Wrong*.
When Things appear *unnatural* or *hard*,
Consult your *Author*, with *Himself* compar'd;
Who knows what blessing *Phœbus* may bestow
And future Ages to your Labour owe?   30
Such Secrets are not easily found out,
But, once Discover'd, leave no Room for Doubt.
Truth stamps Conviction in your Ravisht Breast,
And *Peace* and *Joy* attend the glorious Guest.

Truth still is *One* ; *Truth* is Divinely *bright* ;
No cloudy *Doubts* obscure her *Native light* :
While in your *Thoughts* you find the *least* debate,
You may *Confound*, but *never* can *Translate*.
5 Your *Stile* will this through all Disguises show,
For none *explain* more clearly than they *Know* :
He only proves he *Vnderstands* a Text,
Whose *Exposition* leaves it *unperplex'd*.
They who too faithfully on *Names* insist
10 Rather Create than *Dissipate* the *Mist*,
And grow *Vnjust* by being *over nice*,
For *Superstitious Virtue* turns to *Vice*.
Let *Crassus's* Ghost and *Labienus* tell
How twice in *Parthian* plains their *Legions* fell,
15 Since *Rome* hath been so Jealous of her Fame,
That few know *Pacorus* or *Monœses* Name.

Hor. l. 3.
Od. 6.

Words in One Language Elegantly us'd
Will hardly in another be excus'd,
And some that *Rome* admir'd in *Cæsars* Time
20 May neither suit *Our Genius* nor our *Clime*.
The *Genuine Sence, intelligibly* Told,
Shews a *Translator* both *Discreet* and *Bold*.
Excursions are *inexpiably Bad*,
And 'tis much safer to leave out than *Add*.
25 Abstruse and Mystick thoughts you must express
With painful care but seeming easiness,
For truth shines brightest through the plainest dress.
Th' *Ænæan Muse*, when she appears in *state*,
Makes all *Joves Thunder* on her *Verses* wait,
30 Yet writes sometimes as soft and moving things
As *Venus* speaks or *Philomela* sings.
Your Author alwayes will the best advise :
Fall, when *He falls*; and when *He Rises, Rise*.
Affected *Noise* is the most *wretched* Thing

That to *Contempt* can *Empty Scriblers* bring.
Vowels and *Accents*, *Regularly plac'd*
On *even Syllables*, and still the *Last*,
Tho gross, innumerable *Faults* abound,
In spight of non sense never *fail* of *Sound*.   5
But this is meant of *even Verse* alone,
As being most harmonious and most known ;
For if you will unequal numbers try,
There accents on odd *Syllables* must lie.
Whatever Sister of the learned Nine   10
Do's to your suit a willing Ear incline,
Urge your success, deserve a lasting *Name*,
She'l crown a *Grateful* and a *Constant Flame*.
But if a wild *Vncertainty* prevail,
And turn your *Veering heart* with *ev'ry Gale*,   15
You lose the *Fruit* of all your *former care*
For the sad *Prospect* of a *Just Despair*.

A *Quack*, too scandalously mean to Name,
Had by *Man-Midwifry* got *Wealth* and *Fame* ;
As if *Lucina* had forgot her *Trade*,   20
The *Lab'ring wife* invok's *his surer Aid*.
Well-season'd Bowls the Gossips Spirits raise,
Who, while she Guzzles, Chats the *Doctor's* Praise.
And largely what she wants in *Words* supplies
With *Maudlin-Eloquence* of *trickling Eyes*.   25
But what a thoughtless *Animal* is *Man*,
How very *Active* in his own *Trepan* !
For greedy of *Physicians* frequent *Fees*,
From *Female Mellow Praise* He takes Degrees,
Struts in a new *Vnlicens'd Gown*, and then,   30
From *saving Women* falls to *Killing Men*.
Another Such had left the *Nation Thin*,
In spight of all the *Children* he brought in.
His *Pills* as thick as *Hand Granadoes* flew,

And where they *Fell,* as Certainly they *slew.*
His *Name* struck ev'ry where as great a *Damp*
As *Archimedes* through the *Roman Camp.*
With this the *Doctors Pride* began to *Cool,*
5 For *Smarting soundly* may *convince* a Fool.
But now *Repentance* came too late for *Grace,*
And meager *Famine* star'd him in the Face.
Fain would he to the *Wives* be reconcil'd,
But found no *Husband* left *to own a Child*;
10 The *Friends* that *got* the Brats were poyson'd too;
In this sad case what could our *Vermin* do?
Worry'd with *Debts* and past all *Hope* of *Bail,*
Th' unpity'd wretch lies *Roting* in a *Jail,*
And There, with *Basket-Alms* scarce kept *Alive,*
15 Shows how *Mistaken Talents* ought to *Thrive.*

I pity from my Soul Unhappy men,
Compell'd by *want* to *Prostitute* their *Pen,*
Who must, like *Lawyers,* either *Starve* or *Plead,*
And *follow,* right or wrong, where *Guynny's Lead*;
20 But you, *Pompilian, wealthy, pamper'd Heirs,*
Who to your *Country* owe your *Swords* and *Cares,*
Let no vain hope your easie mind seduce,
For *Rich Ill Poets* are without *Excuse.*
'Tis very Dangerous *Tampring* with a *Muse*:
25 The *Profit's small,* and you have *much* to *lose*;
For, tho *true Wit adorns* your *Birth* or *Place,*
Degenerate lines *degrade* th' *attainted Race.*
No Poet any *Passion* can Excite,
But what they feel transport them when they write.
30 Have you been led through the *Cumæan Cave,*
And heard th' Impatient Maid *Divinely Rave*?
I hear her now; I see her Rowling Eyes;
And panting, *Lo!* the *God,* the *God,* she cries;
With words not *Hers,* and more than *humane sound,*

She makes th' obedient *Ghosts* peep trembling thro the
    ground.
But tho we *must obey* when *heaven Commands,*
And man in vain the *Sacred Call withstands,*
Beware *what Spirit* rages in your breast ;   5
For ten inspir'd ten thousand are Possest.
Thus make the *proper use* of each *Extream,*
And *write* with *fury,* but *correct* with *Phleam* ;
As when the Chearful hours too freely Pass,
And sparkling wine smiles in the tempting Glass,   10
Your *Pulse* advises and Begins to beat
Through Every swelling Vein a *loud Retreat.*
So when a *Muse Propitiously invites,*
Improve her favours and *Indulge* her flights ;
But when you find that vigorous heat *abate,*   15
Leave off, and for *another Summons* wait.
Before the *Radiant Sun* a *Glimmering Lamp,*
Adult'rate Metals to the *Sterling Stamp,*
Appear not *meaner* than *mere humane Lines,*
Compar'd with those whose *Inspiration shines* ;   20
These Nervous, bold ; those Languid and *remiss* ;
There, cold salutes ; But *here* a *Lovers kiss.*
Thus have I seen a Rapid, headlong Tide,
With foaming Waves the Passive *Soan* Divide,
Whose Lazy Waters without Motion lay,   25
While he, with eager force, urg'd his Impetuous way.

    The *Priviledge* that Ancient Poets claim,
Now turn'd to *License* by too *just* a Name,
Belongs to none but an *Establisht Fame,*
Which *scorns* to *Take* it.——   30
Absur'd Expressions, crude, Abortive Thoughts,
All the lewd *Legion* of *Exploded fau'ts,*
Base Fugitives, to that *Asylum* fly,
And sacred *Laws* with *Insolence* Defy.

Not thus our *Heroes* of the *former* Days
Deserv'd and *Gain'd* their never fading *Bayes*;
For I mistake, or far the greatest Part
Of what some call *Neglect* was *study'd Art.*
5 When *Virgil* seems to *Trifle* in a Line,
'Tis like a *Warning-piece*, which gives the *Sign*
To *Wake* your *Fancy* and *prepare* your *Sight*,
To reach the noble Height of some *unusual Flight.*
I lose my Patience, when, with *Sawcy Pride*,
10 By *untun'd Ears* I hear *His Numbers* try'd.
Reverse of *Nature*! shall *such Copies*, then,
Arraign th' *Originals* of *Maro's* Pen,
And the *rude Notions* of *Pedantick Schools*
Blaspheme the sacred *Founder* of *Our Rules*!

15   The Delicacy of the nicest Ear
Finds nothing *harsh* or out of *Order* There.
Sublime or *Low*, *unbended* or *Intense*,
The *sound* is still a *Comment* to the *Sense.*

    A skilful *Ear* in *Numbers* shou'd preside,
20 And all *Disputes* without *Appeal* decide.
This ancient Rome and *Elder Athens* found,
Before *mistaken stops debauch'd* the *sound.*

    When, by Impulse from Heaven, *Tyrtæus* Sung,
In drooping Souldiers a new Courage sprung;
25 *Reviving Sparta* now the fight maintain'd,
And what *Two Gen'rals Lost*, a *Poet Gain'd.*
By secret influence of Indulgent Skyes,
Empire and *Poesy Together* rise.
True Poets are the *Guardians* of a *State*,
30 And, when *They Fail*, portend approaching *Fate*,
For that which *Rome* to *Conquest* did Inspire
Was not the *Vestal*, but the *Muses fire*;

Heaven joyns the *Blessings*; no *declining* Age
E're felt .the *Raptures* of *Poetick Rage.*

Of many faults *Rhyme* is perhaps the *Cause*;
Too *strict* to *Rhyme*, We slight more *useful* Laws;
For *That* in *Greece* or *Rome* was never *known*,   5
Till, by *Barbarian* Deluges *o'reflown*,
Subdu'd, Undone, They did at last *Obey*,
And change their *Own* for their *Invaders* way.

I grant that from some *Mossie Idol Oak,*
In *Double Rhymes* our *Thor* and *Woden* Spoke;   10
And by *Succession* of unlearned Times,
As *Bards began,* so *Monks Rung on* the *Chimes.*

But now that *Phœbus* and the *sacred Nine*
With all their Beams on our blest Island shine,
Why should not *We* their *ancient Rites restore,*   15
And *be* what *Rome* or *Athens* were *Before*?

An Essay
on blanc
verse out
of the 6th
Book of
Paradise
Lost.

Have we forgot how Raphaels *Num'rous Prose*
Led our exalted Souls through heavenly Camps,
And mark'd the ground where proud Apostate Thrones
Defy'd Jehovah? *Here, 'twixt Host and Host,*   20
(A narrow but a dreadful Interval)
Portentous sight! before the Cloudy van
Satan with vast and haughty Strides advanc'd,
Came tow'ring arm'd in Adamant and Gold.
There Bellowing Engines, with their fiery Tubes,   25
Dispers'd Æthereal forms, and down they fell
By thousands, Angels on Arch-Angels rowl'd;
Recover'd, to the hills they ran, they flew,
Which (with their pond'rous load, Rocks, Waters, Woods)
From their firm Seats torn by the Shaggy Tops,   30
They bore like shields before them through the Air,
Till more incens'd they hurl'd them at their Foes.
All was confusion; Heavens Foundations Shook,

Threatning no less than Universal Wrack,
For Michael's *arm main Promontories flung,*
And over prest whole Legions weak with Sin ;
For they Blasphem'd and struggled as they lay,
5 *Till the great Ensign of* Messiah *blaz'd,*
And, arm'd with vengeance, Gods Victorious Son
(Effulgence of Eternal Deity),
Grasping ten thousand Thunders in his hand,
Drove th' old Original Rebels headlong down,
10 *And sent them flameing to the vast Abysse.*

O may I live to hail the Glorious day,
And sing loud *Pæans* through the crowded way,
When in Triumphant State the *British* Muse,
True to her self, shall barb'rous aid Refuse,
15 And in the *Roman* Majesty appear,
Which none know better, and none come so near.

APPENDIX

JOHN EVELYN

I. LETTER TO SIR PETER WYCHE

1665

To Sr Peter Wyche, Knt.

S^r,

This crude paper (which beggs y^r pardon) I should not have presum'd to transmit in this manner, but to obey y^r co'mands, and to save the imputation of being 5 thought unwilling to labour, though it be but in gathering straw. My greate infelicity is that the meeting being on Tuesdays in ye afternoone, I am in a kind of despaire of ever gratifying myne inclinations in a conversation w^h I so infinitely honor, & that would be so much to mine 10 advantage; because the very houre interferes wth an employment, w^h being of publiq concernement, I can in no way dispense with : I mention this to deplore myne owne misfortune onely, not as it can signifie to any losse of yours; w^h cannot be sensible of so inconsiderable a 15 member. I send you notwithstanding these indigested thoughts, and that attempt upon Cicero wch you enjoin'd me.

I conceive the reason both of additions to, and the corruption of, the English language, as of most other tongues, has proceeded from the same causes ; namely, 20 from victories, plantations, frontieres, staples of com'erce, pedantry of schooles, affectation of travellers, translations, fancy and style of Court, vernility & mincing of citizens, pulpits, political remonstrances, theatres, shopps, &c.

The parts affected wth it we find to be the accent, 25 analogy, direct interpretation, tropes, phrases, and the like.

1. I would therefore humbly propose that there might first be compil'd a Gram'ar for the præcepts, which (as did the Roman, when Crates transferr'd the art to that city,

follow'd by Diomedes, Priscianus, and others who under-
tooke it) might only insist on the rules, the sole meanes
to render it a learned & learnable tongue.

2. That with this a more certaine Orthography were
introduc'd, as by leaving out superfluous letters, &c.,
such as *o* in woomen, people, *u* in honour, *a* in reproach,
ugh in though, &c.

3. That there might be invented some new periods and
accents, besides such as our gram'arians & critics use,
to assist, inspirit, and modifie the pronunciation of sentences,
& to stand as markes before hand how the voice & tone is
to be govern'd, as in reciting of playes, reading of verses,
&c., for the varying the tone of the voyce and affections, &c.

4. To this might follow a Lexicon or collection of all the
pure English words by themselves; then those w^h are
derivative from others, with their prime, certaine, and
natural signification; then, the symbolical: so as no
innovation might be us'd or favour'd, at least 'till there
should arise some necessity of providing a new edition, &
of amplifying the old upon mature advice.

5. That in order to this, some were appointed to collect
all the technical words, especially those of the more
generous employments, as the author of the 'Essaies des
Merveilles de la Nature et des plus nobles Artifices' has
don for the French, Francis Junius and others have
endeavor'd for the Latine; but this must be gleaned from
shops, not bookes, & has ben of late attempted by Mr.
Moxon.

6. That things difficult to be translated or express'd, and
such as are, as it were, inco'mensurable one to another (as
determinations of weights and measures, coines, honors,
national habits, armes, dishes, drinkes, municipal con-
stitutions of courts, old and abrogated costomes, &c.) were
better interpreted than as yet we find them in dictionaries,
glossaries, and noted in the lexicon.

7. That a full catalogue of exotic words, such as are daily
minted by our *Logodædali*, were exhibited, and that it were
resolved on what should be sufficient to render them
current, *ut Civitate donentur*, since, without restraining that
same *indomitam novandi verba licentiam*, it will in time quite
disguise the language: there are some elegant words introduc'd by physitians chiefely and philosophers, worthy to be

retained ; others, it may be, fitter to be abrogated ; since there ought to be a law as well as a liberty in this particular. And in this choyce there would be some reguard had to the well sounding and more harmonious words, and such as are numerous and apt to fall gracefully into their cadences 5 and periods, and so recommend themselves at the very first sight, as it were ; others, which (like false stones) will never shine, in whatever light they be placed, but embase the rest. And here I note that such as have lived long in Universities doe greately affect words and expressions 10 no where in use besides, as may be observed in Cleaveland's Poems for Cambridg ; and there are also some Oxford words us'd by others, as I might instance in severall.

8. Previous to this it would be enquir'd what particular 15 dialects, idiomes, and proverbs were in use in every several county of England ; for the words of ye present age being properly the *vernacula*, or classic rather, special reguard is to be had of them, and this consideration admits of infinite improvements. 20

9. And happly it were not amisse that we had a collection of ye most quaint and courtly expressions, by way of *florilegium*, or phrases distinct from the proverbs ; for we are infinitely defective as to civil addresses, excuses, & formes upon suddaine and unpremeditated though 25 ordinary encounters : in which the French, Italians, & Spanyards have a kind of natural grace & talent, which furnishes the conversation, and renders it very agreeable : here may come in synonimes, homoinymes, &c.

10. And since there is likewise a manifest rotation and 30 circling of words, which goe in & out like the mode & fashion, bookes would be consulted for the reduction of some of the old layd-aside words and expressions had formerly *in delicijs* ; for our language is in some places sterile and barren by reason of this depopulation, as I may 35 call it ; and therefore such places should be new cultivated, and enrich'd either wth the former (if significant) or some other ; for example, we have hardly any words that do so fully expresse the French *clinquant, naïveté, ennuy, bizarre, concert, façoniere, chicaneries, consummé, emotion,* 40 *defer, effort, chocq, entours, débouche,* or the Italian *vaghezze, garbato, svelto,* &c. Let us therefore (as ye Romans did

the Greeke) make as many of these do homage as are like
to prove good citizens.

11. Something might likewise be well translated out
of the best orators & poets, Greek and Latin, and even out
5 of yᵉ moderne languages, that so some judgement might be
made concerning the elegancy of yᵉ style, and so a laudable
& unaffected imitation of the best reco'mended to writers.

12. Finaly, there must be a stock of reputation gain'd by
some public writings and compositions of yᵉ Members
10 of this Assembly, and so others may not thinke it dishonor
to come under the test, or accept them for judges and
approbators; and if yᵉ designe were ariv'd thus far, I
conceive a very small matter would dispatch the art of
rhetoric, which the French propos'd as one of the first
15 things they reco'mended to their late academitians.

I am, Sʳ,

Yʳ most, &c.

Says-Court, 20 June, 1665.

II. LETTER TO SAMUEL PEPYS

1689

To Mr. Pepys.

Sir,

20 I was on Wednesday last (afternoone) to kisse your
hands; but finding you abroad, and my selfe obliged to
returne that evening, that I might receive the Countess of
Sunderland, who sent me word she would call at my house
the next morning early, before her embarkment for Holland,
25 I do now write what I should have said to you, if time had
permitted; and that is to let you know that, upon your late
communicating to me your desire of adorning your choice
library with the pictures of men illustrious for their parts
and erudition, I did not in the least suspect your intention
30 of placing my shallow head amongst those heroes, who,
knowing my unworthynesse of that honour, will in spight
of your good opinion of Mr. Kneller for his skill of drawing
to the life, either condemne his colouring, that he made
me not blush, or me for impudence that I did not. But

this is not all; for men will question your judgment or
suspect you of flattery, if you take it not downe; for, in
good earnest, when I seriously consider how unfit I am to
appeare in the classe of those learned gentlemen, I am
perfectly asham'd, & should say with much more reason 5
than Marullus (after a recension of the famous poets)

Nos, si quis inter cæteros locat Vates,
—Onerat, quam honorat verius.

'Tis pitty, and a diminution, so elegant a place & precious
collection should have any thing in it of vulgar, but such 10
as Paulus Jovius has celebrated, and such as you told
me you were procuring, the Boyles, the Gales, & the
Newtons of our nation: what, in God's name, should
a planter of colewort do amongst such worthies? Setting
him aside, I confesse to you I was not displeas'd with the 15
fancy of the late Lord Chancellor Hyde, when to adorne
his stately palace (since demolished) he collected the pictures of as many of our famous countrymen as he could
purchase or procure, instead of the heads and busts of
forreiners, whose names, thro' the unpardonable mistake or 20
(shall I call it?) pride of painters, they scorne to put to
their pieces, imagining it would dishonour their art, should
they transmit every thing valuable to posterity besides
faces, which signifie nothing to the possessor (vnlesse
their relations were to live for ever, & allways in being), 25
so as one cannot tell whether they were drawn from any
of their friends or ancestors, or the picture of some porter
or squalid chimney sweeper, whose prolix beard and
wrinkled forehead might passe him for a philosopher. I
am in perfect indignation at this folly, as oft as I consider 30
what extravagant sums are given for a dry scalp of some
(forsooth) Italian painting, be it of Raphael or Titian himselfe, which would be infinitely more estimable, were we
assured it was the picture of the learned Count of Mirandula,
Politian, Guicciardini, Machiavel, Petrarch, Ariosto, or 35
Tasso; or some famous pope, prince, poet, or other hero of
those times. Give me Carolus Magnus, a Tamerlaine, a
Scanderbeg, Solyman the Magnificent, Matt. Corvinus,
Lorenzo, Cosimo Medicis, Andrea Doria, Ferdinando Cortez,
Columbus, Americus Vesputius, Castracani Castruccio, and 40
a Sforza; the effigies of Cardan, and both the Scaligers,

Tycho Brahe, Copernicus, and Galileo. I say, give me the portraits of an Isabella of Arragon or Castile, and her foure daughters ; Lucretia d'Este (to whom our Queene is related), Victoria Colonna, Hippolita Strozzi, Petrarch's Laura, Anna Maria Schurman, and above all Hellen Cornaro, daughter of a procurator of St. Marco (one of the most illustrious families of Venice), who received the degree of Doctoresse at Padua for her universal knowledge & erudition, upon the importunity of that famous University prevailing on her modesty. She had ben often sought in honorable marriage by many greate persons ; but, preferring the Muses before all other considerations, she preserved herselfe a virgin, and being not long since deceased, had her obsequies celebrated at Rome by a solemn procession, & elogie of all the witts of that renowned citty. Nor may I forget the illustrious of our owne nation of both sexes ; the Westons, Moores, Seymours, Sir J. Cheke. Ann Countess of Oxon (whose monument is in Westminster Abbey), the late Mrs. Philips, & Princesse Elizabeth, eldest daughter to the unfortunate Queen of Bohemia, to whom the greate Des Cartes dedicates his bookes, with a world of more renowned characters, famous for armes & arts ; rather than the most beautiful courtezan or prostitute of them all, who has nothing to commend her but her impudence & that she was a painted strumpet. Did it ever prejudice the glory of the inimitable Holbein, for putting the names of our greate Duke of Norfolk, Henry the Eighth, when lesse corpulent, Edward the Sixth, & Treasurer Cromwell, Jane Seymour, Anne Bulleyn, Charles Brandon, Althea Talbot, Countesse of Arundel, Card. Wolsey, Sr Thomas More & his learned daughters, Sr Brian Tuke, Dr. Nowel, Erasmus, Melancthon, and even honest Frobenius, among innumerable other illustrious of that age for learning & other vertues ? I aske if this were the least diminution to the fame of one who realy painted to the life beyond any man this day living ? But, in truth, they seeme from the beginning jealous of their owne honour, & afraid of being forgotten ; hence we find ΓΛΥΚΩΝ ΑΘΗΝΑΙΟΣ ΕΠΟΙΕΙ insculpt on the Farnesian Hercules, and *Michael Angelo fecit, P. P. Rubens pinxit, Marc. Antonio cœlavit, &c.* There is not that wretched print but weares the name of no-artist, whilst

our painters take no care to transmitt to posterity the names
of the persons whom they represent; through which negligence so many excellent pieces come after a while to be
dispers'd amongst brokers and up-holsters, who expose
them to the streetes in every dirty and infamous corner. 5
'Tis amongst their dusty lumber we frequently meete with
Queene Elizabeth, Mary Q. of Scots, the Countesse of
Pembroke, Earles of Leycester and Essex, Sir Walter
Raleigh, Sr Philip Sidney, Cecil, Buckhurst, Walsingham,
Sir Francis Bacon, King James and his favourite Bucking- 10
ham, and others who made the greate figure in this nation,
of John Husse, Zisca, Luther, Calvine, Beza, Socinus,
William & Maurice, Princes of Orange, Charles the Fifth,
Philip the Second, Francis the First, the Dukes of Alba,
Parma, Don John of Austria, and Count Egmont, authors 15
of sects, great captaines and politicians (famous in our
historie in other countries), flung many times behind the
hangings, covered with dust and cobwebs. Upon this
account it is, men curious of books & antiquities have ever
had medals in such estimation, & rendered them a most 20
necessary furniture to their libraries, because by them we
are not onely inform'd whose real image & superscription
they beare, but have discovered to us, in their reverses,
what heroical exploits they perform'd;— their famous
temples, bazilicæ, thermæ, amphitheaters, aquæducts, 25
circuses, naumachias, bridges, triumphal arches, columns,
historical & other pompous structures & erections by them,
and which have ben greately assistant to ye recovery of the
antient & magnificent architecture, whose real monuments
had ben so barbarously defac'd by the Goths & other 30
truculent invaders, that without this light (& some few
ruines yet extant justifie those types) that so vsefull order
and ornament of columns & their concomitant members
were hardly to be known by the text of Vitruvius and all
his learned Commentators, and till Daniel Barbaro, Leon 35
Alberto, Raphael, M. Angelo, & others raised it out of the
dust & restor'd that noble art, by their owne and other
learned men consulting & comparing the reverses of
medals and medalions: besides what they farther contribute to the elucidation of many passages in historie, 40
chronologie, and geography. So as I do not see how
Mr. Pepys's library can be long without this necessary

adjunct. It is amongst the medals we meete the ancient legislators, Lycurgus, Solon, Numa, &c. There we find Orpheus, Linus, & the old bards, and there is mention of Numus Homericus by Strabo, & (if I well remember) by Aristotle himselfe too; as there is stil extant those of the brave Hector & Achilles: so as among them we may see what kind of persons were Aristides, Themistocles, Epaminondas, Miltiades, Alexander, & Cyrus, Darius, &c. The grave philosophers, Socrates, Pythagoras, Plato, Aristotle, Epicurus, Zeno, and Demosthenes, shew their faces to this day revered in our medals. Those of the Hebrew represent to us the rod of Aaron & pot of manna, & shew how Juda was led captive. We come by medals to understand the antient weight⟨s⟩ & measures, and the value of monies: you will see there when it was that princes assum'd the radiant crownes, and what the diademe was. I might proceede to yᵉ Punic Hanibal, Juba, &c., to the Consular & Imperial of the Romans from Romulus, the Scipios, Catos, down to this age of ours, if after Pertinax, and decline of that empire, sculpture & all good arts had not fall'n with it. You will therefore be curious of having the first Cæsars, the greate Julius (after his Pharsalian victorie) being the first honour'd with having his effigies, old, leane, & bald as he was, in medal, or rather in monie, which are rare to procure in gold or small copper. There are of these and the other Emperors with Greeke inscriptions also. Who is not delighted to behold the true effigies of the famous Augustus, cruel Nero & his master Seneca, Vespasian, Titus, Nerva, Trajan, Antoninus, Severus, the greate Constantine & his devout mother Helena? For we have in medals the beautiful Cleopatra & her paramour, Drusilla, Livia, Julia, Agrippina, Antonia, Valeria, Messalina, Octavia, Poppæa Sabina, all of them Augustas, and sundry more of the faire sex who rul'd the world. I have seene a series of the Popes from St. Peter, & amongst the reputed Heresiarcs, that medalion of John Huss & Hierome of Prague's martyrdome, with the memorable inscription, *Post centum annos vos Cito,* which fell out at the appearing of Martin Luther exactly at that period. But, Sir, I am sensible I have quite tir'd you by this time with medals, & therefore I will say nothing concerning those observations in the filing, sharpnes, & due extancie, vernish, & other markes, necessary to be critically skill'd in to prevent the being cheated & impos'd upon by copies & counterfeits for antique & original (tho' yet all copies, if well dissembled, stamp'd, or cast, are not to be rejected), because you will, both for this and all the rest, consult Fulvius Ursinus, 5 Goltzius, Monsr St. Amant, Otto, Dr Spon, Vaillant, Dr. Patin, and (*instar omnium*) the most learned Spanhemius in that treatise *de præstantia et usu Numismatum Antiquorum*. You will likewise make vse of your friends, Dr Gale, Mr Henshaw, Hill, and Mr Justell, vpon whose 10 skill & judgment you may relie, tho' even the most skillful may now & then be mistaken : but you shall be sure not to be paied with trash, such as I do not (as I say'd) call the Antiquo Moderno, if well imitated. These persons, y^r friends whom I mention'd, will, I am sure, be ready to 15 assist you in this laudable curiositie. And if they can be purchas'd together, as accidentaly they sometimes may, it will save you a greate deale of paines, & enrich you at once. But otherwise, they are likeliest met withall amongst the goldsmiths, & casualy as one walkes the streetes on 20 foot, & passes by the stalls. Mr. Ashmole, our common friend, had collected all the antient & modern coines of this kingdome, which were very rare, together with seuerall medalls of our British, Saxon, & other Kings, vpon occasion of births, coronations, marriages, & other solemnities. I 25 know not whether they escap'd the burning of his study at the Middle Temple. But for the most accurate ordering & disposing of medals, so as one may more commodiously take them out of their repositories, Mr. Charleton of that Society has a peculiar method, as he is the most elegant 30 & rarely furnish'd in all his other collections. In the meane time, the curious of this sort of erudition (I meane of medalls) were formerly, & I believe at present, very few in England. For besides Sr Robert Cotton, Mr Selden, Sr Simon D'Ewes, Sr Tho. Hanmer of Hanmer, Sr Willm 35 Paston, and the late Mr Hervey, I find hardly any. That greate lover of antiquity, Thomas Earle of Arundel, had a very rich collection as well of medalls as other intaglias, belonging to the cabinet he purchas'd of Daniel Nice at the cost of ten thousand pounds, which, with innumerable 40 other rarities, haue ben scatter'd & squander'd away by his Countesse, when she got that treasure to Amsterdam,

whilst my Lord was in Italy, where he died. Aboundance
of them she bestow'd also on the late vnhappy Viscount
Stafford, her beloved son ; & such as remained, Lely,
Wright, & the rest of the painters, panders, and misses,
5 haue cheated the late Duke of Norfolk of. The same fate
befell a noble collection of medals belonging to the then
curious Sʳ Simon Fanshaw of Ware-park ; they were after
his decease thrown about the house (as that worthy gent:
his son Sʳ Richard, Lᵈ Ambassʳ in Spain, from whom I
10 had the relation, has told me) for children to play at
counter with ; as were those elegant types of Sʳ Henry
Savills at Eaton, which that learned Knight procur'd with
greate cost for his edition of St. Chrysostome, & as it
com'only fares with such curiosities, where the next heire
15 is not a virtuoso. So vaine a thing it is to set ones heart
vpon any thing of this nature with that passion & mania,
that unsatiable Earle whom I mention'd did, to the
detriment of his estate and family,—*mediocria firmu*. The
medals in our Universitie Libraries are not yet at all con-
20 siderable, tho' Obadiah Walker were an industrious pro-
moter of it, & not vnskillfull in them. Mr. Ralph Sheldon,
of Weston in Warwickshire, left a very handsome collection
both of gold, silver, & copper, antient & moderne, part of
which were bequeathed to a sister of my Lady Tuke's, who
25 not long since offer'd to haue sold them. I brought Monsʳ
Justell to see them, but they were much ouer-valued, &
whether she haue since dispos'd of them I neuer inquir'd.
At present I know of none who can show a better chosen
set of medals than the Earle of Clarendon, to whose late
30 father (after all this tedious parenthesis) I returne, & haue
a mind to entertaine you a while longer with what I had
begun, where I spake of his purpose to furnish all the
roomes of state and other apartments with the pictures of
the most illustrious of our nation, especially of his Loᵖˢ
35 time & acquaintance, & of diuers before it. There were at
full length, and as I doubt not but you well remember to
haue seene, the greate Duke of Buckingham, the brave Sʳ
Horace & Francis Vere, Sʳ Walt. Raleigh, Sʳ Phil. Sidney,
the greate Earle of Leicester, Treasurer Buckhurst, Bur-
40 leigh, Walsingham, Cecil, Lᵈ Chanʳ Bacon, Elsmere, &
I think all the late Chancelors & graue Judges in the
reignes of Q. Elizabeth & her successors, James &

Charles the First. For there was Treas^r Weston, Cotting-
ton, Duke Hamilton, the magnificent Earle of Carlisle,
Earles of Carnarvon, Bristol, Holland, Lindsey, Northum-
berland, Kingston, and Southampton, Lords Falkland and
Digby (I name them promiscuously as they come into 5
my memorie); & of Charles the Second, besides the Royal
Family, the Dukes of Albemarle and Newcastle, Earles of
Derby, Shrewsbery, St. Alban's, the brave Montrósse,
Sandwich, Manchester, &c.; and of the coife, S^r Ed. Coke,
Judge Berkeley, Bramston, Sr Orlando Bridgman, Jeofry 10
Palmer, Selden, Vaughan, Sr Rob. Cotton, Dugdale, Mr.
Camden, Mr. Hales of Eton. The Archbishops Abbot &
Laud, Bishops Juxon, Sheldon, Morley, and Duppa, Dr.
Sanderson, Brownrig, Dr. Donne, Chillingworth, & seuerall
of the Cleargie, & others of the former & present age. For 15
there were the pictures of Fisher, Fox, Sr Tho. More, Tho.
Lord Cromwell, Dr. Nowel, &c. And what was most
agreeable to his L^{is} general humor, old Chaucer, Shakspere,
Beaumont & Fletcher, who were both in one piece, Spencer,
Mr. Waller, Cowley, Hudibras, which last he plac'd in 20
the roome where he vs'd to eate & dine in publiq, most of
which, if not all, are at the present at Cornebery in
Oxfordshire, together with the library, which ye present
Earle has considerably improv'd, besides what bookes he
has at Swalowfield not contemptible, & the manuscript 25
copies of what concernes the Parliamentary Records,
Journals, & Transactions, which I haue heard both himself & the late vnfortunate Earl of Essex (who had also
the same curiosity) affirme cost them £500 transcribing &
binding, & indeede furnish a prety large roome. To com- 30
pleate & encourage this noble and singular collection, I sent
his L^p a list of the names following: Cardinals Pole and
Wolsey, Gardner Bp. of Winchester, Cranmer, Ridley,
old Latimer, Bp. Usher, Mr. Hooker, Occham, Ridley,
John Duns, Roger Bacon, Suisset, Tunstal Bp. of Duresme 35
(correspondent with Erasmus), Tompson, Ven: Bede, if at
least to be met with in some ancient office or masse booke,
where I haue seene some of those old famous persons ac-
curately painted either from the life or from copies:
Sr John Cheke, Sr Tho. Bodley, Smith, Jo. Berkeley, Mr. 40
Ascham, Sr Fulk Greuil, Buchannan, Dr Harvey, Gilbert,
Mr. Oughtred, Sr Hen. Wotton (I still recite them promis-

cuously & not like an herauld), Sr Fra. Drake, Sr Rich.
Hawkins, Mr. Cavendish, Martine Frobisher, &c.; some of
which his Lo^p procured, but was, you know, interrupted,
and after all this apparatus and grandeure died an exile,
5 & in the displeasure of his Majesty & others who envied
his rise & fortune—*tam breves Populi Romani amores!*
But I shall say no more of his ministrie, and what was
the pretence of his fall, than that we haue liued to see
greate revolutions.   The buffoons, parasites, pimps, & con-
10 cubines, who supplanted him at Court, came to nothing
not long after, and were as little pitied.   'Tis something
yet too early to publish the names of his delators, for fear
of one's teeth.   But time will speake truth, and sure I am
the event has made it good.   Things were infinitely worse
15 manag'd since his disgrace, & both their late Maties fell into
as pernicious counsels as euer Princes did, whilst what
euer my Ld Chancel^rs skill, whether in law or politics, the
offices of State & Justice were filled with men of old
English honor & probitie; lesse open bribery & ostenta-
20 tion; there was at least something of more grauity and
forme kept up (things, however railled at, necessary in
Courts): magnificence & antient hospitalitie in his Maties
houses, more agreeable to the genius of this nation than the
open & avowed luxurie & prophaneness which succeeded,
25 *à la mode de France*, to which this favorite was a declared
enemy, vpon my certaine knowledge.   There were indeede
heinous matters laied to his charge, which I could neuer
see prov'd; & you & I can tell of many that haue fall'n
and yet suffer under that calamitie.
30   But what's all this, you'll say, to our subject? Yes, he
was a greate lover at least of books, & furnish'd a very
ample library, writ himselfe an elegant style, fauour'd &
promoted the designe of the Royal Society; and it was
for this, and in particular for his being very kind to me
35 both abroad & at home, that I sent Naudæus to him in
a dedicatory Addresse, of which I am not so much asham'd
as of the Translation.   There be some who, not displeas'd
with the style of that Epistle, are angrie at the application.
But they do not consider that greate persons, & such as
40 are in place to doe greate & noble things, whateuer their
other defects may be, are to be panegyrized into the
culture of those vertues, without which 'tis to be suppos'd

they had neuer ariv'd to a power of being able to encourage
them. *Qui monet vt facias*—you remember the sequel.
And 'tis a justifiable figure; nor is it properly adulation,
but a civilitie due to their characters. As for the Translation, it has ben so insufferably abus'd at the presse, that 5
the shame any uncorrected copy should come abroad has
made me suppresse as many as I could light on, not without purpose of publishing a new edition, and which now
perhaps might be more seasonable, since the humor of
exposing books *sub hastâ* is become so epidemical, that it 10
may possibly afford some direction to gentlemen who are
making collections out of them. Besides, the first impression is, I heare, prety well worne out, and I should
be very unfortunate if it should miscarry twice, or meete
with such another accident as happen'd, it seemes, to the 15
blotted manuscript at Oxford, the circumstances whereof
I will not now trouble you withall.

And so I haue don with my Ld Chancelor. But not so
soone with my worthy friend Mr. Pepys, to whose learned
& laudable curiosity of still improving his choice collection 20
I should not aduise a solicitous expense of hauing the
pictures of so many greate persons paynted in oyle, which
were a vast & unnecessary charge, tho' not so extraordinary
a one to my Ld Chancel^r, as one may imagine, because,
when his designe was once made known, euery body who 25
either had them of their owne or could purchase them at
any price, strove to make their court by these presents;
by which meanes he got many excellent pieces of Vandyke,
and other originals of Lely, & the best of our modern
masters hands. But if, insteade of these, you think fit to 30
add to your title-pages, in a distinct volume, the heads &
effigies of such as I haue enumerated, and of as many
other as either in this or any other age have ben famous
for armes or arts, in *taille douce*, and with very tollerable
expense to be procur'd amongst the print-sellers, I should 35
not reprove it; I am sure you would be infinitely delighted
with the assembly, and some are so very well don to the
life, that they may stand in competition wth the best
paintings. This were a cheape and so much a more
vsefull curiosity, as they seldome are without their names, 40
ages, and elogies of the persons whose portraits they
represent: I say you will be exceedingly pleas'd to con-

template the effigies of those who haue made such a noise
& bustle in the world, either by their madnesse & folly, or
a more conspicuous figure by their wit & learning.   Nor
would I yet confine you to stop here, but to be continualy
5 gathering as you happen to meete wth other instructive
types.   For vnder this classe may come in batails, sieges,
triumphs, justes & tournaments, coronations, cavalcads, &
entries of ambassadors, processions, funebral & other
pomps, tombs, tryals & executions;   stately edifices,
10 machines, antique vases, spoiles, basse relievos, intaglios,
& cameos taken from achates, onyxes, cornelians, & other
precious stones;   ruines, landskips, if from real subjects,
not fancies which are innumerable & not necessary, but
such as relate to historie, and for reasons specified more
15 at large in my Treatise on Chalcographie.   Your library
being by this accession made suitable to your generous
mind & steady virtue, I know none liuing master of more
happinesse, since, besides the possession of soe many
curiosities, you vnderstand to vse & improue them likewise,
20 & haue declar'd that you will endeauour to secure what
with so much cost & industrie you haue collected, from the
sad dispersions many noble libraries & cabinets haue
suffer'd in these late times,—one auction, I may call it
diminution, of a day or two, hauing scatter'd what has
25 ben gathering many yeares.   Hence it is that we are in
England so defectiue of good libraries among the gentlemen & in our greatest townes; Paris alone, I am persuaded,
being able to shew more than all the three nations of Greate
Britaine : those of Mem'ius, Puteane, Thuanus, Cordesius,
30 Seguier, Colbert, Condé, & others innumerable of bishops,
abbots, advocates, antiquaries, & a world of learned persons of the long robe, besides the publiq libraries at St.
Victoire, the Sorbonne, & aboue all, that of Mazarin (now,
with Richelieu's & sundry others, swallow'd vp in the
35 present King's) far exceeding any thing we can shew at
home, tho' we have as much (if not greater) plenty &
variety of the best books as any country in the learned
world.   But, as I said, they are in private cabinets, &
seldome well chosen, vnlesse in the Vniuersities, where, if
40 one may judge by the few productions of so many learned
men as are there at leasure, they signifie so very little to
the learned world.   This greate & august citty of London,

abounding with so many wits and letter'd persons, has
scarce one library furnish'd and indow'd for the publiq.
Sr John Cotton's, collected by his noble vncle, is without
dispute the most valuable in MSS., especialy of British
and Saxon antiquities ; but he refuses to impart to vs the 5
catalogue of this treasure, for feare, he tells me, of being
disturb'd. That of Westminster is not much considerable,
still less that of Syon Colledge. But there is hope 'his
Maties at St. James's may emerge & be in some measure
restor'd againe, now that it comes vnder the inspection of 10
the learned Mons. Justell, who, you know, was owner of
a very considerable one at Paris. There are in it a greate
many noble manuscripts yet remaining, besides the Tecla;
and more would be, did some royal or generous hand
cause those to be brought back to it, which still are lying 15
in mercenary hands for want of two or three hundred
pounds to pay for their binding ; many of which, being of
the oriental tongues, will soone else find Jewes & chap-
men that will purchase & transport them, from whence we
shall neuer retreiue them againe. For thus has a cabinet 20
of ten thousand medals, not inferior to most abroad, & far
superior to any at home, which were collected by that
hopefull cherisher of greate and noble things, Prince
Henry, been imbezil'd and carried away during our late
barbarous rebellion, by whom & whither none can or is like 25
to discouer. What that collection was, not onely of bookes
and medals, but of statues & other elegant furniture, let
the learned library-keeper, Patritius Junius, tell you in his
notes ad Epist. S^ti Clementis ad Corinthios : 'quem locum'
(speaking of St. James's) 'si vicinam pinacothecam biblio- 30
thecæ celeberrimæ conjunctam, si numismata antiqua
Græca ac Romana, si statuas & signa ex ære et marmore
consideres, non im'erito thesaurum antiquitatis et ταμιεῖον
instructissimum nominare potes,' &c.

Were not this losse enough to break a lover's heart ? 35
The Royal Society at Gresham Colledge has a mixture,
tho' little apposite to the institution & designe of that
worthy assembly, yet of many excellent books and some
few MSS. given them at my instance by the late Duke of
Norfolck, w^h is but a part of that rare collection of good 40
authors which by the industrie & direction of Francis
Junius, the learned son of the learned Patrick, Mr. Selden,

& the purchase of what was brought at once out of Germanie, was left neglected at Arundel House before it was demolished & converted into tenements. I now mention Mr. Selden. There is a fragment of that great antiquarie's
5 librarie at the Middle Temple; but his manuscripts & best collections were bequeath'd to the Bodleian at Oxford, to which both himselfe & especialy Archbishop Laude were the most munificent benefactors, tho', with all these, so poore in manuscripts that they were ashamed to publish
10 their catalogue with that of the *impressorum*, but which might yet have ben equaly inriched with any perhaps in Europe, had they purchas'd what was lately offer'd them by the executors of Isaac Vossius, tho' indeede at a great price, who have since carried them back into Holland,
15 where they expect a quicker mercate. I wished with all my heart some brave and noble Maecenas would have made a present of them to Trinity Colledge in Cambridge, where that sumptuous structure (design'd for a library) would have ben the fittest repository for such a treasure.
20 Where are our Suissets, Bodleys, Lauds, Sheldons, bishops & opulent chancelors? Will the *Nepotismo* neuer be satisfied—*Sed præstat motus componere.* The next to that of the Bodleian are the librarys of Magdalen Coll., Christ Church, University, & Baliol, which last is furnish'd
25 with diuers considerable MSS., & lately (thro' the bounty of Sir Tho. Wendie) with a number of other curious books. But to returne againe neerer this Citty: That at Lambeth, replenish'd at present with excellent books, ebbs & flows like the Thames running by it, at every prelat's succession
30 or translation: there's at present a good assembly of manuscripts in a roome by themselues. The Bishop of Ely has a very well stor'd library; but the very best is what Dr. Stillingfleete, Deane of St. Paules, has at Twicknam, ten miles out of towne. Onely that good & learned man,
35 Dr. Tennison of St. Martine's, neere you, has begun a charity, for so I reckon it as well as that of his two scholes, &c., worthy his publiq & generous spirit, and the esteeme of all who know him. Our famous lawyer Sʳ Edw. Coke purchas'd a very choice library of Greeke & other MSS.
40 which were sold him by Dr. Meric Casaubon, son of the learned Isaac; & these together wᵗʰ his delicious villa, Durdens, came to yᵉ possession of yᵉ present Earle of

Berkley from his unkle Sr Robert Cook. He has sometimes told me he would build a convenient repository for
them, which should be publiq for the use of the cleargie of
Surrey ; but what he has don, or thinks to do herein, I
know not. Why is not such provision made by a publiq 5
law & contribution in euery county of England ? But this
genius dos not allways preside in our representatiues.
I haue heard that Sr Henry Sauill was master of many
precious MSS., & he is frequently celebrated for it by the
learned Valesius, almost in euery page of that learned 10
man's annotations on Eusebius & the ecclesiastical historians publish'd by him. The late Mr. Hales of Eton,
whom I mention'd, had likewise a very good library, and
so had Dr. Cosin, late Bishop of Duresme, a considerable
part of which I had agreed with him for my selfe during 15
his exile abroad, as I can shew under his owne hand ; but
his late daughter, since my Lady Garret, thought I had
not offer'd enough, & made difficulty in deliuering them to
me 'till neere the time of his Maties restauration, & after
that, the Deane her father, becoming Bishop of that 20
opulent see, bestow'd them on the library there. But the
Ld Primate Usher was inferior to none I haue named
among the cleargie for rare MSS., a greate part of which,
being brought out of Ireland, & left his son-in-law S^r
Timothy Tirrill, was dispos'd of to giue bread to that in- 25
comparable prelate during the late fanatic war ; such as
remain'd yet at Dublin were preserv'd, and by a publiq
purse restored & placed in the colledge library of that citty.
I haue already mention'd what Isaac Vossius brought ouer,
that had been his learned father's, & many other manu- 30
scripts which Isaac had himselfe brought from Queene
Christina out of Sweden in recompense of his honorarie,
whilst he was invited thither with Salmasius, Des Cartes,
Blundel, & others, by the heroic and royal errant. But
those birds, as I sayd, haue taken their flight, & are gon. 35
I forbear to name the late Earle of Bristol's & his kinsman
Sr Kenelm Digby's libraries, of more pomp than intrinsic
value, as chiefly consisting of modern poets, romances,
chymical & astrological bookes, for I had the Catalogue in
my possession before they were disposed of, put into my 40
hands by my Lord Danby, then Treasurer, who desir'd me
to giue my opinion of them, which I faithfully did. As for

those of Sr Kenelm's, the Catalogue was printed, & most
of them sold in Paris, as many better haue lately ben in
London. The Duke of Lauderdaile's is yet intire, choicely
bound, & to be sold by a friend of mine, to whom they are
5 pawn'd ; but it comes far short of his relation's, the Lord
Maitland's, which was certainely the noblest, most substantial, & accomplished library that euer pass'd vnder the
speare, and it heartily grieu'd me to behold its limbs, like
those of the chaste Hippolytus, separated & torne from
10 that so well chosen & compacted body. The Earle of
Anglesey's, & severall others since, by I know not what
invidious fate, pass'd the same fortune, to what euer
influence & constellation now reigning malevolent to books
& libraries, which can portend no good to the future age.
15 And now I haue in good earnest don with libraries,
but yet not quite with Mr. Pepys. For I mention none
of all these as if I thought it necessary euery private
gentleman's study should be made common, but wish we
had some more communicatiue & better furnish'd with
20 good books, in one of the greatest citties of the universe,
London ; & for that end that a stately portico were so
contriu'd at the west end of St. Paule's as might support
a palatine capable of such a designe ; & that every company
and corporation of the Citty, euery apprentise at his
25 freedom, assisted at first by a general collection thro-out
the nation, a copy of euery booke printed within the Citty
& Vniversities, did cast in their symbols for a present
stock & a future ample funde. But this we are to expect
when kings are philosophers, or philosophers kings ;
30 which I think may happen not in this but in Plato's
revolution. All that I shall add concerning gentlemen
being furnish'd with competent libraries & for most part
residing in towne is how obliging a thing it were, & of
infinite effect to the promoting a noble and vsefull con-
35 versation of learned gentlemen, if, as there is a Society
for the Improvement of Natural Knowledge, and which
was fit should be first, since things were before words, so
there was an Academie for that of Art & Improvement of
speaking & writing well ; of which sort there are, you
40 know, some in Paris, & almost in euery considerable citty
of Italy, which go under the devises of *La Crusca,
Humoristi, Insensati,* &c.; as that of the *Beaux Esprits* in

France, set vp by the late greate Cardinal de Richelieu
for the polishing & in-riching of the language, publishing
those many accurate pieces which it has from time to time
produc'd. It is in these assemblies, where a select number
of learned men, persons of the first qualitie, not onely 5
come to heare, but esteeme it an honour to haue their
ingenious exercises passe the test & censure of so many
ciuil & polish'd wits. And all the apparatus for this is
onely the use of one competent roome in the gentleman's
house, where there are chaires & a table, where the person 10
who declaimes being seated with a little more eminency,
like the Roman rostrum, & choosing his subject in prose
or verse, recites or reades his composures before the
company. This, for being but one halfe day or afternoone
in the weeke, & retiring in due houre, is of very little 15
inconveniency to the master of the house. Here it is,
I say, gentlemen & scholars bring their essays, poems,
translations, and other oratorious productions vpon a
thousand curious subjects. Here they giue law to words
& phrases, & the *Norma loquendi*. These passe censure 20
& bring authors to the touch, reject or entertaine, &
indenizon exotics, &c. I neede not inlarge to Mr. Pepys
the benefit & noblenesse of such assemblies, who has himselfe seene what illustrious persons vs'd to honor Mr.
Justell: how many greate dukes and blewe-ribbons, 25
ambassadors as well as bishops, abbots, presidents, and
other learned men & trauellers, this brought together into
conversation the most humane and obliging in the world ;
& how exceedingly to be wish'd some noble & worthy
gent. would giue a diuersion so becoming & usefully enter- 30
taining as it would be. We should not then haue so
many crude and fulsome rhapsodies impos'd vpon the
English world for genuine witt, language, & the stage, as
well as on the auditors and spectators, which would be
purg'd from things intollerable. It would inflame, inspire, 35
& kindle another genius and tone of writing, with nervous,
natural strength & beauty, genuine and of our owne growth,
without allways borrowing & filching from our neighbours.
And indeede such was once design'd since the restauration
of Charles the Second (1665), and in order to it three or 40
fowre meetings were begun at Gray's Inn, by Mr. Cowley,
Dr. Sprat, Mr. Waller, the D. of Buckingham, Matt.

Clifford, Mr. Dryden, & some other promoters of it. But
by the death of the incomparable Mr. Cowley, distance
& inconvenience of the place, the contagion, & other
circumstances intervening, it crumbled away & came to
5 nothing : what straw I had gather'd towards the bricks for
that intended pyramid (having the honour to be admitted
an inferior labourer) you may command & dispose of, if
you can suffer my impertinences, and that which I haue
not shew'd you, the plan I drew & was laying before them
10 for that designe, which was, I said, the polishing of the
English tongue, & to be one of the first intentions and
chiefest subjects of the Academicians.

And now for shame haue don ! Methinks I heare you
cry out, 'What a ramble has Mr. Evelyn made ! what
15 a deale of ground for so little game ! ' Well, you see what
the setting up an empty noddle has produc'd, what a deale
of inke is run to waste. And indeede I had ben criminaly
vnanswerable of detriment to the publique as well as to
your owne repose, should I haue dar'd to debauch you
20 with so tedious & intemperate a scribble, whilst you were
not (*tuo jure*) your owne man. But if for all that, this prove
an affliction also, as I haue cause to apprehend it may, the
only expedient to rid yourselfe of such impertinents will
be to assume your late buisy and honourable charge
25 againe, when no man can be so impudently vnciuil as to
expect you should reade his long letters, when he considers how many you will then be obliged to write.

Says-Court, 12 Aug. 1689.

NOTES

SIR WILLIAM DAVENANT (1606-1668)

The preface to *Gondibert* was published separately at Paris, 'chez Matthieu Guillemot,' in 1650, as *A Discourse upon Gondibert, An Heroick Poem, written by S*^r *William D'Avenant: With an Answer to it by M*^r *Hobbs.* Davenant's discourse and Hobbes's reply were reprinted in 1651 at London, prefixed to the poem itself: this edition has been adopted as the basis of the present text, but a few errors have been corrected by reference to the 1673 folio of Davenant's *Works*.

The preface was written in Paris, under the influences then at work in French culture : Davenant had evidently read Chapelain's preface to the *Adone* of Marino, the prefaces to the heroic romances (e. g. Scudéry's to *Ibrahim ou l'Illustre Bassa,* 1641), Scaliger's *Poetice*, and the discourses of Tasso (cf. *infra,* note to 9. 7). The same influences produced much the same results in France : from the time of Le Moyne's *Saint Louis,* 1651, epic after epic, each with its critical preface, appeared within a score of years.

PAGE 3. 24 sq. The contention that Lucan is an historian rather than a poet, which owes its origin to Petronius, *Satyr.* 118, though implied by the converse statement in Aristotle, *Poet.* ix. 2, that ' the work of Herodotus might be put into verse and it would still be a species of history ', was often repeated by Renaissance critics : e. g. Ronsard, *Œuvres*, ed. Blanchemain, vii. 322, Harington's *Brief Apology*, in Gregory Smith, i. 196, Dryden, *Essays*, ed. Ker, i. 11 ; but cf. Scaliger, *Poet.* i. 2, vi. 6 (ed. 1617, pp. 7, 778).

PAGE 5. 4. Professor Ker's statement that ' references to Dante are not frequent in this age ' (*Essays of Dryden*, i. 295) must not be interpreted too literally ; Mr. K. C. M. Sills has collected a respectable number of such references in *Modern Philology*, 1905, iii. 99.

20–33. Davenant's condemnation of supernatural machinery foreshadows the attitude of the school of Boileau (cf. the *Art Poétique*, iii. 193, and Dryden's comment on the passage, in *Essays*, ed. Ker, i. 32, and note).   The French critics of the later Renaissance had urged the substitution of Christian for heathen machinery in tragedy and the epic (cf. Vauquelin de la Fresnaye, *Art Poétique*, ed. Pellissier, 1885, pp. xcii–xcvi).

PAGE 6. 10. Cf. i. 34. 21.

PAGE 9. 7. Davenant's conclusions in regard to the proper theme and characters for the epic appear to be in agreement with Tasso's, in his *Discorsi del Poema Eroico*, then recently rendered into French by Jean Baudoin (*Traité du Poëme épique de T. Tasso*, 1638).   The preference for a Christian theme and Christian characters (9. 7—10. 28): ' Oltre a ciò chi vuol formare l'idea d'un perfetto Cavaliere, non so per qual cagione gli nieghi questa lode di pietà e di religione : laonde preporrei di gran lunga la persona di Carlo e di Artù a quella di Teseo e di Giasone. Ultimamente, dovendo il poeta aver molto riguardo al giovamento, molto meglio accenderà l'animo de' nostri cavalieri coll' esempio de' fedeli che degli infideli . . . Dee dunque l'argomento del poema epico esser derivato da vera istoria, e non da falsa religione' (Tasso, *Opere*, ed. Rosini, 1823, xii. 45 sq.).   The preference for a former age and a distant century (10. 29—11. 33): ' Non debbono le cose presenti, o quelle che sono passate di poco tempo, esser soggetto del poema eroico,' etc. (*ibid.* xii. 47 sq.).

PAGE 19. 11 sq. Cf. i. 210. 8–12, and the discussions of the stanza form in Drayton's preface to *Englands Heroicall Epistles*, 1630, and Dryden's preface to *Annus Mirabilis*, 1666.

PAGE 28. 25. *Two Colleagues*, i. e. Cowley and Waller, whose commendatory verses on *Gondibert* follow this preface in the original.

PAGE 49. 32. *Menenius Agrippa*. Livy, ii. 32.

PAGE 50. 5. Cf. note on i. 118. 6–9.

PAGE 52. 3. Plato, *Rep*. iii. 398.

17 sq. *The Scholler of Plato . . . an absolute Monarch over Arts*. Cf. Scaliger, *Poet*. vii. 2. 1 : ' Aristoteles imperator noster, omnium bonarum artium dictator perpetuus.'

THOMAS HOBBES (1588–1679)

Hobbes's reply to Davenant has been reprinted from the 1651 edition of *Gondibert* (cf. *supra*, p. 331).

PAGE 56. 4. The first collection of the *Quatrains* of Gui du Faur, seigneur de Pibrac, appeared in 1574 ; they were translated into English by Sylvester and into German by Opitz.

PAGE 57. 23 sq. On these figures, cf. Gregory Smith, *Eliz. Crit. Essays*, ii. 95, and note.

PAGE 64. 20. For the history of ' admiration' as a critical term, cf. Gregory Smith, i. 392 (note on i. 177).

23–7. On Hobbes's theory of laughter, see his *Human Nature*, 1650, ix. 13.

32. It will be observed that here (and *infra*, 68. 31) Hobbes does not agree with Davenant in the acceptance of technical terms from ' any Science, as well mechanicall as liberall' (*supra*, 26. 1). The latter is in agreement with the theory and practice of the Pléiade, and is followed by Dryden in the preface to the *Annus Mirabilis*. Hobbes's argument is that of the more purely classical school in its preference for general terms, and Dryden, in his later utterances, accepts this point of view (cf. Ker's *Dryden*, i. p. xxxiii). Rymer illustrates the growing mania for abstract terms (e. g. *infra*, 181. 1, 2) ; and Dennis commends Boileau for poetically speaking of himself as forty, though really forty-six, for ' poetry admits of no odd Numbers above Nine' (*Miscellanies in Prose and Verse*, 1693, p. 50, n.). This theory of numbers persisted into the nineteenth century: cf. Gustave Flaubert, *Correspondance*, ii. 258.

PAGE 72. 34. Lucan, *Phars.* i. 128.

PAGE 73. 16. Quintilian, *Inst.* x. 1. 90.

PAGE 75. 14. Scaliger, *Poet.* v. 3 : ' Non si ipse Iupiter poeta fuit, melius loquatur.'

19. This epigram, wrongly ascribed to Antipater of Sidon or Antipater of Thessalonica, is found in the Planudean Antho-logy (*Anth. Graeca*, ed. Jacobs, ii. 714 ; app. Plan. no. 293).

PAGE 76. 11. John Ogilby (1600–1676): his translation of Homer (*Iliad*, 1660, *Odyssey*, 1665) was ridiculed by Dryden and Pope.

ABRAHAM COWLEY (1618–1667)

PAGE 77. 4. *The Iron Age*, i. e. *The Foure Ages of England, or the Iron Age, with other select poems*, 1648.

PAGE 80. 23 sq. An early *locus* in English of that phase of criticism, initiated by Longinus, which is concerned with the relation between literature and its *milieu*.

PAGE 81. 1–27. Cowley is echoing Ovid, *Trist.* i. 1. 39 sq. ; cf. Guarini, *Pastor Fido*, iv. 1, and Dryden, *Works*, ed. Scott-Saintsbury, xi. 121.

14. Ovid, *Met.* xv. 871.

PAGE 82. 13. Horace, *Epist.* i. 1. 45.

19. *Ibid.* i. 11. 9.

22. Donne, *The Will* (*Poems*, ed. E. K. Chambers, i. 61) :
'And all your graces no more use shall have
Than a sun-dial in a grave.'

29. Martial, viii. 69.

PAGE 83. 30. This passage (to 84. 25) was omitted in all the editions after the Restoration.

PAGE 85. 8. Virgil, *Georg.* iii. 244.

11. Théodore de Bèze published a volume of Latin verse in his youth (*Juvenilia*, 1548), which he attempted later to suppress.

18. Virgil, *Ecl.* iii. 89.

PAGE 86. 9. Dionysius Halicarnassus, *De Vet. Script. Censura*, ii. 8.

26. Horace, *A. P.* 240 sq.

PAGE 88. 2 sq. Cf. *supra*, note to 5. 20–33. The religious epic had again become popular in France when Cowley was writing (e. g. Saint-Amant, *Moyse sauvé*, 1653; Godeau, *Saint Paul*, 1654). Vauquelin (*Art Poétique*, 1605) and Godeau (*Discours de la Poésie Chrestienne*, 1635) had urged the use of scriptural themes; and Desmarets de Saint Sorlin was soon to start a running fire of argument (*Clovis*, 1657 ; *Les Délices de l'Esprit*, 1658 ; *La Comparaison de la Poësie françoise avec la grecque et la latine*, 1670; *Défense du Poëme héroïque*, 1674).

30 sq. *Lying is Essential to good Poetry.* Renaissance criticism commences with a refutation of this conventional

charge (Boccaccio, *Genealogia degli Dei*, trad. Betussi, 1547, p. 257 sq., 'che i poeti non sono bugiardi'), and for many generations the critics continued to have their fling at it (e. g. Sidney, *Defence*, in Gregory Smith, i. 183 sq.).

PAGE 90. 11. Francis Quarles, *A Feast of Wormes*, 1620, *Job Militant*, 1624, &c.

12. Thomas Heywood, *The Hierarchy of the Blessed Angels*, 1635.

RICHARD FLECKNOE (*d.* 1678?)

The *Short Discourse of the English Stage* has been reprinted from *Love's Kingdom, A Pastoral Trage-Comedy : Not as it was Acted at the Theatre near Lincolns-Inn, but as it was written, and since corrected, By Richard Flecknoe. With a short Treatise of the English Stage, &c., by the same Author* (London : Printed by R. Wood for the Author, 1664).

PAGE 91. 7. *De Porta*, i. e. Giambattista della Porta (1535–1615): his comedy of *La Sorella* was the basis of Middleton's *No Wit, No Help like a Woman's* and of Rotrou's *La Sœur*, and his *Astrologo* was reproduced in Tomkis' *Albumazar*.

PAGE 93. 17. Cf. i. 182. 13, and note.

PAGE 96. 25 sq. The Italians were the masters of stage machinery in this age, and their technical works were in advance of all others (e. g. N. Sabbattini, *Pratica di fabricar scene e machine ne' teatri*, 2nd ed., Ravenna, 1638) ; but the French had been paying no small attention to the subject (e. g. J. de la Mesnardière, *Poétique*, 1640, ch. xi, and d'Aubignac, *Pratique du théâtre*, 1657, bk. ii. ch. 13). There was no contemporary equivalent for these in English.

SIR ROBERT HOWARD (1626-1698)

PAGE 97. 22. Henry Herringman, the publisher of Howard's plays.

PAGE 101. 6. Horace, *A. P.* 272-3.

8 sq. Howard here answers Dryden's defence of rhyming plays in the dedicatory epistle of the *Rival Ladies*, 1664.

PAGE 102. 32. Roger Boyle, Earl of Orrery (1621-1679).

PAGE 106. 12. Howard's arguments against rhyming plays are taken up by Crites, and refuted by Neander, in Dryden's *Essay of Dramatic Poesy*, 1668; and it has therefore been assumed that Howard himself is the original of Crites, though in all other respects their points of view are antipodal. Howard now proceeds to answer Neander's arguments.

19. Lucan, *Pharsalia*, i. 12 (cf. Ker's *Dryden*, i. 119).

30. *Don Quixote*, pt. ii. ch. 47.

31 sq. This is Molière's argument, in *La Critique de l'École des Femmes*, 1663, sc. vi: 'Car enfin, si les pièces qui sont selon les règles ne plaisent pas et que celles qui plaisent ne soient pas selon les règles, il faudroit de nécessité que les règles eussent été mal faites. Moquons-nous donc de cette chicane où ils veulent assujettir le goût du public, et ne consultons dans une comédie que l'effet qu'elle fait sur nous,' &c.

PAGE 108. 1 sq. Cf. Dryden, *Essays*, ed. Ker, i. 104, 105, and Dryden's answer, *ibid.* 117.

6. *Shutting a door.* Cf. *ibid.* i. 117, and *supra*, 102. 26, 27.

7. Seneca, *Hippolytus*, 863.

30. For the origin of the dramatic unities, see my *Lit. Crit. in the Ren.* pp. 89-101, 290-92 (cf. also the references cited by Gregory Smith, *Eliz. Crit. Essays*, i. 399, and Ebner, *Gesch. der dram. Einheiten in Italien*, pp. 1-5); for their later history, see D. Nichol Smith, *Eighteenth Century Essays on Shakespeare*, p. 322, and L. Morandi, *Voltaire contro Shakespeare, Baretti contro Voltaire*, ed. 1884, pp. 86-122. Dryden's position is summed up by Ker, *op. cit.*, i. p. xxxix sq.

PAGE 111. 9. Dryden's answer to this preface, *A Defence of an Essay of Dramatic Poesy*, was prefixed to the second edition of his *Indian Emperor*, 1668. Sir Robert's brother, Edward Howard, in the preface to the *Usurper*, 1668, had mildly argued against rhyming plays, and later, in the preface to the *Women's Conquest*, 1671, took up the cudgels for his brother with more vigour. It was to Edward Howard that Richard Flecknoe addressed his *Letter* in reply to Dryden's *Defence* (cf. Pepys, *Diary*, Sept. 20, 1668).

THOMAS SPRAT (1635-1713)

PAGE 112. 1. The preceding section of the *History* contains an account of the French Academy, based on Pellisson's *Histoire de l'Académie françoise*, 1653 (English translation by H. R., *History of the French Academy*, 1657): Sprat now proceeds to urge the formation of a similar body in England as an arbiter in matters of language and style. The Royal Society had already made abortive efforts in this direction by appointing a committee 'for improving the English tongue' on December 7, 1664, with Sir Peter Wyche as Chairman, and including Evelyn, Waller, Sir John Berkenhead, and Dryden, who earlier in the same year had included a plea for an Academy in the dedicatory epistle of his *Rival Ladies* (T. Birch, *History of the Royal Society*, 1746, i. 499, 500, ii 7, &c.). The discussions of this committee doubtless occasioned Evelyn's letter to Wyche in June, 1665 (*infra*, 310. 1 sq.), and out of it grew those other meetings which Evelyn describes as having taken place at Gray's Inn (*infra*, 328. 39 sq.), but which ceased at the death of Cowley in the very year in which Sprat published his *History*. Somewhat later a similar attempt was inaugurated by Roscommon, assisted by Dryden, but it came to nothing (Johnson, *Works*, London, 1824, ix. 213).

On the earlier interest in academies, cf. Einstein, *Italian Renaissance in England*, pp. 146, 357, 358, *Archaeologia*, xxxii. 132-49, and *D. N. B.* s. v. Edmund Bolton and Sir Francis Kynaston. 'It importes no little disgrace to our Nation,' wrote Richard Carew to Sir Robert Cotton in 1605 (Ellis, *Orig. Letters of Eminent Men*, p. 99), 'that others have so many Academyes, and wee none at all'; and Milton, in 1641, said a few words in favour of ' the learned and affable meeting of frequent Academies' (i. 198. 20). In the next century Swift returned to the subject in his *Proposal for Correcting, Improving, and Ascertaining the English Tongue*, 1712, which is discussed by Voltaire, in his *Lettres philosophiques*, 1734 (*Œuvres*, ed. Moland, xxii. 183); and Addison, in the *Spectator*, no. 135, August 4, 1711, Warton, in his *Essay on Pope*, 3rd ed. i. 203, and Goldsmith, in the *Present State of Polite Learning*, 1759, ch. iv, touch on it lightly. The subject was a pet aversion of Dr. Johnson (*Works*, ii. 64, vii. 244, ix. 214), who dismisses it ironically by making Dick Minim its spokesman and supporter (*Idler*, June 15, 1759).

Sprat's *History* was translated into French as *L'Histoire de l'institution, dessein, et progrès de la Société Royale de Londres*, Geneva, 1669, Paris, 1670.

PAGE 115. 6. Cf. Cicero, *Brutus*, 64, and *Leges*, i. 2.

PAGE 117. 2 sq. Cf. Locke, *Human Understanding*, bk. iii. ch. x. § 34, on the abuse of rhetorical figures ; and Samuel Parker, *Censure of the Platonick Philosophy*, 2nd ed. 1667, p. 77, on the viciousness of 'a huge and lushious style'.

PAGE 119. 17. This *Account* was prefixed to the first collected edition of *The Works of Mr. Abraham Cowley*, published by Herringman in 1668, and a Latin abridgement of it appeared in the *Poemata Latina* in the same year. Martin Clifford, to whom the *Account* is addressed, became master of the Charterhouse in 1671, and died in 1677.

PAGE 121. 18. *In the thirteenth year of his age there came forth a little Book under his name.* Fifteenth? The *Poetical Blossoms* appeared in 1633.

PAGE 122. 29. John Hervey (1616-1679), treasurer to Catherine of Braganza.

31. Henry Jermyn, first Earl of St. Albans (*d.* 1684).

PAGE 124. 22. Sir Charles Scarburgh (1616-1694), physician to the King.

31 sq. An allusion to 83. 30—84. 25.

PAGE 127. 24. *Duke of Buckingham*, i. e. George Villiers, author of the *Rehearsal*.

PAGE 129. 26 sq. Cf. i. 21. 11–16, and note.

PAGE 131. 30. Horace, *Od.* iv. 2.

PAGE 132. 20-2. Cf. *infra*, 173. 34, and 265. 19-30, and notes. The more important critical utterances on the Pindaric Ode were collected by Blount, in his *De Re Poetica*, 1694, p. 65 sq.

PAGE 137. 8 sq. 'What literary man has not regretted the prudery of Sprat in refusing to let his friend Cowley appear in his slippers and dressing gown?' Coleridge, *Biogr. Lit.* ch. iii.

THOMAS SHADWELL (1642 ?–1692)

PAGE 148. 17. Molière's *Les Fâcheux* was acted in 1661, and printed in 1662.

PAGE 149. 6. *The Scenes unbroken.* Shadwell is thinking of Dryden's 'exactest rules by which a play is wrought' (prol. to *Maiden Queen*, 1668):

> 'The Unities of Action, Place, and Time;
> The scenes unbroken.'

This is the *liaison des scènes* introduced by the French as a rule of the theatre; Corneille, in his *Discours des Trois Unités*, 1660, had said of it: 'La liaison des scènes, qui unit toutes les actions particulières de chaque acte l'une avec l'autre, est un grand ornement dans un poëme, et qui sert beaucoup à former une continuité d'action par la continuité de la représentation; mais enfin ce n'est qu'un ornement et non pas une règle.'

32. Horace, *A. P.* 125-7.

PAGE 150. 7–11. *Most other Authors.* Dryden?

20 sq. Shadwell is hinting at a passage in the *Essay of Dramatic Poesy*, 1668, on wit and humour in Jonson and Beaumont and Fletcher (Ker's *Dryden*, i. 81): 'One cannot say that he [Jonson] wanted wit, but rather that he was frugal of it.' 'They [Beaumont and Fletcher] understood and imitated the conversation of gentlemen much better; whose wild debaucheries and quickness of wit in repartees, no poet can ever paint as they have done.' Buckingham, in the *Rehearsal*, 1671, act iii. sc. i, echoes Shadwell's contempt for repartee. It is interesting to note that Sir Robert Howard, who also answered the *Essay of Dramatic Poesy*, is represented as Sir Positive At-all in the *Sullen Lovers* (Pepys, *Diary*, May 4, 1668). Dryden did not allow either of his opponents to remain uncontroverted; he answered Shadwell in the preface to the *Mock Astrologer*, 1671.

PAGE 152. 22 sq. *She would if she could*, by Sir George Etherege. Pepys saw it played Feb. 6, 1668, but thought 'nothing in the world good in it, and few people pleased in it'.

PAGE 153. 20. Shadwell here proceeds to reply to the preface of the *Mock Astrologer*. But Dryden had not quite committed himself as yet to the assertion that 'the ultimate end of the Poet is to delight, *without correction or instruction*'. In answering Howard in 1668 he had said that 'delight is the chief, if not the only, end of poesy: instruction can be admitted but in the second place, for poesy only instructs as it delights' (Ker's *Dryden*, i. 113); in the answer to Shadwell he distinguished between tragedy and comedy: 'Thus tragedy fulfills one great part of its institution, which is by example to instruct. But in comedy it is not so, for the chief end of it is divertisement and delight, and that so much that ... instruction . . . can be but its secondary end' (*ibid.* i. 143). Cf. *supra*, 81. 10.

28. Horace, *Epist.* ii. 1. 123.

Page 155. 6. *A. P.* 334.

10. *Od.* iii. 1. 1.

28. *Epist.* ii. 1. 202.

Page 156. 3–9. Shadwell's sincerity is at least open to suspicion. Gossip had already attached a real name to Sir Positive At-all in the *Sullen Lovers*; and later, in the *Virtuoso*, Robert Boyle is certainly portrayed in the guise of Sir Nicholas Gimcrack: 'He is the most admirable Person in the *Meletetiques*, viz., in Reflections and Meditations, in the whole World' (an allusion to the science of 'meleteticks' in Boyle's *Occasional Reflections*, 1665).

Page 157. 22. Cf. Ker's *Dryden*, i. 137, ll. 26–9. Jonson had indignantly denied the charge (see i. 13. 17 sq.).

25–32. 'I admire and applaud him [Jonson] where I ought: those who do more, do but value themselves in their admiration of him; and by telling you they extol Ben Johnson's way, would insinuate to you that they can practise it' (Ker's *Dryden*, i. 138).

34. *My particular friend*, i.e. Dryden.

Page 158. 9. *Phaedrus*, 249 D.

12. 'For my part, I declare that I want judgment to imitate him [Jonson], and should think it a great impudence in myself to attempt it' (Ker, *loc. cit.*).

Page 159. 9. Horace, *Epist.* ii. 1. 73.

12. Cf. Ker's *Dryden*, i. 138, l. 21 sq.

27. Cf. *ibid.* i. 139, l. 24 sq.

Page 160. 26, 27. *Sir John Dawe* and *Sir Amorous la Foole*, characters in Jonson's *Silent Woman*.

PAGE 161. 25. Horace, *Epist.* ii. 1. 168 sq.

PAGE 162. 8. These two prefaces bring out clearly the fundamental opposition between Dryden's 'wit' and Shadwell's
'humour'. In the next year Dryden, with great moderation,
attempted to close the discussion ('I will not contest farther
with my friends,' Ker, i. 172), but Shadwell returned to it in the
preface of the *Royal Shepherdess*, and with increased bitterness
in the dedication, prologue, and epilogue of the *Virtuoso*. The
later stages of the controversy, however, interest rather the
historian of manners than of criticism.

THOMAS RYMER (1641–1713)

I. The Reverend Father René Rapin (1621–1687) published
his *Réflexions sur la Poëtique d'Aristote et sur les ouvrages des
poëtes anciens et modernes* in 1674, and it was translated by
Rymer in the same year, with an original preface which is here
reprinted. Rymer's version was later included in Basil Kennet's
Whole Critical Works of Rapin, which reached a third edition in
1731.

II. *The Tragedies of the Last Age*, addressed to Sir Fleetwood
Sheppard (1634–1698), was licensed July 17, 1677, and was published in November (Arber, *Term Catalogues*, i. 294): the title-
page bears the date 1678. After a brief introduction, Rymer
devotes himself to three of Beaumont and Fletcher's plays : the
critiques of *Rollo* and *A King and no King* are here omitted ;
and of the 144 pages of the original, pages 1–16 and 104–44 are
here included. The treatise was reprinted in 1692, with ' Part I
on the title-page. It provoked Dryden to write his *Heads of an
Answer to Rymer* (*Works*, ed. Scott-Saintsbury, xv. 378), and
Butler to compose the doggerel included in this volume, but
neither was published during the lifetime of its author.

III. The *Short View of Tragedy* appeared late in 1692, and
was reviewed in December by Motteux in the *Gentleman's
Journal* and by Dunton in the *Compleat Library*. The title-page
bears the date 1693. Of the eight chapters in the original, the
first and the seventh are here included : these constitute in bulk
somewhat less than half of the whole work. In the citations from

Othello, I have preserved Rymer's text, which seems in general to follow the Players' Quarto of 1687. Dryden was annoyed by the veiled antagonism to him throughout the *Short View*, and replied bitterly in the dedication of the *Third Miscellany*, 1693; in the following year Gildon included *Some Reflections on Mr. Rymer's Short View of Tragedy, and an Attempt at a Vindication of Shakespear, in an Essay directed to John Dryden, Esq.*, in his *Miscellaneous Letters and Essays on several Subjects.* Another reply, Dennis's *Impartial Critick*, is reprinted in vol. iii.

PAGE 163. 15. Cf. notes on i. 206. 16. Rymer is echoing Rapin; these and other contemporary sketches of the history of criticism were collected by Blount, *De Re Poetica*, 1694, p. 113 sq.

12. The Accademia della Crusca was founded in 1572, and published its Dictionary in 1612.

18. Clément Marot (1495–1544); Jean Antoine de Baïf (1532–1589).

PAGE 164. 3. The *Cid* was acted in 1636; on the controversy which it occasioned, cf. Gasté, *La Querelle du Cid*, Paris, 1898.

35 sq. Rymer had been reading the *Discoveries*; cf. i. 55, 56.

PAGE 165. 13. Cf. Aristotle, *Opera omnia cum Averrois commentariis*, Venice, 1560, iii. 159. Averroës (1126–1198) made an abridged Arabic version of the *Poetics*, which was translated into Latin and exercised some influence on later mediaeval thought: cf. my *Critica letteraria nel Rinascimento*, trad. da A. Fusco, 1905, pp. 20–22.

27–9. Cf. Bouhours, *Entretiens d'Ariste et d'Eugène*, 1671, iv. 'Le bel Esprit :' 'C'est une chose singulière qu'un bel esprit Allemand ou Moscovite, reprit Eugene; & s'il y en a a quelques-uns au monde, ils sont de la nature de ces esprits qui n'apparoissent jamais sans causer de l'étonnement . . . J'avouë, interrompit Ariste, que les beaux esprits sont un peu plus rares dans les païs froids, parce que la nature y est plus languissante & plus morne pour parler ainsi. Avoüez plûtost, dit Eugene, que le bel esprit tel que vous l'avez defini, ne s'accommode point du tout avec les temperamens grossiers & les corps massifs des peuples du Nord,' &c.

34 sq. Rapin, *Réflexions*, 1674, pt. ii. § 23.

PAGE 166. 7 sq. *Ibid.* ii. 20.

29 marg. *Mesnardire*, i.e. J. de la Mesnardière, *La Poëtique*,

1640, p. 371, ' Rudesse de la langue françoise dans les expressions amoureuses.' Bouhours, *Entretiens*, 1671, p. 67, holds a position the very reverse of this ; these thirty years had done much to strengthen French self-esteem.

30. *Kitchin-language* (marg. *lingua di masserizie*). A common taunt ; cf. Mandeville, *Fable of the Bees*, ed. 1755, ii. 281 : ' The French . . . is really a charming language . . . to one that loves his belly ; for it is very copious in the art of cookery, and every thing that belongs to eating and drinking.'

Page 167. 12 marg. Robert Sheringham (1602–1678), fellow of Caius College, Cambridge, is apparently alluded to ; but no treatise of his on the epic is extant.

18 marg. Étienne Pasquier (1529–1615), in his *Recherches de la France*, vii. 3 (*Œuvres*, ed. 1723, i. 690), says of the authors of the *Roman de la Rose* : ' De ce mesme temps (je veux dire souz le regne de S. Louys) nous eusmes Guillaume de Lorry, & sous Philippe le Bel, Jean de Mehum, lesquels quelques-uns des nostres ont voulu comparer à Dante Poëte Italien : Et moy je les opposerois volontiers à tous les Poëtes d'Italie.' Pasquier also compares the poets of the Pléiade with their Italian predecessors ; but the praise of the *Roman de la Rose* in the *Défense et Illustration de la langue françoise*, ii. 2, may account for the allusion to ' Bellay ' in the margin.

19. Sir Richard Baker (1568–1645), author of the *Chronicle of the Kings of England*, 1643.

Page 168. 22 marg. *Aen.* iii. 343.

Page 170. 31. Cf. *supra*, 56. 4, and note.

Page 171. 34 marg. Stobaeus, *Florilegium*, ed. Gaisford, 1822, ii. 95 : Ἀείσω συνετοῖσι, θύρας δ' ἐπίθεσθε βέβηλοι.

Page 172. 35 sq. Tasso, in a letter to Scipione Gonzaga, April 3, 1575, wrote : ' Io ho già condennato con irrevocabil sentenza alla morte l'episodio di Sofronia, perchè in vero era troppo lirico' (*Lettere Poetiche*, in *Opere*, ed. Rosini, xv. 98) ; he accordingly omitted the episode from the *Gerusalemme Conquistata*, the revised version of his epic.

Page 173. 5. Sidney, *Defence of Poesy*, in Gregory Smith, i. 195.

34. The poems of Urban VIII (Maffeo Barberini, 1568–1644) were published at Paris under the editorship of Peiresc

in 1620, and were often reprinted : he was an admirer and imitator of Gabriello Chiabrera (1552–1638), who revived and perfected the Italian Pindaric, doubtless in imitation of Ronsard's Odes or the still earlier tentatives of Trissino, Minturno, and Alamanni. In all these poets the attempt was made to preserve the regularity of the Pindaric form ; and Cowley's irregular Ode has little in common with theirs. Cf. *infra*, note on 265. 20 sq.

PAGE 174. 10. Scaliger has devoted one of the books of his *Poetice*, lib. v. *qui et Criticus*, to a comparison of classical poets according to their treatment of such ' commonplaces ' as *tempestas, pestilentia, dirae*, and the like ; the passages on Night by Apollonius and Virgil, cited here, are contrasted by Scaliger in ch. vi (ed. 1617, p. 587 sq.), and Rymer's originality consists in carrying on the contrast in passages from Italian, French, and English poetry.

11. Macrobius, in the fifth and sixth books of the *Saturnalia*, has contrasted Virgil with Homer and other poets.

11. *Agellius*, i. e. Antonio Agelli (1532–1608), author of Commentaries on various books of the Old Testament.

20. Apollonius Rhodius, *Argonautica*, iii. 744.

PAGE 175. 15. *Aen.* iv. 522.

PAGE 176. 23. Tasso, *Gerusalemme Liberata*, ii. 96, and repeated in the *Gerusalemme Conquistata*, iii. 93. Note that Rymer (ll. 31–3) refers to the *Liberata* as the revised form (cf. Solerti, *Vita di T. Tasso*, 1895, i. 206–7) ; but he seems to have preferred the *Conquistata* (197. 28).

PAGE 178. 1. Chapelain spent twenty years in writing his epic, *La Pucelle* (first twelve cantos published 1656, privilège dated 1546) : these are the opening lines of the second book.

33. The *Saint Louis* of Pierre Le Moyne, in 18 cantos, appeared in 1651–53. Cf. Duchesne, *Histoire des poèmes épiques français du XVIIe siècle*, Paris, 1870.

34. *Our Critick*, i. e. Rapin, *Réflexions*, pt. i. § 31.

PAGE 179. 30. From Dryden's heroic play, *The Indian Emperor, or the Conquest of Mexico by the Spaniards*, 1667, act iii. sc. 2.

PAGE 180. 11. Statius, *Silvae*, v. 4. 4.

PAGE 183. 5. Dryden follows Rymer in calling the unities

'the mechanic beauties of the plot' (Ker, i. 212, and note): cf. Rapin, *Réflexions*, pt. i. § 21.

19 sq. Cf. Molière, *La Critique de l'Ecole des Femmes*, 1663, sc. vi: 'Il semble, à vous ouïr parler, que ces règles de l'art soient les plus grands mystères du monde; et cependant ce ne sont que quelques observations aisées, que le bon sens a faites sur ce qui peut ôter le plaisir que l'on prend à ces sortes de poëmes; et le même bon sens qui a fait autrefois ces observations les fait aisément tous les jours, sans le secours d'Horace et d'Aristote.' In the first book of the *Pratique du Théâtre*, the abbé d'Aubignac answers objections similar to those which Rymer discusses in the following pages, but unlike Rymer he does not believe that 'common sense suffices' without a knowledge of the Rules; Dennis goes a step farther in adding taste to good sense (*Remarks on Prince Arthur*, 1696, p. 41).

PAGE 184. 3. Charles Hart (*d.* 1683), who acted the part of Arbaces in *A King and no King*.

10 sq. Cf. Scaliger, *Poet.* i. 11.

14. *Poet.* xiv. 1, 2.

17 sq. Cf. Racine, pref. to *Iphigénie*, 1675: 'J'ai reconnu avec plaisir, par l'effet qu'a produit sur notre théâtre tout ce que j'ai imité ou d'Homère ou d'Euripide, que le bon sens et la raison étoient les mêmes dans tous les siècles. Le goût de Paris s'est trouvé conforme à celui d'Athènes. Mes spectateurs ont été émus des mêmes choses qui ont mis autrefois en larmes le plus savant peuple de la Grèce.'

PAGE 185. 14-23. Cf. *supra*, 70. 6-19.

PAGE 186. 25. Rapin, *Réflexions*, pt. ii. § 20.

note 1. Alessandro Tassoni, *Pensieri Diversi*, ed. Venice, 1636, p. 483.

30. Tasso's tragedy of *Torrismondo* was published in 1587.

PAGE 187. note 1. Horace, *A. P.* 220; Juvenal, i. 44.

PAGE 189. note 1. *Poet.* ix. 3.

PAGE 190. 9 sq. Rymer has here taken a hint from Tassoni (*op. cit.* p. 385), who objects to the title of the *Orlando Furioso* on the ground that it refers to a subsidiary incident of the poem, and who suggests such other titles for it as 'La Guerra del Re Agramante' and 'Carlo Vittorioso'. But the subject of titles troubled all the critical casuists; cf. La Mesnardière,

Poëtique, 1640, p. 47, Scaliger, *Poet.* iii. 96, 126, and B. Fioretti, *Proginnasmi Poetici di Udeno Nisiely*, ed. 1695, iv. 11.

PAGE 192. note 1. Euripides, *Hippolytus*, 377.

note 2. Seneca, *Hippolytus*, 143-4.

PAGE 193. 5 sq. Cf. Rapin, *Réflexions*, pt. i. § 25 (Rymer's transl.): 'The Angelica of Ariosto is too immodest ; the Armida of Tasso is too free and impudent : these two poets rob Women of their Character, which is Modesty.'

PAGE 195. 1 sq. Rymer's utterances on the treatment of kings in tragedy should be compared with Corneille's, in the *examen* of *Clitandre* (the dissertation of a chamberlain rather than of a critic, as M. Lemaître says), and especially with Mesnardière's, in his *Poëtique*, 1640, p. 104 : 'Si le Poëte me veut croire, il ne permettra iamais que la plus iuste colere emporte si fort son Héros, qu'il en perde & le iugement & le respect qui est deu aux Potentats de la terre ; ' and p. 120 : ' Un Roy qui paroist au Théatre doit estre si courageux qu'il n'appréhende aucun danger. . . . Il doit estre si prudent, qu'il n'ait iamais aucun sujet de rétracter ses iugemens, ni d'en condamner les succés... Enfin il doit estre si bon, qu'il viue auec ses sujets comme il eût voulu que le Prince eût traitté auec lui-mesme, s'il eût été homme priué.'

6. *Perillus's Bull*, i. e. the bull which the sculptor Perillus fashioned for the victims of Phalaris.

14. *Aen.* ii. 79, 80.

PAGE 196. 13-16. Euripides, *Medea*, 61, 83.

PAGE 197. 11. *All the clashing is among friends.* Cf. Aristotle, *Poet.* xiv. 4.

12. *Pitty and terror.* The ἔλεος and φόβος of Aristotle's definition of tragedy, *Poet.* vi. 2.

21. *Aen.* x. 870.

28. *Gerusalemme Conquistata*, xxiv. 98.

PAGE 199. 29. *Aen.* vi. 854.

PAGE 200. note 1. Horace, *A. P.* 126, 127.

PAGE 204. 2, 3. The characters of the *Commedia dell' arte*, popular in France for some time, were not without influence in England : in the very year in which Rymer was writing, Ravenscroft had published his *Scara-mouch, a Philosopher ; Harlequin, a School Boy ; Bravo, a Merchant and Magician* :

A Comedy, after the Italian Manner, largely stolen from Molière.

8, 9. Euripides, *Iphigenia in Tauris*, 772 sq. (cf. Aristotle, *Poet.* xiv. 9; xvii. 3).

25. Terence, *Eunuchus*, i. 1. 18.

PAGE 205. 32. After the Restoration, Hart played *Amintor*; Mohun, *Melantius*; and Mrs. Marshall, *Evadne*.

PAGE 206. 2. *The two former*, i.e. *Rollo* and *A King and no King*; Rymer's discussion of them precedes that of the *Maid's Tragedy* in the original.

23 sq. Rymer is at one with Dryden (cf. *supra*, note on 150. 20), but he seems to have chiefly in mind the arguments of Corneille in the *Discours du Poëme dramatique*, 1660.

31. *Knew.* Orig. 'know.'

PAGE 208. 7. John Selden, *Titles of Honor*, pt. ii. ch. 1. § 43 (3rd ed. 1672, p. 336).

PAGE 209. 14. Racine reintroduced the chorus in his *Esther*, 1689, and *Athalie*, 1691; his example was followed by the abbé Claude Boyer (1618–1698) in his *Jephté*, 1692. Rymer's arguments in favour of the chorus are very much like those of Dacier, *La Poëtique d'Aristote*, Paris, 1692, p. 312 sq., and D'Aubignac, *Whole Art of the Stage*, 1684, pp. 118-32. Cf. note to i. 209. 1.

26. Cf. *Poet.* xv. 9, also vi. 19, xiv. 1–3, and Scaliger, *Poet.* i. 11: 'Sane caetera ad aures, apparatus ad oculos.'

34 sq. Cf. *supra*, 184. 3–16.

27. *The Rehearsal*, 1671, act iii. sc. 1: ' Now, Sir, I gad, this is the bane of all us Writers; let us soar never so little above the common pitch, I gad, all's spoiled; for the vulgar never understand us, they can never conceive you, Sir, the excellencie of these things.' Rymer's allusions to the character of Bayes were too frequent to please Dryden.

PAGE 210. 4. Horace, *Epist.* ii. 1. 206.

7. *Mamamouchi*, an imaginary dignity conferred by the Sultan on Monsieur Jourdain in Molière's *Bourgeois Gentilhomme*, act iv. sc. 3. Ravenscroft called his version of the latter, *Mamamouchi, or the Citizen turn'd Gentleman*, 1675.

21–25. ' I suppose two Kings to be of the same place, as for example at Brentford,' says Bayes, in *The Rehearsal*, act i;

and in the last act the Kings 'descend in the Clouds, singing in white garments', and dance a Coranto.

PAGE 212. 10. From Waller's commendatory verses prefixed to Roscommon's translation of Horace's *Ars Poetica*, 1680.

PAGE 213. 14. In Pellisson's *Histoire de l'Académie françoise* (ed. 1672, p. 125) the phrase is 'Cela est beau comme le Cid' (cf. note on 112. 1).

18–26, and n. 3. *Le Parnasse réformé*, Paris, 1668, p. 41 sq. This work, by Gabriel Guéret (1641–1688), is an amusing skit after the manner of Boccalini's *Ragguagli di Parnaso*. The prose tragedy, *Thomas Morus*, by Jean de la Serre (1600–1665), was acted in 1641.

23. Thomas Jordan, author of *Money is an Ass*, 1663.

PAGE 214. 3. Horace, *Epist.* ii. 1. 188 ('incertos oculos', &c.).

20. Waller, in *Verses writ in the Tasso of Her Royal Highness* (ed. Drury, p. 216).

22. Rymer probably has in mind Bouhours's *Pensées Ingénieuses des Anciens et des Modernes*, Paris, 1689.

23. *Baptista*, i. e. Giovanni Battista Lully (1633–1687), the favourite operatic composer of the French court.

PAGE 215. 1–11. Pellisson, *Histoire de l'Académie françoise*, ed. 1672, pp. 108–9.

PAGE 217. 3 sq. The suggestion for an ideal plot of this sort doubtless came from Scaliger, *Poet.* iii. 96 (ed. 1617, p. 335). Le Bossu, in his *Traité du Poëme épique*, 1675, i. 7, sketches the plot of an ideal epic (cf. Rapin, *Réflexions*, ii. 4).

PAGE 219. 9. *Pit, Box, and Gallery*, a phrase used by Bayes in *The Rehearsal*, act i. The compliment to Dryden is double-edged. It should also be remembered that Dryden had recently translated Bouhours's *Life of Francis Xavier* (cf. 218. 34).

PAGE 220. 4. Shakespeare's indebtedness to the *Ecatommiti* (1565) of Giambattista Giraldi Cintio for the plot of *Othello* had already been pointed out by Dryden (pref. to *Mock Astrologer*, 1671) and Langbaine (*Acct. of Engl. Dram. Poets*, 1691).

27. *A. P.* 12.

PAGE 221. 15. *Ecatommiti*, iii. 7.

PAGE 222. 9. *Aqua Tetrachymagogon*. On this absurd name, see W. King, *Orig. Works*, 1776, i. 202, and the *Tatler*, no. 240.

19. *A. P.* 114, 118.

Page 223. 6. *Aen.* iv. 628.

33. *A. P.* 121.

Page 226. 36. Aristophanes, *Knights, passim.*

19. *Say.* Orig. 'sad', and so the 1655 quarto of *Othello.*

Page 227. 4-14. Rabelais, *Gargantua*, ch. xxxix.

Page 230. 21. Cf. note on 210. 21-5.

24-34. *The Rehearsal*, act iii. sc. 2.

Page 231. 7. Rabelais, *Tiers livre*, ch. xxi. I have adopted the text of Marty-Laveaux's edition (Paris, 1870, ii. 107). The poem is really by Guillaume Crétin (*d.* 1525), who has therefore been assumed to be the original of Raminagrobis.

Page 234. 19 sq. This refers to an extract from the Registers of the French Parliament, December 9, 1541 (translated by Rymer on p. 53 sq. of the *Short View*, and cited in French on p. 170 sq.), in which it is charged that the strolling players 'had undertaken to represent *Christ's Passion* and the *Acts* of the *Apostles*, and therein had employed mean illiterate fellows who were cunning in those matters, as a Carpenter, a Bum-Bailiff, a Weaver, and others, who had committed divers faults, both in the *Fiction* and in their *Action*, and to lengthen out the time had interlarded many *Apocryphal* matters'.

Page 239. 19. *Pantagruel*, ch. xix.

Page 242. 21. *Gorboduc*, act iv, sc. 2. Rymer had characterized this tragedy in an earlier chapter (*Short View*, p. 84): 'And after that were reckon'd for Comedy, *Edward* Earl of *Oxford*; for Tragedy, amongst others, *Thomas* Lord of *Buckhurst*, whose *Gorboduck* is a fable doubtless better turn'd for Tragedy than any on this side the *Alps* in his time, and might have been a better direction to *Shakespear* and *Ben. Johnson* than any guide they have had the luck to follow.'

Page 249. 2. *Salsa, O picante.* Rymer probably wrote *salsa picante* (i. e. piquant sauce); in any case, the disjunctive *o* (i. e. or) seems preferable to the interjection *O*.

4. Ovid, *Trist.* ii. 409.

Page 250. 17. Catullus, v. 4.

27. Suetonius, *Tib.* 21.

Page 251. 4. Quintilian, *Inst.* vi. 1. 36.

26. *Rehearsal*, act iv. sc. 1.

35. John Hamsteed (1646-1719), astronomer royal.

PAGE 252. 2. *Gresham Colledge*, i. e. the **Royal Society**, which held its meetings there.

PAGE 253. 33. *John an Oaks* and *John a Stiles*, fictitious names used in a legal action (cf. ' John Doe ').

3. *Poet.* ix. 3.

EDWARD PHILLIPS (1630–1696 ?)

The *Theatrum Poetarum*, the preface to which is here re-printed, appeared in 1675 : it is a chaotic collection of bio-graphical notices, arranged for the most part according to the alphabetical order of the poets' Christian names. In 1669 (though I have seen no edition earlier than 1679) Phillips had used some of the same material, arranged in the form of an historical narrative, in his *Compendiosa Enumeratio Poetarum qui a tempore Dantis Aligerii usque ad hanc ætatem claruerunt*, appended, with a *Tractatulus de Carmine Dramatico Poetarum præsertim in Choris Tragicis et veteris Comœdiæ*, to the seventeenth edition of Buchler's poetic dictionary, *Sacrarum Profanarumque Phrasium Poeticarum Thesaurus*. This preface, addressed to Thomas Stanley (1625–1678), the historian of philosophy, and Sir Edward Sherburne (1618–1702), both poets and scholars of no slight distinction, is on a plane so much higher than the other work of Phillips that the assistance of his uncle, Milton, has been suspected (cf. i. 194–209).

PAGE 265. 20 sq. Cf. *supra*, 132. 20 sq., 173. 34, and notes. Dr. Johnson's assertion that Congreve ' first taught the English writers that Pindar's odes were regular ' has become a common-place of literary history, though Phillips in this passage has preceded Congreve by over a quarter of a century, and though Milton before him was acquainted with the nature of Pindar's strophic structure. The Italian critics of the sixteenth century had formulated the latter correctly, e. g. Minturno, *Arte Poetica*, Venice, 1564, p. 182. As early as 1584, John Soothern, in his *Pandora*, had echoed the boast of Ronsard, that

'never man before
Now in England knewe Pindar's string '
(cf. Puttenham, *Arte of English Poesie*, ed. Arber, p. 259 sq.).

and Jonson had essayed the regular Pindaric Ode in *Under-woods*.

29. Cf. i. 209. 5, and note.

PAGE 269. 28. *Argalus* and *Parthenia*, characters in Sidney's *Arcadia* : their names are joined in the title of a poetic romance by Quarles and of a tragedy by Glapthorne.

34. Aristotle, *Poet*. i. 5.

PAGE 271. 34. *Poetic Energie*. See Gregory Smith, ii. 148, and note ; and cf. Du Bellay, *Defense et Illustration*, 1549, i. 6 : 'Bref, ceste energie, et ne scay quel esprit, qui est en leurs ecriz, que les Latins appelleroient *genius*.'

JOSEPH GLANVILL (1636-1680)

The *Essay on Preaching* was approved by the Bishop of London on December 6, 1677, and appeared early in 1678 ; it was followed in the same year by *A Seasonable Defence of Preaching, and the Plain Way of it*. The extract occupies pages 12-28 in the original edition. The origins of the movement toward simplicity in preaching, and Glanvill's indebtedness to Eachard and others, are discussed in the Introduction. On Glanvill's critical theories in general, cf. Ferris Greenslet, *Joseph Glanvill*, 1900, pp. 185-92.

PAGE 274. 5. *A late writer*. Nathaniel Fairfax (1637-1690), author of *A Treatise of the Bulk and Selvedge of the World*, 1674.

SAMUEL BUTLER (1612-1680)

The poem *Upon Critics* has been transcribed from the original MS. in the British Museum (Add. MS. 32625, Remains of Samuel Butler, ff. 124, 125). It is without a title in the MS., and I have retained that given to it by the first editor (R. Thyer, *Genuine Remains of Samuel Butler*, 1759, i. 161). I have also omitted four lines which precede 279. 4-7, and which the latter were apparently intended to recast and supersede. The poem was called forth by Rymer's critique of Beaumont and Fletcher in *The Tragedies of the Last Age* (*supra*, pp. 181-208), and was therefore written between November, 1677, and September, 1680. Rymer's critical opinions must be kept continually in mind in reading this reply.

PAGE 278. 2. 'The Poet here very wittily considers the Muse, under the tyrannous Direction of Critics, as a Person found Idiot or Lunatick by a Jury, who is not at liberty to act for himself, but as his Guardian shall order' (Thyer). The legal imagery is sustained throughout, with an occasional use of legal terms (e. g. ' Tales,' 280. 19 ; ' Trover,' 280. 34).

16. *Torricellian Glasses*, i. e. the barometer, invented by Evangelista Torricelli in 1643.

PAGE 279. 4. The allusion is to Rymer's incessant harping on Aristotle's definition of tragedy ; cf. *supra*, 197. 12, and note.

11–34. Another allusion to Rymer's Aristotelianism : cf. *Poet*. xiii. 2–4, where the tragic hero is defined as a man between the extremes of goodness and badness, whose misfortunes are brought about, not by depravity, but by some error or frailty.

PAGE 280. 5. See Thyer's note, *op. cit.* i. 164.

25. *A Forraine Lawyer & his Pupils*, i. e. Aristotle and his commentators, especially the Italians ('virtuosi-Tuscans,' l. 26).

29. Sperone Speroni (1500–1588) gained his European reputation as a critic by reason of his relations with Tasso in the composition and revision of the *Gerusalemme* (cf. Zaniboni, *Torquato Tasso e Sperone Speroni*, 1891); this, rather than his *Dialoghi*, or his tragedy of *Canace* and the controversy which raged about it, is probably responsible for his mention here.

30. Lope de Vega stole nothing from Speroni, but was indebted to other Italian critics in his *Arte Nuevo de hacer comedias*, 1609 (cf. note on i. 65. 15): Butler, in selecting it as a representative of classical tendencies, was at odds with seventeenth-century opinion, which regarded it as a strong protest against the Rules (cf. Rodenburg, *Eglentiers Poëtens Borst-weringh*, 1619, p. 97; Mairet, *Epistre familière*, 1637; La Mesnardière, *Poëtique*, 1640, pref., pp. T, V, DDD ; Chapelain, *Lettres*, ii. 236; Rapin, *Réflexions*, 1674, pref.; Dryden, 1695, in Ker, ii. 139; but cf. Lessing, *Hamb. Dram.* no. 69).

31. *The French Filew* (i. e. *filou*) *Corneele*, i. e. Corneille as propounder of rules and theories in his *discours* and *examens*. With this attack on the legislators of Parnassus, cf. Farquhar's, in his *Discourse upon Comedy*, 1702, and Gildon's answer in the *Laws of Poetry*, 1721, p. 11.

EARL OF ROCHESTER (1647–1680)

The *Allusion to Horace* was first printed in *Poems on Several Occasions, By the Right Honourable the E. of R——*, Antwerp (i. e. London), 1680; this volume was reprinted in 1685 with the title, *Poems on Several Occasions : Written by a late Person of Honour.* The present text follows the reading of the latter edition, but the names of contemporaries, represented merely by initials in the original, have been given in full, in accordance with the almost unanimous consensus of seventeenth and early eighteenth century editions. A few important variants in the later editions are indicated below.

PAGE 283. 14. *Sense.* So orig. Later eds. ' Scenes '.

17, 18. The allusion is to Nathaniel Lee's *Sophonisba, or Hannibal's Overthrow*, 1676.

20. Richard Busby (1606–1695), the famous head master of Westminster School.

30. Lansdowne replied to this characterization of Wycherley in *Poems upon Several Occasions*, 1712, p. 178.

33. *Best.* So orig. Later eds. ' rest '.

PAGE 284. 4. *Buckhurst*, i. e. Charles Sackville, Earl of Dorset. Cf. Ker's *Dryden*, ii. 18 sq.

8. *Please.* So orig. Later eds. ' warm '.

9. *Sidley*, i. e. Sir Charles Sedley.

24 sq. This is an allusion to the epilogue and the ' Defence of the Epilogue' appended to the second part of the *Conquest of Granada*, 1672 (Dryden, ed. Scott-Saintsbury, iv. 224–46). Many of Dryden's contemporaries, notably Langbaine, were offended by the tone of both.

PAGE 285. 4. *Mustapha, or the Son of Solyman the Magnificent*, an heroic play by the Earl of Orrery, 1668.

4. *The English Princess, or the Death of Richard the Third*, an heroic play by John Caryl, 1667. Some later eds. read ' *Island Princess* '.

19. Betty Morice, or Morris, is said to be the Betty celebrated by Lord Buckhurst, later Earl of Dorset, in his song, ' Methinks the poor town has been troubled too long,' and

other poems (*Gentleman's Magazine*, 1780, p. 218). For 'Bawdy' (l. 20), the later eds. read ' Buckhurst's' or ' Buckley's '.

23. *The Pur-blind Knight.* An allusion apparently to Sir Carr Scrope (1649–1680), who at least so understood it; he replied in a *Defence of Satire*, which was in turn answered by Rochester in the verses *To Sir Car Scrope.*

29. *Shephard,* i. e. Sir Fleetwood Sheppard.

EARL OF MULGRAVE (1648–1721)

The text of the *Essay upon Poetry* has been transcribed from the Bodleian copy of the first edition (1682). Mulgrave's name appeared for the first time on the title-page of the second edition : this was published in 1691, and was accompanied by a Latin translation of the poem by John Morris. French translations appeared in 1764 (*Essai sur la Poésie,* in *Mélanges de Poésie angloise*) and in 1775 (*Mélanges de Littérature, de Morale, et de Physique,* t. vi). 'Upon this piece he appears to have set a high value; for he was all his lifetime improving it by successive revisals, so that there is scarcely any poem to be found of which the last edition differs more from the first. Amongst other changes, mention is made of some compositions of Dryden, which were written after the first appearance of the Essay.' (Johnson, *Life of Sheffield, Duke of Buckinghamshire.*) An elaborate commentary on the poem is contained in Charles Gildon's *The Laws of Poetry, as laid down by the Duke of Buckinghamshire in his Essay on Poetry, by the Earl of Roscommon in his Essay on Translated Verse, and by the Lord Lansdowne on Unnatural Flights in Poetry, Explain'd and Illustrated,* 1721.

PAGE 287. 21. Mulgrave is disingenuous: he owes not a little to Horace and Vida, but his model, in proceeding to discuss the various kinds of poetry after the introductory remarks on the necessity of genius and judgement, seems rather to have been Boileau's *Art Poétique,* which he imitates throughout.

PAGE 288. 5 sq. Cf. Boileau, *A. P.* ii. 168–204.

17. Cf. Dryden, pref. to *State of Innocence,* 1677 (Ker, i. 190, and note): ' The definition of Wit (which has been so often attempted, and ever unsuccessfully, by many poets) is

only this: it is a propriety of thoughts and words.' Addison criticizes this definition in the *Spectator*, no. 62.

24. *The late Convert*, i. e. the Earl of Rochester: the allusion is to his death-bed conversion by Burnet in 1680. The later eds. read 'a late author'.

32 sq. Cf. Boileau, *A. P.* ii. 38 sq.

PAGE 289. 22. *Cooper's Hill*, by Sir John Denham.

23 sq. Cf. Boileau, *A. P.* ii. 58 sq.

PAGE 290. 27. *Punish'd for another's Rimes*, i. e. for the stinging passage on Rochester in Mulgrave's *Essay on Satire*, 1680. Rochester held Dryden responsible for the attack, and had him beaten by hired ruffians. *Mac-Flecknoe* was published in October, 1682.

PAGE 291. 23. Cf. Corneille, *Discours du Poëme dramatique*, 1660: 'Ce n'est pas que je veuille dire que quand un acteur parle seul, il ne puisse instruire l'auditeur de beaucoup de choses; mais il faut que ce soit par les sentiments d'une passion qui l'agite, et non pas par une simple narration;' and the *examen* of *Clitandre*: 'Les monologues sont trop longs et trop fréquents en cette pièce ; c'étoit une beauté en ce temps-là ... La mode a si bien changé, que la plupart de mes derniers ouvrages n'en ont aucun.' Cf. d'Aubignac, *Pratique du Théâtre*, iii. 8, 9.

30. *Bellario*, in Beaumont and Fletcher's *Philaster*.

PAGES 291. 31—292. 8. In the *Rehearsal*, act ii. sc. 3, Bayes enunciates the ' general Rule : you must ever make similes when you are surpris'd ; 'tis the new way of writing'. Dryden took the lesson to heart, and in the preface to *Troilus and Cressida*, 1679, he says : 'There is yet another obstacle to be removed, which is pointed wit, and sentences affected out of season : there is nothing of kin to the violence of passion ; no man is at leisure to make sentences and similes, when his soul is in agony.' Cf. Boileau, *A. P.* iii. 135 sq., and Rapin, *Réflexions*, pt. i. § 34.

PAGE 293. 3 sq. Cf. Boileau, *A. P.* iii. 104 :

' Des héros de roman fuyez les petitesses ;

Toutefois aux grands cœurs donnez quelques foiblesses,' &c. Johnson compares Mulgrave's 'faultless Monster' with Scaliger's ' sine labe monstrum '. Cf. Shaftesbury, *Characteristicks*, 1711, iii. 262, *n.*, 'a compleat and perfect Character is the greatest monster,' &c.

21 sq. Cf. Boileau, *A. P.* iii. 345 sq.

33 sq. Cf. *ibid.* iii. 413 sq.

PAGE 294. 6. *Sheer Wit.* Bayes, in the *Rehearsal*, act iii. sc. 1, is an advocate of 'sheer wit' (cf. the strictures of Warton, *Essay on Pope*, 3rd ed. i. 161).

PAGE 295. 16 sq. Cf. Rapin, *Réflexions sur la Poëtique*, 1674 (Rymer's transl.): 'The Epick Poem is that which is the greatest and most noble in Poesy; it is the greatest work that human Wit is capable of,' &c.

32. René Le Bossu, *Traité du Poëme épique*, 1675 (Engl. transl. 1695). Le Bossu shared, with Rapin, Dacier, and Boileau, the worship of the later wits (cf. Congreve, *Double Dealer*, ii. 2). Dryden, in 1679, had called him 'the best of modern critics' (Ker, i. 211), and in 1697 thought that 'Spenser wanted only to have read the rules of Bossu' for complete success in epic poetry. Shaftesbury (*Characteristicks*, 1711, i. 142, *n.*) echoes Dryden's praise of him ; Dennis borrowed freely from his work in the critique of *Prince Arthur*, and Addison in that of *Paradise Lost*; and as late as 1753, Joseph Warton admired 'the regularity of his plan and the exactness of his method' (*Adventurer*, no. 49; cf. Pope, *Works*, ed. Elwin and Courthope, x. 401). In the dozen years between *Tom Jones*, xi. 1, and *Tristram Shandy*, iii. 12, his fame withered and died.

PAGE 296. 18, 19. ' At the time when this work first appeared, Milton's fame was not yet fully established, and therefore Tasso and Spenser were set before him ... The last line in succeeding editions was shortened, and the order of names continued ; but now Milton is at last advanced to the highest place, and the passage thus adjusted :

"Must above Tasso's lofty flights prevail,
Succeed where Spenser, and ev'n Milton, fail." '

(Johnson, *Life of Sheffield.*)

EARL OF ROSCOMMON (1633 ?-1685)

The *Essay on Translated Verse* was brought out by Tonson in 1684. The significant Miltonic imitation in blank verse (308. 17 – 309. 10) was added to 'the second edition, corrected and enlarged ', which appeared in the following year ; and the latter edition has accordingly been adopted as the basis of the present text. A Latin version by L. Eusden appeared in 1717, and an extended commentary by Gildon in 1721 (*Laws of Poetry*, pp. 281–339).

PAGE 297. 1. Mulgrave's *Essay upon Poetry*.

PAGE 298. 17–22. The allusion is to André Dacier's translation of Horace into French prose ; the first volume appeared in 1681.

PAGE 299. 7–12. Cf. Boileau, *A. P.* iv. 121–4.

19–22. Cf. Ker's *Dryden*, ii. 164 (note to l. 34).

PAGE 300. 4. Cf. Pope's ' Search then the ruling passion ' (*Moral Essays*, i. 174 sq.).

10. Cf. i. 54. 1 sq.

23 sq. Cf. *supra*, 288. 22 sq., and Boileau, *A. P.* ii. 173 sq.

PAGE 301. 14 sq. Roscommon has in mind Vida, *De Arte Poetica*, ii. 179 sq., or the flings at Homer in Scaliger, *Poet.* v. 3. Homer's similes were censured by Desmarets de Saint-Sorlin, Perrault, Fontenelle, Houdar de la Motte, and other French critics (cf. Goujet, *Bibliothèque françoise*, 1744, iv. 48–149).

PAGE 304. 18—305. 15. Imitated from Boileau, *A. P.* iv. 1 sq.

PAGE 305. 28, 29. Cf. Horace, *A. P.* 102, 103, and Boileau, *A. P.* iii. 142.

PAGE 307. 18. *The sound is still a Comment to the Sense.* Vida, in his *De Arte Poetica*, iii. 367, seems to have given its modern prestige to the law of imitative harmony first enunciated by Dionysius of Halicarnassus :

'Omnia sed numeris vocum concordibus aptant,

Atque sono quaecunque canunt imitantur,' &c. ;
and Bembo, Dolce, and other Italian and Spanish rhetoricians proceeded to study the poetic effects of the various vocalic and consonantal sounds : cf. Juan de la Cueva, *Egemplar Poético*, 1606 (Sedano, *Parnaso Español*, 1774, viii. 48) :

'De la R usurás quando el violento

Euro contrasta al Boreas poderoso

Con horrido furor su movimiento,' &c.
Cowley, in the notes to the first book of his *Davideis*, naturalized the idea in England : ' The disposition of words and numbers should be such, as that out of the order and sound of them, the things themselves may be represented ; ' and Pope, in the

Essay on Criticism, has followed Roscommon : 'The sound must seem an echo to the sense.' It was a favourite observation of Dick Minim (*Idler*, no. 60, June 9, 1759; cf. *Rambler*, no. 92, Feb. 2, 1751).

PAGE 308. 17. A significant *locus* in the history of Milton's fame. In 1690, the Swiss scholar, Minutoli, wrote to Bayle : 'All the educated Englishmen I have known extol to the skies a poem written in English by Milton and called *Adam ;* they speak of it as the *non plus ultra* of the human spirit' (Gigas, *Correspondance Inédite de Pierre Bayle*, Copenhagen, 1890, p. 579).

APPENDIX

Evelyn's letters to Sir Peter Wyche (1628–1699 ?) and Samuel Pepys (1633–1703) have been transcribed from Bray's edition of the *Memoirs of John Evelyn*, London, 1827, vol. iv. pp. 144-9, 296-323. The originals of these and other letters are now at Wotton Court, in Surrey, but are not accessible to scholars (see my letter in the New York *Nation*, August 30, 1906), Of the three or four hundred names in the letter to Pepys, those which may be readily identified in such works as the *Dictionary of National Biography* and the *Nouvelle Biographie Générale* have not, except for special reasons, received any attention here.

PAGE 310. 7. On the 'meeting' which was the occasion of this letter see *supra*, p. 337.

29. Suetonius, *De Grammaticis*, 2.

PAGE 311. 4-7. Similar suggestions had already been made by Howell in 1650 (*Familiar Letters*, ed. Jacobs, p. 510), acting on the example of the French Academy. On the reform of orthography in France during the seventeenth century, cf. Petit de Julleville, *Hist. de la langue et de la litt. française*, vol. v. pt. ii. p. 778 sq. Evelyn may have seen Corneille's preface to the 1663 edition of his collected plays, in which a strong plea is made for simplified spelling (*Œuvres*, ed. Marty-Laveaux, i. 4-12).

23. The *Essai des merveilles de la nature et des plus nobles artifices : pièce très nécessaire à tous ceux qui font profession d'eloquence*, by René François (i. e. Étienne Binet, 1569-1639), appeared in 1621, and was often reprinted (13th ed. 1657) :

it is   cyclopaedia of arts and sciences, with explanations of technical terms, intended as a handbook for writers and preachers.

25. Francis Junius, or du Jon (1589–1677) : his lexico-graphical work is almost wholly concerned with the Germanic tongues (see *D. N. B.*). Is this a slip for Adrianus Junius, the author of the *Nomenclator*? Evelyn, in the preface to his *Account of Architects and Architecture*, 1697 (*Lit. Remains*, ed. Upcott, pp. 353–4), repeats this plea for a collection of technical terms, and couples Adrianus Junius and the *Essai des merveilles de la nature* as illustrations of the work needed in English.

28. Joseph Moxon (1627–1677), in his *Mechanick Exercises* and *Mathematicks made easie*, both then still unpublished.

PAGE 312. 12. John Cleveland (1613–1658).

PAGE 314. 6. *Marullus*, i. e. Michele Marullo (*d.* 1500).

11. *Such as Paulus Jovius has celebrated*, i. e. in his own ' museum ' (cf. Evelyn, *Diary*, Oct. 22, 1644), and in his *Elogia doctorum Virorum* and *Elogia Virorum bellica virtute illustrium*, which contain the portraits of his heroes. The practice of com-bining portrait and eulogy was popular on the continent up to Evelyn's time : e. g. Fulvio Orsini's *Imagines et Elogia virorum illustrium et eruditorum*, 1570, Reusner's *Icones virorum litteris illustrium in Germania*, 1587, and *Icones litteris clarorum virorum Italiae, Germaniae, Galliae, Angliae*, 1589, Crasso's *Elogii d'Huomini letterati*, 1666, and Perrault's *Hommes Illustres qui ont paru en France*, 1696–1700.

PAGE 317. 4. *Numus Homericus*, a brass coin of Smyrna, as the reputed birthplace of Homer (Strabo, *Geog.* xiv. i. 37) : it is described and figured in J. Spon's *Miscellanea Eruditae Anti-quitatis*, Leydon, 1685, p. 140, and Nuñez's commentary on Goltzius's *Graeciae eiusque insularum et Asiae Minoris Numis-mata*, Antwerp, 1644, p. 250, to both of which books Evelyn refers *infra*, 318. 6.

38. *Post centum annos vos cito*, the prophetic words ascribed to Jerome of Prague at his trial (*Historia et Monumenta Ioannis Hus atque Hieronymi Pragensis*, 1715, ii. 526). The medallion to which Evelyn apparently refers was executed for the centenary of Huss in 1515, and contains the inscription, ' Centum revolutis annis Deo respondebitis et mihi : ' it is reproduced on the title-

page of Seyfried's *Dissertatio Historica de Iohannis Hussi ortu, educatione*, &c., Jena, 1711, and described on pp. 124–7. See also the *Trésor de Numismatique et de Glyptique* (*Choix de Médailles exécutées en Allemagne aux XVIe et XVIIe siècles*, 1841, p. 2, and pl. 1, no. 1); the various volumes of this collection reproduce many other of the medallions mentioned by Evelyn. For the earlier English interest in medals and coins, see Peacham's *Compleat Gentleman*, ch. xii.

PAGE 318. 5. *Fulvius Ursinus*, i. e. Fulvio Orsini (1529–1600), author of the *Imagines* (*v. sup.*) and *Familiae Romanae*, 1577.

6, 7. Jean Tristan, sieur de Saint-Amant (1595–1656), author of *Commentaires Historiques contenant en abrégé les Vies des Empereurs romains*, 1635; Joannes Otho, of Bruges, author of *Introductio in Historiam Romanam, ex fide marmorum, numismatum, et veterum historiarum restituta*, 1565; Jean Foy-Vaillant (1632–1706), author of *Numismata Imperatorum Romanorum*, 1674; Charles Patin (1633–1693), author of *Introduction à la Connoissance des médailles*, 1665, and other numismatic works. On Ezekiel Spanheim (1629–1710), see Evelyn, *Diary*, Sept. 31, 1675; on Jacob Spon (1647–1685) and Hubert Goltzius (1526–1583), see note to 317. 4.

29. Charleton's collection, purchased later by Sir Hans Sloane, was often visited by Evelyn (*Diary*, Dec. 16, 1686, March 11, Dec. 30, 1690).

35. Sir Thomas Hanmer, the grandfather of the editor of Shakespeare.

PAGE 319. 7–9. Sir Simon Fanshawe (1604–1680) was the elder brother, not the father, of Sir Richard, the translator of Guarini.

PAGE 321. 6. Tacitus, *Ann.* ii. 41.

35. *Naudæus.* Evelyn's version of Gabriel Naudé's *Advis pour dresser une Bibliothèque* appeared in 1661 (cf. *Diary*, Nov. 16, Dec. 3, 1661).

PAGE 322. 2. Ovid, *Fast.* vi. 647:

'Sic agitur censura, et sic exempla parantur,
　　Cum vindex, alios quod monet, ipse facit.'

PAGE 323. 15. Evelyn's *Sculptura, or the History and Art of Chalcography and Engraving in Copper*, appeared in 1662.

29. *Mem'ius.* The noble house of Mesmes possessed an

historic library, celebrated by Turnebus and Pibrac. Naudé
dedicated his *Advis pour dresser une Bibliothèque* to the President
de Mesmes in 1627. For a contemporary account of the public
and private libraries referred to by Evelyn in the passage which
follows, see P. Le Gallois, *Traitté des plus belles Bibliothèques de
l'Europe*, 1685, pp. 147-65 (paraphrased in the *Critical and
Historical Account of all the celebrated Libraries in Foreign
Countries : By a Gentleman of the Temple*, 1739, pp. 119-33).

29. *Puteane* (Puteanus), i. e. Jacques Dupuy (1586-1656),
who bequeathed the library of nine thousand volumes, collected
by himself and his brother Pierre, to the Bibliothèque du Roi.

29. *Thuanus*, i. e. the historian Jacques-Auguste de Thou
(1553-1617): Jacques and Pierre Dupuy (Puteanus) prepared
the catalogue of his library (*Catalogus Bibliothecae Thuanae*,
1679).

29. *Cordesius*, i. e. Jean de Cordes (1570-1642): his library
was catalogued by Naudé (*Bibliothecae Cordesianae Catalogus*,
1653).

30. The Chancellor Pierre Seguier (1588-1672) bequeathed
his library to the abbey of Saint-Germain-des-Prés. A *Catalogue
des Manuscrits de la Bibliothèque du Chancelier Seguier* appeared
in 1685.

30. The splendid library of the finance minister, Colbert,
was in charge of Étienne Baluze until 1700, and was acquired
by the Bibliothèque du Roi in 1732; a catalogue was printed in
1728. The great Condé collected a large library, which was
augmented by his son, and ultimately passed to the national
collection.

33. The famous library of the Augustinian house of St. Victor
was founded by Francis I. Cardinal Mazarin's library was
opened to the public in 1648.

Page 325. 22. Virgil, *Aen.* i. 135.

Page 326. 11. Valesius (Henry de Valois, 1603-1676) published
his edition of Eusebius in 1659.

Page 327. 1. Sir Kenelm Digby's books were sold April 19,
1680, and fetched £908. The printed catalogue to which Evelyn
refers, *Bibliotheca Digbeiana, sive Catalogus librorum quos post
K. Digbeium possedit Georgius Comes Bristol*, is described in
Repertorium Bibliographicum, London, 1819, p. 439 sq.

41-42. The Accademia della Crusca was founded at Florence in 1572, the Umoristi at Rome about 1600, and the Insensati at Perugia in 1561 : for the history of these and other Italian academies, see Quadrio, *Storia e Ragione d' ogni Poesia,* 1739, i. 51-113. Evelyn, during his Italian tour, had attended a meeting of the Umoristi (*Diary,* Feb. 17, 1644-5) and visited the hall of La Crusca (*ib.* May 26, 1645).

42. *The Beaux Esprits,* i. e. the French Academy. The founders adopted the present name on March 20, 1634, but others were current at the time (Pellisson, *Hist.,* ed. 1672, p. 19): ' quelques-uns l'ont nommée depuis *l'Académie des beaux esprits,* quelques autres *l'Académie de l'Eloquence.*' The first of these unofficial titles was widely disseminated ; several years after the foundation of the academy Howell spoke of it as ' the new Academy of Wits call'd *l'Academie de beaux esprits,* which the late Cardinal Richlieu founded in Paris ' (*Fam. Letters,* ed. Jacobs, p. 510).

PAGE 328. 22—329. 13. Cf. *supra,* p. 337.